D0875679

International Finance and the Developing Economies

Also by Graham Bird

THE INTERNATIONAL MONETARY SYSTEM AND THE LESS DEVELOPED COUNTRIES (1978)

WORLD FINANCE AND ADJUSTMENT: An Agenda for Reform (1985)

INTERNATIONAL FINANCIAL POLICY AND ECONOMIC DEVELOPMENT: A Disaggregated Approach (1987)

INTERNATIONAL MACROECONOMICS: Theory, Policy and Applications (1987)

MANAGING GLOBAL MONEY (1988)

THIRD WORLD DEBT: The Search for a Solution (1989)

COMMERCIAL BANK LENDING AND THIRD WORLD DEBT (1989)

THE INTERNATIONAL FINANCIAL REGIME (1990)

CONTEMPORARY ISSUES IN APPLIED ECONOMICS (1991)

ECONOMIC REFORM IN EASTERN EUROPE (1992)

INTERNATIONAL ASPECTS OF ECONOMIC DEVELOPMENT (1992)

LATIN AMERICA'S ECONOMIC FUTURE (1994)

IMF LENDING TO DEVELOPING COUNTRIES: Issues and Evidence (1995)

CLASSICAL WRITINGS IN INTERNATIONAL DEBT (1995)

THE IMF AND THE FUTURE; Issues and Options Facing the Fund (2003)

International Finance and the Developing Economies

Graham Bird
Director,
Surrey Centre for International Economic Studies,
Professor of Economics,
University of Surrey, UK

For details of previous publication of chapters see Acknowledgements page.

First published 2004 by
PALGRAVE MACMILLAN
Houndmills, Basingstoke, Hampshire RG21 6XS and
175 Fifth Avenue, New York, N.Y. 10010
Companies and representatives throughout the world

PALGRAVE MACMILLAN is the global academic imprint of the Palgrave Macmillan division of St. Martin's Press, LLC and of Palgrave Macmillan Ltd. Macmillan® is a registered trademark in the United States, United Kingdom and other countries. Palgrave is a registered trademark in the European Union and other countries.

ISBN 0–333–73397–5

This book is printed on paper suitable for recycling and made from fully managed and sustained forest sources.

A catalogue record for this book is available from the British Library.

Library of Congress Cataloging-in-Publication Data
Bird, Graham R.
    International finance and the developing economies / Graham Bird.
      p. cm.
    Includes bibliographical references and index.
    ISBN 0–333–73397–5
      1. International finance. 2. Finance – Developing countries. 3. International Monetary Fund – Developing countries. 4. Structural adjustment (Economic policy) – Developing countries. I. Title.

HG3881.B5359 2003
332'.042'091724—dc21   2003040524

10 9 8 7 6 5 4 3 2 1
13 12 11 10 09 08 07 06 05 04

Printed and bound in Great Britain by
Antony Rowe Ltd, Chippenham and Eastbourne

Contents

Acknowledgements

Chapters 1 and 6 first appeared in *Third World Quarterly*, vol. 22, no. 1, pp. 37–49 and vol. 20, no. 2, pp. 421–437 respectively and are reprinted here by kind permission of the editors of that journal.

Chapter 2 first appeared in *World Development*, vol. 25, no. 9, pp. 1409–1420 and is reprinted here by kind permission of the editors of that journal.

Chapters 3, 4 and 5 first appeared in *World Economics*, vol. 3, no. 1, vol. 2, no. 1 and vol. 2, no. 4 respectively and are reprinted here by kind permission of the editors of that journal.

Chapter 7 first appeared in *International Organization*, vol. 50, no. 3, pp. 477–511 and is reprinted here by kind permission of the editors of that journal.

Chapter 8 first appeared in *Global Governance*, vol. 7, no. 1 and is reprinted here by kind permission of the editors of that journal.

Chapters 9 and 11 first appeared in *Journal of International Development*, vol. 11, no. 1, pp. 1–26 and vol. 13, no. 1, pp. 1–24 respectively and are reprinted here by kind permission of the editors of that journal.

Chapter 10 first appeared in *Economics Notes*, vol. 22, no. 2, pp. 141–156 and is reprinted here by kind permission of the editors of that journal.

Chapters 12 and 15 first appeared in *World Economy*, vol. 20, no. 7, pp. 967–991 and vol. 26, no. 1, pp. 43–59 respectively and are reprinted here by kind permission of the editors of that journal.

Chapter 13 first appeared in *Zagreb Review of Economics and Business*, vol. 2, no. 2, pp. 1–24 and is reprinted here by kind permission of the editors of that journal.

Chapter 14 first appeared in *Essays in International Finance*, no. 193 and is reprinted here by kind permission of the editors of that journal.

Chapter 15 first appeared in *The World Economy*, vol. 26, no. 1, pp. 43–59.

Preface

This book draws together various previously published papers. The unifying theme relates to macroeconomic policy and international financial issues in the context of developing countries and the sequence in which the chapters appear is designed to follow a logical path as explained below. The book starts from a point at which macroeconomic disequilibria are assumed to exist and only incidentally analyses their causes, except in the sense that the design of appropriate policy needs to take this into account.

Chapter 1 examines the extent to which conventional analysis of fiscal and monetary policy is appropriate for developing countries. It also discusses whether longer term supply-side or structural policies may influence the effectiveness of traditional aggregate demand management tools. Chapter 2 develops this theme further by looking at the mix between adjustment and financing as ways of dealing with balance of payment deficits. It may be the binding nature of the external financing constraint that dictates the nature and speed of adjustment. The chapters look at the role of international financial institutions in relaxing this constraint.

Apart from monetary and fiscal policy, another adjustment tool is exchange rate policy. Chapter 3 reviews the issues surrounding the choice of exchange rate regime. Following the East Asian crisis in 1997/98 a consensus had emerged suggesting that developing countries should opt either for firmly fixed exchange rates or free flexibility but this chapter suggests that the choice may be more nuanced. Chapter 4 takes the extreme of dollarisation and examines the extent to which this would be a sensible choice for the countries of Latin America.

It was in Latin America as well as elsewhere in the developing world that countries began to pursue policies of macroeconomic stabilisation and economic liberalisation at the beginning of the 1990s. Chapter 5 discusses the record of the so-called 'Washington Consensus' that advocated these policies and shows how the consensus has changed over the years. While it was perhaps frustration with the failure of populist policies as much as confidence in policies of economic liberalisation that led to their adoption in Latin America and Africa, the growth record of East Asian economies had been held up as an example of what could be achieved by disciplined economic management and an export orientation. Seen by some as a 'miracle' that was difficult to explain in terms of conventional theory, the economic and financial performance of the region suffered an abrupt deterioration with the crisis in 1997/98. Chapter 6 examines the crisis and the transformation from 'miracle' to 'meltdown'.

It was in the context of this crisis that the IMF came in for much criticism. Chapter 7 reviews the issues raised and the evidence surrounding the IMF's involvement in developing countries and goes on to examine and assess some of the policy options. Some commentators have suggested that the multilateral financial institutions are in need of deep and fundamental reform as part of establishing a 'new international financial architecture'. Chapter 8 examines the extent to which remodelling is required.

For many better-off developing countries and for lengthy periods of time private capital inflows have been more important than inflows from the multilaterals. Chapter 9 examines the extent to which private inflows can be influenced by potential recipients via their pursuit of sound macroeconomics. The following three chapters examine other aspects of private capital flows. Chapter 10 weighs up the arguments for and against capital account liberalisation. Does this provide developing countries with an opportunity to improve their access to international capital and further alleviate financing constraints on their development or does it expose them to greater risks associated with capital instability? Chapter 11 examines whether international currency taxation could be used to reduce such instability. The chapter points out that if capital movements are insensitive to such a tax the implication is that the tax would be effective in raising revenue. Could this revenue be used to alleviate the financial problems encountered by developing countries? Chapter 12 connects the discussion of the multilaterals with that of private capital markets by investigating the so-called catalytic effect by which it is often assumed that IMF and World Bank conditionality may induce others to lend to developing countries. To the extent that it exists, the evidence suggests that catalysis may be stronger in the case of official flows.

Chapters 13, 14 and 15 discuss other aspects of foreign aid. Chapter 13 investigates the decline in aid flows during the 1990s drawing on both economic and political factors. Chapter 14 examines the idea of linking the provision of aid with the creation of Special Drawing Rights as one way of increasing the flow of resources to low-income countries. Chapter 15 analyses debt relief as another way of providing financial assistance to highly indebted poor countries and assesses debt relief in relation to other forms of aid.

Although essentially a collection of essays, they have been selected in order to offer a coherent structure to the book, which explores both adjustment policy and financing options. I am grateful for the various anonymous referees who commented on early drafts of the chapters, which in their revised versions appear here. I am also grateful to the publishers of the journals for allowing me to reproduce them. I am most of all grateful to my collaborators, Joe Joyce, Alistair Milne, Kishen Rajan and Dane Rowlands not only for the stimulation they provided in association with our joint work but also for their willingness to let me use the outcome of their endeavours in this book. A final mention goes to my family: Heather, Alan, Anne, Simon and Tom. Family life is also quite a lot about adjustment and financing.

1
Conducting Macroeconomic Policy in Developing Countries: Piece of Cake or Mission Impossible?

Graham Bird

Recent economic crises in East Asia and Latin America have once again raised serious questions about the conduct of macroeconomic policy in developing countries. In the early 1980s the Latin America debt crisis was attributed by some observers to domestic economic mismanagement in the indebted countries. Similarly, Africa's poor economic performance has often been put down to overexpansionary monetary and fiscal policy and currency overvaluation.

But what is the scope for macroeconomic management in developing countries? Is it the same as in industrial economies where good economic performance, according to most conventional macroeconomic criteria at the beginning of the 2000s, might seem to suggest that macroeconomic policy has been successful? Should the international financial institutions that assist developing countries expect macroeconomic policy to deliver improved macroeconomic performance in developing countries, and should they rely heavily on it?

This chapter examines these questions, drawing both on theoretical analysis and empirical evidence. The layout of the chapter is as follows. The following section provides a brief summary of how ideas relating to the design of macroeconomic policy have changed since the 1970s. Against this backdrop, the third section examines the scope for macroeconomic management in developing countries by focusing on the three key tools of policy: monetary policy, fiscal policy and exchange rate policy. Section four then looks at ways in which the efficiency of macroeconomic policy could be improved. The next section evaluates the potential and actual role of the International Monetary Fund (IMF) in influencing the conduct of economic policy in developing countries, before a few concluding critical observations about some current proposals for reform, are offered in the final section.

1

Different approaches to macroeconomic management

How should countries conduct macroeconomic policy? While there is a consensus that they should avoid fiscal and monetary excesses, opinions vary about the emphasis that should be placed on monetary policy, fiscal policy and exchange rate policy as tools of macroeconomic management. Generally speaking, opinions change over time; usually because one particular approach is seen as falling short.

Up to the mid-1970s, the dominant macro model was Keynesian. The emphasis was placed on managing aggregate demand through fiscal policy. Policy makers believed in a Phillips curve trade-off between inflation and unemployment and this resulted in the evolution of stop–go policies: stop, in the form of fiscal contraction, when inflation and related balance of payments deficits were seen as the principal problems; and go, in the form of fiscal expansion, when economies were experiencing relatively high levels of unemployment and low rates of economic growth.

In the mid-1970s, however, the economic problem became one of simultaneously rapid inflation and high unemployment. The conventional Phillips curve no longer seemed to fit the facts. Policy makers abandoned Keynesianism in favour of monetarism. Monetarists and their new classical macroeconomics successors emphasised adaptive and rational expectations respectively, offering an explanation as to why the Phillips curve no longer seemed to exist, either in the long run according to adaptive expectations or even in the short run according to rational expectations.

Even in the short run, new classical macroeconomics claimed that it was possible to reduce inflation without causing unemployment to rise. This offered an attractive prospectus to politicians who seized upon it. Thus in the late 1970s and early 1980s the focus of macroeconomic policy changed. Emphasis was now placed on controlling monetary aggregates.[1] Fiscal policy was no longer seen as a demand management tool – indeed, the whole idea of managing aggregate demand went out of fashion. Instead, fiscal policy as it related to the structure of taxes and government expenditure was seen as a microeconomic tool that exerted an effect on individuals' incentives to work and save, and on firms' incentives to invest. There was a supply-side revolution.

However, monetarist policies assumed first that the authorities could both define and control the relevant monetary aggregate, and second that the demand for money was stable. Whereas old-fashioned monetarists did warn that their policies could lead to a temporary increase in unemployment above the 'natural' rate, policy makers who consulted new classical macroeconomists for advice assumed that unemployment would not increase much, if at all. In practice, none of these assumptions seemed to hold. As a consequence, monetarist policies were quietly dropped.[2] When there was a stock market crash in 1987, the fear was that this would result in an essentially Keynesian recession, and the policy adopted to raise aggregate demand was accordingly Keynesian in nature.

Having abandoned one policy rule relating to the growth of monetary aggregates, some countries looked for another rule to replace it in the form of pegged exchange rates. This was particularly visible in Europe and the Exchange Rate Mechanism (ERM) of the European Monetary System. However, the trials, tribulations and near collapse of the ERM in the early 1990s induced two responses. For some European economies, the lesson was that pegged exchange rates should be replaced with a single currency.[3] For others – the UK in particular – the lesson was that it should no longer commit itself to a pegged exchange rate. But what was left as a focus for macroeconomic policy if the exchange rate target was abandoned? The UK now joined the ranks of some other industrial economies, including the USA, that targeted inflation rather than the exchange rate. Interest rate policy became the principal instrument through which the authorities – usually in the guise of an independent central bank – sought to deliver low inflation. Inflation targeting replaced exchange rate targeting.

By the end of the 1990s strong economic growth, which in practice had probably little to do with macroeconomic policy, was reducing fiscal deficits and was also helping to reduce unemployment. Although the stance of macroeconomic policy was no longer so closely linked to any particular underlying macroeconomic ideology, macroeconomic performance was sufficiently good that satisficing policy makers were under no pressure to make sharp policy changes.

But to what extent is this an industrial country story? Has a similar course of events occurred in developing countries? And, more importantly, do developing countries encounter easier or harder problems in the conduct of macroeconomic policy?

Macroeconomic policy in developing countries

In this section, we shall again concentrate on the three principal macroeconomic policy instruments: monetary policy, fiscal policy and exchange rate policy. Conventional macroeconomic theory tells us that the effectiveness of monetary policy based on controlling monetary aggregates hinges on the stability of the demand for money, the interest rate elasticity of the demand for money, the interest rate elasticity of expenditure and the ability of the authorities to control the money supply.

Because of ill-developed financial markets and few substitutes for money, it might be assumed that the demand for money will be relatively stable in developing countries, and will exhibit a relatively low interest rate elasticity. It was these features that led some monetarists to believe that policies based on controlling the supply of money would be particularly effective in a developing country context. However, subsequent empirical work has challenged these theoretical priors.[4] Moreover, given the size of fiscal deficits and the limited scope for financing them by issuing bonds rather than by allowing the money supply to increase, as well as the problems in controlling the money supply when exchange rates are pegged, it transpired that monetarist policies were difficult to implement effectively.

On top of this, controlling the supply of money was inconsistent with the frequent desire in developing countries to cap interest rates. Financial repression aimed to keep interest rates below the equilibrium rate, partly to encourage investment but also to reduce the costs of servicing government debt and to allow governments to allocate credit in ways that they favoured. This certainly did not guarantee that scarce credit would flow to where it yielded the highest rate of return.

At the same time the new structuralists argued that in developing countries many firms, especially new ones, relied heavily on bank credit. Rising interest rates therefore meant rising costs which would be passed on to consumers in the form of higher prices. Contractionary monetary policy would therefore be cost inflationary. Distributionally, the higher cost of credit would hit embryonic firms particularly hard, and these firms, so it was argued, offered the greatest potential source of future export growth.

Although it was rarely argued that developing countries ran the risk of falling into a liquidity trap, the basic conclusion was much the same,[5] monetary policy would be relatively ineffective. Moreover, for as long as fiscal deficits were endemic and exchange rates were pegged, it was difficult to see that developing countries would possess the credentials necessary for effective monetary policy based on the control of monetary aggregates.

But what about fiscal policy? Fiscal deficits often seem to have lain at the heart of macroeconomic disequilibrium and instability in developing countries.[6] Surely more restrictive fiscal policy was the key to improved macroeconomic management. Why not just tighten fiscal policy?

Again, of course, there was the conventional monetarist critique of fiscal policy, namely that, because the demand for money was insensitive to interest rate changes, fiscal expansion or contraction would merely lead to changes in interest rates with little change in real output. In other words, fiscal expansion would lead to the crowding out of private investment. But this would only happen if the money supply were to be fixed. In practice, fiscal deficits were often accommodated by monetary expansion because financial markets were thin and governments did not want interest rates to rise.

So some way needed to be found to reduce budget deficits rather than finance them. This has proved to be far from easy for developing countries. Political pressures make it difficult to cut government expenditure, particularly current expenditure, since this often involves cutting welfare programmes or the wages of public employees. At the same time, it may be equally difficult to increase tax revenue. The tax base may be limited, and raising tax rates may simply lead to more tax evasion. There may be a developing country version of the Laffer curve where higher tax rates lead to greater incentives to evade tax and a decline in tax revenue. Moreover, the fiscal drag encountered in industrial countries may be replaced by fiscal thrust in developing countries as inflation not only creates pressures on governments to maintain the real value of welfare payments, but also pushes people into higher rates of tax that they then seek to avoid. Inflation, which may in part be a consequence of fiscal deficits, then itself results in larger fiscal deficits; a vicious circle develops.

New structuralists have emphasised another problem with fiscal policy in developing countries by pointing out that, to a significant degree, fiscal deficits are exogenous and beyond the control of domestic policy makers.[7] Developing countries rely heavily on trade taxes such as taxes on exports. But what if there is a recession in the industrial countries that comprise the markets for their exports? Or what if there is a bad harvest that limits exports? It is possible that, as a consequence, exports will fall, as will the revenue from export taxes.

It is not just tax revenue that may be affected by exogenous shocks. Many developing countries have high levels of sovereign external debt denominated in a foreign currency such as the US dollar. As world interest rates rise to reflect monetary conditions in industrial countries, or as the value of the US dollar appreciates, the domestic currency cost of servicing external debt rises. In other words, government expenditure increases. The exposure to external shocks may call on fiscal policy to be more flexible in developing countries than it is in industrial countries, when the reality is that it is likely to be less flexible.

Some of the external shocks mentioned above could be avoided by pegging the value of the domestic currency to (say) the US dollar – at least this might mitigate the effects of a dollar appreciation on the domestic currency costs of servicing external debt. Furthermore, given endemic inflation inertia in many developing countries there has been a nominal anchor argument for pegged exchange rates. Like some industrial countries, more than a few developing countries have opted for exchange rate-based stabilisation. The idea is in effect to import a lower rate of inflation from the country to whose currency you peg.[8] However, this policy too has been shown to have its shortcomings. It is not enough that the policy reduces the domestic rate of inflation. In fact, many developing countries showed considerable success at reducing their inflation rates in the first half of the 1990s.[9] But they were still unable to avoid balance of payments crises. The problem is that, if inflation remains high relative to that in countries with which there is trade, the associated appreciation in the real exchange rate will erode competitiveness.[10]

There will be no mechanism for maintaining the real exchange rate at an equilibrium level if inflation is relatively fast, or for altering equilibrium rates in the event of permanent real shocks such as a change in the terms of trade.

For these reasons developing countries have been increasingly tempted to opt for flexible exchange rates.[11] But this is not an ideal solution either. With ill-developed markets, demand and supply elasticities may be relatively low. While they may comply with Marshall–Lerner conditions which dictate whether devaluation will be effective in strengthening the current account of the balance of payments, the response to exchange rate changes may not be as great in developing countries as it is in industrial countries.[12]

Moreover, with thin foreign exchange markets, flexible exchange rates may be highly unstable and vulnerable to speculative attack. Developing countries still lack access to the range of hedging devices by which industrial countries seek to minimise such risks. Where the exchange rate is driven sharply down, the danger is that it may set off additional inflation. Again, a vicious circle can be established between inflation and devaluation and yet more inflation. The inflation will then negate the extra competitiveness associated with the devaluation and may in turn result in fiscal thrust. One can see why nominal anchors were attractive, even though their durability hinged on developing countries being able to show success in an area where they had historically been weak – the control of inflation.[13]

If nominal anchors in the form of pegged exchange rates have been insufficiently effective, what about the idea of inflation targeting as favoured by many industrial economies in the late 1990s and early 2000s? Is this a feasible policy option for developing countries? Inflation targeting relies on a number of conditions being met. Inflation forecasting needs to be well developed and accurate. There has to be an autonomous or independent central bank that is free to set interest rates at a level deemed appropriate to achieve the inflation target, and the monetary authorities have to be under little pressure to finance fiscal deficits; there has to be no 'fiscal dominance'. Unfortunately these conditions do not generally hold in developing countries, where historically the monetary authorities have financed deficits by issuing credit to the government. There can therefore be no presumption that inflation targeting will work in developing countries. This conclusion is strengthened by the weak reputation many developing countries have as inflation fighters, such that inflation targeting might be expected to carry little credibility. Moreover, it is by no means obvious that interest rate policy would be an effective counter-inflationary tool. Most studies show saving to be insensitive to interest rate changes in developing countries.

Where does this leave us? Is it the case that developing countries have no effective means of managing their macroeconomies? Should they focus on avoiding the worst excesses of fiscal and monetary expansion in order to maintain inflation at a moderate level, and on monitoring the exchange rate to prevent severe currency overvaluation? If this is the case, developing countries can claim significant success. Fiscal deficits have been narrowed, rates of monetary expansion have been reduced and inflation rates have fallen. Empirical evidence in support of these claims is provided in Tables 1.1 and 1.2. Table 1.1 presents data on central government fiscal deficits as a percentage of GDP over the period 1992–99. By the early 1990s fiscal deficits were lower in developing countries than they were in advanced economies, where, in 1992, the central government fiscal deficit was 4.1 per cent of GDP, as compared with 3 per cent in developing countries. Until 1996 developing countries as a group continued to reduce their fiscal deficits. However, there were regional differences. While, for example, this measure of fiscal improvement was most marked in Africa, in Latin America fiscal deficits increased slightly, although remaining below those in advanced economies. At the end of the period shown in the table, between 1997 and 1999 the fiscal stance became more relaxed for developing countries as a group. This was particularly marked in Latin America. However, fiscal deficits among developing countries at the end of the 1990s were still no higher than they had been in advanced economies at the beginning of the period.

What about monetary growth? The data in Table 1.2 show the considerable success achieved by developing countries during the 1990s in more tightly controlling the growth of monetary aggregates. Particularly eye-catching is the experience in the developing countries of the Western

Table 1.1   Developing countries: central government fiscal balances (% of GDP)

	1992	1993	1994	1995	1996	1997	1998	1999
Developing countries	−3.0	−3.2	−2.7	−2.7	−2.4	−2.6	−4.0	−4.4
Africa	−6.8	−7.3	−5.1	−3.8	−2.9	−3.9	−3.5	
Sub-Sahara	−8.1	−7.9	−5.7	−4.0	−3.6	−3.6	−4.1	−4.3
Excluding Nigeria and South Africa	−9.8	−7.6	−6.1	−4.9	−4.3	−3.9	−4.0	−4.5
Asia	−2.9	−2.9	−2.5	−2.4	−2.1	−2.6	−3.8	−4.4
Excluding China and India	−1.8	−1.9	−1.2	−0.8	−0.8	−1.8	−3.1	−3.5
Middle East and Europe	−5.6	−7.6	−5.9	−4.5	−4.5	−4.0	−7.1	−6.2
Western Hemisphere	−0.4	−0.2	−0.9	−1.9	−1.8	−1.6	−3.2	−4.1
Advanced economies	−4.1	−4.4	−3.7	−3.3	−2.7	−1.5	−1.1	−0.8

Source: *World Economic Outlook*, IMF, May 2000.

Table 1.2   Developing countries: broad money aggregates (annual % change)

	1992	1993	1994	1995	1996	1997	1998	1999
Developing countries	107.9	117.8	94.5	25.1	22.1	20.2	17.0	16.9
Africa	32.0	27.5	38.6	23.6	21.0	18.6	16.6	19.2
Sub-Sahara	36.8	31.5	47.5	28.6	24.2	19.8	18.1	21.8
Asia	22.7	27.5	24.8	23.4	21.1	18.0	18.3	14.4
Excluding China and India	20.2	21.8	18.6	22.5	19.8	17.0	20.9	12.2
Middle East and Europe	27.7	26.9	40.4	33.4	34.2	26.4	27.2	25.8
Western Hemisphere	367.7	414.5	246.2	24.1	19.5	20.6	12.1	15.9

Source: *World Economic Outlook*, IMF, May 2000.

Hemisphere, where the growth in the money supply fell from 414.5 per cent in 1993 to 12.1 per cent in 1998.

Thus the evidence does seem to support the idea that in the developing world as a whole there has been an increasing awareness of the dangers of macroeconomic excesses and a substantial degree of success in avoiding them. But should the focus of macroeconomic policy simply be to avoid large fiscal deficits and excessive monetary growth?

As mentioned in the previous section, industrial countries have tended to shift away from placing emphasis on controlling monetary aggregates and have instead focused on counter-inflationary interest rate policy. They have also reinterpreted fiscal policy as a microeconomic tool rather than a macro-economic one for managing aggregate demand, although sustained economic growth has enabled them to reduce overall fiscal deficits. Are there lessons here for developing countries? We have already seen that many developing countries do not possess the characteristics to make inflation targeting work, although this is no justification for ignoring interest rates. But what about fiscal policy and exchange rate policy? And should a distinction be made between what can be achieved in the long run compared with the short run?

What to do? Lessons for the design of policy

Although the above discussion is negative in as much as it emphasises the problems encountered by many developing countries in conducting macro-economic policy, it also has a more positive side by hinting at what needs to be done to make things work better. The overall message is that developing countries need to strengthen the supply side of their economies.

First and foremost, attention needs to focus on encouraging non-inflationary economic growth. The message here is simultaneously simple and difficult. Macroeconomic disequilibria reflect imbalances between aggregate demand and aggregate supply. They may, therefore, be corrected either by reducing aggregate demand or by increasing aggregate supply. The latter is the more attractive option. From both an economic and political perspective, it is easier to manage a growing economy. From an economic perspective, economic growth is likely to be associated with rising tax revenue and perhaps falling government expenditure. The fiscal balance will therefore improve. This will reduce the need to create credit, so money supply growth can be reduced. In any case as an economy grows the demand for money increases and monetary expansion can be accommodated without causing inflation. From a political perspective, poverty alleviation through economic growth leads to fewer problems than poverty alleviation via income redistribution.[14]

The more difficult question, then, is how to encourage economic growth? Unfortunately, at present, we have no clear and unambiguous answer to this question, although there is some indication that reasonably liberal, open and market-based systems have a better record.[15] If this is the case, developing countries need to expand and strengthen their market structures. By making markets work better there is a presumption that a whole range of price elasticities will rise in value, spanning goods markets and financial markets. The important point here is that, by increasing the value of these price elasticities, the effectiveness of the traditional tools of macroeconomic policy will increase.[16] For example, by increasing the price elasticity of export supply, exchange rate devaluation will become a more effective way of strengthening the current account of the balance of payments. By developing domestic financial markets, saving may be made more responsive to changes in interest rates.

If, at the same time, governments broaden the tax base and reduce the reliance on trade taxes, the fiscal balance will become less vulnerable to external shocks and more responsive to changes in domestic policy. Fiscal deficits can also be reduced by reducing the degree of state ownership of industry and by encouraging governments to focus instead on the provision of public goods and on creating an appropriate regulatory environment in which markets may function without adversely affecting social welfare.

The general point is that the efficiency of monetary policy, fiscal policy and exchange rate policy in the long run can be increased by structural change which strengthens the supply side of developing economies.

Who can help and do they? The role of the IMF

There is a problem with the strategy outlined above. Supply-side changes are unlikely to have an immediate effect. While they may be the most appropriate way of dealing with macroeconomic disequilibria in the long run, what happens in the short run? If they were sufficiently farsighted and confident in the ultimate success of a supply-side approach, private international capital markets might be expected to provide the necessary short-term financing. But the reality is that, in the case of many developing countries, they do not – a situation that is unlikely to change in the foreseeable future. Here, then, is a role for international agencies, such as the IMF. Providing medium-to-long-term financing to developing countries bypassed by private capital markets is an international public good. Does the IMF provide it?

The answer is only in part. Conventional IMF conditionality focuses precisely on the areas of macroeconomic management where developing countries are likely to encounter problems. IMF programmes invariably incorporate conditions relating to the growth of domestic credit, the size of fiscal deficits and the value of the domestic currency.[17] On the basis of the above analysis it might be expected that developing countries will find it difficult to deliver on these policy variables and this is what the evidence shows.[18] Apart from the exchange rate, IMF programmes do not generally have statistically significant effects on fiscal deficits and do not reduce the growth of monetary aggregates. Since compliance with performance criteria is required in order to gain access to later instalments of a Fund loan it is therefore unsurprising to find that the majority of IMF programmes in developing countries break down and remain uncompleted.[19]

Since the late 1980s some attempt has been made by the IMF to deal with the problems of supply-side weakness in developing countries by introducing structural adjustment lending and structural conditionality in the form of the Structural Adjustment Facility (SAF) and Enhanced Structural Adjustment Facility (ESAF).[20] However, the problem has been that structural conditions have been added to conventional conditions relating to macroeconomic management, and these programmes have shown an even greater tendency to break down.

Some critics have used this experience as a reason to argue that the Fund should return to its core area of competence: macroeconomic management of aggregate demand.[21] The International Financial Institution Advisory Commission (IFIAC) has, in a similar vein, recommended that the Fund should withdraw from medium-to-long-term lending to developing countries and should abandon the ESAF (now renamed the Poverty Reduction and Growth Facility).

According to the analysis in this chapter, however, such reforms would do nothing to improve the economic performance of developing countries and could make it worse. Instead, reform needs to focus initially on creating the economic circumstances in which the traditional tools of macroeconomic management will work. This is not an argument for ignoring the demand side; uncontrolled fiscal deficits, rapid monetary expansion and severely overvalued exchange rates clearly need to be avoided. But it is an argument for not expecting too much from the principal macroeconomic policy tools and for not expecting developing countries to be able to exert the same degree of control over them as might be expected of industrial economies – which have, of course, themselves often run large fiscal deficits, been unable to control monetary aggregates and allowed exchange rates to become significantly overvalued.

This general conclusion is more applicable to some macro policy tools than others. Developing countries can, for example, exert more control over their exchange rates than over monetary growth. IMF programmes have exerted a greater effect on exchange rates than monetary growth. And exchange rate devaluation is more likely to be associated with export expansion and economic growth. While devaluation could be made more effective by raising foreign trade price elasticities, there is evidence that it is already an effective policy instrument that meets the requirements of a reasonable performance criterion for IMF programmes.[22]

At the same time, fiscal conditionality should be modified to relate less to the overall budgetary balance, which may be affected by exogenous factors, and more to the microeconomic components of taxation policy and government expenditure. Again, the evidence on the effects of IMF programmes suggests that countries have found it easier to comply with such conditions than conditions relating to the overall fiscal deficit.[23]

Concluding remarks

Developing countries encounter many problems in seeking to manage their economies. First, they are particularly vulnerable to external shocks of one type or another. These can be related both to trade, as the terms of trade move against them, and to finance as world interest rates rise and capital flows dry up.[24] Second, faced with the resultant instability, it may be expected that the traditional macroeconomic stabilisation policies will be relatively ineffective because of the economic features that frequently characterise developing countries.

Some of the current proposals for the reform of the international financial architecture ignore these problems and argue that developing countries should rely yet more heavily on these traditional policies, even though IMF-supported programmes that have emphasised them in the past have generally not worked, except perhaps in strengthening the balance of payments.[25] While any country ignores fiscal and monetary excesses at its peril, the evidence on why countries turn to the IMF does not support the claim that developing countries are always the worst offenders.[26] This chapter has argued that developing countries need to focus on long-term structural change aimed at reducing their vulnerability to external shocks and creating an economic environment which allows traditional measures of macroeconomic policy to work better. They need to broaden and deepen financial markets so that governments are better able to finance fiscal deficits, improve the operation of goods markets to raise price elasticities, improve the structure of taxation to increase the tax base and strengthen their ability to raise tax revenue and redefine the role of the government to focus on the provision of public goods.

The IMF (and World Bank) have an important role to play in facilitating this transition, but they can also miss the opportunity. While the movement towards structural adjustment has been a step in the right direction, the continuing preoccupation with controlling monetary aggregates has prevented this initiative from being as effective as it could otherwise have been. IMF programmes need to be redesigned to match the realities found in developing countries. There is no point in looking for more than can be realistically expected or achieved. Otherwise, the failure rate will be high and there will be damage to the credibility of economic reform which will undermine future attempts at stabilisation.

Macroeconomic management is never likely to be a 'piece of cake' and good economic performance is, in any case, not simply a function of good macroeconomic management alone. But the continuation of appropriate supply-side reform should mean that developing countries will encounter fewer problems in conducting effective macroeconomic policy in the future. Abandoning it would make the effective pursuit of macroeconomic stability much more of an impossible mission. Economists based in industrial countries might do better to advise their own governments to maintain economic growth and stability and thereby help create a global economic environment which is conducive to sustainable economic growth in developing countries.

References

Bird, G (1996) The International Monetary Fund and developing countries: a review of the evidence and policy options, *International Organization*, 50(3), pp 477–511.

Bird, G (1998a) Exchange rate policy in developing countries: what is left of the nominal anchor approach?, *Third World Quarterly*, 19(2), pp 255–76.

Bird, G (1998b) Convertibility and volatility: the pros and cons of liberalising the capital account, *Economic Notes*, 27(2), pp 141–56.

Bird, G and Helwege, A (1997) Can liberalisation survive in Latin America?, *Millennium: Journal of International Studies*, 26(1), pp 31–56.

Conway, P (1994) IMF lending programmes: participation and impact, *Journal of Development Economics*, 45, pp 365–91.

Dicks-Mireaux, L, Mecagni, M and Schadler, S (2000) Evaluating the effect of IMF lending to low-income countries, *Journal of Development Economics*, 61(2), pp 495–526.

Easterly, W and Schmidt-Hebbel, K (1993) Fiscal deficits and macroeconomic performance in developing countries, *World Bank Research Observer*, 8(2), pp 211–38.

Edwards, S (1989) The IMF and the developing countries: a critical evaluation, *Carnegie–Rochester Conference Series on Public Policy*, 31 (Amsterdam: North Holland) pp 7–68.

Edwards, S (1998) Openness, productivity and growth: what do we really know?, *Economic Journal*, 108, pp 383–99.

Fanelli, J M, Frenkel, R and Taylor L (1994) Is the market-friendly approach friendly to development? A critical assessment, in G Bird and A Helwege (eds), *Latin America's Economic Future* (London: Academic Press).

Kamin, S (1988) Devaluation, external balance and macroeconomic performance: a look at the numbers, *Princeton Studies in International Finance*, 62.

Haque, N and Khan, M (1998) Do IMF-supported programmes work? A survey of the cross-country empirical evidence, IMF *Working Paper* 98/169, December, Washington, DC: IMF.

Killick, T (1995a) *IMF Programmes in Developing Countries: Design and Impact* (London: Routledge).

Killick, T (1995b) Can the IMF help low-income countries? experiences with its structural adjustment facilities, *The World Economy*, 18(4), pp 603–16.

Mosley, P (2000) Globalisation, economic policy and convergence, *The World Economy*, 23(5), pp 613–34.

Mussa, M and Savastano, M (1999) The IMF approach to economic stabilisation, *IMF Working Paper* 99/104, July, Washington, DC: IMF.

Page, S (ed.) (1993) *Monetary Policy in Developing Countries* (London: Routledge).

Rodrik, D (1996) Understanding economic policy reform, *Journal of Economic Literature*, 34(1), pp 9–41.

Sachs, J D and Warner, A (1995) Economic reform and the process of global integration, *Brookings Papers on Economic Activity*, pp 1–65.

Santaella, J (1995) Four decades of Fund arrangements: macroeconomic stylised facts before the adjustment programmes, IMF *Working Paper* 95/74, Washington, DC: IMF.

Schadler, S, Rozwadowski, F, Tiwari, S and Robinson, D G (1993) Economic adjustment in low-income countries: experience under the Enhanced Structural Adjustment Facility, Occasional Paper No 106, Washington, DC: IMF.

Summers, L (1999) Speech to London Business School, 14 December 1999, reported in *Financial Times*, 15 December 1999.

2
External Financing and Balance of Payments Adjustment in Developing Countries: Getting a Better Policy Mix

Graham Bird

Introduction

There are a number of alternative strategies for dealing with current account balance of payments deficits. One is to ignore them altogether on the grounds that they do not matter. Here the argument is that in the long term the imbalance between domestic investment and savings, which the deficit reflects, will be automatically corrected and that, mindful of this, private external finance will be available to cover excess expenditure in the short term; net capital inflows will finance short-term net inward transfers of real resources. If, in long-run equilibrium, there is a close positive correlation between investment and saving across countries, net external financing will be merely a cyclical deviation from this.[1]

Where current account imbalances, however, are not automatically eliminated, or where the process of automatic adjustment is too prolonged and uncertain for markets to be prepared to finance it, governments will have to take policy actions in order to shorten its duration or improve the flow of information about it in order to raise market confidence.

In as much as current account deficits reveal an excess of aggregate domestic demand over and above aggregate supply they may be corrected either by reducing the former or by raising the latter. Financing balance of payments (BoP) deficits involves either reducing international reserves, or international borrowing. Governments will explicitly or implicitly calculate the optimum combination of policies depending upon their relative costs. The choice will, however, be constrained in various ways. First, anxious to maintain power, governments will factor in political as well as economic costs. An adjustment strategy needs to incorporate a judgement about the political scope for implementation. Second, international reserves may be too low to allow countries to finance their preferred adjustment strategy by

14

decumulating international reserves, and yet, at the same time, and in part because of low reserves, international creditors may be unwilling to lend the amounts of finance that countries wish to borrow. In these circumstances of balance of payments need, governments may turn to the International Monetary Fund (IMF) for financial support. But, while this will relax one constraint, it will impose others since the Fund will only lend where it approves an adjustment program.

Different countries will experience these constraints with different degrees of acuity. To the extent that international creditworthiness is positively associated with the level of economic development, developing countries, and in particular the poorest among them, will face constraints that are more binding than those facing developed countries and, in this sense, the "new" theory of the balance of payments, which downplays the significance of current account deficits, will be less relevant to them.

Through credit rationing, private international capital markets and the IMF may therefore preclude developing countries from implementing their preferred mix of adjustment and external financing, forcing them to opt for shorter-term adjustment-intensive strategies. But will this lead to a better mix of policies?

The next section of this chapter informally explores a simple theoretical framework within which the factors impinging on the final outcome may be analyzed. This framework allows for interaction between those factors which influence countries' preferred choices and the constraints which limit their choice. This section also examines the nature of the relationship between adjustment and financing; are they substitutes or complements? The section that follows traces out how the mix between adjustment and financing has changed since the early 1970s, and investigates the extent to which observed changes have been desirable. The last section goes on briefly to explore policy options that would shift countries toward a mix of adjustment and external financing that the theoretical analysis and empirical evidence suggests would be better. Given the involvement of the Fund in balance of payments policy in developing countries, the chapter also covers the Fund's role in bringing about an appropriate blend of adjustment and financing, and touches on the part played by conditionality in securing it.

An informal theoretical framework

Basic ideas

Unless countries are unconstrained in their levels of external indebtedness, they will be unable to run current account deficits in perpetuity. They cannot therefore, in the long run, avoid adjustment; in essence, this is what lies behind the concept of a "sustainable" BoP current account deficit. What they can do, however, is to choose what they perceive as the optimal intertemporal distribution of that adjustment. They can therefore opt for more or for less adjustment in any one particular time period. Where their preference is to defer adjustment, postponing it to the future or spreading it out over time, they will need to finance the ongoing current account deficit. They will only be able to do this, however, if they possess sufficient international reserves to finance the excess imports that are not financed from current export earnings, or alternatively if they can borrow from international capital markets. They will only be able to borrow if they retain creditworthiness, and, in large measure, this will depend upon the credibility of the government's program for eliminating current account deficits. Where markets lack confidence, creditworthiness will decline and countries will be forced to modify their programs to coincide more closely with what markets deem to be appropriate. Almost certainly this will imply bringing adjustment forward in time.

Where macroeconomic disequilibria are not self-correcting, or where government policies designed to induce adjustment lack credibility with markets, countries will be unable to substitute external financing for economic adjustment. On the other hand, for as long as they can retain credibility, governments may trade-off the speed of adjustment against external financing.

While external financing allows adjustment to be phased over a longer time period, it also increases its non-discounted costs since loans have to be serviced and repaid. While rapid adjustment involves sacrifices of consumption early on, external financing involves subsequent sacrifices of consumption, with the size of these sacrifices varying positively with the rate of interest. Governments will, however, have a rate of time preference; future sacrifices will be less important to them than current sacrifices. For as long as their positive discount rate exceeds the rate of interest, it may be expected that they will try to substitute external financing for current-period adjustment. With other things equal, an increase in interest rates or a fall in the government's rate of discount will lead to a drop in demand for external financing. A recently elected government may, for example, believe that there is a "honeymoon period" during which economic sacrifices in consumption are more acceptable politically, with the result that the relative costs of current adjustment fall relative to those of future adjustment, and, in these circumstances, the speed of adjustment will increase.

The unconstrained optimum mix of policy occurs where the marginal rate of substitution between current and future expenditure equals the marginal rate of transformation between the sacrifice of current expenditure (current adjustment) and the sacrifice of future expenditure (current financing/ future adjustment); here the intertemporal distribution of the adjustment burden is deemed to be optimal by the relevant government.

This optimal combination of adjustment and financing will be disturbed first, if preferences alter, or second, if the relative costs of adjustment and financing change. Thus a strengthening preference for current expenditure will increase the degree of financing and encourage countries to substitute *out of* current adjustment, while an increase in the relative cost of external financing will encourage countries to substitute *into* current adjustment.

If developing countries in general encounter relatively high financing costs, then, other things being equal, they will be encouraged to make relatively greater use of current adjustment. But if they possess a relatively strong preference to avoid sacrificing current expenditure they will, other things being equal, tend to make relatively greater use of external financing. It is therefore difficult to say *a priori* whether they will prefer near-term adjustment-intensive or financing-intensive BoP strategies. Of course, were external financing to be subsidized and provided at concessional rates, this would reinforce the natural political inclination to avoid the immediate sacrifice that current adjustment involves and to postpone it. For many developing countries, however, postponing adjustment may not turn out to be a realistic option since, in practice, they often come up against an availability constraint in terms of external financing. They will therefore be precluded from using the combination of adjustment and financing which they would have chosen had no such constraint existed. Where the external financing constraint is effective, they will be forced to make greater use of current adjustment and less use of financing than they would have preferred.

Extending the analysis

The above analysis provides some useful insights into a government's preferred and actual mix between adjustment and external financing as a means of coping with balance of payments deficits – showing as it does the interplay of preferences and constraints. But it remains rudimentary and potentially misplaced and misleading. It implicitly assumes that the availability and cost of external financing affect only the intertemporal distribution of a given adjustment burden, modified to allow for a positive interest rate. This is consistent with viewing the balance of payments in a dynamic setting where deficits, financed by decumulating international reserves or by foreign borrowing, smooth domestic consumption. In practice, however, the availability of external financing affects the design and type of adjustment, and this has implications for the total costs of adjustment, as well as for the distribution of a given cost over time. Where external financing is strictly limited, adjustment will have to be achieved rapidly. Since it is generally easier for governments to exert a more direct and faster influence over aggregate demand than over aggregate supply, adjustment will have to focus on reducing aggregate domestic demand.

If an economy is close to full productive capacity, and therefore short-run aggregate supply is effectively fixed, short-run adjustment will have to focus on depressing consumption, investment, and/or government expenditure. A problem here is that reducing consumption or the current component of government expenditure may lead to social and political difficulties. Government employees may be expected to resist cuts in their wages, welfare recipients and the beneficiaries of price subsidies will also resist attempts to cut these elements of government expenditure. To the extent that at least a part of current government expenditure is directed toward efficient poverty alleviation, there will therefore be social costs associated with adjustment. But even if governments' perceptions are that these costs are outweighed by the need to correct the BoP deficit, the incidence of the costs may create sufficient political resistance as to make it impossible to implement this particular adjustment strategy.

Attention may therefore shift to reducing investment and the capital component of government expenditure as measures which will circumvent short-term political resistance. These measures, however, are likely to have an adverse effect on future aggregate supply. Even where the entire discrepancy between aggregate domestic demand and aggregate supply is eliminated in the current time period, adjustment costs will still, therefore, be carried over into future time periods because of the diminished physical and human capital stock that is passed on.

To the extent that future aggregate supply is a function of current aggregate demand, short-term demand-based BoP adjustment will create macroeconomic difficulties in the form of future balance of payments deficits; difficulties that could have been avoided had adjustment been achieved by increasing aggregate supply.

Much the same result emerges from an analytical approach which focuses on savings-investment imbalances. To the extent that it is difficult to increase savings in the short run, adjustment must reduce investment, but, by adversely affecting income growth, this reduces future period savings below what they would otherwise have been.

With fewer constraints on external financing, not only may reductions in aggregate demand be phased over a longer period, but, more importantly, the design of adjustment may switch toward slower-acting supply-side measures or structural adjustment. Here the emphasis is placed on correcting macroeconomic imbalances by raising aggregate supply and by increasing domestic savings rather than by reducing aggregate demand and domestic investment; the intention is to combine adjustment with economic growth. Of course, even with economic growth, correcting a balance of payments deficit continues to involve a sacrifice in terms of consumption foregone, but the sacrifice is now in the form of a reduced rate of improvement in living standards, and this will be politically easier to manage than adjustment that cuts existing living standards.

Moreover, while economic growth does not inevitably imply human and social development, other things being equal, it is more likely to create an environment within which these goals may be attained than one where there is economic stagnation and recession.

This leads on to another problem with the earlier analysis, which may too easily be interpreted to imply that there is a trade off between external financing and adjustment *per se*. Loosely seen in this way, external financing is often presented as allowing countries to "escape" adjustment, whereas credit rationing is seen as forcing them to undertake necessary adjustment. In fact the relationships between adjustment and external financing are much more subtle and complex, as more detailed analysis reveals. The true trade-off is between external financing and the speed, and therefore the nature, of adjustment. While external financing may be a substitute for short-term demand-deflation, it is a complement to longer-term and structurally oriented adjustment. If, furthermore, it can be argued that longer-term and supply-based adjustment is superior, because it protects economic growth, helps avoid social costs and political resistance, and therefore enhances the probability of implementation, external financing is appropriately seen as contributing positively to adjustment.

Can it be expected that markets will provide the external finance required to support longer-term adjustment? After all BoP deficits will now be more persistent. The problem is that structural adjustment and external financing come as a policy package. If either element is missing, the package as a whole will fail unless exogenous factors change for the better. Dynamically a vicious circle may be established in which inadequate external financing causes attempts at structural adjustment to fail. In turn the perceived failure of structural adjustment then makes it less likely that private capital will support further attempts, which means that the chances of success recede still further over time. The challenge is to transform this vicious circle into a virtuous one in which adequate external financing facilitates successful adjustment, which then reduces the BoP need for further external financing. While longer-term adjustment means that more external finance will be needed in the near term, it also means that less external finance will be needed later on, once structural adjustment has been successful.

Taking a long-term view, structural adjustment programs that succeed will require less external finance than demand-based adjustment programs that persistently fail because of their in-built political and intertemporal inconsistencies. But will private capital markets take this long-term view? There are sound reasons for believing that they will not, and will therefore, in general, undersupply the external finance needed to support structural adjustment. A socially optimal mix of adjustment and external financing is unlikely.

Because of the uncertainties surrounding longer-term structural adjustment and lack of confidence in the commitment and ability of governments to carry programs through to completion, creditors may demand high rates of interest which, particularly if they exceed the borrowers' rate of discount, will reduce the demand for external financing and may rule out structural adjustment. More likely, there will be credit rationing. Borrowers will be constrained by the availability of external finance and will therefore have to modify the design of adjustment away from longer-term supply-side measures and toward ones that focus on short-term demand. If demand-based adjustment is ineffective and inefficient, however, the gloomy expectations of creditors with respect to the success of adjustment will be fulfilled, and will therefore be reinforced at the next stage. Countries needing to adjust may find it increasingly difficult to attract financial support from private capital markets whatever adjustment strategy they adopt.

If creditors are short-termist in their outlook, it is also easy to see how they will be overinfluenced by transient changes in a country's economic performance, such as sudden changes in the terms of trade, rather than by longer-term economic fundamentals related to structural change. The combination of highly elastic expectations and contagion effects creates volatility and the scope for both capital shortfalls and capital surges. From time to time the availability of external financing may exceed the optimum, and governments may then be induced to postpone adjustment altogether, a strategy which they perceive as reducing near-term social and political costs.[2] To the extent that postponing adjustment causes macroeconomic disequilibria to deepen, however, future adjustment costs will also tend to rise (Edwards and Montiel, 1989). If private capital is volatile, an excess inflow will be followed by a deficiency, and countries which have deferred adjustment will then be forced to opt for yet more rapid correction of their BoP deficits. In as much as the underlying disequilibria are now larger, the degree of demand contraction will also need to be larger.

International agencies and non-optimal external financing

If private capital markets supply non-optimal amounts of external finance in support of economic adjustment, what may be done to correct this source of market failure? In principle, there appears to be a role for international agencies, although it is a role that has a number of facets. Here we concentrate on the IMF, although much of what follows could also apply to the World Bank. First, the Fund could seek to ensure that informational errors are corrected, and that private lenders are better informed about, and therefore pay greater attention to "economic fundamentals"; assuming, of course, that the Fund is itself well informed about such things. Second, it could seek both to increase the commitment of governments to the process of adjustment, and to raise market confidence in that commitment, and the appropriateness of economic policy; a key question here is whether IMF conditionality, as it has conventionally been used, is the best means of achieving these objectives. Third, it could provide its own finance in order to close any gap between what it deemed to be the appropriate provision of external finance and the actual provision from private capital markets. This implies a relatively long-term lending role for the Fund in some countries, but possibly a short-term lending role in others where the Fund is attempting to compensate for sudden and ill-based capital outflows.[3] It also begs the question of the appropriate modalities through which lending occurs.

Where there is asymmetrical information, an alternative possibility would be for the Fund to subsidize commercial lending or itself borrow directly from international capital markets and then on-lend.

The involvement of the Fund in securing a particular mix of financing and adjustment via conditional lending requires a slight modification to the earlier analysis. From the borrower's viewpoint the cost of Fund finance includes a loss of national sovereignty in the design of macroeconomic policy. It is not that the Fund shifts the blend of policy toward adjustment. Indeed, without the Fund's financial support adjustment would, in principle, need to be more rapid. It is instead that the Fund exerts an influence over the design of adjustment. The extent to which countries perceive this as a cost depends on the size of the discrepancy between their own favored program and the one favored by the Fund. In principle therefore, the perceived cost of Fund support will fall as a consequence of either the Fund redesigning its conditionality to match more closely the preferences of borrowing governments, or borrowing governments changing their own views about adjustment in such a way that they come closer to those held by the Fund.

Even where a gap exists between the preferences of governments and those of the Fund, however, the borrower's perceived cost of IMF conditionality will be a decreasing function of the need to comply with it. Thus,

$$C^b = \alpha(A^b - A^f) \tag{1}$$

where C^b is the borrower's perceived cost of IMF conditionality, A^b is the vector of policies which the borrower would prefer, A^f is the vector of policies that the Fund is prepared to support, and α is the compliance ratio, describing the extent to which Fund-supported policies need to be implemented in order to gain access to Fund finance. As α falls toward zero, the perceived costs of conditionality will fall. But, α will not reach zero because the Fund will almost certainly require "prior actions" to be undertaken before any finance is released. A borrowing country will therefore have to implement some Fund-backed policy changes in order to gain access to any finance from the Fund. For any given value of α, the perceived costs of conditionality will be an increasing function of the inequality between A^b and A^f.

An extra twist is added to this analysis by the fact that, for any given value of α, α^*, or the *actual* degree to which Fund-backed policies are implemented, will be a decreasing function of $(A^b - A^f)$.

Where does this theoretical discussion leave us? Faced with BoP deficits, governments will have a preferred mix of current adjustment and external financing. Although high interest rates will disincline them from foreign borrowing, for developing countries this is likely to be offset by a high social discount rate and by the perceived social and political costs of short-term adjustment. Given the opportunity to finance BoP deficits by borrowing, it might be expected that most developing country governments would opt for this alternative. Many developing countries however, will encounter a constraint on the availability of external financing, although the effectiveness of this constraint will vary from country to country as well as from time to time. Less financing means that adjustment needs to be more rapid and this is likely to imply a greater emphasis on deflating domestic aggregate demand. While unrestrained external financing could mean that adjustment is ignored or inadequate, unduly restrained financing will mean that excessive emphasis is placed on short-term demand management, and this will have potential dangers for economic growth and longer-term economic development.

For developing countries that are vulnerable to world economic shocks, adjustment has to encourage structural diversification and increased economic flexibility. Short-term adjustment which focuses on aggregate demand management may do little to help induce necessary structural changes. Indeed structural change may even be needed in order to make effective the conventional monetary and fiscal tools of demand management as well as exchange rate devaluation. Increasing the rate of economic growth clearly provides a preferable long-run form of adjustment. But for as long as BoP deficits persist, external financing will be needed. Yet there is little theoretical reason to believe that private capital markets will supply the optimal amount of financing, and this therefore raises the question of what the international financial institutions, particularly the IMF and World Bank, should do to offset this source of market failure.

External financing and balance of payments adjustment in practice: experience in the 1980s

How has the mix between external financing and adjustment changed over recent years, and have the changes been in a desirable direction? Following a significant increase in the quantity of international liquidity in the early 1970s, the global redistributional effects of rising oil prices in 1973–74 served to increase the lending capacity of the private international banks which attracted deposits from the oil-exporting countries. Petrodollars were recycled to oil-importing developing countries, as well as to some oil-producing countries which wished to take early advantage of their oil wealth. Bank lending was largely unconditional and borrowing countries were able to by-pass adjustment. With low world interest rates there were clear incentives to opt for financing-intensive BoP strategies. Although much less significant in quantitative terms, the Fund also sought to recycle petrodollars and help finance BoP deficits through a new Oil Facility (OF);

drawings on the OF by the least developed countries were made available at subsidized interest rates, with resources provided by the Trust Fund which itself was financed by IMF sales of gold. The liberalization of its Compensatory Financing Facility (CFF) in the mid-1970s also meant that a relatively large proportion of Fund support was being offered on low conditionality terms, which made it an attractive source of finance.

For some developing countries, either under or outside the auspices of the IMF, there was an opportunity to temporally avoid adjustment and to substitute external financing, and many of them grasped it.

Systemically the justification for a financing-intensive response to the then existing global disequilibria was that they were short-term and self-correcting. Adjustment was therefore inappropriate. But with the second large increase in oil prices at the end of the 1970s this interpretation changed. The international financial institutions (IFIs) began to accentuate the need for adjustment. In response to the global disequilibria existing at the beginning of the 1980s, the IMF resisted any temptation to reactivate the by then defunct Oil Facility and, moreover, modified the CFF in such ways as to effectively eliminate its low conditionality properties. Meanwhile, the World Bank embarked on a new program of structural adjustment lending.

The debt crisis also meant that the commercial banks became much less willing to lend voluntarily to governments in general support of the balance of payments, and, in any case, as real interest rates rose sharply, external financing became less attractive to potential borrowers. Early diagnosis of the debt crisis still emphasized its liquidity as opposed to its solvency aspects and international policy initially focused on trying to galvanize new financial flows. But the market mood took a contrary view and the multilateral debt strategy soon switched toward a stronger emphasis on economic adjustment in the highly indebted countries combined with debt rescheduling. The 1980s witnessed a fairly general increase in conditionality, and a move towards adjustment rather than external financing as the most appropriate way of dealing with BoP deficits in developing countries.

As the 1980s progressed there was also a growing consensus upon what constituted the key components of such adjustment – the so-called Washington consensus. This comprised elements to induce macroeconomic stability, microeconomic efficiency, and openness. While conventional tools of macroeconomic management remained important, they were now apparently to be augmented by structural or supply-side measures which were frequently based on reducing state regulation and involvement in economic activity. Thus, at the same time as there was an undeniable shift toward adjustment, it was also argued by the IFIs that the nature of adjustment was changing. Certainly the Fund claimed to be reorientating its conditionality toward the supply-side in support of structural adjustment and, as if to emphasize the point, introduced its own structural adjustment lending facilities (the SAP and ESAF). Moreover, while the Fund became involved in an increasing number of developing countries such that the number of outstanding Fund arrangements increased, there were no significant increases in the amount of Fund lending, and, for most of the period since the mid-1980s, the repayment of old loans by developing countries has exceeded the receipt of new ones.

Here, however, are the beginnings of a number of fundamental inconsistencies. As was seen in the previous section, reduced external financing is consistent with more adjustment if this is of a conventional demand-side type. Short-run adjustment acts as a substitute for external financing. Reduced financing by the Fund would therefore be quite consistent with an increase in the speed of adjustment. But the IMF and the World Bank were claiming that they had encompassed structural adjustment. In the context of this form of adjustment, however, external financing is a complement rather than a substitute. It might have been expected, therefore, that a move toward structural adjustment would go hand in hand with an increase in lending by the IFIs. Without such an increase, the presumption might reasonably be that external financing would remain an effective constraint, and that there would be, in reality, a continuing and even enhanced emphasis on demand-side adjustment. Moreover, if the analysis of the need for structural adjustment is accurate, it would be further expected that demand-side adjustment would be relatively ineffective at curing supply-side problems; negative effects on investment, economic growth and aggregate supply could be anticipated.

The potential inconsistency between reductions in IFI financing and a shift toward structural adjustment could, however, in principle, also be resolved in another way. Increases in the need for external financing could still be met alongside reduced IFI lending if other sources of funding filled the gap. Indeed the IFIs, and in particular the IMF, claimed that there was an important link between their involvement and other financial flows; the so-called catalytic effect. Here, potential private investors and public aid agencies would be disinclined to lend to some countries without the involvement of the IFIs but would become inclined to do so with such involvement.

The theory underpinning the catalytic effect is unclear, however. To the extent that financial liberalization leads to higher interest rates, and exchange rate liberalization leads to currency depreciation, it could be argued that additional private capital would be attracted to countries implementing a standard demand-based stabilization program. But what if rising domestic interest rates cause economic recession? Direct and portfolio investment, as well as bank lending, could in these circumstances seem less attractive. Moreover, what if exchange rate devaluation is interpreted to signal reduced government commitment to economic stabilization and an increased probability of further devaluation?

Moreover, external financing has public good characteristics. While individual investors may perceive that developing countries need critical masses of external finance in order to support structural adjustment, they do not perceive it to be in their own interests to provide finance in isolation; there is a coordination problem which may be more evident in the case of nonbank lending. If individual private lending institutions believe that IFI involvement is unlikely to induce others to lend, they will themselves become more reluctant to do so, and this strategy will then reaffirm market expectations in general.

All creditors lend on the basis of an expectation of the economic performance of debtors. Does IFI involvement stand as a reasonable guarantee of improved economic performance? This is both a theoretical and an empirical issue, but it essentially reduces to the question of whether IFI involvement will be perceived as significantly increasing the probability that policies which are deemed appropriate by potential private lenders will be identified and implemented. This perception is in turn likely to depend heavily on the IFIs' track record and less on an independent assessment of economic policy. Again there is a potentially fundamental inconsistency. The catalytic effect will be strong if IFI involvement in the past has had a significant and beneficial impact on the economic performance of the countries involved. It will be weak where the IFIs' track record has been one of apparently only very limited success. But what if the poor track record reflects inadequate external financing in support of economic adjustment? There will have to be some mechanism for breaking out of the vicious circle. On the basis of this analysis, relying on the catalytic effect is most unlikely to provide that mechanism.

Data from the World Bank's *World Development Report* (World Bank various years) show that over 1980–91, nineteen low-income countries and twenty-five middle-income countries experienced negative per capita economic growth. Whatever policies were being pursued, they clearly did not raise aggregate supply. Over the same period, thirteen low-income countries and thirty-two middle-income countries experienced declines in gross domestic investment. The relationship between economic growth and investment is complex, with causality running in both directions. Moreover, there is a far from perfect statistical match between those developing countries experiencing negative economic growth, and falling investment. For example, four of the low-income countries (LICs) with declining investment avoided negative economic growth. But nonetheless the evidence is consistent with the broad claim that during the 1980s many developing countries encountered external financing constraints which forced them to adopt policies of adjustment, based on aggregate demand deflation, and that these policies were unable to insulate investment. This conclusion is reinforced by data on domestic saving and investment ratios across developing countries, taken from the IMF's *World Economic Outlook* (IMF, various years). These show that during the 1980s, and outside Asia, adjustment, to the extent it occurred, took place by means of investment falling rather than saving increasing.[4] Again, there is no overall evidence of a successful shift toward structural adjustment during the 1980s aimed at increasing productive potential.

Studies of the effects of Fund-backed balance of payments adjustment provide much the same conclusion. The conventional caricature of Fund conditionality as relying on devaluation of the exchange rate and deflation of domestic aggregate demand seems to have been increasingly accurate during the post 1982 years (Edwards, 1989). Although there have been changes in conditionality, these have largely involved extending it to incorporate additional supply-side conditions. The hard core of Fund-backed programs has not changed, (Killick, 1992; Knight and Santaella, 1994), and remains based on reducing aggregate demand. One of the most robust conclusions of empirical research into the economic effects of programs supported by the IFIs is that they have a significantly adverse effect on domestic investment. Indeed, it is reduced investment which carries the largest share of falling levels of domestic absorption, suggesting that short-term social and political factors force governments to adopt high social discount rates in designing their BoP strategy.

The evidence on economic growth is less clear-cut. Although some recent studies suggest that programs backed by the IMF may have a negative short-run effect, other research suggests that these adverse growth effects may be offset to some extent by incorporating supply-side measures, and studies of World Bank structural adjustment lending have generally identified a positive effect on economic growth.[5]

Overall there is at least some empirical support for the theoretical expectations formulated earlier. The reduced availability of external financing in support of the balance of payments during the 1980s, as well as the increasing cost of such finance, pushed developing countries toward greater adjustment. However, and again as theory predicts, it pushed them into a form of adjustment (reductions in domestic aggregate demand) which was a short-term substitute for external financing, and not into longer-term supply-side adjustment, which required additional short-term financing.

Even where the fundamental economic problems facing developing countries relate to the supply-side of their economies, demand-based adjustment may still have the short-term effect of reducing BoP deficits, but it is unlikely to strengthen the balance of payments in the long term, as it adversely affects both physical and human capital formation.

The deterioration in the balance of payments of developing countries at the beginning of the 1990s (shown in Table 2.1) aptly illustrates that to the extent that adjustment had occurred, it had been inadequate to eliminate their vulnerability to swings in global economic activity (something that structural adjustment is designed to reduce).

Empirical evidence also suggests that it is unwise to rely on the catalytic effects of IFI lending in order to generate adequate amounts of external

Table 2.1 Balance of payments on current account (in billions of US dollars)

Year	All developing countries	Africa	Asia	Western Hemisphere
1977	−0.1	−10.4	−0.9	−11.6
1978	−36.2	−15.4	−8.9	−19.4
1979	0.2	−6.6	−15.2	−21.7
1980	22.6	−5.3	−21.8	−29.3
1981	−56.3	−25.2	−23.4	−43.1
1982	−99.6	−24.4	−19.8	−42.1
1983	−70.5	−15.5	−16.3	−11.7
1984	−43.9	−10.9	−7.9	−5.5
1985	−44.2	−9.8	−8.2	−7.5
1986	−46.4	−9.1	4.3	−16.4
1987	−5.3	−4.0	22.0	−10.4
1988	−22.9	−9.1	10.7	−11.7
1989	−15.4	−7.1	2.6	−8.5
1990	−9.8	−2.9	−0.7	−6.7
1991	−86.7	−4.4	−1.0	−21.0

Source: IMF, *World Economic Outlook* (October 1994).

financing. The catalytic effect is more of a myth than a reality. Although there may be instances where programs backed by the IFIs coincide with additional capital inflows from other sources, IFI involvement appears to be neither a necessary nor a sufficient condition. Moreover, in individual cases where there does seem to be some empirical support for its existence, the catalytic effect appears to be limited to public flows. Although clearly something that could be explained through disaggregation, the overall observation that increases in the number of IMF arrangements coincided with reduced private capital inflows to developing countries during the 1980s is also inconsistent with the idea of a catalytic effect.

Taking all this together there is considerable empirical support for the claim that during the 1980s the blend of external financing and BoP adjustment in developing countries was suboptimal; there was inadequate external finance and there was therefore excessive emphasis on short-run demand-side adjustment which, in large measure concentrated on reducing investment. Structural adjustment designed to increase aggregate supply relative to aggregate demand, and to improve the sustainability of the current account of the balance of payments did not, in general, take place.

It does not follow, however, that it would have been better to have had more external financing and a *spreading out* of demand-based adjustment. Instead what is needed is a shift toward longer-term structural adjustment which focuses on raising long-run aggregate supply.

Evidence from the early 1990s seems, perhaps, to be at odds with the hypothesis of deficient external financing. After all the early 1990s saw a surge of capital flows to Latin America, as well as apparently strengthening government commitment to the notion of structural adjustment in many developing countries. Moreover, there was some confidence that changes in the mechanisms through which capital was flowing into developing countries (direct and portfolio investment and bond issues) represented a systemic improvement which would avoid a repeat of the consequences of the surge of private bank lending that there had been in the 1970s. While the IFIs did little to increase their own lending to developing countries, it perhaps seemed that private capital markets, buoyed up by the conversion of many developing country governments to market-based policies, were now effectively providing adequate complementary external financing.

As the Mexican peso crisis aptly demonstrated, however, confidence that a more appropriate blend between structural adjustment and external financing had been found was misplaced. First, there was the issue of whether developing countries had actually discovered a set of appropriate economic policies. Second, there was the question of the extent to which these policies could reasonably be expected to generate an upturn in economic performance within the time-frame set by commercial lenders, and the extent to which lenders were influenced by the actions of other lenders rather than by economic fundamentals, creating conditions under which speculative bubbles could occur. Third, there was the question of whether the new forms of private lending were actually any more secure and stable than earlier bank lending, and whether, if mishandled, they could not themselves be destabilizing through their effects on exchange rates and money supplies. Fourth, there was the question of the distribution of private capital flows across developing countries. In fact the surge of new lending had been heavily concentrated on a narrow range of better-off developing counties (the emerging markets) and had bypassed the vast majority of poor countries.

The Mexican peso crisis in fact nicely illustrated the problem of non-optimal external financing. Except in this case, external financing was in excess of the needs of structural adjustment and led to too much macroeconomic relaxation. Although not being typical of the scenario that this paper focuses on, where shortages of external finance force countries to place too much emphasis on short-term policies which may be inappropriate in a longer-term context, the Mexican case still implies that relying on private capital markets is unlikely to result in the best mix of short-run macroeconomic stabilization, long-run economic adjustment and external financing in developing countries.

Implications for international public policy

The IFIs need a coherent strategy for offsetting sources of market failure, encompassing both adjustment and external financing components. It is also important that the strategy allows for interactions between adjustment and external financing in the design of policy. The focus needs to shift from designing adjustment programs that are consistent with existing financing constraints toward relaxing these constraints to generate adequate external finance in support of adjustment programs which best meet the needs of individual developing countries. This may sometimes imply rapid demand-based adjustment with little external financing, but more commonly than in the past, it may involve longer-term structural adjustment combined with larger and more appropriately tailored forms of external financing.

Policy with respect to adjustment needs to address the issues of both design and implementation. An appropriately designed adjustment program will only be effective if it is implemented. What are the relevant incentives? Implementation will be a positive function of "ownership", and by implication, a function of the size and intertemporal distribution of the net benefits as perceived by the relevant government. It will also be a positive function of the amount of external financial assistance, and the costs of noncompliance. Policy has to address each of these issues. Taking the example of the IMF, attempts should be made to strengthen the feeling of ownership among borrowing governments by narrowing the gap between A^b and A^f. This could clearly be achieved both by altering the preferences of governments through "education" and by modifying the design of conditionality. It would also have the advantage of encouraging countries to turn to the Fund at an earlier stage in the development of their BoP problems, and this would allow a longer process of program negotiation and a focus on forming a broad coalition of support, rather than a short-term solution in a crisis environment, when it may be difficult to put such a coalition together.

The literature on negotiation has drawn a distinction between advisers as "oracles" and as "attendants". Oracle advisers view clients as "empty vessels to be filled with the adviser's wisdom," whereas attendant advisers view their task as helping clients draw on (their) own knowledge and experience in determining a course of action necessary to solve the client's problem (Salacuse, 1994, p. 9). This latter type of adviser considers the client to be "an important, if not primary, source of information and knowledge" and the adviser's role as "helping the client identify, organize, evaluate and apply knowledge and information that the client already has". Indeed, adviser roles are characterized by two factors – the extent to which the adviser draws on the client's knowledge, experience and information, and the extent to which the client participates in formulating the course of action to be followed. IFI advice is more likely to be heeded where client countries feel that they have been fully involved in the process of negotiating programs, and that, in areas where they have superior information, this has influenced the final outcome.

The size of perceived net benefits could be increased and their intertemporal distribution made more attractive by improving the design and therefore the effectiveness of adjustment programs, by strengthening the catalytic effect, and by providing external finance which enables short-term costs to be ameliorated. There is an element of the chicken and the egg here. The strength of the catalytic effect will depend on the past effectiveness of IFI-backed programs. But the effectiveness of programs depends on the degree of implementation, which in turn depends, in part, on the availability and terms of accompanying finance. This suggests that initially at least relatively heavy claims will be put on the IFIs to provide the needed finance in support of adjustment, with the financing role gradually being shared with and ultimately largely borne by private capital markets once the credibility of IFI-backed adjustment has been enhanced. It also calls for close cooperation between the IMF and the World Bank in terms of the design and financing of an appropriate adjustment strategy.

Credibility in the eyes of private capital markets could also be raised in the short term by means of the IFIs imposing greater penalties on noncompliance, since this would, other things being equal, raise a government's commitment to implement an agreed program. With little penalty on noncompliance the degree of commitment would remain in doubt.

The degree of implementation may, however, also be influenced by changes in economic conditions which were not foreseen at the time when the program was designed. It is therefore important to provide contingent resources in these circumstances.

There is always the danger, of course, that additional external financing will be used by governments as a substitute for adjustment.[6] In these circumstances additional financing would not lead to a superior mix of policies but simply a different but still suboptimal mix. For this reason it may be preferable, and certainly more politically realistic, to respond to the shortcomings of IFI conditionality by modifying it rather than abandoning it altogether. Moreover, the idea that the IFIs should provide additional financial support to developing countries in pursuit of structural adjustment begs the question of where the extra resources will come from, and this itself raises questions relating to the future of the SDR, the provision of IMF subsidies, and the reform of IMF quotas. None of these questions present insuperable difficulties in themselves. The difficulty instead lies in convincing the IFI's principal shareholders that such a re-mix in favor of, IFI-based financing is desirable.

In this context, it is important to stress that economic adjustment and the provision of external finance are interrelated components of one BoP package. Longer-term adjustment initially requires more financing, but, by being more successful in raising rates of economic growth, the increased need for finance will not be permanent. More BoP financing early on permits less financing later on. Furthermore, as adjustment becomes more successful, not only will the demand for finance from the IFIs decline, but also countries will enjoy greater access to commercial financing. In this sense it is improvements in the effectiveness of conditionality that lie at the heart of the Fund's catalytic effect. For as long as conditionality is perceived as ineffective it will fail to catalyze private capital inflows. Other things being equal, long-term private capital is unlikely to be attracted to countries in which domestic demand is being deflated, unless this is clearly seen as a precursor of faster economic growth. There is also considerable evidence to support the claim that it is by encouraging economic growth that the Fund can hope to reduce the future demand for its resources.

Compensating for the inadequacies of private capital markets does not necessarily mean that the IFIs need to replace them as a source of finance. Another approach is to analyze more carefully the reasons why private capital markets fail and to seek to correct them. Clearly one problem may be that individual market participants have insufficient information and may fail to interpret accurately the information that they do have. If the IFIs have fuller information and greater expertise in analyzing it then, in principle, they could improve the efficiency of capital markets by making both the information and their own analyses more openly available. Here the Fund's systemic policy role needs to be separated from its role as a lending institution.[7]

Concluding remarks

The mix between adjustment and external financing as a means of dealing with BoP deficits has altered significantly since the 1970s. Although there have been notable exceptions from time to time, for many developing countries the scope for financing them has fallen. The shift toward greater emphasis on adjustment, however, has incorporated a fundamental inconsistency. Although, the accent has, in principle, increasingly been placed on the need for supply enhancement and therefore for long-run structural adjustment, in practice and in the context of binding external financing constraints, developing countries have often been forced to rely heavily on the short-run management of aggregate domestic demand whether under or outside the auspices of the IFIs.

While macroeconomic instability may clearly adversely affect long-run aggregate supply, economic adjustment via the compression of aggregate demand may also itself have adverse long-run consequences for the supply side. Where reduced external financing implies quicker adjustment this adverse effect will be reinforced.

Longer-run adjustment implies an increased need for external financing in the short run. The appropriate mix between current adjustment and external financing depends therefore on the type of adjustment that is envisaged. Starving structural adjustment of required external financing in its early stages will reduce the probability of success.

Private capital markets cannot be confidently expected to supply the needed capital inflows in support of structural adjustment. The lack of confidence which they have in longer-term adjustment may prove self-fulfilling and self-perpetuating, and, in these circumstances, the international financial institutions such as the IMF need to take on the role not only of creating an economic environment in which private markets will be prepared to lend, but also of providing direct finance themselves. Enhancing the role of the IMF involves institutional changes, measures to raise its own financing capacity, and modifications to the design and modalities of conditionality.

Recent reform proposals put forward by the G-7, while in part addressing the question of information and the lending capacity of the Fund in emergency circumstances, unfortunately do not address the more deep-seated difficulties upon which this paper concentrates. Indeed, by urging the Fund to concentrate on its core concern of macroeconomic stability, the G-7 proposals tend to point in the opposite direction to the one that is favored here.

In circumstances where many of the Fund's major shareholders are anxious to limit (or reduce) their own levels of government expenditure, they will be unenthusiastic about increasing their contributions to IFIs. In seeking to justify such a policy it is convenient to argue that the Fund should focus on its core concern of encouraging macroeconomic stability, since this de-emphasizes the need for additional external financing. But, if the Fund is also unable to catalyze and stabilize external financing from private capital markets, the prospects for economic growth in many developing countries, let alone social and human development, look bleak. Poor economic and social performance reflect in part the wrong mix of policy. Although developing countries are not powerless in seeking to change the mix, there remains a key role for international public policy.

Acknowledgements

This chapter is based on research sponsored by the Office of Development Studies of the United Nations Development Programme. Their support is gratefully acknowledged as are the comments of the referees. The usual disclaimer applies.

References

Bird, G. (1995) *IMF Lending to Developing Countries: Issues and Evidence.* Routledge, London.

Corden, M. (1991) Does the current account matter? The old and the new. In *International Financial Policy: Essays in Honour of Jacques J. Polak,* eds. J. Frenkel and M. Goldstein. IMF, Washington D.C.

Edwards, S. (1989) The IMF and developing countries: A critical evaluation. *Carnegie–Rochester Conference Series on Public Policy* 31.

Edwards, S. and Montiel, P. (1989) Devaluation crises and the macroeconomic consequences of postponed adjustment in developing countries. *IMF Staff Papers,* December.

Feldstein, M. and Horioka, C. (1980) Domestic saving and international capital flows. *Economic Journal* **90**.

Ghosh, A. R. (1995) International capital mobility amongst the major industrialised countries: Too little or too much. *Economic Journal* **105**.

IMF (various years) *World Economic Outlook*. IMF, Washington D.C.

Killick, T. (1992) *Continuity and Change in IMF Programme Design, 1982–92*, ODI Working Paper 69. Overseas Development Institute, London.

Killick, T. and Malik, M. (1992) Country experiences with IMF programmes in the 1980s. *The World Economy* **5**.

Knight, M. and Santaella, J. A. (1994) Economic determinants of Fund financial arrangements. *IMF Working Paper*, WP/94/36. IMF, Washington D.C.

Salacuse, J. W. (1994) *The Art of Advice*. Time Books, New York.

World Bank (various years) *World Development Report*. Oxford University Press, New York.

3
Where do we Stand on Choosing Exchange Rate Regimes in Developing and Emerging Economies?

Graham Bird

Introduction

The question of what is the best exchange rate regime for a country to adopt has been an important part of the macroeconomic policy debate for as long as here has been a debate about macroeconomic policy. It has indeed sometimes been the dominant issue. An historical review could easily go back to the nineteenth century and the debate over the gold standard and the bimetallic standard, or could go back to the interwar period and the debate over the return to gold and the abandonment of the gold standard in favour of exchange rate flexibility. Or it could focus on the exchange rate arrangements incorporated into the Bretton Woods system devised in 1944 and the final collapse of those arrangements in favour of generalised flexible exchange rates in 1973.

All textbooks in international economics will have a section dealing with the arguments for and against different exchange rate regimes, particularly fixed versus flexible exchange rates. However, although it is relatively easy to assemble a list of the principal issues from a theoretical perspective, the choice of exchange rate regime also needs to be informed by empirical evidence. What does experience tell us?

By the beginning of the twenty-first century the consensus view was that experience favoured the extremes and disfavoured the middle ground. The 1990s had been characterised by a series of economic crises that had frequently been associated with attempts by governments to defend pegged exchange rates in conditions of evaporating credibility. According to this view countries should opt either for immutably fixed exchange rates, in the form of close monetary union, where credibility is assured, or for free floating, where there is no commitment to any particular exchange rate. They should not opt for any regimes lying in between these two poles.

This consensus has been reflected by a series of reports about international monetary reform that basically say as much.[1] However, there is another point of view suggesting that this is an illegitimate response to the crises of the 1990s and that intermediate solutions have not lost all their appeal; at the same time the polar extremes may have their own problems. This implies that inappropriate conclusions may have been drawn from the evidence. But what are the right lessons to draw and does it really matter if we draw the wrong ones?

There is another dimension to this. Many developing countries and emerging economies have borrowed from the International Monetary Fund and may be expected to do so in the future. Fund lending is conditional upon the pursuit of certain macroeconomic policies. A common component of conditionality has related to exchange rate policy, and there is evidence that the Fund exerts a stronger influence over this than over monetary and fiscal policy.[2] If the Fund is persuaded by the consensus view about exchange rate policy this may be reflected in its policy advice. In these circumstances, would the Fund be offering good advice? Might some countries in fact do better to opt for intermediate solutions of one form or another rather than to go for the extremes.

The purpose of this chapter is to offer a judgement on alternative exchange rate regimes for developing and emerging economies, informed by experience since the early 1990s.[3] It explores some of the lessons that may be learned from the currency crises that have occurred, and examines their implications for the design of IMF conditionality.

The following section briefly summarises the range of choices regarding exchange rate regimes. The next section explores the principal analytical issues raised by them. Much of the underlying material is quite familiar and an attempt is therefore made here to offer something other than a simple litany of the possible advantages and disadvantages of the various regimes. The fourth section investigates the extent to which the choice of exchange rate regime really matters. The following section then goes on to summarise the choice of exchange rate policy amongst a number of developing and emerging economies and how it has changed over recent years. It revisits the theoretical issues in the context of evidence drawn from Africa, Asia and Latin America, and attempts to identify the principal lessons that emerge. The final section offers a few concluding remarks that attempt to place exchange rate policy more generally in the context of macroeconomic policy and to examine the implications for the design of IMF conditionality.

The available options

There is a spectrum of choice when it comes to exchange rate regimes. At one end, there is free floating, where a government opts not to intervene at all in the foreign exchange market to influence the price of the currency.

In effect there is no exchange rate policy and no target in terms of the value of the currency. The exchange rate is left 'to find its own level' and does not constrain domestic macroeconomic policy. At the other end there is immutable fixity, in the form of a currency union or dollarisation.[4]

Adopting a single currency such as the Euro in Europe or the US dollar in case of Ecuador and Panama therefore rules out the possibility of changing the value of the national currency in terms of other currencies. Within the union exchange rates as such no longer exist; there is a unified currency. Of course there will still be an exchange rate against the rest of the world. Immutably fixing the exchange rate within the currency union in this way imposes strict constraints on domestic macroeconomic policy; there is no independent monetary policy and this in turn constrains fiscal policy.

In between the two extremes there are a number of intermediate exchange rate regimes that are neither immutably fixed nor freely floating, but are more proximate to one or other of the extremes. The closer the regime is to floating the fewer the constraints on other macroeconomic policies and the closer it is to a fixed rate regime the greater are the constraints. Thus under a currency board arrangement, which is proximate to a fixed exchange rate regime, the national currency is retained but its value is firmly pegged to that of another currency. The authorities then have to desist from neutralising the monetary implications of balance of payments disequilibria and sacrifice monetary independence. Currency boards are, in this respect, similar to the gold standard of the nineteenth and the early twentieth century.

Under an adjustable peg regime, similar to that incorporated in the Bretton Woods system, there is also a commitment to defend a par value for the currency, with macroeconomic policy, in principle, being designed to this end. However, this regime has an 'escape clause' in the sense that the peg is adjustable; something that is missing in the case of dollarisation and may be less easy to activate in the case of currency boards. The general intention in an adjustable peg regime is that the exchange rate should be adjusted if an inconsistency develops between the internal target in terms of employment and economic growth, and the external target in terms of the balance of payments. The commitment to the peg is contingent, and may therefore appear less strong and carry less credibility in the eyes of private capital markets. Under adjustable peg systems exchange rate changes tend to be infrequent, and large and also therefore directionally predictable. As a consequence, and with free capital mobility, such regimes are susceptible to speculative attack. They leave little or no discretion in terms of domestic monetary policy since domestic interest rates need to be set with a view to affecting capital flows. For this reason they have, in practice, commonly been supported by capital controls, reflecting the inability of combining an exchange rate peg, with independent monetary policy and free capital mobility. This 'impossible triad' says that it is only feasible to have any two of them at any one time.

Crawling pegs substitute small and frequent changes in the peg for large and infrequent ones. They thereby attempt to minimise the extent to which fundamental disequilibria are allowed to build up, and, by doing so, also aim to minimise speculation. The peg may crawl according to a pre-announced schedule with the authorities attempting to actively lead the market or it may respond passively and retrospectively to market pressures, in which case the commitment to any particular currency value will be less strong.

Instead of targeting a particular value, as is the case with the adjustable peg and crawling peg regimes, governments may merely establish limits on the range of values that the exchange rate is allowed to take. They may set out to constrain the value of the currency to lie within a 'target zone'. The basic nature of the target zone regime depends on where in the zone the currency's value is located. Inside the margins its value will be left to be determined by market forces and in many respects the regime is then much like a free floating regime. At the margins, it assumes the characteristics of a pegged regime with the domestic monetary authorities attempting to prevent the value of the currency from moving outside the zone's limits. As with other pegged systems, they may do this by means of direct intervention in the foreign exchange market – for example buying the domestic currency when it is being heavily sold by others – or by interest rate policy. There are variations on the general theme of target zones. The zone may be wide or narrow and therefore the regime may be closer to free floating or pegging respectively. It may be explicit or implicit, depending on the extent to which the authorities clearly spell out or announce the margins of the zone. And it may be 'hard' or 'soft' depending on the level of commitment with which the authorities defend the margins. Indeed where the zone or band within which the value of the currency is allowed to fluctuate is altered, the regime becomes an adjustable or crawling zone or sliding band.

In a sense, whether static or moving, a target zone represents an example of managed floating in as much as floating is permitted but only inside the zone. However, more generally, managed floating can be a way of describing any exchange rate regime where the authorities are prepared, in some circumstances, to intervene in order to influence the exchange rate and to limit the effect of market pressures. How far the system deviates from free floating then depends on the extent of management. How narrow and binding are the constraints. Managed floating will exist in basically any flexible exchange rate regime where the authorities eschew a policy of 'benign neglect'.

The analytics

How will governments select from this range of choice with respect to exchange rate regime? Many attempts to answer this question weigh up the pros and cons of the different regimes. A slightly different approach to the question is to place it in context of the underlying macroeconomics of the country concerned and various other country characteristics. Lurking behind the choice of exchange rate regime is some fairly fundamental macroeconomics.

First, altering the exchange rate is one means of attempting to engender economic adjustment. The need to adjust will depend on the incidence of macroeconomic disequilibria. Faced with disequilibria, governments will wish to retain policy instruments that are effective and efficient. But, as noted above, there are trade-offs here. Pegging the exchange rate constrains monetary independence. If monetary and fiscal policy have proved effective policy tools in the past, governments may be reluctant to constrain their ability to use them in the future by targeting a particular exchange rate. If, on the other hand, indisciplined monetary policy has been a feature of the past, imposing an exchange rate constraint may be seen as an advantage. Choice therefore depends on the relative merits of alternative macroeconomic policy instruments.

Second, macroeconomic disequilibria are ultimately corrected either by price changes or by quantity changes or by some combination of the two. Indeed the debates surrounding macroeconomics that have existed ever since the subject began have largely revolved around the extent to which prices or quantities change in both the short and long run. In essence the exchange rate is a price variable. The choice of exchange rate regime will therefore depend on whether the exchange rate is perceived as being an effective way of altering relative prices, and as more effective than other ways of altering relative prices. It will also depend on the extent to which governments wish to avoid correcting disequilibria by means of changing the quantity of output and employment.[5] Faced with a balance of payments deficit, reflecting excess aggregate domestic demand relative to aggregate supply, adjustment could in principle occur through a devaluation of the currency, which will drive up the price level and drive down real wages, or through a fall in real wages facilitated by a flexible labour market. In the absence of flexible real wages via either route, adjustment will involve increasing unemployment. Either a price variable or a quantity variable will have to change. Economics is all about minding 'P's' and 'Q's'. If the labour market is inflexible, but there is a strong desire to avoid recession and unemployment, there may also be expected to be a desire to retain the option of altering the exchange rate. If labour markets are flexible or unemployment is, up to a point, acceptable, perhaps because fiscal policy is seen to be an effective way of dealing with it, then there will be a smaller cost associated with pegging the exchange rate. This will especially be the case where devaluation is thought to be rather ineffective at reducing real wages because of real wage resistance or where the inflation induced by devaluation prevents it from depreciating the real exchange rate.

Third, there is an important time dimension in assessing the exchange rate regime. Adjustment to balance of payments deficits may in the long run occur via labour market flexibility or via rising unemployment. But the adjustment speed may be slow. In this case the deficit will have to be financed by borrowing or by decumulating international reserves. Again, in the absence of short-term price adjustment, a quantity variable of some type will change. But what if the financing option is unavailable because of low holdings of international reserves or poor international creditworthiness, then an adjustment policy is needed that will work fairly rapidly. The appeal of the exchange rate instrument will therefore, in part, depend on how fast it is thought to work as compared with alternative adjustment mechanisms.[6]

Fourth, and leading on from the trade-off between price and output adjustment, there is the conventional trade-off between inflation and unemployment. The choice of the exchange rate regime will reflect a government's preferences as between inflation and unemployment. Perhaps the principal appeal of a pegged exchange rate regime is its potentially counter-inflationary property. This feature will be particularly attractive to countries that, while having a poor record with respect to inflation and little scope for fighting inflation via the domestic control of monetary aggregates or via inflation targeting, at the same time, face high inflationary expectations. However, there is a catch, or perhaps even a Catch 22. For, in countries, with historically high inflation, any counter-inflationary policy may carry only limited credibility. If firm exchange rate pegging fails to alter inflationary expectations, it will either result in rising unemployment automatically as the money supply falls, or as governments are forced to pursue contractionary fiscal policies to defend the peg, or the abandonment of the peg in an attempt to neutralise the effect of inertial inflation on the real exchange rate and the balance of payments. However, once abandoned, future attempts to peg may then carry even less credibility than they did before. While building some flexibility into the peg by means of crawling may allow inflation to be reduced more gradually and may permit a lower rate of appreciation in the real exchange rate as a consequence of inflation, it may also bring into question the resolution of the government to lower inflation. This may in turn limit the impact on inflationary expectations, with the end result that the crawling peg is actually associated with further real appreciation.[7] In order to make counter-inflationary policy credible, governments may therefore need to contemplate regimes that effectively rule out future devaluations completely. This is the central attraction of currency boards, and, even more so, dollarisation and currency union. Ironically, the problem with any escape route in this context is that it may be used; and this creates a moral hazard problem. Regimes that are less flexible and more difficult to exit from have the advantage of suggesting a stronger commitment by the government to fighting inflation but have the disadvantage of being more likely to be associated with balance of payments disequilibria.

The inflation–unemployment trade-off also illustrates the political economy of exchange rate choice. Which is more unpopular, a combination of devaluation and inflation, or unemployment and recession? The choice of exchange rate will therefore tend to be path-dependent. Countries with a history of high inflation may be more tempted to opt for currency pegging that those with a history of high unemployment; for at least as long as it takes to break inflationary expectations.

Fifth, exchange rate choice is also related to the size, openness and integration of the countries concerned. However, the relationship is complex. Openness may be measured in terms of the average or the marginal propensity to import or the share of tradables versus non-tradables. On balance a small open economy with a low degree of product diversification may see advantage in pegging its currency. A flexible exchange rate could be unstable particularly if the world price of the country's major export is unstable, or if there are trade shocks. Given the importance of tradables, instability in the exchange rate would then cause domestic price instability. Moreover, in these circumstances, the impact of devaluation on real wages would likely be neutralised by some form of wage indexation, since the impact of exchange rate changes on the price level would be more transparent; it would therefore become a less effective adjustment tool. Meanwhile, the automatic stabilisation associated with the monetary repercussions of balance of payments disequilibria in pegged rate regimes would be more powerful where the marginal propensity to import is high. Less contraction would be needed to generate a given absolute decline in imports. More generally, domestic macroeconomic stabilisation would be more effective in correcting payments disequilibria in open economies and this would allow output and employment to be more stable than in less open economies.

In highly integrated economies, coordinated macroeconomic policies will, in any event, reduce the incidence of asymmetrical policy-related shocks. Economic integration is also likely to be associated with both enhanced labour mobility, which could substitute for adjustment via the exchange rate, and closer financial integration and fiscal federalism, which could more easily enable countries to finance balance of payments deficits, and therefore bypass one of the conventional shortcomings of pegged exchange rate regimes.

Larger, more diversified and therefore less open economies might want to retain the option of a flexible exchange rate, even though or partly because greater diversification should make their balance of payments more stable so that exchange rate flexibility is needed less. By the same token, the vulnerability of undiversified economies to shocks provides some justification for retaining a degree of exchange rate flexibility. To this extent, small economies that are both undiversified and open may face a trade-off with respect to the choice of exchange rate regime. The source of shocks combined with the degree of openness will be important. A completely closed economy will be insulated from external shocks, but will be unable to export internal shocks abroad via the balance of payments. An open economy, on the other hand, will be vulnerable to external shocks but at the same time will be able to mitigate the domestic effects of internal shocks. Thus expansionary demand policies will lead to less domestic inflation since some of the excess demand will spillover into imports. An open economy may seek to insulate itself from external shocks by using the exchange rate as a shock absorber, but may be tempted to opt for a pegged exchange rate if internal shocks are more common so that it can export their effects and minimise their domestic repercussions.

There are other potential conundrums associated with integration. The advantage of a fixed exchange rate will rise as the extent of economic integration increases because the gains from exchange rate stability in terms of reduced risk will increase. A larger part of a country's trade will now escape exchange rate risk, and lower exchange rate risk may encourage investment and economic growth by reducing the interest rate premium associated with the possibility of exchange rate changes. However, greater integration may be expected to lead to greater specialisation via exploiting comparative advantage, and this increases vulnerability to asymmetrical product shocks. This source of potential instability then needs to be weighed up against the gains from the reduced incidence of policy shocks resulting from closer policy coordination as well as from closer correlation between national incomes that will probably follow from closer integration and will reduce the incidence of disequilibria.[8]

Another consideration is that integration may be as much a function of the exchange rate regime as the exchange rate regime is a function of integration. Where countries wish to become more fully integrated with a neighbouring economy or group of economies, pegging the exchange rate or forming a currency union may be seen as a way of encouraging this development. Trade will be diverted away from third countries, where an exchange rate risk continues to exist, towards countries in the economic union where it does not.

Even where closer integration with a group of partner countries is not envisaged, a government may still be contemplating trade liberalisation and a switch from an 'inward' to an 'outward' orientation. In these circumstances it may refrain from ruling out the possibility of exchange rate adjustment as a way of offsetting the effects of tariff reductions on the balance of payments. To peg the exchange rate in advance of trade liberalisation may undermine the credibility and sustainability of the peg.[9]

Sixth, the credibility of pegging and its susceptibility to speculative attack, will, in any case, be an important factor in choosing an exchange rate regime. It is indeed largely this factor that has made the intermediate exchange rate regimes appear unattractive, unless they are buttressed by capital controls of one form or another. A high degree of financial integration may then point towards full currency union where private markets will no longer doubt or challenge the commitment to a fairly pegged exchange rate. Otherwise higher capital mobility may point towards free floating and a regime in which disequilibrium in the foreign exchange market leads to immediate as opposed to postponed changes in exchange rates, and, in principle, the possibility of upward as well as downward movements in the value of currencies, something that may increase risk and discourage speculation.[10] However, with flexible exchange rates, there will always be a question of whether markets know best. Leaving things to the market may result in excessive short-term instability with possibly adverse effects on trade and investment, and long-term currency misalignment with adverse consequences for the allocation of resources. Will speculation smooth market fluctuations or make them more pronounced, and do countries have access to the necessary instruments to hedge against exchange rate risk and at what cost? Are foreign exchange markets dominated by those who are well informed about the long run equilibrium exchange rate and possess inelastic expectations, or by those who are short-termist or have elastic expectations, taking a move in the exchange rate in one direction as an indication that there will be a further movement in the same direction?[11]

Does the choice matter?

This analysis shows that choosing the best exchange rate regime is a complex issue. It depends on many things about which governments will be uncertain and where signals may be conflicting. But does it matter if the wrong choice is made? Again there are arguments on both sides. No exchange rate regime is a substitute for well-designed macroeconomic policy. A government that persistently runs large fiscal deficits is likely to encounter exchange rate problems, irrespective of its regime choice. Similarly a country that avoids long-term fiscal deficits and monetary excesses and is unaffected by economic shocks is likely to encounter few exchange rate problems, whether it opts for a flexible or a fixed exchange rate regime or something in between the two. Moreover, a country experiencing a sudden inflow of capital will find that its real exchange rate appreciates whether its exchange rate is flexible or pegged. In the former case the nominal value of the currency will rise, whereas in the latter the domestic money supply will increase, leading to inflation. It is certainly possible to make too much of choosing the right exchange rate regime.

On the other hand, it is also misguided to regard the choice as an issue of little or no importance. After all, the exchange rate is probably the most significant relative price in the economy affecting or as it does the relative price of both goods and assets. If prices 'matter', it is difficult to argue that the exchange rate does not. The choice of exchange rate regime has implications for employment, output, economic growth and inflation.

It may influence capital flows, international reserve levels, trade and investment. It has repercussions for the conduct of other macroeconomic policies and will have serious political ramifications not least for the future of the politicians who make the choice. Moreover, it will help to determine an economy's response to global shocks. While a sudden inflow of capital will result in exchange rate appreciation in some way or another, an appreciation in the nominal value of the currency will tend to be domestically counter-inflationary and may have a de-industrialising effect whereas an increase in the domestic money supply will be inflationary. A negative shock in the form of a capital outflow will tend to lead to recession and unemployment if nominal wages are inflexible, but it may be possible to avoid these effects if there is a devaluation which stimulates the traded goods sector. As part of a comprehensive macroeconomic strategy it is therefore reasonable to conclude that the choice of exchange rate regime is important. It is therefore also important to try and move beyond the 'ifs', 'buts' and 'maybes' to some firmer conclusions. The 1990s and early 2000s provide a considerable amount of evidence on the choice of exchange rate regime. Does an assessment of this evidence yield any general lessons that can be applied to future choices and have the appropriate lessons been drawn?

As noted in the Introduction the consensus at the beginning of the twenty-first century was that events during the 1990s pointed towards corner solutions and away from interior solutions. According to this view countries should be persuaded to opt either for complete flexibility or for some form of immutable fixity but not for the options lying between these extremes. Is this judgement well founded or is it premature?[12]

Drawing lessons from the evidence of the 1990s and early 2000s

The 1990s and early 2000s have experienced a number of currency crises in many parts of the world and provide a rich source of evidence on the issues raised earlier in the analytical part of this chapter.[13] Although most of the crises have occurred in developing and emerging economies, even advanced economies have not been exempt, as the crisis in the Exchange Rate Mechanism of the European Monetary System revealed in 1992 and 1993.[14] It is possible to tell a story about each of these crisis episodes and much time and effort has been spent trying to account for them. Rather than adopting a country-by-country approach, investigating the pathology of the crises in detail, our approach here is to take some propositions surrounding the exchange rate issue and briefly investigate the extent to which recent evidence is or is not consistent with them. However, it may not be sensible to concentrate on crises alone. Although it is certainly possible to learn important lessons from them it may be just as important to think about countries that were able to avoid crises during a globally crisis-ridden period. To what extent was this because of their choice of exchange rate regime?

A lesson from the early part of the 1990s is that exchange rate pegging either in the form of an adjustable peg or a crawling peg regime can certainly be an important component of a counter-inflationary strategy. In both the case of Mexico in the early 1990s and Brazil under the Real Plan an exchange rate peg was used as a nominal anchor and as a part of a successful attempt to reduce inflation. However, these experiences, alongside the East Asian crisis also show clearly that these regimes have significant practical short-comings. Invariably the real exchange rate appreciates, the current account balance of payments weakens, international reserves are decumulated and the regime becomes vulnerable to speculative attack. This pattern has been repeated often throughout the 1990s; in the case of Mexico in 1994 it was an increase in consumption financed by capital inflows that was the source of disequilibrium, in Thailand in 1997 it was an increase in private investment, and in Russia in 1998 and Brazil in 1999 it was public sector fiscal expansion. Earlier devaluation, although an almost self-evident way of avoiding the incipient climb towards currency overvaluation and eventual crisis, seems to encounter problems in practice; it appears much easier to be wise after the event than before it.[15] Governments become reluctant to abandon an exchange rate peg once it has been installed. The evidence seems to suggest that pegged exchange rates are only abandoned in a crisis. The fear seems to be that devaluation will reignite inflation and inflation-ary expectations by suggesting that the government has become less committed to reducing inflation. This fear also raises doubts about the effec-tiveness of devaluation in strengthening the current account. There is then a danger that private capital markets will react negatively to it. Governments may also be concerned about the income redistributive effects and their implications for their political popularity. Devaluation is seen as a badge of failure and governments that pursue it frequently fall. Certainly such fears seem to have been present in both Mexico's and Brazil's decision to delay devaluation. They also exerted a significant influence over Argentina's deci-sion to adopt a currency board arrangement in 1991 and Ecuador's move towards dollarisation in 2000.[16] However, case study evidence from the 1990s challenges the view that devaluation will necessarily be inflationary; much depends on whether it is accompanied by fiscal discipline. Inflation did not accelerate significantly following devaluation in Mexico in 1994 or the Franc Zone in 1994, or East Asia in 1997/1998 (with the exception of Indonesia where accompanying policies were not disciplined) or Brazil in 1999. If a nominal anchor of some type is believed to be helpful in reduc-ing inflation an alternative is to use inflation targeting; this has become fashionable over recent years. Experience so far suggests that currency pegging is not a necessary condition for low inflation. Of course if interest rates are to be set in order to meet an inflation target they cannot be used to defend a currency peg, so inflation targeting implies exchange rate flexibility. In the latter part of the 1990s, Mexico, Chile and Brazil seem to have had some success with a combination of inflation targeting and flexible exchange rate. However this policy combination appears to have worked in cases where inflationary expectations had already been reduced. Inflation targeting might not be so successful at reducing inflation rates from a hyperinflationary level. Because of the greater flexibility that inflation targeting allows, it may carry less credibility where inflation is rapid and inflationary expectations are firmly entrenched. Fixing the exchange rate in the context of an adjustable peg or crawling peg regime may then be helpful for a time to signal a strong counter-inflationary commitment and may seem attractive in spite of the difficulties in exiting from the regime which may be seen to be some way off and heavily discounted.[17] Again, it was this belief that pushed Argentina towards a currency board and Ecuador towards dollarisation. Exit problems can be avoided if there is no exit. For a currency board to be sustainable, evidence from Argentina confirms that there has to be a very strong public desire to reduce inflation and keep it low, as well as a willingness to face the consequences; something that may depend on a country's inflationary history. Gaining credibility as an inflation fighter is the principal gain. However, there is a downside that may be large enough to severely challenge the long-term durability of a currency board and may therefore make it still vulnerable to speculative attack. Asymmetric shocks can create severe macroeconomic disequilibria, as the Mexican and Brazilian crises did in Argentina. Capital inflows can lead to inflation and an appreciation in the real exchange rate and capital outflows can cause deep recession as the domestic money supply falls. The effective exchange rate will appreciate if the anchor currency's value rises, as happened in Argentina with the rise in the value of the US dollar in the second half of the 1990s. Fiscal deficits will drive up interest rates as they now have to be financed by issuing bonds rather than by monetisation; something that may also happen if there is a default risk or a risk that the currency board will be abandoned. Furthermore, Argentina's experiences during the 1990s clearly illustrate the trade-off between exchange rate stability and domestic economic stability. Greater exchange rate stability tends to mean greater domestic instability. Defending an exchange rate in an economy that faces balance of payments deficits and has limited labour market flexibility implies large potential output losses and unemployment, and these will challenge the counter-inflationary commitment of the government and may lead to speculative pressures that undermine the sustainability of the pegged exchange rate. To reaffirm such commitment it may be then necessary to consider even more immutable fixity in the form of dollarisation; hence Argentina's flirtation with dollarisation in 2000/2001. To abandon a currency board in favour of floating would be to risk sacrificing the hard-fought gains in terms of credibility. Moreover, Argentina illustrates the underlying dilemma for relatively small and open economies. While flexible exchange rates may lead to instability in both the exchange rate and the domestic price level, and may be relatively ineffective because of high inflation pass-through, fixed exchange rates will redistribute adjustment towards interest rates, output and employment.

Evidence from the 1990s further shows why it may still be attractive to seek the benefits of fixity whilst retaining the option of exchange rate adjustment in the event of fundamental disequilibrium. The Bretton Woods system aimed to deliver this but illustrated that such a regime probably needs to be supported, particularly in times of crises, by capital controls. In this regard it is noteworthy that Chile, Malaysia, China and India were relatively successful in minimising contagion from the Mexican peso crisis and the East Asian financial crisis, although in the first three countries the fundamentals were almost certainly stronger as well. Chile's unremunerated deposit requirement (UDR) scheme was designed in part to avoid the exchange rate appreciation associated with capital inflows that were themselves encouraged by the high interest rates aimed at restraining inflation, and to push capital flows to the longer end of the market where they would be less volatile. Malaysia imposed controls on outflows in order to drive a wedge between domestic and world interest rates and allow for more independence in domestic monetary policy. But here the desire was to deal with the recessionary effects of the East Asian financial crisis. Neither China nor India are renowned for their unreservedly enthusiastic pursuit of liberalised markets and did seem able to avoid the large devaluations and severe recessions that many other Asian economies experienced in part by using capital controls. However, a danger with controls is that there will be attempts to evade them, and a parallel market may arise where the exchange rate differs significantly from the official one. Controls are unlikely to work where they are used in an attempt to defend rates that have become severely overvalued. The implication is that controls over capital movements should not be used as a substitute for appropriate macroeconomic and indeed microeconomic policies but merely as a way of offsetting excessive instability. Thus to the extent that controls appear to have been used reasonably successful in the 'headline' cases of Chile and Malaysia, this may be largely to do with the basically sound fundamentals in the two economies. It does not mean that controls are a viable way of protecting any exchange rate.

Another lesson from the East Asian crisis has been that large devaluations which are conventionally viewed as expansionary because of their expenditure-switching effects, may be severely contractionary, at least in the short run and before the expansionary effects materialise. This may happen where the private financial sector holds unhedged liabilities denominated in foreign currencies but assets which are denominated in domestic currency. Devaluation may then need to be accompanied by a more lax fiscal stance than would otherwise be the case. A similar problem had arisen during the

Mexican crisis when the authorities had issued dollar-denominated bonds (tesobonos), which were not fully backed by foreign exchange reserves. Problems occurred in spite of the fact that the underlying fiscal deficit in Mexico was not large by international standards. The motivation in this case seems to have been to signal the government's commitment to maintaining the value of the currency and to attempt to take advantage of the lower interest rate that the dollar guarantee allowed. The eventual devaluation of the peso increased the peso value of government expenditure, which in isolation increased the fiscal deficit. At the same time, however, the strong export response encouraged economic recovery and this helped increase tax revenue. This again suggests that, aside from the recessionary effects arising from unhedged foreign currency denominated liabilities, exchange rate flexibility will allow current accounts to be corrected by export expansion rather than solely by import compression which may be the consequence in a pegged rate regime where deficits result in monetary contraction.

So where does this leave us? First, the transition from high to low inflation may be assisted by pegging the exchange rate, but it is usually difficult to exit from such a regime except in the midst of a crisis. Are the inflationary gains worth the cost of the crisis? Second, disciplined fiscal and monetary policy will contribute to exchange rate stability irrespective of the choice of the exchange rate regime. By the same token fiscal and monetary excesses or a weak domestic banking and financial system will cause problems whether exchange rates are fixed or flexible. Turkey in 2000 provides further evidence for this. Third, capital controls of one form or another may be a useful way of supporting a pegged exchange rate and of neutralising the effect of capital volatility. Fourth, devaluation or exchange rate depreciation in the context of a flexible exchange rate regime may have recessionary effects in the short run where there are 'balance sheet' problems but devaluation is still likely to be an effective way of depreciating the real exchange rate and of correcting current account deficits. It will not necessarily lead to higher inflation if other forms of counter-inflationary policy are credible. Fifth, crawling peg regimes seem to encounter similar problems to those associated with adjustable pegs although they may allow the eventual crisis to be postponed. Sixth, currency boards or dollarisation may be feasible where there is a history of hyperinflation and a strong desire to eliminate inflationary expectations that have perhaps been built up by previous cycles of inflation and devaluation. But sustaining immutable fixed exchange rates have ramifications for economic growth and employment and this will test the commitment to the pegged exchange rate specially when there is an escape route available. Faced with a balance of payments deficit the recessionary implications can be severe. Immutable fixing may make more sense in the context of broader moves towards economic integration. Even Argentina modified its exchange rate arrangements in June 2001 in order to reduce the real appreciation in the peso that had resulted from the rise in the value of the dollar, and moved towards pegging against a basket containing the Euro as well as the dollar. Seventh, while free floating may, in principle, lead to short-term instability and medium-term currency misalignment, with potentially adverse consequences for trade, investment and resource allocation, the evidence amongst emerging economies at present is limited on this. Many emerging economies still seem somewhat reluctant to freely float their currencies, especially where they want to replenish the international reserves lost during failed attempts to protect a previous peg. Those that have adopted floating rates have not experienced instability but have generally provided supportive monetary and fiscal policy. Eighth, and finally, the choice of exchange rate regime is a complex issue with conflicting arguments, trade-offs and a volatile mixture of economics and politics. There are rarely likely to be clear-cut and unambiguous answers. It is a matter of weighing up the arguments on both sides of any option. What may be best for one country may not be for another or indeed the same one at another point in time. Although attempts to peg exchange rates in an environment of high capital mobility failed during the 1990s this should not be taken to imply that the extremes of immutable fixing or free floating will therefore be problem-free. Moreover, it does not mean that a pegged exchange rate supported in the short term by capital controls or used in countries where capital instability is not a problem must be automatically dismissed. Whereas it is unwise to defend severely disequilibrium real exchange rates – because in the long run it is impossible to defend them – this does not systemically preclude regimes where pegged exchange rates are periodically adjusted or where essentially floating exchange rates are managed so that the floating is bounded. A flexible exchange rate regime does not have to signal complete indifference on the part of the government with respect to the currency's value.

Thus although it is easy to see why in response to the crises of the 1990s the consensus view emerged that exchange rates should either be firmly fixed or freely flexible, this judgement is perhaps overly simplistic and premature.

Concluding remarks

Choosing an exchange rate regime involves many complex issues. There are advantages and disadvantages associated with any choice although these may be perceived in different ways by different countries or by the same country at different times. The 1990s and early 2000s have experienced a spate of currency crises. All of them shared the common component that there was an attempt to defend a particular parity or parity range that failed. By definition if the defence had been successful there would have been less of a perceived currency crisis. Successes are less visible than failures and this creates an attention bias. The crises of the 1990s have suggested to some that we can now be more confident at least about what is a bad choice. The consensus emerged at the beginning of the twenty-first century that any attempt to peg the exchange rate in anything other than an immutable way was doomed to fail in the long run, especially in a global environment of high capital mobility. Countries needed to be persuaded to move out of the middle ground and towards the extremes either in the form of immutable fixity via a monetary union or dollarisation or perhaps a currency board (though here the exchange rate is not completely immutable), or in the form of free floating.

The analysis in this chapter has shown that there may indeed be circumstances in which such choices are appropriate. However, there are other circumstances in which they are not. There may also still remain situations in which the middle ground is fertile. The choice of exchange rate regime needs to reflect a country's economic characteristics. Since these differ, so should the choice of exchange rate regime. Moreover, the choice should not be an isolated one. The exchange rate is only one potential policy instrument; there is also monetary policy and fiscal policy. Choosing the exchange rate regime should therefore represent a consistent part of choosing a coherent macroeconomic strategy. If not viewed in this way any regime is likely to fail because inconsistencies will arise. Thus if a pegged exchange rate is to be abandoned in favour of floating in order to address the problem of currency misalignment some other aspect of policy needs to focus on controlling inflation. If maintaining an equilibrium real exchange rate is deemed to be best achieved by a flexible nominal exchange rate, reflecting the view that this is the comparative advantage of the exchange rate instrument, then the interest rate needs to be directed towards achieving an inflation target. If a pegged exchange rate is deemed to be a better way of instilling counter-inflationary discipline, and monetary policy is therefore directed towards maintaining the peg, then fiscal policy must assume an important role in maintaining stable output and employment.

The IMF has a big part to play in all of this. For many developing and emerging economies the IMF becomes involved at precisely the time that the existing exchange rate regime appears to have demonstrably failed. Less complex will be advice that with an unsustainable current account balance of payments deficits the currency is overvalued; although even here assessing the size of the needed devaluation and the short run and long run effects of the devaluation may not be straightforward. More complex will be advice with regards the choice of exchange rate regime. Although it may be tempting to advise a country simply to abandon its existing regime because it is this that has apparently failed, an alternative prescription may be that it has been other policies that have failed rather than exchange rate policy. Perhaps it is these other policies that need to be altered. Perhaps the crises in Mexico, Thailand and other parts of East Asia, as well as in Brazil, Turkey and Argentina represented failures in terms of fiscal policy or monetary policy or banking policy more so than failures in the exchange rate regime as such.[18] The exchange rate needs to be seen in 'general' rather than 'partial terms', with the ramifications of the exchange rate choice for other policies being fully explored. Governments have a range of policy targets in terms of inflation, output, employment and the balance of payments, and a range of policy instruments which they orchestrate in an attempt to achieve their targets. The orchestration will depend on the priorities attached to the different targets and the effectiveness of the different instruments. To simply draw the blanket conclusion from the experience of the 1990s and early 2000s that any form of pegging or even managed floating is bound to fail and should be rejected, and that corner solutions offer the only feasible alternatives would almost certainly lead to exchange rate advice that results in further crises of one form or another. When it comes to exchange rate choice there are few if any easy solutions, and almost certainly no more now than there used to be.

References

Bird, Graham (1998) 'Exchange Rate Policy in Developing Countries: What is Left of the Nominal Anchor Approach?' *Third World Quarterly*, 19, 2, pp 255–76.

Bird, Graham (2001) 'Is Dollarisation a Viable Option for Latin America,' *World Economics*, 2, 1, pp 137–47.

Bird, Graham and Ramkishen S. Rajan (2001) 'All at SEA: Exchange Rate Policy in Developing Countries After Nomina Anchor,' mimeographed.

Corden, W. Max (2002) *Too Sensational on the Choice of Exchange Rate Regimes*, Cambridge, MA, The MIT Press.

Council on Foreign Relations (1999) *Safeguarding Prosperity in a Global Financial System: the Future International Financial Architecture*, Task Force Report, Washington DC, Institute for International Economics.

Eichengreen, Barry, Paul Masson, Miguel Savastano and Sunil Sharma (1999) *Transition Strategies and Nominal Anchors on the Road to Greater Exchange Rate Flexibility*, Essays in International Finance, No 213, Princeton NJ, Princeton University Press.

Frankel, Jeffrey A. (1999) *No Single Currency Regime is Right for All Countries or at All Times*, Essays in International Finance, No 213, Princeton NJ, Princeton University Press.

International Financial Institution Advisory Commission (2000) *Report of the International Financial Institution Advisory Commission* (the Meltzer Report), Washington DC.

Killick, Tony (1995) *IMF Programmes in Developing Countries: Design and Effects*, London, Routledge.

Williamson, John (1999) 'Future Exchange Rate Regimes for Developing East Asia: Exploring the Policy Options' paper presented at a conference on Asia in Economic Recovery: Policy Options for Growth and Stability' Singapore, 21–22 June.

4

Is Dollarisation a Viable Option for Latin America?

Graham Bird

Introduction

In January 2000 Ecuador announced that it was replacing its own currency (the sucre) with the US dollar; a process known as 'dollarisation'. Although in parts of Latin America the dollar has been used unofficially as a medium of exchange for many years and frequently has been preferred by some nationals to their domestic currency, this was the first time that a country that had previously had its own currency had opted to abandon it and to replace it officially with the US dollar. Panama, which also uses the dollar as legal tender, has never had its own currency. Argentina, with a currency board arrangement in place since 1991 (effectively tying the quantity of pesos to foreign exchange reserves), has seriously contemplated going to the next stage in the form of dollarisation but has yet to make the move.

At a time when there is a great deal of discussion of exchange rate policy and monetary policy in developing countries, following economic crises in Mexico, Brazil and East Asia, does dollarisation offer a viable and attractive option, particularly for countries in Latin America? Certainly it seems to be consistent with the advice given by the Council on Foreign Relations and by the Meltzer Commission suggesting that developing countries should opt for either flexible exchange rates or for 'firm fixity', and should not use pegged exchange rates, which were seen as contributing to the crises. It is more difficult to make the exchange rate firmly fixed than to give it up altogether by abandoning the domestic currency. In the case of a dollarised country the exchange rate is simply the dollar exchange rate *vis à vis* other currencies; the country becomes an 'exchange rate taker' and does not have its own exchange rate as such. Furthermore, dollarisation seems to be in step with developments in Europe, where euroland countries are in the process of abandoning their own currencies in favour of a common currency. Is there a global momentum behind the move to single currencies; the euro in Europe and the US dollar in North America and Latin America?

Up until recently, international financial institutions and academic opinion has generally opposed dollarisation. The IMF sought to dissuade Ecuador from dollarising, and key outside economic advisers took a similar line.

However, the Fund's position is noticeably softening; dollarisation is now being afforded the status of warranting serious scrutiny rather than being rejected out of hand. Its apparent early success in Ecuador in helping to stabilise what was a very unstable situation has also caused academic economists – particularly those involved in giving advice in Latin America – to have second thoughts and to become a little more agnostic in their attitude.

This chapter identifies and assesses the issues involved and draws on the evidence from Ecuador to see whether any conclusions may be reached about dollarisation. The difficulty is that there are arguments for and against any exchange rate regime and dollarisation is no exception. The policy choice therefore involves a balancing act. Moreover, what makes sense in one set of circumstances may not make sense in another set. However, a feature of dollarisation is that it is much less easy to reverse than a commitment to a pegged exchange rate or even membership of a currency board. Will Ecuador live to regret its decision or are other Latin American economies well advised to follow suit?

The layout of the chapter is as follows. The next section briefly places dollarisation in the context of the evolution of exchange rate policy in developing countries. The following section discusses its potential advantages, while the fourth section responds with potential disadvantages. The section titled 'Assessing the arguments' offers an assessment of the arguments and counter-arguments drawing on the case of Ecuador as an example; and evaluates the extent to which dollarisation is likely to be adopted by other Latin American economies. The final section offers a few concluding remarks.

The historical background to exchange rate policy

Exchange rate policy has been a contentious issue in Latin America and other parts of the developing world for many years. Developing countries in general were critical of the move towards flexible exchange rates at the global level in 1973 fearing that there would be adverse repercussions on their trade growth, because of uncertainty and their poor access to forward cover, on their real terms of trade and on the adequacy of their reserves. The clear majority decided to retain some form of currency peg, and from amongst the alternatives, the US dollar was the favoured currency against which to peg. Since then, the trend has been towards greater exchange rate flexibility. However, during the 1980s and early 1990s the idea of pegging made something of a comeback in the context of exchange rate based stabilisation. A pegged exchange rate was now presented as a nominal anchor for the conduct of macroeconomic policy; its defence was a central component of a counter-inflationary economic strategy. Viewed in this way, exchange rate pegging became more acceptable to the IMF, which had traditionally favoured more flexible exchange rate regimes.

Whilst the debate was still ongoing, currency crises in Mexico in 1994, East Asia in 1997/1998 and Brazil in 1999 swung the argument against nominal anchors. In each case a reluctance by governments to allow the exchange rate to be devalued was seen as contributing to the severity of the crisis. For a range of both economic and political reasons, countries tend to postpone devaluation even where their currencies appear to be often quite severely overvalued. Economic reasons include the fear that devaluation will spark off further inflation which will in turn weaken the effect of the devaluation on competitiveness, that it will lead to increased interest rates and therefore threaten domestic financial and corporate stability, and that the domestic currency costs of servicing external debt denominated in dollars will rise. Political reasons include the income redistributive effects of devaluation which often hit the politically important urban poor. In Mexico there was the fear that devaluation would be interpreted in the US as a hostile economic act designed to take away more US jobs at a time when this was a sensitive issue in the context of NAFTA. Besides, devaluation is normally seen as a badge of economic failure and incumbent governments are unlikely to rush to pin it on, unless of course, in the case of a new government, it can pin the responsibility for the devaluation on the outgoing administration.

It was against the background of the crises of the 1990s that the Council on Foreign Relations Task Force advised that developing countries should 'just say no to pegged exchange rates'. However, not without reason, many developing countries remain reluctant to adopt completely flexible exchange rates. At the very least they remain concerned that the exchange rate will be unstable given the thinness of foreign exchange markets. Moreover, there is the problem of how to orchestrate a move from pegged to flexible exchange rates without encouraging a speculative attack. If, for this reason, a flexible exchange rate is unattractive, what about firm fixity in the form of dollarisation?

Dollarisation: potential advantages

If exchange rate pegging has become unattractive because of its susceptibility to crisis, with speculation driving down the value of a currency below its fundamental equilibrium level, it is easy to see why dollarisation may be appealing. In a dollarised country there is no exchange rate and there cannot therefore be an exchange rate crisis. Since the domestic currency cannot be devalued the need for domestic interest rates to offer a premium to cover the risk of a devaluation is also eliminated. With lower interest rates, fiscal problems may be eased as the cost of servicing government debt is reduced, and private investment may be encouraged fostering faster economic growth.

At the same time since the monetary authorities can no longer finance fiscal deficits by increasing the domestic money supply, dollarisation imposes a measure of counter-inflationary discipline on the authorities and also, to the extent that this is understood, on labour markets as well. The domestic monetisation of fiscal deficits has been an enduring problem in many Latin American countries. For countries wishing to bring a history of rapid inflation to an end, the counter-inflationary aspects of dollarisation may be of particular appeal.

For many Latin American economies devaluation has been seen as part of the problem of securing lasting economic stability rather than as the solution for neutralising the effects of excessive inflation. There has been a vicious circle revolving around inflation, devaluation and further inflation. Because of its inflationary effects, devaluation is politically unpopular domestically. A government's popularity may be closely correlated with the value of the currency. Dollarisation offers a way of breaking the circle.

But why not simply commit to a pegged exchange rate or establish a currency board? The problem here is that these commitments can be relatively easily broken, and this may be a significant problem in countries that do not have a strong reputation for sound macroeconomic management. There will be a time consistency problem. People may realise that what governments say may not be what they do. To engender confidence and enhance the credibility of policy reform a step needs to be taken that is much harder to reverse. The government needs to lock itself in. It is more difficult to reverse a decision that leads to the abandonment of the domestic currency than one that retains it. It is therefore largely the credibility gain that distinguishes dollarisation from currency boards, just as it was the credibility gain that encouraged Europe to move from the Exchange Rate Mechanism to the euro.

Moreover, just as the euro is intended to foster trade within Europe, using the US dollar as official legal tender in Latin America could encourage trade with the US; uncertainties regarding the exchange rate with the dollar would be eliminated, as would be the transactions costs associated with moving between the dollar and domestic currencies. But the benefits could go beyond trade with the US. The dollar is after all the principal international currency and dollarisation could therefore encourage all trade denominated in dollars. The extent of these benefits will depend in essence on how often a dollarised country has to move out of the dollar and back into it. If it doesn't have to do this at all, dollarisation eliminates all exchange rate risk. If it does have to do it, there may still be a significant gain from the dollar's greater stability *vis à vis* other currencies. Thus Latin American dollarisation could encourage trade within Latin America as well as trade with the United States.

Finally, the efficiency of the domestic financial sector, which has frequently been an area of weakness in developing countries, could be increased by the entry of foreign financial firms that would be encouraged by dollarisation.

However, to weigh up against these potential advantages, dollarisation has a down side.

Dollarisation: potential disadvantages

By dollarising a country, in essence, gives up its exchange rate policy and monetary policy, and also severely constrains its fiscal policy. There is therefore a loss of national sovereignty over the design of macroeconomic policy; although there is a legitimate question about the degree of discretion that governments in any case enjoy in an economic environment where they have to keep happy foreign capital markets and international financial institutions.

By giving up its ability to print money, the government of a dollarising country loses seigniorage – the difference between the costs of producing domestic currency and its purchasing power. The loss of independent monetary policy and exchange rate policy makes it harder for the government to manage the domestic economy since there will be fewer policy instruments with which to try and achieve a given number of targets, such as high economic growth and employment, and low inflation. Since it can no longer monetise them, fiscal deficits will be constrained by the government's ability and willingness to borrow.

The central bank can no longer fulfil some of its textbook functions in a dollarised situation. As it no longer creates money, it also loses much of its ability to act as a lender of last resort. If central banks conventionally fulfil this function in order to generate confidence during times of domestic financial instability, does the loss of this function make the domestic financial sector more vulnerable to crises of confidence?

Finally, since key balance of payments policies now lie beyond the scope of the government, how will balance of payments deficits be handled? Dollarisation is not the same as a unified currency within a nation state, and there is no reason to believe that dollarised countries running persistent deficits will have them financed by loans or by aid from elsewhere. Balance of payments correction and measures to eliminate currency overvaluation will be needed and will have to rely on contractionary fiscal policy. If domestic prices and wages are downwardly inflexible this will in turn imply recession and rising unemployment. Balance of payments correction will involve compressing imports, and this could have a deleterious effect not only on current national income but also on economic growth and development.

Assessing the arguments: yes or no to dollarisation

Assuming that governments make reasonably well-informed and rational choices, it must be that Ecuador saw the balance of the above arguments lying in favour of dollarisation while Argentina and other Latin American economies have, for now at least, seen them as lying the other way.[1] This suggests that saying yes or no to dollarisation is a country-specific decision. There is no universally right or wrong answer. Frustratingly, the general answer is that it all depends. However, at least we can say upon what it depends. It depends on a range of economic and political factors. In order to reach a measured conclusion we need to know the answers to the following questions.

To what extent will dollarisation reduce risk premia? How high are these and do they result from the risk of devaluation or from the risk of default? Is default risk linked to devaluation and if so how closely? How large is seigniorage? Will it in any case fall as interest rates rise in connection with domestic financial liberalisation, with financial broadening increasing the range of money substitutes, and as inflation falls?[2] If there is a seigniorage loss associated with dollarisation that can be expressed as a percentage of GDP, how does this compare with the additional growth in GDP that may be associated with any increased stability and investment associated with dollarisation? Is printing money as part of the lender of last resort role really a sensible way of dealing with financial crises? What scope is there for reducing domestic inflation and, if little, are recessions politically acceptable? If unacceptable, are they more or less acceptable than devaluation? Do countries need to retain a 'get out' option in the form of devaluation, or is the sacrifice of this option needed in order to establish credibility? How strong is the national commitment to the domestic currency?

Since a dollarised country gives up discretion over its exchange rate and monetary policy and limits the scope for fiscal policy, an important question is whether these policies have been used well in the past. If the economy has been well managed and economically stable, flexibility in the exchange rate offers a way of protecting this stability from instability in the rest of the world. Insulation is a classic argument for exchange rate flexibility. If, on the other hand, it is the domestic economy that has been macroeconomically unstable and the rest of the world that has been more stable, there is less to be lost from giving up domestic policy instruments and more to be gained by forging a stronger link with a more stable economy outside.

This is where Ecuador found itself in January 2000. There was a large fiscal deficit, and rapid monetary growth. The rate of inflation was easily the fastest in Latin America – running at 55 per cent in 1999 compared with a regional average of just under 9 per cent – and the exchange rate was depreciating rapidly as both foreign investors and nationals lost confidence. The balance of payments had been hit by low oil prices and by poor export performance in shrimps and bananas. This also had a negative impact on the revenue from export taxes and therefore the fiscal deficit. The government enjoyed little credibility and was suffering from the unpopularity associated with sharp economic recession and devaluation. While Latin America as a whole had (barely) positive real growth, real GDP in Ecuador fell by 9.0 per cent in 1999. Policy makers faced an awkward dilemma. While raising the interest rate might arrest the decline in the value of the sucre, there was no guarantee given the lack of confidence. Moreover, it would deepen the recession and destabilise the domestic financial system further. Whereas in Europe the adoption of a single currency was seen as the final outcome of a lengthy period of macroeconomic stabilisation and convergence, in Ecuador it was the outcome of a short-term crisis. Why the difference? In Europe the adoption of a single currency is generally acknowledged to have been driven by long-term political considerations. In Latin America these are lacking. Without them in Europe it is extremely unlikely that the euro would have been established. Without them in Latin America it needed a crisis to push Ecuador to dollarisation. In Argentina, while the economic situation was weak, it was less critical, some of the benefits associated with dollarisation were already being delivered by the currency board arrangement, the additional benefits from dollarisation were uncertain, and there was probably perceived to be a stronger sense of national pride in and commitment to the domestic currency.

It was almost certainly these considerations that drove the decision to say yes to dollarisation in Ecuador and no, for now, to it in Argentina, rather than a belief that Ecuador was a uniquely strong candidate in terms of the conventional theory of optimum currency areas which stresses factor mobility, openness, diversification, and macroeconomic characteristics. It would also be difficult to argue that Ecuador has particularly close economic ties with the US by comparison with other Latin American economies.

Will dollarisation survive in Ecuador?[3] Might it become more appealing over time to other countries in Latin America? It will become less popular in Ecuador if balance of payments deficits require rapid adjustment to take place, since, in the short term, restoration of macroeconomic equilibrium will have to rely almost exclusively on contractionary fiscal policy. Deep recession and rising unemployment could undermine dollarisation. The durability of dollarisation therefore depends on the government's ability to bring about needed structural change, since this will reduce the need for short-term contraction in domestic aggregate demand. If dollarisation creates the breathing space needed to implement appropriate structural policies, it may prove to have been a sensible choice and durable. If however the opportunity is wasted, there is little reason to believe that dollarisation will have a lasting impact on Ecuador's economic performance.

What about the rest of Latin America? Dollarisation in the not-too-distant future may prove more likely in those Central American states where there is already a high degree of unofficial dollarisation, where the domestic currency is weak and unattractive even to residents, and where geographical proximity to the US drives the pattern of trade. For the larger economies of

South America these characteristics are absent. For them, it might need another financial crisis to push them towards dollarisation. However, there is a rather different long-term scenario. Should a free trade area for the Americas become a significant possibility, there would be associated arguments for a unified currency to encourage intra-area trade. In Europe, political imperatives dictated that this needed to be a new currency. In an all-American free trade area the dollar would unambiguously dominate and the advantages of a single currency could lead to universal dollarisation. There would also be network externalities associated with using the dollar that would be absent in the case of a new currency and this would make it in the interests of Latin American countries to use the dollar. As part of this type of regional arrangement, a mechanism for distributing a part of the seigniorage from dollar creation across all participants could also be negotiated, which would make dollarisation a more attractive proposition.

Concluding remarks

Having one's own currency has sometimes been seen as a mark of nationhood. In this sense giving it up is an unlikely move. Moreover, losing control over the exchange rate and monetary policy implies a loss of sovereignty over macroeconomic policy and a truncated ability to manage the domestic economy. In a world that believes in the importance of relative prices, the exchange rate may be seen to be too important a relative price to abandon.

However, for a range of reasons it has proved difficult to conduct macroeconomic policy in Latin America. Exchange rate devaluation has had inflationary repercussions and faces strong political resistance, fiscal deficits are affected by external shocks that may affect both tax revenue and government expenditure in terms of debt servicing, and partly for this reason monetary aggregates are difficult to control. There is some general evidence that macroeconomic policy is more effective when it is linked to a policy rule, and given the difficulties with monetary rules and inflation targeting in developing countries, dollarisation may be seen as offering an alternative policy approach.

Certainly, views have been changing. Economic crises in Latin America and elsewhere have led to a broad consensus against currency pegging. Events in Europe suggest that there may be advantages with single currencies and numerous influential Reports have encouraged developing countries to opt for either free exchange rate flexibility or firm fixity. Fears that flexible exchange rates may be unstable has focused renewed attention on dollarisation. In crisis conditions Ecuador has already made the move, opting to abandon its currency – other than in the form of small coins.

It is too early to judge how successful dollarisation has been or will be. Certainly the economy has stabilised and inflation has fallen (as has the President who chose to dollarise!). But other things have moved to

Ecuador's advantage – in particular the price of oil, which has also assisted other Latin American economies such as Venezuela that were in economic difficult – so it is difficult to say how much of the improvement may be attributed to dollarisation. The attitude of the IMF is changing and, while a failure to undertake the necessary structural changes in Ecuador could undermine the experiment with dollarisation, further financial crises hitting the region in the short run, or a strong movement towards economic integration between Latin America and North America in the long run, could result in a broader adoption of the US dollar in place of national currencies.

5
What Happened to the Washington Consensus?

Graham Bird

Introduction

The phrase, 'The Washington Consensus' was, so the story goes, coined by John Williamson at a conference in response to the suggestion that, during the 1980s, countries in Latin America were being confronted with conflicting, and therefore confusing, advice from the International Monetary Fund and the World Bank. Williamson's response was that there was, in fact, a strong consensus about policy across the Washington-based institutions around the need for macroeconomic stability, microeconomic liberalisation and openness. Their advice was therefore not conflicting but reinforcing.

Either because of cajoling by the Fund and the Bank, or as a consequence of coming to believe in the superiority of neo-liberal policies, or because it was felt that private capital markets would be impressed by them, many countries throughout the world certainly adopted the types of policies generally associated with the Washington Consensus (WC). Thus, broadly similar policies were adopted in many parts of Latin America, Africa, and Asia, as well as in the Countries in Transition (CITs) in Central and Eastern Europe. Greater emphasis was placed on fiscal rectitude, financial markets were liberalised, state monopolies were privatised, tariffs were reduced, and foreign direct investment encouraged.

How have things panned out? Has the economic performance of these countries improved? If so, it might be expected that this would have had the effect of drawing in detractors from the WC, which, as a result, would have become progressively stronger. Alternatively, if their economic performance has been disappointing, or at least patchy, it might be anticipated that the WC view of the world would have begun to appear tarnished. Divergence away from the WC rather than further convergence towards it might be expected, calling into question whether there is sufficient agreement to warrant using the term 'consensus' at all.

The purpose of this chapter is to examine the record of the WC and to assess its current status. Is there still a consensus view about economic policy that underpins the advice given by the IMF and the World Bank? Moreover, does the answer to this question have implications for the future design of the Washington-based institutions themselves given the contemporary debate about the way in which they should evolve?

The layout of the chapter is as follows. The following section discusses the WC in a little more detail, identifying the kinds of policies with which it is conventionally associated. Was it legitimate to think in terms of a high degree of unanimity of view with respect to these policies at the beginning of the 1990s?

The section 'From design to implementation' discusses the channels through which countries were exposed to the WC and assesses the extent to which it influenced the design of economic policy worldwide. The next section examines briefly the overall economic performance of countries that adopted WC policies as well as the performance of the global economy as a whole. It reveals a nuanced picture. The section titled 'Judging the components' goes on to look at individual policies that formed components of the WC and assesses their track record. Have some components done better than others? Might there be more consensus about certain components of the WC than others? The final section then assesses the extent to which the degree of consensus over economic policy has changed and the implications of this for the Washington-based institutions.

An important issue here relates to conditionality. If there is a strong consensus about economic policy, it may be reasonable that this should be reflected in the conditionality of the Fund and the Bank. But what if there is little consensus?

The Washington Consensus: conception and design

When they were originally established there was a fairly clear division of labour between the IMF and the World Bank. The IMF was a balance of payments agency dealing with the demand side and influencing macroeconomic policy. Its focus was on the short term. In contrast, the World Bank was responsible for longer-term development issues. Through its project assistance, it focused on the microeconomics of the supply side. Although this difference in focus created the scope for disagreement, it was during the 1980s, and in the context of structural adjustment, that the spheres of influence of the two institutions began to overlap, creating more potential for direct disagreement and conflict.[1] Although the details of the case are complex, this potential appeared to have become a reality in Argentina towards the end of the 1980s as the Fund withdrew its support, and under pressure from the US, the Bank in effect took over much of the Fund's role. There appeared to be 'Washington dissent'.[2]

However, with a change in administration in the US which allowed the Bank to withdraw from Argentina, a concordat between the institutions which sought to re-emphasise their primary areas of responsibility, and a continuing upswing in the general popularity of neo-liberal economics, the view, which found expression in Williamson's phrase, was that by the beginning of the 1990s consensus rather than dissent was the order of the day. Although never defined in precise detail, the WC was widely regarded as comprising a number of elements. These included: fiscal and monetary discipline, in particular avoiding excessive fiscal deficits that would fuel monetary expansion; tax reform designed to widen the tax base and increase tax revenue; tight control of public expenditure, with a redirection of it towards areas such as health and education which would not be supplied adequately by the private sector; financial liberalisation designed to encourage domestic saving and to raise the marginal efficiency of investment; the elimination of over-valued exchange rates, in order to strengthen the current account of the balance of payments and discourage capital flight; trade liberalisation designed with the objective of raising domestic economic efficiency and exploiting comparative advantage; encouragement of foreign direct investment as a means of facilitating technology transfer; privatisation and deregulation as ways of overcoming the inefficiencies of state monopolies, increasing competitiveness and raising efficiency; and the establishment of systems of property rights, where these were missing, in order to facilitate the operation of markets.

The WC therefore constituted a package of policies that aimed to establish macroeconomic stability by eliminating inflation and currency overvaluation, and to raise domestic economic efficiency by means of economic liberalisation in goods and financial markets. Although both the Fund and the Bank might have had their own institutional comparative advantage in terms of the above components, the idea of a WC suggested that there was little disagreement about the appropriate overall direction and design of economic policy.

This is probably a reasonable description of the situation at the beginning of the 1990s. In both institutions there was a commitment to the need for macroeconomic stabilisation and the superiority of liberalised markets over state provision or intervention. There was also broad agreement about the details of economic policies needed to deliver these objectives. In a sense the enormity of the challenge facing CITs sharpened the focus on areas of agreement. With large fiscal deficits, rapid monetary expansion, and hyperinflation being characteristic of these economies, macroeconomic stabilisation was a necessary prerequisite to reform. At the same time, the fall of Communism seemed to provide direct testimony to the superiority of market-based systems thus reinforcing the consensus around economic liberalisation.

From design to implementation

The impact of the WC only in part resulted directly from the coincidence of view about the broad direction of economic reform across the IMF and the

World Bank. The diffusion of the WC was encouraged by the fact that a relatively large number of countries throughout the world were drawing resources from the Washington-based institutions at the beginning of the 1990s. For example, in 1990 a record fifty-one IMF arrangements were in effect. For comparison, there had been only twelve arrangements in 1975, twenty-nine in 1980, and thirty in 1985. Under the direct tutelage of the Fund and the Bank, an historically large number of countries began to pursue broadly similar policies.

However, the impact of the WC was even greater than is suggested by the number of countries that were drawing resources from the Fund and the Bank. Generally speaking, borrowing from the IMF is regarded as a last resort. For a range of reasons countries prefer to avoid the Fund if at all possible. Their chances of doing so are higher if they can retain access to private international capital markets. How can they do this? Partly by pursuing the kinds of policies of which the private markets approve. But how do private markets form a view about what policies are appropriate? To a significant degree they may do this by observing the policies that are favoured by the IMF, and, probably to a lesser extent, the World Bank.[3] But how much importance will they attach to the views of the Fund and the Bank? Probably much more where there is perceived to be a clear consensus emerging from the institutions. By this mechanism the impact of the WC moved well beyond those countries that came directly under the influence of the Washington-based institutions. Although difficult to quantify, it is likely that the indirect effect of the WC on countries not drawing resources from the Fund or the Bank was at least as important. The idea of a consensus perhaps served to create it as much as it reflected it.[4]

The broad consensus covering macroeconomic stabilisation, microeconomic liberalisation and openness may also have contributed to the increase in the dimensions of IMF and World Bank conditionality that occurred towards the end of the 1980s and at the beginning of the 1990s. IMF conditionally now went beyond conventional demand-side policies and incorporated detailed structural conditionality, such as pricing policy. Had there been no consensus outside the need for macro stability, the Fund might have been less prepared to extend the range of its conditionality.[5] But with the broad consensus view in Washington, the Fund seemed to have few such inhibitions. The WC therefore incorporated a number of 'multiplier effects', with the Fund and the Bank exerting both a direct and indirect influence over an increasingly wide array of policies. How effective have these policies been?

Economic performance in the aftermath of the Washington Consensus

Since the WC incorporates policies which might be expected to exert their influence only in the long run, it is premature to try and reach a firm conclusion about their effects. Having said this it may nevertheless be legitimate to make a few preliminary remarks.

First, the era of the WC coincided with a surge of capital into developing countries. Was there a connection? Certainly some early studies claimed that it was the adoption of WC-type policies that enticed private capital markets to lend, and the discussion above suggests that the catalytic effect of the Fund and the Bank might be expected to be stronger where there is a clear consensus surrounding economic policy. The WC may then have contributed to the increase in capital flows. However, the contribution should not be overstated. Not all countries pursuing WC-type policies experienced large capital inflows, and subsequent more detailed research suggests that the surge of capital towards Latin America and East Asia was at least as much to do with relatively low interest rates and economic stagnation in the US. Capital was therefore being 'pushed' towards certain developing countries by external events rather than being 'pulled' in by the pursuit of policies which carried a strong endorsement from the Fund and the Bank.[6] Thus while it may have been true that policy designed in Washington did indeed have an effect on capital flows perhaps it was policy designed at the Federal Reserve, the Treasury, and on Capitol Hill rather than at the IMF and World Bank. If countries were persuaded to adopt WC-type policies in the belief that it would induce private capital inflows the lesson was that this certainly could not be guaranteed.

For low-income countries there was never a reasonable chance that pursuing WC policies would lead to significant private capital flows. Here the hope was that by adopting such policies there might be a catalytic effect on aid flows. In some respects aid agencies were after all part of the WC and were involved in the design of policy. In fact what happened was that aid flows fell in the mid-1990s.[7] To the extent that economic reform complying with the WC had a positive effect it was overpowered by other negative influences.

Second, did compliance with the WC bring about an improvement in domestic economic performance irrespective of its effects on capital flows? Again the answer might, at first sight and based on evidence from the early 1990s, seem to be quite positive. In Latin America not only was the pursuit of WC-type policies associated with a surge of capital inflows, but it also seemed to be associated with falling inflation and increasing economic growth as shown in Table 5.1. Fiscal deficits that had been equivalent to about 7 per cent of GDP in 1987 had been virtually eliminated by 1993, taking the region as a whole. It is tempting to attribute a causal connection between the WC and this improvement in economic performance and it is, of course, quite valid to suggest that economic performance should improve where sensible economic policies replace inappropriate ones. Few would argue that macroeconomic instability is preferable to stability. But in claiming that the improved economic performance in Latin America in the early

Table 5.1 Macroeconomic performance in Latin America in the aftermath of the Washington Consensus

	1990	1991	1992	1993	1994	1995
Economic growth[a]	1.1	3.3	2.8	3.2	4.7	0.9
Inflation[a]	438.7	128.8	151.5	209.5	210.9	35.6
Balance of payments[b] on current account	−1.4	−17.0	−34.0	−45.0	−49.5	−33.2

Notes
[a] Per cent change.
[b] In billions of US dollars.
Source: *World Economic Outlook*, IMF.

1990s can be attributed to policies associated with the WC a number of issues need to be addressed. Many commentators believe that the important factor in explaining the change in economic policy was the growing belief within the countries themselves that economic reform was needed. They came to 'own' the policies. Perhaps the 'Latin American Consensus' was more important than the WC. The question then is the extent to which the existence of the WC helped bring about this change in policy direction in Latin America. At best the connection is probably indirect and loose and, in any case, the influence of the Fund and the Bank is likely to have developed over a number of years. It was not that the WC brought about a discrete and sudden change.

In principle there is a reasonable presumption that, to the extent that they were aimed at increasing efficiency, WC policies should have paid off in terms of an increase in the rate of economic growth. Although this improvement initially occurred, it may have been more to do with the capital inflows reported above and the expectations associated with the policy change. After the initial improvement, economic growth actually faltered in the mid-to-late 1990s. Explaining economic growth is, of course, notoriously difficult, but at a superficial level the adoption of WC policies failed to create sustained economic growth.

This brings us to a third point. The growth record of the liberalisation policies incorporated as part of the WC might have been more pronounced had it not been for the Mexican peso crisis in 1994 and the East Asian crisis in 1997/98. Did these crises disrupt what would otherwise have been a clearer record of success? The problem here is that the liberalisation policies that formed a central element of the WC may themselves have contributed to the crises. At a global level it is the economic and financial crises of the 1990s that raise the most serious doubts about the unrestrained pursuit of economic liberalisation.

Fourth, but combined with this, concerns that the WC paid insufficient attention to the balance of payments and income inequality – issues that in the longer run could constrain the pursuit of the policies of economic liberalisation favoured in Washington – proved to have some empirical justification. Economic growth proved inadequate to reduce poverty, and policies to reduce income inequality did not form a part of the WC. Economic liberalisation failed to change the structure of trade in the near term and this meant that many countries that had adopted measures of trade liberalisation remained vulnerable to commodity instability as well as a secular deterioration in their terms of trade.[8] Meanwhile, capital account liberalisation, which facilitated capital inflows in the early 1990s, also facilitated capital outflows later in the decade. Again, the importance of closer financial supervision and prudential control that many commentators began to accentuate in the aftermath of the financial crises had not featured within the WC of the early 1990s. The crises also demonstrated that, to the extent that the exchange rate policies associated with the WC were adopted, they were unable to prevent currency overvaluation.

While open to a number of interpretations one reading of the evidence is that the establishment of the WC had a short-run impact on expectations that was then not matched by changes in fundamentals. There was therefore a short-run effect on capital inflows and on economic growth, which was not sustained. Moreover in both cases the early 1990s followed a 'lost decade of development' in Latin America when private capital flows had been adversely affected by the debt crisis, suggesting that there was some catching up to do. Over the longer term there seems to be little evidence that WC policies have led to an increase in domestic savings rates, the marginal efficiency of investment or the rate of productivity growth.

A perhaps more enduring effect of the WC seems to be in terms of the higher priority accorded to macroeconomic stabilisation. Fiscal deficits, the rate of growth of monetary aggregates and inflation all tended to fall in the first half of the 1990s. But even here there are some contraindications as fiscal deficits began to rise again in Latin America in the second half of the 1990s and over-expansionary fiscal policy was seen as a contributor to the Brazilian crisis in 1999. In any case using restrictionary fiscal policy as a means of moderating inflation and avoiding severe macroeconomic disequilibria is not a defining feature of the WC. It could, after all, be viewed as fairly conventional Keynesianism. Even new structuralists who roundly criticise the Fund conditionality as stagflationary do not advocate macroeconomic indiscipline or currency overvaluation.

Judging the components of the Washington Consensus

The previous section suggests that the adoption of the policies associated with the WC did not result in sustained or universal success in terms of conventional macroeconomic performance indicators. It is difficult to support the claim that economic reform based on the WC transformed those economies that complied with it. Moreover, rapid liberalisation and inappropriate sequencing of reform may have contributed to the economic and financial crises that were a feature of the 1990s. But what about the individual elements of economic policy that go to make up the WC? Do we know more about them at the beginning of the 2000s than we did at the beginning of the 1990s?

First, with regard to fiscal deficits, we certainly know that large deficits can create problems in terms of inflation and currency overvaluation, but we also know that economic crises may arise even when fiscal deficits are not large, as in the case in East Asia in the mid-1990s. Reducing fiscal deficits may not be appropriate where there is a private sector surplus or where the recessionary effects of an economic crisis are likely to reduce private sector investment. Reducing fiscal deficits may not even improve the current account of the balance of payments if accompanied by an increase in private sector consumption. The wisdom of reducing or seeking to eliminate fiscal deficits therefore depends on the circumstances at hand.

Second, with regard to domestic financial liberalisation, while continuing to recognise the problems associated with financial repression in terms of discouraging saving, permitting inefficient investment, encouraging capital flight, and, through credit rationing, allowing scope for the inefficient allocation of scarce loanable funds, we also know that, if pursued too rapidly and vigorously, financial liberalisation may lead to problems for the domestic banking and financial sectors as well as the corporate sector as interest rates rise sharply. Moreover, they may encourage excessive capital inflows that are macroeconomically destabilising as they drive up the value of the domestic currency, or lead to inflation when the government intervenes to prevent exchange rate appreciation, or, because of sterilisation designed to prevent this, are self-perpetuating as interest rates remain high.[9] There is also as yet little evidence to support the claim that financial liberalisation increases domestic saving or increases the efficiency of investment.

Third, with regard to capital account liberalisation, and as a consequence of the East Asian crisis and other crises, we are now aware of the fact that, while capital mobility may basically be a good thing, especially in a first-best world, it is possible to have too much of it in a world that is not first-best. Whether seen as a basic cause of the financial crises of the 1990s, or as a facilitator of crises that have different fundamental causes, capital mobility is now seen as being often only a short step away from capital volatility. There is a growing acknowledgement that the regulation of capital movements may be appropriate in certain circumstances.[10] Moreover, it is now widely agreed that capital account liberalisation should be sequenced to follow domestic financial liberalisation and the introduction of adequate prudential supervision and regulation.

Fourth, with regard to exchange rate policy, experience in Mexico, Thailand and elsewhere led to a rapid erosion of the case for exchange rate management. The 'nominal anchor' approach to exchange rate policy lost ground to the 'real targets' approach. Initially the response of many commentators was to advocate one or other of the 'corner solutions'; either exchange rate flexibility or firmly pegged exchange rates in the form of currency boards or dollarisation. While exchange rate flexibility was consistent with the WC, since it implied the liberalisation of foreign exchange markets, currency boards and dollarisation were not. More recently the 'corner solution consensus' itself appears to have broken down with a number of influential economists arguing that intermediate exchange rate regimes may still be appropriate.[11] The conclusion emerges that perhaps any exchange rate regime ranging from complete exchange rate flexibility, through managed floating or some form of optimal peg, to firmly fixed exchange rates, even as far as a single currency, may be appropriate in different sets of circumstances.

Fifth, with regard to openness and trade liberalisation, although some studies have appeared during the 1990s suggesting that openness is indeed the key to continued economic growth, others have more recently questioned the evidential support for this contention.[12] For many developing countries conventional arguments in favour of some degree of protection to support infant industries, to generate tax revenue, and to allow countries to dynamically change their comparative advantage in order to avoid the problems associated with concentrating on the production and exporting of primary products have proved quite resilient. Especially under the umbrella of a World Trade Organisation in which they feel that their interests are poorly represented, commitment to unfettered trade liberalisation may be weak. It may be difficult to persuade developing countries of the advantages of trade liberalisation in circumstances where they continue to encounter protectionist measures in advanced countries against their own exports.[13]

Sixth, with regard to privatisation, there has been a gradual shift in emphasis. In the early 1990s privatisation was commonly viewed as a way of getting away from inefficient loss-making state monopolies, the financing of which created a drain on government resources. With a softening attitude to foreign direct investment there was a trend towards selling them off to foreign purchasers. Such sales did indeed contribute towards reducing fiscal deficits, not only in terms of avoiding the ongoing need to cover losses but also in terms of the one-off revenue generated by the sale of the enterprises. It was also seen as a conduit for technology transfer and as a way of encouraging less volatile capital inflows. However, over time a counter-view has been in the ascendancy claiming that little may be gained from using privatisation simply as a vehicle for moving from a state monopoly to a private monopoly. This view stresses that privatisation needs to be used to break up monopolies if it is to generate the greater efficiency that will be associated with competition.

Finally, the WC incorporated the view that the state had a minimal role to play. Generally the view was that, in many developing countries and certainly in CITs the state had taken on too many functions; the government sector had become too large relative to other sectors of the economy. Not only was the government sector seen as being relatively inefficient by comparison with the private sector, but also it was seen as being in competition with it. Government expenditure supposedly 'crowded out' private expenditure. WC policies focused on reducing public expenditure. During the 1990s the consensus within economics has probably shifted somewhat. The emphasis has changed towards considering how best the state can support markets and help avoid their worst excesses, through appropriate regulation. The state is seen more as a facilitator creating a political and institutional environment which allows markets to operate in a socially acceptable way. While the WC stressed financial 'crowding out', it is now more widely accepted that there may be an element of real 'crowding in' as the state provides both physical and social infrastructural investment. There has, in short, been something of a backlash to the simplistic approach to the role of the state which the WC was seen as embodying.[14]

What is left to the Washington Consensus?

Where does all this leave the Washington Consensus? Given the lack of precision surrounding the original concept, this is a difficult question to answer precisely. However, there are a number of ways of describing what has happened. One is that the WC has softened. 'Black and white' has been replaced by 'grey'. 'Definites' have been replaced by 'maybes'. There is a greater awareness of, and greater legitimacy attached to, counter views. This claim might suggest that there is a consensus around agnosticism concerning economic policy, if this is not a contradiction in terms. While there has probably been a move in this direction, there is another way of describing what has happened. Although some people still stick firmly to the old WC policies, there are now more detractors or, at least, more agnostics. These would include those who subscribe to the view that one size is unlikely to fit all and that, outside some fairly broad generalisations concerning the avoidance of macroeconomic disequilibrium, the design of economic policy should be country-specific and made to measure. The question then becomes whether there are enough detractors to undermine the legitimacy of the very concept of a consensus and whether these detractors are located inside the Fund and the Bank.

If it is now widely accepted that in some circumstances fiscal deficits may be warranted or even needed, that financial liberalisation may lead to banking and corporate failures and economic recession, that capital account liberalisation may need to be postponed because it encourages capital volatility, that exchange rates may need to be pegged, that trade liberalisation may create difficulties for tax revenue and may fail to correct balance of payments problems, that privatisation may not lead to greater economic efficiency, and that there is an important economic role for the state, then it is difficult to talk about a consensus around any specific combination of policies.

Even in Washington there appear to be disagreements between the Fund and the Bank. Thus Stiglitz, a former Chief Economist at the Bank, reports that the Bank was highly critical of the Fund's conditionality in East Asia arguing that it was badly designed and would lead to economic recession.[15] At the same time Collier, another senior economist at the Bank, has been critical of conditionality in general and of the sequencing of policy favoured by the IMF within the context of its Enhanced Structural Adjustment Facility in particular.[16] This evidence suggests that there is at least a significant degree of dissent in Washington.

Is there a new consensus emerging? Implications for conditionality

If consensus surrounding many of the original components of what might be called the 'old Washington Consensus' has now disappeared, has a different sort of consensus emerged covering other issues? The new consensus, to the extent that it exists, is more limited in scope. It retains a belief in the need for macroeconomic stability and the overall superiority of markets over planning, although accepting that the state has a positive role to play. This is hardly stunning. More particularly, it assigns a higher priority to domestic financial regulation and prudential control as necessary preconditions for financial liberalisation. It accepts that the sequencing of policy is important and that capital account liberalisation should probably come at the end of the sequence. It also gives greater weight to the importance of 'ownership' in helping to ensure that economic reform is actually implemented. Furthermore it *appears* to suggest that economic growth and poverty reduction should be primary objectives for both the Fund and the Bank.[17]

However, there is a fundamental inconsistency between this 'new' consensus and the 'old' one. Ownership is more likely to be achieved if the Fund and the Bank are less prescriptive. Subject to constraints, this means supporting the policy preferences of client countries rather than inducing them to accept a standard package of policies emanating from Washington. The new Washington consensus may, in effect, therefore be to avoid forcing countries to accept all the policies associated with the old 'Washington Consensus'.

Concluding remarks

It is difficult to know what degree of agreement is needed in order to constitute a 'consensus'. The 'turf wars' that took place between the IMF and the World Bank towards the end of the 1980s seemed to imply institutions at loggerheads, but they concealed important areas of agreement about the general direction of economic reform in client countries; there was probably more that united the institutions than divided them. However, there are certainly things to suggest that this underlying uniformity of view became particularly marked at the beginning of the 1990s. The World Bank produced a *World Development Report* in 1991 strongly advocating a market-oriented approach to economic development, which coincided with the Fund's view of the world. The continued success of the East Asian economies seemed to support the case for firm macroeconomic discipline and for an outward orientation. Meanwhile, and most noticeably, the collapse of Communism suggested that the command and control system did not work. Countries that had staunchly resisted neo-liberal policies in the past began to embark on them. This was the heyday of the WC.

The consensus within the Fund and the Bank in turn reflected the dominant view within the economics profession at the time. Outside the Washington-based institutions there remained detractors, of course, in the form of the 'new structuralists' and others who, while not subscribing to the new structuralist model, retained doubts about full-blown economic liberalisation, but these commentators did not appear to have much influence with the Fund and the Bank.

This chapter suggests that during the 1990s the consensus weakened. Although no one argues that macroeconomic instability is a good thing there is increasing disagreement about what is needed to stabilise an economy. Just how vital is it to cut fiscal deficits and by how much? Particularly in the context of its policies in East Asia there was concern, even within the World Bank, that the Fund's policies had involved overkill and led to unnecessary recession. With regards economic liberalisation there is growing agreement that this can be taken too far too fast. In many areas of policy the WC of the early 1990s has broken down, to be replaced by a more agnostic approach. This is nicely captured by the Fund's evolving attitude towards capital account liberalisation which shifted from strong advocacy to more muted support emphasising the necessary conditions for it. To the extent that a well-defined consensus exists the focus is now more on issues that did not form a part of the original WC. This new consensus concentrates on poor financial regulation as a contributory cause of economic crises, and on the need for better financial supervision and prudential control as a way of helping to prevent future crises. It has shifted attention towards the implementation of programmes and not just their contents. Indeed improving the record of compliance may dictate a more flexible approach to content. Thus both the Bank and the Fund have formally begun to stress the importance of country ownership and have introduced organisational changes to encourage it. Closer coordination under the umbrella of the Heavily Indebted Poor Country initiative (HIPC) and the Poverty Reduction and Growth Facility (PRGF) may be expected to increase the overlap between the institutions and may encourage convergence towards a kind of consensus. At least it may force differences to the surface where they can be resolved.

If, as some recent reports on the institutions advocate, the Fund and the Bank were to be returned to their 'core competencies' with the Fund focusing on short-term macroeconomic stabilisation and the Bank on long-term development, this could heighten institutional conflict and truncate some of these emerging areas of coordination.[18] Policies designed to induce rapid stabilisation may at least in the short run have adverse effects on output and economic growth. Finding the optimal point on any such trade-off may become more difficult in the future if the trends of recent years are reversed. Although the original WC has in large measure been lost, it is perhaps being replaced by closer coordination. This could be threatened by proposals to lodge the responsibility for stabilisation exclusively with the Fund and for economic development with the Bank.

References

Bird, Graham (1994), 'Changing Partners: Perspectives and Policies of the Bretton Woods Institutions', *Third World Quarterly*, 15, 3, pp 483–503.

Bird, Graham (1999), 'How Important is Sound Domestic Macroeconomics in Attracting Capital Inflows to Developing Countries?', *Journal of International Development*, 11, pp 1–26.

Bird, Graham and R Rajan (2000), 'All at Sea: Exchange Rate Policy in Developing Countries after Nominal Anchors', mimeographed.

Calvo, G A, L Leiderman and C M Reinhart (1996), 'Inflows of Capital to Developing Countries in the 1990s', *Journal of Economic Perspectives*, 10, 2, pp 125–39.

Collier, Paul (1997), 'The Failure of Conditionality', in C Gwin and J Nelson, eds, *Perspectives on Aid and Development* ODC Policy Essay No 22, Washington DC, Overseas Development Council.

Collier, Paul and Jan Willem Gunning (1999), 'The IMF's Role in Structural Adjustment', *Economic Journal*, 109, F, pp 634–51.

Edwards, S (1998), 'Openness, Productivity and Growth: What Do We Really Know?', *Economic Journal*, 108, pp 383–99.

Feinberg, Richard E (1988), 'The Changing Relationship Between the World Bank and the International Monetary Fund', *International Organization*, Summer.

Fischer, Stanley et al. (1998), 'Should the IMF Pursue Capital Account Convertibility?', *Essays in International Finance*, No 207, May, Princeton NJ, Princeton University Press.

Frankel, Jeffrey A (1999), 'No Single Currency Regime is Right for All Countries at All Times', *Essays in International Finance*, No 215, August, Princeton NJ, Princeton University Press.

Grindle, Merilee S (1994), 'Sustaining Economic Recovery in Latin America: State Capacity, Markets and Politics', in G Bird and A Helwege, eds, *Latin America's Economic Future*, London, Academic Press, pp 303–24.

Killick, Tony (1989a), 'Issues Arising from the Spread of Obligatory Adjustment', in Graham Bird, ed, *Third World Debt: The Search for a Solution*, Aldershot, Edward Elgar, pp 78–117.

Killick, Tony (1989b), *A Reaction Too Far: Economic Theory and the Role of the State in Developing Countries*, London, Overseas Development Institute.

Mosley, P (2000), 'Globalisation, Economic Policy and Convergence', *The World Economy*, pp 613–34.

Polak, J J (1991), 'The Changing Nature of IMF Conditionally', *Essays in International Finance*, No 84, September, Princeton NJ, Princeton University Press.

Puyana, Alicia (1994), 'The External Sector and the Latin American Economy in the 1990s: Is there Hope for Sustainable Growth?', in G Bird and A Helwege, eds, *Latin America's Economic Future*, London, Academic Press, pp 51–80.

Rodrik, Dani (1999a), 'Governing the Global Economy: Does One Architectural Style Fit All?', paper prepared for the Brookings Institution Trade Policy Forum Conference on Governing in a Global Economy, April 15–16.

Rodrik, Dani (1999b), *The New Global Economy and Developing Countries: Making Openness Work*, Policy Essay 24, Washington DC, Overseas Development Council.

Sachs, J and A Warner (1995), 'Economic Reform and the Process of Global Integration', *Brookings Papers in Economic Activity*, 1, pp 1–117.

Stiglitz, Joseph (2000), 'What I Learned at the World Economic Crisis', *New Republic*, April.

Tussie, Diana and M Botzman (1990), 'Sweet Entanglement: Argentina and the World Bank 1985–9', *Development Policy Review*, 8, 4, pp 391–409.

Williamson, John (1999), 'Future Exchange Rate Regimes for Developing East Asia', paper presented at a conference on 'Asia in Economic Recovery: Policy Options for Growth and Stability' organised by the Institute of Policy Studies, Singapore, June 21–22.

Williamson, John (2000), 'The Role of the IMF: A Guide to the Reports', paper presented to a conference on Developing Countries and the Global Financial Architecture organised by the Commonwealth Secretariat and the World Bank, London, 22–23 June.

6
Miracle to Meltdown: A Pathology of the East Asian Financial Crisis

Graham Bird and Alistair Milne

For most of the 1980s and the first half of the 1990s the newly industrialising countries of East Asia were held up as the world's most dramatic economic success story. They were characterised by exceptionally rapid rates of economic growth and human development, by relatively low inflation and by an absence of balance of payments difficulties. During the 1980s, when Latin America was experiencing severe debt crises, East Asia managed to avoid them. The size of capital inflows to the region in the first half of the 1990s suggested that capital markets expected the East Asian success story to continue.

As many parts of the developing world, including Latin America and Africa, began to review their economic structures as well as their economic policies, with the objective of raising future rates of economic growth, East Asia was frequently cited as a model of what could be achieved.

However, as it received closer scrutiny, economics often seemed unable to provide an entirely satisfactory explanation of the East Asian growth experience, which therefore became referred to as a 'miracle', the very choice of the term implying that the phenomenon was beyond purely scientific explanation.

Then, in 1997/98, quite suddenly it seemed, the success turned sour and the economies of East Asia experienced an economic reversal of such proportions that it was generally regarded as warranting the overused description of a 'crisis'. The crisis saw sharply depreciating exchange rates, a big reduction in the rate of economic growth, rising unemployment, a large turnaround in capital flows from inflows to outflows and – a sure sign of economic distress – the involvement of the IMF.

But just as economics had struggled to find a fully convincing explanation of the East Asian growth 'miracle', so it now struggled to explain the 'meltdown'. Certainly the conventional analysis of speculative currency crises that had been honed over the previous twenty years did not appear to fit the facts neatly. One feature of the Asian crisis, differentiating it from previous crises which have affected the international financial system, is that repayment difficulties have largely related to short-term international bank loans to *private* sector borrowers. Previous crises – over the repayment of sovereign bonds (in the nineteenth century and in the 1930s), long-term syndicated bank lending to sovereign borrowers (the 1980s debt crises), and short-term bills (the dollar-denominated *tesobonos* issued by the Mexican government in 1993 and 1994) – were all associated with *public sector* borrowing. Reflecting this, the crisis had not been widely predicted. Credit rating agencies only marked down Southeast Asian and South Korean bonds after the crisis, and spreads on bond issues and syndicated loans actually fell between mid-1995 and mid-1997.

It is in the nature of economics that it is better at explaining the past than at anticipating the future. After the event, there is clearly more information upon which to draw. The problem with prediction is not usually in identifying the relevant indicators, but in attaching appropriate weight to them.

This chapter is an exercise in retrospection. However, retrospection is important in as much as it may lead to a reassessment of the weight that should be attached to different economic indicators. This would certainly appear to be the legacy of the East Asian crisis from which there are important lessons to be learned.

The layout of the chapter is as follows. The following section briefly discusses the 'miracle' phase and assesses the extent to which conventional economic analysis explains it. Was the East Asian miracle as miraculous after all? The next section examines the 'crisis' or 'meltdown' phase, and assesses a number of hypotheses that have been put forward to account for it. What, in particular, was it that created an unsustainable situation in East Asia in 1997 and 1998. The section on policy failures discusses the weaknesses of the policy response to the crisis. The final section attempts to extract lessons from the East Asian experience that may be helpful in avoiding similar crises in the future.

East Asia: the miracle phase

As a comprehensive study by the World Bank conducted in the first half of the 1990s showed (Page *et al.*, 1993), there was no uni-causal explanation of rapid East Asian economic growth during 1965–90. However, although the study identified wide divergences across countries, it concluded that common elements were to be found in sound domestic macroeconomic management, in strong export orientation and in political stability. East Asian economies had been able to avoid the fiscal deficits and current account balance of payments deficits that had often constrained economic growth in developing countries. The idea that growth was associated with a unique 'Asian development model' based on strategic government intervention in trade or industry found less support, with the picture differing significantly between countries.

At the same time as the World Bank was producing its study, other analyses of East Asia based on growth accounting were producing results which strongly challenged the 'miracle' orthodoxy (Young, 1995). Here the contention was that East Asian growth was largely attributable to both physical and human capital accumulation rather than to any miraculous increase in total factor productivity. It was increasing inputs, rather than rapid increases in output per unit of input, which lay behind East Asian growth.

While interesting in itself, this finding was more relevant in terms of its message for future economic growth in the region. With diminishing returns, it was most unlikely that East Asian economies would be able to sustain the rates of economic growth that they had achieved throughout the 1980s and early 1990s. Far from being miraculous, their experience now appeared to be entirely consistent with neoclassical growth theory.[1] Economies with high saving and investment rates will accumulate capital and grow up to a point; but beyond that point economic growth will decline. High savings rates will not sustain economic growth in perpetuity. In the long run this model says that economic growth depends on the growth of productivity. To the extent that there was a miracle in East Asia, it was to do with the rapid accumulation of capital, and the willingness to sacrifice current consumption in favour of future consumption.

However, whereas neoclassical growth theory was consistent with a slowdown in East Asian growth, it was certainly not directly consistent with an economic crisis. Why should a fall in economic growth to a less spectacular but still impressive rate create a crisis? Indirectly, of course, a slowdown in economic growth that had been unexpected by the markets could, in principle, have sparked a discrete downward reassessment of future growth prospects and a sudden outflow of capital, with this in turn creating a liquidity crisis. However, it is much more likely that this reassessment would have been gradual. Moreover, in practice it was the crisis that reduced the rate of economic growth rather than the other way around. Asian economic growth during the first half of the 1990s had if anything been faster than it had been during the 1980s.[2] So what did cause the crisis?

East Asia: the meltdown phase

Just as there was no uni-causal explanation of East Asia's rapid growth in the 1980s and 1990s, there is no uni-causal explanation of the crisis in 1997/98. Furthermore, just as differences existed across East Asian economies in terms of the nature of their growth performance, differences also existed in the nature of the crisis that they encountered.[3] In Indonesia, Korea, Malaysia, the Philippines and Singapore an important element of the crisis was the contagion effect from Thailand. Clearly, for the initiating country contagion was not relevant.

While the IMF has claimed that economic crises do not occur in the absence of fundamental economic imbalances and weaknesses (or, more picturesquely, 'out of a clear blue sky'), by the same token not all situations of fundamental economic weakness result in crises. For a crisis to occur, therefore, it would seem necessary for fundamental economic weakness to be combined with a 'trigger' that sets it off. Something happened in East Asia that converted a situation that appeared sustainable into one that became unsustainable.

But again, while the economic situation became unsustainable in Thailand, Korea and Indonesia, it remained sustainable in Malaysia, Hong Kong and Singapore, in the sense that these countries avoided having to borrow from the IMF; why was this?

There are a number of elements to the concept of sustainability.[4] These include underlying structural features, including the structure and pattern of trade, and the balance between domestic saving and investment; the stance of macroeconomic policy in terms of fiscal, monetary and exchange rate policy; vulnerability and exposure to external trading and financial shocks, reflecting the degree of export concentration and the maturity of external debt, as well as swings in international capital market perceptions; and, finally, the scope for economic adjustment, which depends largely on the political economy of policy reform.

This classification suggests that sustainability may be affected by both domestic and external factors, although of course this causal distinction is not always clear cut, since a given external shock may be better or less well handled by domestic policy makers. Thus it was that the deteriorating global economic environment at the beginning of the 1980s was better handled by East Asian than by Latin American countries. In principle, at least, it could be that East Asian policy makers simply became less good at navigating their way through turbulent global economic waters in the mid-1990s. In practice, while there is little doubt that some policy mistakes were made, the global economic environment in the mid-1990s was not very turbulent. In many respects the global economy was performing well according to conventional indicators. This makes the East Asian crisis more intriguing. What do the elements of sustainability suggest about it?

Underlying structural features

Domestic saving rates have remained high in East Asia at more than 30% of GDP; the crisis was not therefore caused by any explosion in consumption. The principal structural factor contributing to the crisis was a rapid growth of bank and other claims on the private sector. During the 1990s these claims increased rapidly as a share of GDP, reaching especially high levels in Thailand and South Korea, even during a period when GDP itself was growing rapidly (Table 6.1).

Table 6.1   GDP growth and bank lending in East Asia, 1985–97

	Thailand	Indonesia	Malaysia	Philippines	South Korea
Annual growth rates of GDP (%)					
1985–90	10.3	6.3	6.8	4.7	10.0
1990–95	8.6	7.1	8.7	2.2	7.5
1995–96	5.5	8.0	8.6	5.8	7.1
1996–97	−0.4	4.6	7.7	9.7	5.5
Ratio of bank claims on private sector to GDP (% end period)					
1990	65	46	71	19	100
1995	98	53	85	38	137
1996	102	55	93	49	141
1997	116	61	108	57	145

Source: *International Financial Statistics.*

The potential for repayment problems is exacerbated by the fact that these claims are largely liabilities of the *corporate* sector not individuals and therefore must be serviced out of corporate profits, the least stable component – relative to wages or rental income – of private sector income. In fact the data in Table 6.1 understate total corporate indebtedness in the Asian economies, since they exclude direct borrowing, which in the case of Indonesian and Korean companies was of a comparable magnitude to their borrowing from domestic banks. The extreme case is South Korea, where many of the industrial conglomerates (the *chaebols*) have ratios of debt to equity in excess of six to one, making some form of debt restructuring unavoidable.

Since bank lending in the Asian countries has primarily been to companies, not to individuals, it is appropriate to compare the data in Table 6.1 with ratios of corporate debt to GDP in the industrialised countries. The ratios of enterprise debt to GDP in 1994 ranged from 55% in Japan and Germany, to 60% in the USA and 65% in the UK (OECD non-financial enterprises, financial statements, 1995). The data thus suggest that, with the exception of the Philippines, corporate debt in the crisis countries had reached levels far higher in relation to national income than in the developed world.

It might still have been possible to service this corporate borrowing, had it been used efficiently to finance profitable investment opportunities. But this was not always the case. In Thailand, and to a lesser extent in Malaysia and the Philippines, there was an excessive allocation of bank loans to property investment. While this was not a classic speculative property boom, in that property prices themselves do not appear to have become grossly inflated, there was an oversupply of commercial property. By the end of 1996 the excess supply of office space in Bangkok had risen to some six years' worth of flow demand, even in good years. With rental levels declining, property developers faced considerable difficulties in maintaining repayments. In the Thai case this led to a suspension of bank loan servicing in January 1997.

In two of the other countries affected by the crisis, Indonesia and South Korea, misallocation of investment occurred because bank credit was allocated in large degree according to political direction. In the Indonesian case this reflected an extreme form of 'crony capitalism' where those with links to President Suharto could access bank credit without regard to the viability of their business enterprises.

In South Korea the mechanism was less crude but also led to great distortion in the allocation of investment funds. South Korea was facing difficult problems of structural adjustment as traditional export industries were being undercut by competition from the lower wage economies of Southeast Asia and the Republic of China. However, instead of confronting the necessity to rationalise and if necessary close loss-making capacity, Korea used government guarantees to sanction a continued flow of borrowing to bridge the financial deficits of the *chaebols*.

These misallocations of investment were a relatively recent problem. As argued by the World Bank in 1993, the Asian economies had hitherto been highly successful in directing investment to areas where there was a high rate of return. While the data in Table 6.2 suggest an upward trend in incremental capital output ratios (ICORs) in the crisis countries, there were no obvious indications in the aggregate data of declining returns to investment until the crisis broke.

Another structural factor was the trade orientation of the Asian economies. Because of their degree of export diversification, East Asian economies do not initially give the impression of being vulnerable to external shocks in the same way that (say) sub-Saharan African economies are (because of their high degree of export concentration on primary products). However, while not exposed to a severe adverse trade shock in the form of a sudden decline in

Table 6.2 Incremental capital output ratios in East Asia, 1987–96

	1987–89	1990–92	1993–95
Indonesia	3.6	3.5	3.9
Korea	3.5	5.2	5.2
Malaysia	3.5	4.5	5.0
Philippines	3.4	23.8	6.2
Thailand	3.0	4.8	5.4

Source: *World Development Indicators*, World Bank.

commodity prices, East Asian export growth was always likely to be liable to increasing international competition. This came from China and Mexico, particularly following the large devaluation of the yuan and the peso in 1994 and 1995, respectively. Korea's export performance, in particular, was hit by the world's oversupply of semi-conductors and immediately before the crisis the terms of trade did move against the East Asian economies.

Structural problems were present but are not of themselves a sufficient explanation of the crisis. Increasing ICORS and a deterioration of the terms of trade would normally be expected to lead to a gradual decline in the rate of economic growth rather than a sudden crisis. It is also necessary to consider macroeconomic and other factors in order to understand what made these economies vulnerable to a sudden shock.

Macroeconomic policy and vulnerability to external shocks

To attribute the 'crisis' to lax macroeconomic policy is at odds with earlier explanations of the 'miracle', which emphasised sound macroeconomics and political stability. Was there really such a sea change? The answer is no; although this is not to say that macroeconomic policy was irrelevant.

IMF data show that Asian inflation increased quite sharply over 1993–95, but then fell from 11.9% in 1995 to a modest 6.7% and 3.9% in 1996 and 1997, respectively. Concentrating on Southeast Asia, inflation actually fell between 1991 and 1996 in Indonesia and Malaysia, and showed little change in Thailand. Government finances were in surplus throughout the region more often than they were in deficit in the years preceding the crisis, and when there were deficits these remained small relative to GDP, and much smaller than fiscal deficits in industrialised countries.

For illustrative purposes Table 6.3 provides selected economic indicators for Thailand over 1994–97. Before 1997 there is little here to suggest an

Table 6.3   Thailand: selected economic indicators

	1994	1995	1996	1997[a]
		(% change)		
Real GDP growth	8.9	8.7	6.4	2.5
Consumer prices	5.3	7.1	4.8	9.5
		(% of GDP)		
Overall public sector balance	1.8	2.5	2.2	−1.6
External current account balance	−5.6	−8.0	−7.9	−5.0
		(months of imports)		
Gross official reserves	6.8	6.3	6.6	4.2

Note: [a] IMF programme targets.

Source: *IMF Survey*, 26, 17 September 1997.

economy in imminent crisis; indeed, it is only the rapid decline in official reserves that hints at the depth of the crisis in 1997. If there was a major lapse in the macroeconomic policy stance it was not to be found in fiscal policy. The weak link in terms of macroeconomic policy, particularly in Thailand but elsewhere in East Asia as well, related to exchange rate policy. Thailand maintained a pegged value for the baht against the dollar. But with relatively fast inflation compared with the USA and other industrial countries, and a 50% appreciation in the value of the US dollar against the Japanese yen over the period 1995–97, the baht became overvalued in real terms. This seriously weakened the current account balance of payments. However, Thailand did not take timely measures to eliminate currency overvaluation. In this respect there were elements of a conventional currency crisis.

Although weaknesses in economic fundamentals and macroeconomic policy were present in Thailand, and to a lesser degree elsewhere in Southeast Asia, these alone would not have made the situation unsustainable. Central to the crisis was the acceleration of capital inflows during 1995 and 1996, which were much greater than earlier in the decade, followed by the sudden outflow of capital after the crisis had begun. This inflow and subsequent outflow was especially associated with over-reliance on short-term bank borrowing. The size of this reversal ($105 billion over 1996–97) is shown in Table 6.4. Only foreign direct investment was exempt from it. Most of the turnaround in capital inflows is accounted for by short-term borrowing from overseas

Table 6.4 Five Asian economies: external financing (US$ billions)

	1994	1995	1996	1997[a]
Current account balance	−24.6	−41.6	−54.9	−26.0
External financing, net	47.4	80.9	92.8	15.2
Private flows, net	40.5	77.4	93.0	−12.1
Equity investment	12.2	15.5	19.1	−4.5
Direct equity	4.7	4.9	7.0	7.2
Portfolio equity	7.6	10.6	12.1	−11.6
Private creditors	28.2	61.8	74.0	−7.6
Commercial banks	24.0	49.5	55.5	−21.3
Non-bank private creditors	4.2	12.4	18.4	13.7
Official flows, net	7.0	3.6	−0.2	27.2
International financial institutions	−0.4	−0.6	−1.0	23.0
Bilateral creditors	7.4	4.2	0.7	4.3
Resident lending/other, net[b]	−17.5	−25.9	−19.6	−11.9
Reserves excluding gold (− = increase)	−5.4	−13.7	−18.3	22.7

Notes: The five economies comprise Indonesia, Korea, Malaysia, the Philippines and Thailand.
[a] Estimate.
[b] Including resident net lending, monetary gold and errors and omissions.

Source: Institute of International Finance.

banks, in both domestic and foreign currencies. Other features of the table are the large fall in international reserves across the region, and the offsetting infusion of finance from the international financial institutions – largely the IMF.

Why were overseas bankers prepared to lend such large sums to the Asian economies and why did their confidence in the region deteriorate so rapidly? To understand this it is necessary to recall the mindset which existed in early 1997. With the exception of the Philippines, export orientation and macroeconomic rectitude had underpinned years of rapid growth. There was no reason to question the political will to continue these policies. Exchange rate instability was perceived as a problem of the profligate economies of Latin America, not something which could possibly affect the miracle economies of Asia.

Lenders also believed that governments would guarantee bank liabilities to overseas creditors, were they to face repayment difficulties. In the Thai case this was made quite explicit by the establishment of the 'international banking facility' which guaranteed domestic bank borrowing from overseas and supported a particularly large inflow of short-term international bank lending.

Following the floating of the baht in June 1997, international investors and domestic banks realised quite suddenly that they had grossly underestimated the risks of exchange rate realignment throughout Southeast Asia. This quickly became a self-fulfilling prophecy. They sought, individually, to reduce their exposure to exchange rate risk. In the case of the international banks this meant that they now sought to decrease, rather than increase, their domestic currency lending to the Southeast Asian economies. The domestic banks meanwhile sought to hedge their exposure to foreign currency liabilities, by conducting offsetting transactions in both spot and future forex markets. The threat of devaluation also led to a substantial, although largely unrecorded, capital flight (hidden in the errors and omissions of the balance of payments). The pressure to devalue became irresistible. This was the mechanism of contagion by which the crisis spread from Thailand to Malaysia, Indonesia and the Philippines. When, in October 1997, banking sector difficulties similar to those which had afflicted Thailand emerged in South Korea, contagion again affected the South Korean won.

Contagion effects were amplified by the close substitutability of exports from the different economies of Southeast Asia. The devaluation of the baht made the exports of Indonesia, Malaysia and the Philippines much less competitive in Japanese and US markets. The competitive effects of devaluation also put considerable pressure on the exchange rates of the Hong Kong dollar and the Chinese yuan, which remained firm only because of the currency board arrangement in Hong Kong and the huge volume of Chinese foreign currency reserves.

Exchange rate overreaction

While the crisis was unanticipated, the mechanisms which initiated it and the process by which it spread among the Asian economies are reasonably well understood. What is less amenable to standard economic analysis is why, after the abandonment of currency pegs, exchange rates depreciated by far more than could possibly be justified in terms of economic fundamentals. As illustrated in Figure 6.1, the exchange rate between the Indonesian rupiah and the dollar fell by 75% before stabilising in early 1998, with the dollar exchange rates of South Korea and the countries of Southeast Asia depreciating by over 30%. These depreciations have been far in excess of what might have been required to restore fundamental exchange rate equilibrium. Excessive currency depreciations have also affected other Asian countries, such as Singapore, Taiwan and India, which had not operated pegged exchange rates before the crisis and were not affected by such severe banking sector problems.

Special factors apply in the case of Indonesia, where a vacillating policy response and continued political uncertainty have undermined confidence in the rupiah. The other countries, however, responded coherently to the crisis, moving swiftly to close down and restructure insolvent financial institutions and maintaining tight monetary policy to prevent any inflationary impact from devaluation. Moreover, their macroeconomic position continues to be strong, with substantial fiscal surpluses, continued high rates of domestic

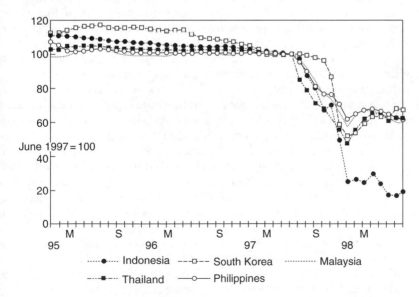

Figure 6.1 Dollar exchange rate indices

saving, and a rapid shift into current account surplus as domestic expenditure has contracted. There is nothing in these economic fundamentals which can explain the magnitude of their exchange rate depreciation.

Two factors seem to be relevant to explaining exchange rate overreaction: investor psychology and the failure of policy makers to deal with the overhang of corporate sector debt. While individually investors can reduce their exposure to particular financial assets, collectively such a reaction produces only a steep decline in prices and worsens their losses. In such circumstances it is common to observe an overreaction of market prices, with the initial decline followed by an eventual correction. This was, for example, exactly what happened following both the 1987 stock market crash and the departure of sterling from the Exchange Rate Mechanism of the European Monetary System in 1992.

Acting rationally, bank creditors of the Asian countries should surely have realised that, after the event, they had little to gain by withdrawing short-term investments since they had already suffered the capital loss. Why would they continue to liquidate their positions and hence weaken exchange rates?

The theory of speculation offers two alternative accounts of such financial crises. Is it that international financial markets are efficient and based on fundamentals, with speculative crises representing the short-term domination of ill-informed speculators who will not survive? Or is it that international financial markets are inherently unstable, and that problems arise when market sentiment becomes biased in one direction? Individual creditors are swayed by market sentiment; their expectations are elastic. The smaller the minority opinion to which they subscribe the more likely they are to abandon it and therefore the smaller the minority becomes. Once foreign lenders began to withdraw from East Asia, the safest bet for the others seemed to be for them to follow suit, regardless of the degree to which exchange rates had departed from fundamental levels.

Instability in exchange rates has been further exacerbated because Southeast Asian economies are not as well integrated into world capital markets as popular characterisation might suppose. Having become so undervalued, the currencies of these countries might have been viewed as highly attractive short-term speculative investments. But the markets in them, unlike those for the currencies of the industrial countries, are relatively illiquid and dominated by trade and investment transactions. Moreover, following the onset of the crisis, liquidity in these forex markets declined dramatically. Few participants were willing to take the kind of speculative trading positions which would have helped move exchange rates back towards their fundamental equilibrium values. By the same token, the orthodox prescription of maintaining high domestic rates of interest in an attempt to encourage short-term capital inflows and strengthen exchange rates has been much less effective in restoring an appropriate real exchange rate than would be the case among industrial countries.

In summary there were, indeed, signs of fundamental disequilibria in the East Asian economies before the crisis in 1997. Inflation was showing signs of accelerating, the current account of the balance of payments had moved into substantial deficit, partly as a result of exchange rate policy and partly as a result of increasing international competition and a slight lapse in the degree of fiscal rectitude.

However, an explanation based on fundamental economic weakness cannot be taken too far. If the sky was not 'clear blue' it was certainly no more than 'partly cloudy'. The East Asian economies continued to exhibit high savings rates, relatively low external debt relative to GDP, relatively rapid rates of economic growth and low rates of unemployment. At worst they appeared to face a period of (slightly) declining economic growth, because of diminishing returns to capital accumulation, and a modest combination of monetary and exchange rate adjustment. Their economic fundamentals did not make them candidates for a crisis.

The three key elements which triggered the East Asian crisis were then, first, the liberalisation of domestic financial markets and the capital account, second, the inappropriate use of capital inflows for sometimes speculative investment and third, and perhaps most importantly, the weaknesses in domestic financial sectors and the problems with resolving excessive corporate indebtedness. These exposed the East Asian economies to the intrinsic volatility of private international capital markets and their vulnerability to mutually re-enforcing mood swings among creditors.

In one sense the East Asian crisis was similar to the Mexican peso crisis that had preceded it, in as much as it was proximately an illiquidity rather than an insolvency crisis. But whereas the Mexican crisis had revolved around an 'old' problem in the form of the short-term indebtedness of the government, the East Asian crisis was 'new' in the sense that it was linked to excessive private sector indebtedness, especially short-term foreign exposure. Hong Kong, Taiwan and Singapore weathered the storm better than the other Southeast and East Asian economies because their corporate sectors were not so overborrowed and because they were less illiquid; their higher holdings of international reserves and their willingness to pursue strict domestic macroeconomic policy moderated the effects of the regional loss of confidence.[5]

Policy failures

Although most macroeconomic fundamentals remain reasonably strong, it is clear that the Asian crisis, far from being close to resolution, may deepen considerably before getting better. While exchange rates have stabilised, current data suggest a substantial contraction of GDP in Southeast Asia and Korea in 1998 which could be as great as 10% of GDP; some commentators anticipate further declines of output in 1999.[6] How is it that the response to the Asian crisis has been such a severe macroeconomic contraction, when the conventional macroeconomic indicators, such as the current account balance of payments, fiscal deficits, real exchange rates and inflation, are all fairly benign?

The principal reason for this sharp output fall is that little is being done as yet to resolve the overhang of corporate debt. In none of the Asian economies are there any bankruptcy procedures which allow an orderly workout of company debt; an exception to this generalisation is Taiwan, where company failure is common (Aw and Roberts, 1997), a fact which may help to explain why Taiwan has been relatively unaffected by the crisis. Unable to either service or reschedule their debts, companies are substantially reducing investment. This reduction in investment is exacerbated by the reduction in the supply of bank loans, as the authorities have taken steps to deal with banking sector problems. While industrial export industries continue to be highly profitable, falling investment, contraction of bank credit and declining consumer confidence are sharply reducing domestic demand.

Excessive currency devaluation is also a contributory factor, in that domestic banks and corporations continue to be net borrowers of foreign exchange and so suffer substantial declines of net worth as the domestic currency depreciates. This mechanism is most pronounced in the case of Indonesia, where at present exchange rates, for example, some 90% of companies quoted on the Jakarta stock market are thought to be insolvent.

But it is also clear that these problems are being exacerbated by some of the policies taken to counter the crisis. In particular the high interest rates imposed in order to maintain international investor confidence (in Thailand and Korea short-term money market rates rose from around 12% before the crisis to nearly 20%, while in Indonesia money market rates reached 60% or more) have led to increased problems of loan repayment and further declines in domestic investment and consumption.

Furthermore, the early reliance placed by the IMF on a substantial fiscal contraction, as a condition for its support, was misplaced. As it subsequently realised, there is little need for sharp fiscal contraction in an economic environment where domestic saving rates remain high and the investment rate is falling. More recent Fund agreements have placed greater emphasis on the reform of the financial sector.

It is therefore unsurprising that several commentators have argued that the policy response of high interest rates and tight control of fiscal spending made matters worse rather than better (Radelet and Sachs, 1998; Feldstein, 1998). Here, however, policy makers are stuck between 'a rock and a hard place': while lowering interest rates would improve the servicing of domestic currency loans, it would, at the same time, lead to greater exchange rate depreciation and a further deterioration in bank balance sheets.

Threats to Asian recovery also come from the deteriorating economic situation in Japan and, potentially, from the problems faced by the banking sector and state-owned industry in China. Japanese banks have been among Southeast Asia's and Korea's major international creditors, and are themselves under a fierce credit squeeze. Depreciation of the yen has had adverse knock-on effects on other Asian currencies. Notwithstanding its huge foreign exchange reserves, domestic economic problems in China could lead to an exchange crisis similar to the one that has afflicted other Asian countries. A further devaluation of the yuan could lead to additional problems throughout Asia.[7]

The basic analytical issue here is the extent to which the Asian economies are facing problems of *illiquidity* rather than *insolvency*. The depth of the crisis and the difficulties of dealing with it are certainly exacerbated by illiquidity. Were the Asian economies able freely to access international capital markets on favourable terms, they could raise sufficient funds to recapitalise their banking systems and restructure corporate debt. This would, in turn, restore investor confidence, allow them to lower domestic rates of interest, and lead to an appreciation of exchange rates back towards fundamental equilibrium levels.

There is also, however, a solvency problem, not at the national level, but in relation to many private sector companies which are unable to service outstanding debts. Ultimately, resolution of the crisis and the restoration of growth will require recognition of the real value of this debt and an allocation of losses between domestic governments and both domestic and international creditors. Bank restucturing, while a necessary response, will not be sufficient on its own to restore the confidence of international investors.

In other words, the real policy failure has been of responding not to the real disease – the unsustainable private sector debt overhang and the lack of international liquidity – with the introduction of bankruptcy procedures and a comprehensive debt restructuring, but of instead treating only the symptoms – banking failures, capital outflows and currency depreciation – with the tools of conventional macroeconomic and regulatory policy.

Conclusions: lessons from the East Asian crisis

The first lesson is that capital inflows need to be handled with care. It is through excessive inflows that past economic success can breed future economic failure. In retrospect, and given the size of the capital inflows, which in the case of Thailand reached about 13% of GDP in 1995, East Asian economies would have been wise to relax their quasi-pegged exchange rate policies. Although the resulting real exchange rate appreciation would no doubt have caused a 'Dutch disease' effect, which would have weakened the current account of the balance of payments, it would also have avoided the domestic inflationary consequences that merely served to appreciate real exchange rates via another route. More importantly, it would have eliminated the problem of excess credibility. Exchange rate risk (exchange rates may depreciate as well as appreciate), would then have moderated future capital inflows. International financial crises reflect capital instability; in other words, excess capital inflows as well as excess capital outflows. The East Asian countries would have done better to have relied on conventional monetary and fiscal policy to control inflation and to have allowed their nominal exchange rates to change in order to maintain real exchange rate equilibrium. The East Asian crisis provides further evidence in favour of the 'real targets' approach to exchange rate policy and against the 'nominal anchor' approach (Bird, 1998).

The second lesson is that liberalisation of the domestic banking and financial sectors should not be allowed to occur too rapidly and in the absence of either adequate prudential supervision and regulation or procedures for corporate bankruptcy. The standard view is now that an essential precondition for successful capital account liberalisation is the introduction of proper regulation and supervision of domestic banking systems (Basle Committee on Banking Supervision, 1997; Folkerts-Landau and Lindgren, 1998).

Over a period of seven years up to 1996, banking claims in Thailand, Korea and Malaysia increased by more than 50% relative to GDP. Moreover, much of the new lending was financed by the banks borrowing offshore, such that the foreign liabilities of the banking and financial system in Thailand reached over 28% of GDP by 1995. Not only this, but an increasing share of the foreign borrowing was short term, especially and significantly in the three crisis countries, Korea, Thailand and Indonesia. Beyond 1994, the ratio of short-term debt to foreign exchange reserves exceeded one in all three countries. With lax regulation of the assets held against these foreign currency denominated short-term liabilities, and the moral hazard effects of any expected bail-out of the banks (Krugman, 1998), the seeds of a liquidity crisis were sown.

Greater supervision of the banks' balance sheets could have helped avert the financial crisis. This lesson is also emerging from more broadly based economic research published by the IMF (Demirguc-Kunt and Detragiache, 1998), which suggests that banking sector problems have played a significant role in a number of other currency crises.

Less standard, but perhaps equally important, is the point that any country attracting substantial foreign capital flows to finance corporate investment, either directly or via the domestic banking system, needs to establish the legal framework and procedures for corporate bankruptcy and debt restructuring. This is crucial for two reasons: first, it provides a mechanism for dealing with an excessive build-up of corporate debt; second, the existence of a recognised bankruptcy procedure encourages local banks and overseas creditors to take into account bankruptcy risk, instead of assuming that the face value of claims will be maintained even when a borrower gets into difficulties.

The third lesson is that liberalisation of the capital account of the balance of payments is a two-edged sword. Capital inflows may overcome shortages of domestic saving and provide finance for long-term investment with a high rate of return. This, of course, is the typical justification for free capital mobility. However, especially in an unregulated market, speculative and volatile short-term capital inflows may just as easily be used to finance speculative investment. This can make the capital importer highly vulnerable to changed capital market perceptions and outside 'push' factors. Sudden capital outflows then create liquidity problems for which there are no easy answers.

Among the push factors are the contagion effects associated with economic crises elsewhere. Capital outflows may therefore create liquidity problems in countries that have generally used capital imports wisely. Externalities will not be internalised and the resulting allocation of global savings will be inefficient. A lesson from Asia is that problems can arise even where capital inflows are not used to finance consumption.

The conventional calculus of capital account liberalisation has underestimated the vulnerability of liberalised international capital markets to crises associated with the clustering of investors' expectations (Dooley, 1996). Financial crises in emerging markets provide timely evidence of how important this phenomenon can be, and advise in favour of a reassessment of the costs and benefits of unabashed capital account liberalisation. While a full blown regime of permanent capital controls may be unworkable and inefficient, the use of capital controls as a short-term measure to regulate capital inflows and outflows at the margins may be an option that should be retained.

Financial crises may be as much (and possibly more) to do with the shortcomings of private international capital markets as they are to do with the deficiencies of domestic economic policy and performance in crisis countries. It would be unwise, therefore, to focus exclusively on economic reform in crisis countries and to ignore global economic reform which seeks to reduce financial instability. But what needs to be done to stabilise international capital markets? There are well known intrinsic difficulties here since, up to a point, capital mobility confers global benefits. It is *excess* capital mobility that is the problem. However, this is much easier to define after a crisis than before it.

In principle there are essentially three ways of dealing with the instability of international capital markets. The first involves capital controls to frustrate the market's wishes. The second involves taxing international currency transactions in an attempt to de-incentivise capital movements. And the third involves establishing an international lender of last resort (ILLR) which swims against the tide of the market mood sufficiently strongly to change it. There are problems with each of these possibilities. Capital controls may not work in the long run because of evasion. Transactions taxes may encounter low elasticities, given the size of the potential gains from currency transactions relative to the size of the tax. And an ILLR requires massive resources given the size of private international capital markets, and also has associated moral hazard problems.

The provision of more information and greater transparency is, in principle, a way of dealing with informational asymmetries which may be part of the problem of international financial instability. But this too may encounter difficulties. It is the distribution of expectations that stabilises non-efficient markets. More (and superior) information will narrow this distribution. If the information is accurate and pertains to fundamentals, foreign lending will become more rational, speculators will in the long run lose out and will be discouraged. However, if the information is inaccurate in terms of the fundamentals it will encourage inappropriate capital flows that then themselves weaken the fundamentals.

In practice the answer to international financial instability is to ensure that the costs of crises are shared across creditors as well as debtors, with private creditors having to reschedule their loans and extend maturities. This will not only help to cure crises that have occurred but, by increasing the perceived risks of foreign lending, will help prevent the crises to which excess lending contributes.

Lesson four is that the policy response to a crisis needs to be based on a careful diagnosis of the underlying economic difficulties. In the Asian case failure to deal with the private sector debt overhang, and over-reliance on conventional macroeconomic policy instruments, has led to a deep and protracted decline in output.

The final lesson is that economics as a subject still has a lot to learn. Over the past ten years economists failed to predict the fall of Communism and the related move to market-based systems, as well as the two major international financial crises that have hit the world economy. At a time when market-based solutions and liberalisation have been in the ascendancy, the Mexican and latterly the East Asian crisis have come along to give pause for thought. There is clearly some distance still to travel along the learning curve.

References

Aw, Bee Yan and Mark J Roberts, 'Firm-level evidence on productivity differentials, turnover and exports in Taiwanese manufacturing', *NBER Working Paper*, 6235, October 1997.

Basle Committee on Banking Supervision, *Core Principles for Effective Banking Supervision*, Basle: Bank for International Settlements, 1997.

Bird, Graham, 'New approaches to country risk assessment', in Graham Bird, *Commercial Bank Lending and Third World Debt*, London: Macmillan, 1989.

Bird, Graham, 'Exchange rate policy in developing countries: what is left of the nominal anchor approach?' *Third World Quarterly*, 19(2) June 1998, pp 255–76.

Demirguc-Kunt, Asli and Enrica Detragiache, 'The determinants of banking crises in developing and developed countries', *IMF Staff Papers*, 45, March 1998, pp 81–109.

Dooley, Michael P, 'A survey of literature on controls over international capital transactions', *IMF Staff Papers*, 24, December 1996, pp 639–87.

Feldstein, N, 'Refocusing the IMF', *Foreign Affairs*, 1998.

Folkerts-Landau, David and Carl-Johan Lindgren, *Towards a Framework for Financial Stability*, Washington, DC: IMF, 1998.

Kaminsky, Graciela, Saul Lizondo and Carmen M Reinhart, 'Leading indicators of currency crises', *IMF Staff Papers*, 45, March 1998, pp 1–48.

Krugman, Paul, 'The myth of Asia's miracle', *Foreign Affairs*, November/December 1994, pp 62–78.

Krugman, Paul, 'What happened to Asia?', unpublished manuscript, January, 1998.

Milesi-Ferretti, Gian and Assaf Razin, *Current Account Sustainability*, Princeton Studies in International Finance, No 81, October 1996.

Page, John et al., *The East Asian Miracle: Economic Growth and Public Policy*, New York: World Bank/Oxford University Press, 1993.

Radelet, Steven and Jeffrey Sachs, 'The East Asian financial crisis: diagnosis, remedies, prospects', paper prepared for the Brookings Panel, Washington DC, 26–27, March 1998.

Young, Alwyn, 'The tyranny of numbers: confronting the statistical realities of the East Asian growth experience', *Quarterly Journal of Economics*, August 1995, pp 641–80.

7

The International Monetary Fund and Developing Countries: A Review of the Evidence and Policy Options

Graham Bird

As its systemic role evaporated with the collapse of the Bretton Woods system, so the International Monetary Fund (IMF) became drawn into a much more specific role in the context of the balance-of-payments (BOP) problems that developing countries were encountering. At its inception, the IMF had been seen as having no specific role in developing countries, but now it became exclusively these countries that formed its clientele. While during the 1970s the IMF had continued to make a few relatively large loans to a limited number of industrial countries (Italy and the United Kingdom), beyond the mid-1970s industrial countries ceased to draw any resources from it.

In the early 1990s the emergence of the Central and East European economies (countries in transition) presented the IMF with a new challenge as well as a new opportunity, but developing countries continued to dominate the pattern of its lending.

The IMF's change in focus provided plenty of ammunition for its critics. At one end of the political spectrum the argument was that it had inappropriately become a development agency. In this context the loss of its systemic role was seen as sufficient reason to close it down. At the other end, nongovernmental organizations (NGOs) argued that the Fund was an inadequate development agency. Here the argument was that IMF-supported policies did more harm than good and that developing countries, particularly the poorest of them, would be better off without it. During 1994, the year of the IMF's fiftieth anniversary, NGOs put together a coalition claiming that "Fifty Years Is Enough."

In the same year the Bretton Woods Commission, under the chairmanship of Paul Volcker, also suggested that the IMF's continuing involvement in developing countries was in many ways unfortunate and misplaced and that it might be sensible at some stage to consider merging the Fund's lending operations with those of the World Bank.

Mexico's economic crisis in early 1995 gave further fuel to the debate over the IMF's role in developing countries. Some saw the crisis as additional evidence of the deficiencies of IMF conditionality; others saw it as justification for increasing the lending capacity of the Fund; and still others saw it as reason for leaving private capital markets and governments to sort things out on their own without the intervention of any outside agency.

At their meeting in June 1995 the Group of 7 (G-7) leaders urged the introduction of a new emergency financing mechanism (EFM) to provide rapid-response finance in Mexico-type situations. But this was to be financed by doubling the size of the general arrangements to borrow (GAB) rather than by increasing IMF quotas. In terms of quotas and special drawing rights (SDRs), the G-7 merely recommended that the existing state of affairs be reviewed. Less ambiguously, however, the leaders argued for strong IMF conditionality and for the Fund to return to its core concern of macro-economic policy.

There is then no shortage of policy proposals with respect to the Fund's future role in developing countries. However, the scholarly basis for many of these is often rather superficial. In this chapter I attempt to provide a more measured review and analysis of the part played by the IMF in developing countries as both a BOP financing and adjustment organization. To do this I survey and draw on the large amount of economic research that is now available. I do not set out to provide a fully comprehensive treatment of this literature, nor do I seek to cover the growing bodies of research into the politics of economic adjustment and the political economy of economic reform, although I allude to both from time to time.

Moreover, as a survey of the IMF and developing countries, I gloss over some important issues. IMF policies and decisions represent the outcome of a complex negotiating process involving various elements of the Fund's management and executive board. The executive board represents different points of view reflecting different political interests. The IMF is clearly not a unified actor. Having said this, however, and for an institution of its size and complexity, reasonably well-defined policies do emerge, especially in the context of its dealings with developing countries, and this probably legitimizes the generalizations that follow.

An additional complication is that individual developing countries differ widely. They face different economic problems, differences in the scope for economic adjustment, and differences in the domestic political context within which adjustment is pursued (or not pursued). They possess different degrees of creditworthiness and experience differences in their appeal to aid donors. Furthermore, they have different degrees of political, military, and strategic importance and may be more, or less, familiar with the way in which the IMF operates. The nexus of support for them within the executive board of the IMF will therefore vary from case to case. All of this leaves plenty of room for studying the details of dealings between individual developing countries and the IMF. Again, however, the focus here is much broader, attempting to extract generalizations from which policy conclusions may be drawn.

I begin by providing a brief account of IMF involvement in developing countries, which shows the twin roles of the Fund as both a financing and an adjustment agency. In subsequent sections I examine each of these roles in turn and show the principal deficiencies that have emerged. In the final section I suggest a policy approach designed to help remedy these deficiencies comprising proposals that are rather different from those advocated by the G-7 leaders at the Halifax summit in 1995.

The IMF and developing countries: country and policy coverage

IMF lending: size and pattern

That the IMF has become heavily involved with developing countries is beyond question. Looking first at the breadth of country coverage, Tables 7.1 and 7.2 show the overall size and pattern of lending to developing countries. At the beginning of the 1980s it was most heavily involved in lending to African and Asian developing countries; but the debt crisis radically changed the picture. The highly indebted countries of Latin America now became major users of IMF financing while loans to Africa actually fell. However, while the Fund continued to be involved with highly indebted developing countries throughout the rest of the 1980s, the surge of lending in the early 1980s turned out to be temporary. For almost the entire period beyond 1986 net IMF credit to developing countries was negative.

A number of other features of IMF lending to developing countries are noteworthy. First, Table 7.3 reveals large swings in the use of individual facilities, particularly the extended fund facility (EFF). This had been the facility under which most of the additional lending to Latin America took place in the early 1980s. By 1987, however, there was only one EFF arrangement. Although the EFF became more popular after 1987, a relatively large proportion of total Fund arrangements now began to take the form of credits to low-income countries under the newly created structural adjustment facility (SAF) and enhanced structural adjustment facility (ESAF). While structural adjustment lending contributed to the widening influence of the Fund, SAF and ESAF arrangements accounted for only a small fraction of the total amount of Fund lending, which remained dominated by a small number of relatively large loans to big middle-income developing countries such as Brazil and Mexico.

Significant changes in the use of other lending facilities also occurred. The Fund's compensatory (and latterly contingency) facility had been an important source of finance to developing countries in the mid-1970s, and even

Table 7.1 Developing countries: net credit from the International Monetary Fund 1982–87 (in billions of U.S. dollars)[a]

	1982	1983	1984	1985	1986	1987
Developing countries by region	6.9	11.0	4.7	0.3	−2.2	−4.7
Africa	2.0	1.3	0.6	0.1	−1.0	−1.1
Asia	2.3	2.5	0.3	−1.0	−0.9	−2.4
Middle East and Europe	1.2	1.1	0.5	−0.2	−0.5	−0.4
Western Hemisphere	1.5	6.1	3.4	1.5	0.1	−0.8
Sub-Saharan Africa	0.7	1.3	0.5	—	−0.4	−0.5
By predominant export						
Fuel	0.2	1.7	1.3	—	0.8	1.0
Nonfuel exports	6.7	9.3	3.5	0.3	−3.0	−5.7
Manufactures	3.6	4.7	3.0	−0.6	−1.0	−4.0
Primary products	1.2	3.4	0.6	1.1	−0.5	−0.3
Services and private transfers	0.6	0.6	—	−0.2	−0.6	−0.6
Diversified export base	1.5	0.5	—	—	−1.0	−0.8
By financial criteria						
Net creditor countries	—	—	—	—	—	—
Net debtor countries	6.9	11.0	4.7	0.3	−2.2	−4.7
Market borrowers	2.0	5.9	4.0	1.2	0.6	−1.8
Official borrowers	1.8	1.6	0.3	−0.2	−1.0	−0.8
Countries with recent debt-servicing difficulties	4.0	7.9	3.8	1.7	−1.0	−1.8
Countries without debt-servicing difficulties	2.9	3.1	0.9	−1.4	−1.2	−2.9
Miscellaneous groups						
Small low-income economies	1.0	1.2	0.2	−0.2	−0.9	−0.6
Fifteen heavily indebted countries	2.2	6.3	3.3	1.6	−0.2	−1.3
Least developed countries	—	—	—	−0.1	−0.3	—
Countries in transition	—	—	—	−0.3	−0.5	−1.1

[a] Includes net disbursements from programs under the general resources account, trust fund, structural adjustment facility, and enhanced structural adjustment facility. The data are on a transaction basis, with conversions to U.S. dollar values at annual exchange rates. Converted to U.S. dollar values at end of period exchange rates.

Sources: International Monetary Fund (IMF). *World Economic Outlook*. Washington, D.C.: May 1991, May 1992, May 1993, and October 1994.

Table 7.2   Developing countries: net credit from the International Monetary Fund, 1988–93 (in billions of U.S. dollars)[a]

	1988	1989	1990	1991	1992	1993[b]
Developing countries by						
region	−4.1	−1.5	−1.9	1.1	−0.2	1.0
Africa	−0.3	0.1	−0.6	0.2	−0.2	1.1
Asia	−2.4	−1.1	−2.4	1.9	1.3	0.7
Middle East and Europe	−0.5	−0.2	−0.1	—	0.4	—
Western Hemisphere	−0.9	−0.2	1.2	−1.0	−1.6	−0.8
Sub-Saharan Africa	−0.2	−0.4	−0.3	—	—	−0.1
By predominant export						
Fuel	—	2.0	2.7	0.3	−1.3	−1.0
Nonfuel exports	−4.1	−3.5	−4.6	0.8	1.2	2.1
Manufactures	−2.9	−2.6	−2.6	1.3	1.1	—
Primary products	−0.4	−1.0	−0.9	−0.8	−0.4	1.0
Services and private						
transfers	−0.6	0.2	−0.4	0.3	0.3	0.3
Diversified export base	−0.3	−0.1	−0.7	0.1	0.1	0.8
By financial criteria						
Net creditor countries	—	—	—	—	—	—
Net debtor countries	−4.1	−1.5	−1.9	1.1	−0.2	1.0
Market borrowers	−1.4	0.2	0.7	−1.2	−1.6	−0.3
Official borrowers	−0.8	−0.2	−1.1	0.3	0.3	−0.1
Countries with recent						
debt-servicing						
difficulties	−1.3	−0.5	0.4	−1.0	−1.8	−0.3
Countries without						
debt-servicing						
difficulties	−2.8	−1.0	−2.3	2.1	1.6	1.3
Miscellaneous groups						
Small low-income						
economies	−0.3	—	−0.6	0.4	0.2	0.1
Fifteen heavily						
indebted countries	−1.4	−0.8	0.6	−1.4	−1.8	−0.8
Least developed						
countries	−0.2	−0.3	−0.4	0.1	0.2	—
Countries in transition	−0.9	−0.9	0.1	3.5	1.7	2.1

[a] Includes net disbursements from programs under the general resources account, trust fund, structural adjustment facility, and enhanced structural adjustment facility. The data are on a transaction basis, with conversions to U.S. dollar values at annual exchange rates. Converted to U.S. dollar values at end of period exchange rates.
[b] Figures for 1993 are estimates.

Sources: International Monetary Fund (IMF). *World Economic Outlook*. Washington, D.C.: May 1991, May 1992, May 1993, and October 1994.

Table 7.3 International Monetary Fund arrangements in effect in the financial years ended 30 April 1975–95, by facility type[a]

Financial year	Standby No.	Standby Amt.[b]	EFF No.	EFF Amt.	SAF No.	SAF Amt.	ESAF No.	ESAF Amt.	Total No.	Total Amt.
1975	12	337	—	—	—	—	—	—	12	337
1976	17	1,159	2	284	—	—	—	—	19	1,443
1977	17	4,673	3	802	—	—	—	—	20	5,475
1978	19	5,075	3	802	—	—	—	—	22	5,877
1979	15	1,033	5	1,611	—	—	—	—	20	2,643
1980	22	2,340	7	1,463	—	—	—	—	29	3,803
1981	22	5,331	15	5,464	—	—	—	—	37	10,795
1982	23	6,296	12	9,910	—	—	—	—	35	16,206
1983	30	9,464	9	15,561	—	—	—	—	39	25,025
1984	30	5,448	5	13,121	—	—	—	—	35	18,569
1985	27	3,925	3	7,750	—	—	—	—	30	11,675
1986	24	4,076	2	831	—	—	—	—	26	4,907
1987	23	4,313	1	750	10	327	—	—	34	5,391
1988	18	2,187	2	995	25	1,357	—	—	45	4,540
1989	14	3,054	2	1,032	23	1,566	7	955	46	6,608
1990	19	3,597	4	7,834	17	1,110	11	1370	51	13,911
1991	14	2,703	5	9,597	12	539	14	1813	45	14,652
1992	22	4,833	7	12,159	8	101	16	2111	53	19,203
1993	15	4,490	6	8,569	3	83	22	2137	45	15,279
1994	16	1,131	6	4,504	3	80	22	2713	47	8,428
1995	19	13,190	9	6,840	1	49	27	3306	56	23,385

[a] EFF = extended fund facility; SAF = structural adjustment facility; ESAF = enhanced structural adjustment facility. Includes arrangements where the three-year commitment period has expired but the third annual arrangement remains in effect (three cases in 1991 and two cases in 1992). The committed amounts exclude these cases. Includes amounts previously committed under SAF arrangements that were replaced by ESAF arrangements.
[b] In millions of special drawing rights (SDRs).

Source: International Monetary Fund, 1996. IMF Annual Report, 1995. Washington, D.C.: International Monetary Fund.

as late as 1982 drawings under the compensatory financing facility (CFF) accounted for about 30 percent of total IMF purchases. But following changes in its design in 1982, which had the effect of making it a high-conditionality facility, the CFF became much less heavily used, and by 1990 drawings under the remodeled compensatory and contingency financing facility (CCFF) were less than SDR 0.1 billion.[1] The Fund's buffer stock financing facility (BSFF) has been used even less.

While the data in Table 7.2 suggest that the number of arrangements has increased steadily since the mid-1980s this gives a misleading impression of the number of countries involved with the IMF. A significant feature of IMF lending to developing countries is the recidivist tendencies of many borrowers – a tendency most pronounced among but by no means limited to low-income countries. Developing countries have often had credit outstanding from the Fund for as many as fifteen consecutive years and, in some cases, have had such an outstanding balance for almost thirty years.[2] The long-term involvement of the IMF in many developing countries calls into question the temporary and revolving character of IMF lending envisaged in its Articles of Agreement.

But how should the IMF respond to such long-term involvement? Two opposing responses are possible. The first argues that its Articles of Agreement remain appropriate and that measures should be taken to shorten the duration of IMF involvement. The second argues that the nature of the problems faced by developing countries requires the Fund to adopt a longer-term perspective than was envisaged when the Articles of Agreement were originally drafted. In this context the word "temporary" needs to be interpreted as meaning "nonpermanent" rather than "short-term."

But if the IMF is to make resources available to developing countries in support of longer-term adjustment as well as shorter-term stabilization, is its existing array of facilities appropriate? What is the logic behind the Fund's portfolio of lending windows, and is there not scope for rationalization? We return to this issue later.

Policy coverage

The IMF exerts an important influence over the design of economic policy in countries that turn to it for financial assistance. This influence is at its strongest in areas where the IMF stipulates preconditions and prior actions or where there are quantified performance criteria. The IMF therefore has a powerful say on the exchange rate, domestic credit creation, interest rates, and fiscal imbalances. But it will also have to approve a much wider range of policies within the context of the "letter of intent" signed by the relevant borrowing government. In particular, in the context of its ESAF, the IMF also has become involved in structural conditionality covering pricing policy, trade liberalization, privatization, the structure of taxes and government expenditure, as well as the reform of the financial sector. Such structural provisions have acquired the status of performance criteria in about 40 per cent of SAF and ESAF arrangements, and this has served to accentuate the trend toward increasing conditionality. Whereas during 1968–77 standby arrangements had on average included fewer than six performance criteria, by 1984–87 this had increased to more than nine.[3] The trend has been further emphasized by more recent moves toward social conditionality under which the Fund seeks to offset the effects of adjustment programs on "vulnerable groups."

Other potential indicators of IMF involvement in the design of economic policy in developing countries are less easy to quantify because of lack of data. It is therefore difficult to comment with authority on the depth of the Fund's policy involvement, since the details of programs generally are not published. To observe that credit ceilings are an ever-present performance criterion only tells part of the story. How restrictive are the ceilings, and how much more restrictive are they than those that might have been set by governments outside the influence of the Fund?

Explaining Fund lending to developing countries

In order for the IMF to provide financial support to a member country, two sets of circumstances have to coexist. First, the country has to demand a loan, and, second, the Fund has to be willing to supply it. In a significant sense, however, the demand side is more important, since the IMF cannot volunteer loans; it can only respond either positively or negatively to requests from members.

Generally speaking, demand may be expected to vary with the state of a country's BOP and the availability (and cost) of alternative sources of finance. This is essentially what is found.[4] Periods of relatively heavy use of IMF credit by developing countries coincide with deteriorating BOP performance and falling creditworthiness. Furthermore, poorer developing countries, where BOP deficits are more severe and creditworthiness is lower, have a more persistent demand for Fund credit than do middle-income countries where the BOP and creditworthiness vary.

From time to time, however, the IMF may exert an influence over the amount of lending by reforming its facilities and by modifying conditionality. The reduced use of the CFF and CCFF in the period since 1982 surely is associated with the deliberalization of the facility that occurred. Moreover, the near abandonment of the EFF in the mid-1980s must to some extent be associated with the IMF's reservations about the effectiveness of extended arrangements – reservations that were relaxed in the late 1980s.

More detailed econometric examination of the economic characteristics of user countries confirms much of the overall picture painted above.[5] Developing countries have drawn more resources from the IMF as their BOP deteriorates – although the cause of the deterioration may be either excessive credit creation and rapid inflation or deteriorating terms of trade. Equally clear is the finding that the IMF is a more important source of finance for the poorer developing countries. Economic growth and development can, so it appears, wean countries away from the Fund. At an early stage of economic development, low-income countries are heavily dependent on the Fund. At an advanced stage high-income countries do not depend on the IMF at all. And, at an intermediate stage, middle-income countries place time-variant demands on the Fund. Yet, strong inertial elements in borrowing exist: countries that have borrowed from the Fund in the recent past are more likely to borrow from it in the reasonably near future.

This perhaps implies some form of threshold. Below it, countries remain reluctant to borrow from the Fund even where their economic situation is weak; the costs of involving the IMF are seen as outweighing the benefits of the additional finance that will be forthcoming. Above it, however, and having once accepted IMF involvement, the costs and benefits are reassessed with the result that future Fund involvement becomes more probable. Either the perceived benefits rise or the perceived costs fall. Perhaps a significant component of the perceived cost of IMF involvement is a fixed cost that, having once been incurred, becomes irrelevant to future decision making over some specific time span.

The evidence reported above has a number of important implications for the design of future policy. First, to the extent that the BOP problems encountered by developing countries are associated with external shocks, such as movements in the terms of trade or interest rates, disengagement from the Fund in the long run will depend on reducing their vulnerability to such shocks. Second, since slow economic growth and low levels of economic development are associated with relatively heavy use of IMF resources, it is important that the interface between economic development and the balance of payments is fully acknowledged. If developing countries are to reduce their reliance on the Fund they must secure economic growth. Adjustment programs supported by the IMF therefore need to ensure that any adverse effects on long-term economic growth are minimized. Third, if there is a demand threshold that is explained by erroneous ex ante expectations concerning the nature of conditionality, these expectations need to be corrected. Otherwise the expectations may become self-fulfilling. Delaying the implementation of an appropriate adjustment strategy is likely to deepen the underlying macroeconomic disequilibrium, and this in turn implies that IMF-supported programs, when eventually adopted, will need to be stricter than they would otherwise have had to have been. Fourth, while the IMF cannot proactively offer financial support in individual circumstances, it has scope to manage the demand for its loans by modifying the facilities under which it lends as well as the nature of its conditionality.

Therefore the Fund's increasing involvement with developing countries can lead to a much more positive and constructive response than discontinuing or off-loading its lending operations. This approach seeks to explain the factors that combine to cause increases in lending, with a view to exerting an influence on them. If we know what causes developing countries to seek assistance from the Fund, we know what needs to happen to reduce demand in the future.

The IMF as a direct and indirect source of external finance: too little, too late

If the Fund did not exist, countries' access to external finance would depend on international capital markets' perceptions of their creditworthiness as well as the proclivities of aid donors. Relying on commercial capital markets would not be a cause for concern if they were both efficient and equitable. Experience suggests otherwise: commercial flows are highly unstable. The feast-and-famine aspects of commercial lending during the 1970s and 1980s provide evidence for this, as do the ebbs and flows of commercial lending to Latin America during the first half of the 1990s.

Where such instabilities reflect the underlying economic performance of countries one might legitimately argue that capital movements are effectively policing economic policy. But much of the observed instability reflects speculation, with strong elements of contagion as problems in one country are quickly transmitted to others. Where short-term financial considerations dominate capital movements, there is little reason to believe that capital will be allocated to uses where the real rate of return is highest.

Moreover, commercial lending may bypass countries that are viewed as uncreditworthy. Although advocates of the market mechanism see this as encouraging such countries to pursue policies that enhance their creditworthiness, others see a commercially based system as imposing severe and unmanageable pressures on countries to correct BOP deficits. In this context markets fail because they are incomplete, and the IMF fills the gap.

The above features of commercial markets imply that the poorest countries in the world will carry a disproportionate share of the global adjustment burden, with damaging consequences for poverty. The alleviation of poverty has proved a long-standing and resilient justification for the sorts of resource transfers that the IMF organizes.

The IMF can, in principle, both provide its own resources in support of adjustment programs and galvanize additional finance from other public and private sources. Although frequently downplayed in assessments of the role of the Fund in developing countries, the availability of finance is usually an effective constraint on the design of an adjustment program, and the Fund's impact on it is therefore of considerable importance.

Much evidence suggests that developing countries use the IMF as a lender of last resort, only turning to it when all other financing options have been exhausted. The economic situation in these circumstances is usually critical with severe BOP difficulties, depleted international reserves, and high levels of external debt. Low investment and slow economic growth are also characteristics of countries borrowing from the Fund.[6]

Yet why should countries put off turning to the IMF if it directly or indirectly provides a significant source of external finance? Clearly, they may prefer to avoid the apparent loss of national sovereignty associated with IMF conditionality. Even here, however, sufficiently large amounts of external finance might be expected to afford compensation. The revealed preferences of developing countries suggest, therefore, that they do not perceive the Fund as providing adequate financial support; the benefits of additional external finance via the Fund do not exceed the costs of the loss of sovereignty over economic policy, except when external finance from other sources has become exceedingly scarce.

Does then the IMF provide adequate direct financial support? The answer depends on the size of the BOP problems that countries face, on the availability of alternative sources of finance, and on the appropriate blend between financing and adjustment in dealing with BOP deficits. Conceptual problems in calculating the implied financing gap mean that it is difficult to measure the extent to which IMF lending is adequate. However, we can gain some insight by examining the success of IMF-backed programs relative to the amount of Fund finance provided. If a lower success rate is associated with smaller amounts of financial assistance this could constitute prima facie evidence that it is the inadequacy of financing that has contributed the low success rate (particularly as the reverse causation is unlikely).

Among thirty-eight developing countries that negotiated programs with the IMF over 1979–89, the average size of Fund credit represented about 30 per cent of the base-year current account BOP deficit. However, when the programs are subdivided into those that were completed and those that were not (with the criterion for completion being that no more than 20 per cent of the credit was left undrawn), and making allowance for interruptions in the flow of credits associated with the suspension or cancellation of programs, it turns out that significantly more IMF finance was provided in the case of completed than uncompleted programs: 50 per cent as opposed to 20 per cent of the base-year current account deficit.[7]

A further analysis of all 266 programs negotiated with the IMF over 1980–90 (excluding SAF credits that were subsequently converted into credits under the ESAF) shows that the majority of these programs (52 per cent) broke down. This suggests that the limited amount of direct Fund finance may be potentially significant in explaining what is a relatively unimpressive performance of IMF-backed programs in developing countries. Could more financial support from the Fund have increased the success rate?

Limited direct financing would be less important were the IMF indeed to act as a gatekeeper, unlocking the door to capital inflows from other sources. This catalyzing role has often been treated almost as a stylized fact. Does it deserve such status? What does the theory of the capital account of the BOP suggest, and what does the empirical evidence reveal?

Theory suggests that the relationship between IMF lending and other forms of lending could cut either way. To the extent that IMF-backed programs are associated with rising domestic interest rates as well as the elimination of currency overvaluation and are seen as part of a coherent economic strategy to which the government is committed, the Fund's involvement should raise investors' confidence. On the other hand, where rising interest rates are seen as a precursor of economic recession and where devaluation generates expectations of further devaluation, there will be incentives for capital to leave. The IMF may be seen as providing a "seal of good housekeeping," but its involvement may also be seen as a summary indication of severe economic distress. Moreover, as will be seen later, the track record of IMF-supported programs is not strong. Combine this with the significant inertial component of Fund lending that was identified earlier, and it becomes unsound to presume that Fund involvement will be short-lived and associated with a significant turnaround in economic performance. Even where an improvement can be anticipated, such improvement may be insufficient to raise creditworthiness enough to affect capital flows. Marginal increases in creditworthiness will only be significant where they alter a country's credit rating.

If the theoretical analysis leads to ambiguous conclusions, what does the empirical evidence show? This also generates mixed results. Some studies do indeed find a positive relationship between borrowing from the Fund and borrowing from private capital markets, but even where this is statistically significant it is generally rather weak. Others find a negative but statistically insignificant relationship.[8] New tests based on 235 observations involving developing countries that made purchases on the Fund during 1980–85 yielded the following correlation coefficients on private borrowing (with F ratios in parentheses): $+0.095$ (4.88), $+0.008$ (3.82), $+0.046$ (1.96), and $+0.018$ (3.23), suggesting, at best, that the catalytic effect is weak.

Further empirical evidence on the catalytic effect may be gleaned by examining the performance of the capital account of the BOP following the negotiation of a program with the IMF (reported more fully later). Based on taking a representative sample of sixteen developing countries over 1979–85, the net effect is found to be a reduced capital inflow. Countries seem to be using a substantial part of any observed improvement in the current account to finance the repayment of foreign loans, which are not then matched by new disbursements. Rather than serving to generate new flows, IMF credits are often in effect repaying other creditors.

This evidence also allows some examination of the claim that the IMF's involvement will have a delayed effect on other forms of lending: is the catalytic effect lagged? In fact, the negative relationship appears to become progressively more pronounced during the three years following the negotiation of a program with the Fund. Perhaps foreign investors start off with higher hopes than are later justified by events.

Case study evidence is also broadly consistent with the conclusion that IMF lending does not have a strong catalytic effect. A reasonably detailed analysis of seventeen countries with IMF programs during 1979–89 reveals a clearly discernible catalytic effect in only two cases (the Gambia and Ghana), and even in these the effect was mainly on noncommercial flows. For the rest, including countries where IMF-backed programs were linked with debt rescheduling, no measurable effect on either public or commercial inflows was found. This case study evidence confirms the results of earlier case study work based on the period 1971–79 which concluded that IMF involvement was neither a necessary nor a sufficient condition for attracting capital from other sources.[9]

Interviews conducted with commercial bank lenders during the late 1980s in the context of debt restructuring provide yet more evidence on the catalytic effect. All banks included IMF involvement in their country-risk matrices, but while some included it with a positive sign seeing the Fund as providing some implicit guarantee of sound economic management, others gave it a negative sign viewing IMF involvement as a indicator of the extreme severity of a country's economic difficulties.[10]

Since the Fund presents its central role as supporting and catalyzing other support for members' economic adjustment efforts, the failure to discover any strong argument for its existence either theoretically or empirically is of considerable relevance. The Fund's seal of approval does not seem to carry a very high market value. Future policy needs to address the apparently mythical status of the catalytic effect. Can it be strengthened? If not, should the IMF itself provide a larger proportion of the necessary external financing? Moreover, should the Fund distinguish more clearly between countries where the catalytic effect may be strong or weak, as well as between the forms of lending it is seeking to catalyze? If the IMF does seek to increase its own lending capacity, it must address a further issue since over the last fifteen years it has usually possessed spare lending capacity. What can it do to encourage its members to turn to it for assistance in situations other than quasi economic crisis? Yet again, a more complex and nuanced reform agenda is implied than one that seeks merely to close down the IMF or merge its lending operations with those of the World Bank.

IMF conditionality: weaknesses in design, but slow to change

Important links exist between flows of external finance and IMF conditionality. First, programs have a greater chance of success if they are adequately financed. Second, the greater the success of IMF conditionality the greater the willingness of countries to turn to the Fund earlier, when they need less financial support, and the greater the willingness of private capital markets and aid donors to provide financial support. But have IMF programs been designed appropriately to meet the economic and political circumstances often found in developing countries? Has the IMF responded to criticisms of conditionality? And have developing countries implemented the programs that they have negotiated?

During the last fifteen years the IMF has probably been criticized more over the issue of conditionality than anything else. Research has attempted to describe the policies favored by the Fund by putting them in the context of an underlying analytical framework. This has then been assessed in terms of its relevance to developing countries.

In essence, IMF-backed programs are based on a monetary (as opposed to monetarist) model of the BOP. This model not only rests on restrictive theoretical assumptions, such as the stability of the demand for money, that do not hold in many developing economies but also leads to policy conclusions that assume a degree of policy control beyond the reach of many developing countries for either technical or political reasons. It is hardly surprising that an essentially monetary framework focuses on the fundamental importance of controlling domestic monetary aggregates. This requires governments to hold credit under ceilings stipulated by the anticipated growth in money demand. But, in practice, the degree of financial control may be highly imperfect because of unreliable data, the difficulties of forecasting and regulating budgetary outcomes, vulnerability to shocks, and the unpredictable responses of banks, financial institutions, and the private sector to government policy.

The model creates an attention bias toward monetary excesses as the principal cause of BOP problems and away from fiscal imbalances and problems that stem from structural weaknesses in production and trade. A danger is that the policy recommendations that follow from it may be at best inefficient, imposing significant costs on borrowing countries in terms of lost output and employment as well as human development, and therefore imposing social and political instability. At worst, these recommendations may be ineffective, failing to induce the sought-after strengthening in the BOP.[11]

In this context, IMF conditionality offers a demand-based solution to what is frequently just as much a supply-side problem. A large amount of evidence shows that BOP difficulties in developing countries are caused by external factors such as adverse movements in the terms of trade or increases in world interest rates as well as by domestic economic mismanagement.[12] Indeed, recent evidence from the IMF shows little support for the idea that it is excessive monetary growth that distinguishes between those developing countries that turn to it and those that do not.[13] Neostructuralist critics have gone on from this to claim that IMF conditionality not only is irrelevant to the real problem but also has a negative effect via its stagflationary consequences.[14]

A more recent source of criticism has been that the financial programming model used by the Fund is too static, failing to deal adequately with the time lags, uncertainties, and elastic expectations that underlie the adjustment process.[15] Moreover, the model clearly is oriented toward BOP stabilization rather than toward economic growth, which is treated as exogenous. Attempts to modify the model to endogenize economic growth therefore serve only to illustrate its fundamental shortcomings. Its inability to deal with economic growth in a formal fashion has, so it is claimed by some critics, resulted in a narrow approach to the supply side of the economy, which concentrates on reducing price distortions, encouraging privatization, and curtailing public expenditure. A shift toward less state intervention and a greater reliance on market forces is seen by the Fund as the principal means by which aggregate supply may be increased.[16]

Excessive reliance on the financial programming model may be a source of much of the inflexibility in implementation and the overemphasis on quantitative targets of which the IMF has been accused. Such preoccupations tend to replace more meaningful qualitative discussion of the overall thrust and complexion of policy, with the result that governments remain uncommitted to the programs that result from negotiations and may even feel alienated from the measures they are supposed to implement. Even when flexibility is present, some critics have claimed that it reflects bargaining power rather than economic circumstances and that it is driven largely by the political self-interests of the Fund's major shareholders.[17]

Using the financial programming model has not, however, prevented the IMF from favoring the exchange rate as an expenditure-switching policy; a subarea of research has concentrated on the likely effects of devaluation in developing countries. Criticisms of devaluation have not only ranged over familiar elasticity pessimism territory and the inflationary consequences of devaluation but have also covered the contractionary effects of devaluation and, more recently, the erosion of counterinflationary credibility that is associated with frequent use of the exchange rate instrument, although the Mexican peso crisis reminds us of the BOP consequences of currency overvaluation.[18]

All this material is contentious, and for each claim there is a counterclaim. To the claim that the financial programming model reveals the underlying monetarist credentials of the Fund is the counterclaim that the model may easily be interpreted in a neo-Keynesian context but that, in any case, IMF missions do not slavishly follow any formal model. To the claim that the Fund is short-termist, there is the counterclaim that it makes loans under a range of medium-term facilities (the EFF and ESAF) and in any case can (and does) engage in a *succession* of programs. To the claim that its favored policies are essentially demand-side is the counterclaim that exchange rate policy, financial liberalization, privatization, and price deregulation are important supply-side measures. The debate goes on in similar vein. Furthermore, the IMF has responded positively to criticisms relating to the design and implementation of its conditionally. In recent years it has reduced its reliance on quantified indicators of demand control, such as ceilings on credit to the public and private sectors. While such "performance criteria" remain central, the Fund now makes greater use of (usually half-yearly) review missions to take an overall view of program execution and adjusts program details in the light of the most recent economic data.

The Fund is also moving away from concentration on simple budgetary aggregates, such as total spending or the budget balance, in favor of paying more attention to the "quality" of fiscal adjustment. Since the economic impact of its fiscal provisions are much affected by which expenditures are trimmed and what is done with taxes, the Fund is becoming more insistent on knowing how a government proposes to implement promised reductions in the budget deficit, increasingly urging governments to install social safety nets and asking awkward questions about military spending.

In other respects, too, it is paying more attention to achieving a better balance between demand-management and supply-side measures, even in its short-term (typically eighteen-month) standby programs. The extension of conditionality into measures bearing directly on productive structure have found further expression in the greater use of structural adjustment arrangements. In the case of the SAF and ESAF, this involves establishing a "policy framework paper," which is to be drafted jointly by borrowing governments, the IMF, and the World Bank.

Under pressures from the United Nations International Children's Emergency Fund (UNICEF) and others, the IMF's managing director, Michel Camdessus, who took office in 1987, has changed its stance on the social effects of its programs. It formerly insisted that it was for national governments to decide whether to protect the poor from hardships resulting from programs. Now, its missions commonly discuss distributional aspects with governments when preparing programs. Policy framework papers must include measures to protect the well-being of vulnerable groups.

However, doubts remain about how much difference these changes have made in practice. Examination of program content reveals considerable continuity in their hard core.[19] Indeed some evidence suggests that devaluation and credit ceilings became increasingly common components of Fund-backed programs during the 1980s.[20] In a recent IMF study, Malcolm Knight and Julio Santaella are able to give a good explanation of the probability that the Fund would offer a financial arrangement by using an empirical specification of its determinants that focuses only on "the core policy variables relating to the demand management aspects of a macroeconomic adjustment program." While acknowledging that the IMF increasingly has emphasized other areas of policy action in recent years (with the result that program design has become more complex and comprehensive), Knight and Santaella also revealingly state that, "a balance of payments deficit usually reflects an excess of aggregate domestic demand relative to domestic supply" and that "Fund programs, which are dedicated to restoring a sustainable external position, must emphasize measures of demand restraint ... as essential ... elements of a stabilization program."[21] IMF-backed programs therefore continue to focus on measures that tighten domestic credit, enhance fiscal revenues, reduce government expenditures, and adjust the exchange rate.

If we know what the basic ingredients of IMF-backed programs look like, do we know the extent to which countries carry them through to completion? As noted earlier, taking as a criterion for noncompletion the extent to which credit remains undrawn, a study of 266 programs over 1980–90 yields the following results.[22] First, the majority of programs break down. Second, EFF arrangements have a greater tendency to break down than do standby arrangements. Third, where programs break down, they often do so quite quickly. Sixteen per cent of all standby programs break down almost immediately with often little or no use of the credit beyond the first installment. Fourth, noncompletion became an increasingly common phenomenon at the end of the 1980s. Of the thirty-nine programs negotiated during 1988–90, 72 per cent broke down, even though this was not a time of particular world economic turbulence. Finally, programs are more likely to break down where the borrowing country is moderately or severely indebted.

But why do programs break down? Potential explanations include: the size of the initial disequilibrium that needs to be corrected; the overambition of the targets set in relation to the country's ability to achieve them; and external disruptions caused by such things as terms of trade movements. However, perhaps even more important is the government's degree of commitment to carrying through the agreed program. Commitment will in large measure depend on the extent to which the government views the program as its own. Certainly, evidence on the World Bank's policy-based lending programs identifies ownership as a highly significant influence on implementation, and there is little reason to believe that anything different would be found in the case of IMF-backed programs.[23] A key problem therefore, becomes that of finding ways in which countries not only may be persuaded to accept the advice offered by the Fund but also may be brought fully on board in agreeing with it.

This problem has spawned a large amount of research into the political economy of adjustment and of economic reform, with a range of hypotheses being offered about the circumstances that are most conducive to the reform process.[24]

A recent study organized by the Institute for International Economics attempts to test various hypotheses against case study evidence. The hypothesis that it is easier to implement reform when there is a "visionary leader," a "coherent team," and a firm "political base" received "strong support." Those that point to the need for a "comprehensive program" (although one that is not spelled out in great detail in advance) and "external aid" command support in "most cases," whereas those that highlight the need for a "crisis" and for governments to use effectively a "honeymoon" period that they may enjoy are relevant in "many cases." The study found earlier notions that implementing reform requires an "authoritarian regime," most probably of a "rightist" inclination, generally to be "invalid."

In the context of implementing IMF-backed programs, notions of a visionary leader, coherent team, and firm political base are likely to be positively associated with ownership. Moreover, the importance of having a comprehensive program and adequate external aid are also important given earlier comments about the narrowness of the hard core of IMF-backed programs, the inadequacies of Fund financial support, and the frequently illusory nature of the catalytic effect.

Even psychologists and others concerned with the art of negotiation have, with relevance to the IMF's dealings with developing countries, considered what factors make it most likely that advice will be accepted and acted upon.[25] An important element here is the extent to which governments feel that their superior knowledge of what is possible in a set of country-specific circumstances is taken into account, and they have been genuinely involved in designing the programs. Should the Fund then be rather more like a psychotherapist who extracts the appropriate solutions from clients than a doctor who simply tells patients what course of action should be followed? The latter approach may work well enough when patients feel unqualified to reach decisions and when the doctor commands respect, but these conditions have not always been met in the case of developing countries and the IMF.

There may, however, have been a change in developing countries' perceptions of the wisdom of Fund advice. For many years the Fund has emphasized the consequences of monetary excesses and currency overvaluation and the advantage of open trade. During the 1990s many developing countries in Africa and Latin America decided in favor of more counter-inflationary and market-friendly policies. However, the economic difficulties encountered by Mexico in 1994 and 1995 have led to a further reassessment of the Fund's conventional wisdom. Mexico had after all followed policies broadly in line with those represented by the so-called Washington consensus for a number of years prior to the peso crisis. Trade had been liberalized, industry privatized, fiscal deficits reduced, and the rate of monetary expansion reduced. Yet these policies, albeit in the company of growing currency overvaluation, failed to generate sustainable economic growth and BOP performance. The degree of confidence that governments have in IMF conditionality depends in part on the effects that it has had in the past. Have IMF-backed programs generally had beneficial effects in those developing countries that have negotiated them?

The muted effects of IMF-backed programs

Programs backed by the IMF primarily set out to effect the BOP, although secondary objectives relate to economic growth and inflation. Critics such as UNICEF and Oxfam have argued that it is more important to concentrate on the effects of programs on poverty and on human and social development.[26] However, these are notoriously awkward to measure, and isolating the effects of IMF-backed programs on them is difficult and complex: falling living standards may simply be a consequence of the initial economic crisis. Clearly, devaluation and price deregulation will raise prices and may therefore tend to erode the living standards of the poor. Similarly, reduced government subsidies will reduce their real income, even though the poor typically receive only a modest share of such subsidies. Rising unemployment and falling real wages need also to be taken into account.

But, at the same time, devaluation helps to enhance competitiveness and create employment. Trade liberalization may benefit domestic consumers, and improving the efficiency of the public sector may help the poor who use public services. Moreover, appropriate economic stabilization and adjustment may be necessary preconditions for the effective long-term alleviation of poverty. In addition, the effects of such policies on the urban and rural poor may differ, and many of the prime sources of poverty – such as the distribution of assets and political power, access to services, and the pattern of demographic dependency – are not directly affected by IMF-backed programs.

To the extent that Fund involvement encourages economic growth it provides an opportunity for helping the poor, even though strengthening the BOP will also absorb some of the additional resources. Whether such help materializes depends on the form that economic growth takes and how governments use the associated benefits. In the same manner, the short-term costs of adjustment on the poor may in principle be offset by appropriate domestic policies. But, in practice, the policies of compensating losers will rarely favor the poor, and even less so the very poor, and the Institute for International Economics case study evidence found little support for the hypothesis that compensating losers was important in determining the implementation of economic reform.

While improvements in economic performance do not, therefore, guarantee human development or falling poverty, economic failure surely will constrain them. In this chapter I therefore focus on the effects of IMF-backed programs on the principal economic variables they set out to influence.

Even here methodological problems abound. We must distinguish between changes that have resulted from a particular adjustment program and those that have occurred for other reasons: the problem of the counterfactual. In practice, there is no completely satisfactory means of making such a sharp distinction. Before-and-after tests implicitly assume that other things remain constant, which they do not. Target–actual tests rely on the appropriateness of the targets that are set. While with–without tests assume that it is possible to formulate an accurate view as to what would have happened in the absence of an IMF-backed program. One way of doing this is to compare a sample of countries that has negotiated Fund programs with a control group of other countries that has not. But the problem of discovering countries that are similar in all respects apart from the involvement of the Fund remains. The very decision as to whether or not to turn to the IMF in similar economic circumstances itself implies a significant difference in the approach to economic adjustment as well as in the political environment in which adjustment takes place, which then invalidates the comparison.

This problem may be overcome by endeavoring to simulate the performance of an individual economy under different sets of policies; but simulation analysis encounters another problem since it relies on being able to specify a model that accurately describes how individual economies function. In fact, economies differ, and no one model is likely to provide an accurate description of all developing countries. A case study methodology offers a way of allowing for such differences but suffers from problems of generalization – unless a similar format is used across a range of cases, which enables common themes to be identified.

Other difficulties that get in the way of an unambiguous assessment of the effects of IMF-backed programs relate to the time period over which the effects are monitored and the range of performance indicators that are studied. There is no reason to presume that program effects follow some linear path over time or that positive effects on some economic variables will be matched by similar positive effects on others. Indeed the contrary often is the case: much BOP analysis implies that economic variables will move in different directions over the short and long terms. Better performance in terms of one variable at one time is likely to be offset by worse performance in that variable at a later time or in another variable at the same time. Unless a sophisticated social welfare function has been specified, it is therefore difficult to say whether things overall have improved or deteriorated.

But what do these methodological difficulties imply? They clearly imply that there is no uniquely correct approach. But they also suggest that an accumulation of evidence using different methodologies will gradually provide an overall picture of the effects of IMF-backed programs. Results that are robust across different methodologies may be stronger than those that are methodology-specific. Recent research carried out at the Overseas Development Institute adds to our knowledge of the effects of IMF programs not only by using a combination of before-and-after tests and case study evidence but also by integrating this with other studies that use different methodologies. It examines the effects of programs over a longer time frame than has conventionally been used and endeavors to differentiate between those programs that were completed and those that were not. It derives performance indicators from econometric studies of the demand for Fund credit, since Fund-backed programs should seek to correct the problems that cause countries to turn to it in the first place. The 1980s time period covered by the research coincides with a time when the Fund dealt only with developing countries that faced severe economic problems. The data examined cover all programs negotiated with the Fund over 1980–90, excluding those SAF arrangements that were subsequently converted into ESAFs, giving a total of 266 programs. The results are summarized briefly in Table 7.4.[27]

Since a prior deterioration in the BOP is an important factor in causing countries to turn to the Fund, it is of particular interest to see what happens to the BOP after the negotiation of a program. The results suggest that both the overall and current account balances strengthen, especially over a three-year period, in part by import compression (rather than import strangulation) but also by relatively large increases in export volume, which rise through time. This performance was secured against a background of deteriorating commodity terms of trade. As anticipated, the catalytic effect on net capital inflows is negative (with the apparently strong positive effect on foreign direct investment disappearing when Dominica is removed from the sample).

Estimation of the demand function for IMF credit suggests that inflation may be another cause of borrowing particularly in cases where it results in currency overvaluation. The negotiation of a program with the Fund does not, however, seem to lead to much significant change in inflation performance. The demand-reducing effects of Fund programs seem to be generally compensated by the price-raising effects of devaluation and financial liberalization. In 40 per cent of the programs the inflation rate increased.

Similarly, the study finds a neutral association with economic growth, although over the longer time frame the association appears to be positive (albeit of only limited statistical significance). This is somewhat surprising in light of the apparent negative effect on fixed investment, suggesting that growth has been achieved through increases in the marginal productivity of capital or that it may represent a temporary recovery from recession. The danger is that countries may not be able to sustain such increases, and the fall investment remains a source of concern for longer-term economic growth – particularly since it persists. Stabilization under the auspices of the Fund generally is achieved by lowering investment rather than by increasing savings. It is investment that carries the main burden of reduced absorption; private and public consumption are apparently little influenced by the negotiation of a program with the Fund (which has some bearing on the debate over the effects of IMF-backed programs on the poor).

The data in Table 7.3 allow a number of other observations. First, while involving the IMF seems to lead to substantial and significant currency depreciation that is sustained in real terms (which helps to explain the

Table 7.4 Results of before–after tests on sixteen developing countries with IMF Program commenced in 1979–85

Variable	Base value				Differences from base value (Years 1 and 2)	
	Years −1 and −2	Year 0	Years 1 and 2	Year 3	Completed programs	Uncompleted programs
Balance of payments (BOP) indicators						
Overall BOP (as % GDP, change in reserves)	−1.2	+0.4****	+1.2*,****	+1.9*,****	+0.7****	+1.5*,****
Current account (as % GDP, excluding official transfers)	−11.2	+1.1	+3.0*,****	+3.8*,****	+4.4**	+2.2**,****
Official transfers (as % GDP)	2.8	−0.2	+0.0****	+0.0****	−1.4****	+0.8****
Capital account						
Direct foreign investment (as % GDP)	0.4	+0.0	+0.1	+0.3**	−0.0	+0.2
Net long-term loans (as % GDP)	5.5	−0.0	−1.2***	−2.0***,****	−1.1****	−1.3****
Terms of trade index (% change)[a]	—	−3.8***,****	−6.5***,****	−8.2***,****	−2.5	−8.8***
Import volume index (% change)	—	−4.6**	−3.1	−4.1	+0.2	−5.0
Export volume index (% change)	—	+3.5****	+9.6*,****	+11.7*,****	+8.7	+10.2*,****
Inflation and growth						
Increase in consumer prices (% per annum)[b]	24.8	+1.7	−1.1***	−0.4	−12.7***	+5.6
GDP growth (% per annum constant prices)	2.1	−0.0	+0.6	+1.2	+1.8	−0.0
Domestic absorption						
Total absorption (as % GDP)	107.5	−2.5*,****	−3.4*,****	−3.3*,****	−1.2	−4.6*,****
Private consumption (as % GDP)	71.6	−0.3	−0.4	+0.2	+1.5	−1.5
Government consumption (as % GDP)	13.7	−0.4	−0.3	−0.4	−1.0**	+0.1
Fixed investment (as % GDP)	21.2	−1.9*,****	−3.1*,****	−3.8*,****	−3.4	−2.9*,****

Table 7.4 (Contd.)

Variable	Base value				Differences from base value (Years 1 and 2)	
	Years −1 and −2	Year 0	Years 1 and 2	Year 3	Completed programs	Uncompleted programs
Policy variables						
Real effective exchange rate index (% change)	—	−7.1**,****	−11.0*,****	−15.0*,****	−18.1**	−7.0****
Total domestic credit						
Growth rate (% per annum)	25.8	−3.4	−3.3****	−4.2**,****	−3.3	−3.2
As % GDP	42.4	−0.4	−0.7	−1.8	+2.0	−2.4
Private sector credit						
Growth rate (% per annum)	23.1	+0.4	+0.8	+0.8	−3.6****	+3.2
As % GDP	18.9	−0.8	−0.8	−0.2	+0.8	−1.6
Credit to central government (as % GDP)c	18.2	+0.2	+0.0	−1.5	+1.0****	−0.6
Central government budget deficit (as % GDP)	−6.7	+0.2	+1.4*	+1.6*	—	—

* Significantly different from zero, under a one-tailed t-test, at the 99 percent confidence level.

** Significantly different from zero, under a one-tailed t-test, at the 95 percent confidence level.

*** Significantly different from zero, under a two-tailed t-test, at the 95 percent confidence level.

**** Significant proportion of program with either a positive or negative change, as compared with a hypothesized equal proportion.

a Completed and uncompleted program values are significantly different from each other at the 90 percent confidence level.

b As above but at the 95 percent confidence level.

c Year-to-year changes in credit to government were too variable for it to be meaningful to calculate changes in growth rates.

Source: Reprinted, in slightly modified form, with kind permission of The World Economy from Killick, Malik, and Manuel 1992, 592.

current account effects reported earlier), there is much less evidence of any influence on monetary variables. Generally, countries have seen only a small and insignificant reduction in the rate of growth of credit and no significant reduction in the share of credit to the government. This is a somewhat surprising finding given the core status of credit restraint within IMF-backed programs. Influence over the budget deficit, on the other hand, is more apparent and significant.

Second, the idea that the IMF is able to orchestrate a "quick fix" is not supported. In general, the impact of the Fund is much more muted in the year in which the program is negotiated than in subsequent years, although the effect on the exchange rate is rapid – which may be one reason the Fund favors devaluation.

Third, there is no clear evidence to suggest that macroeconomic perfor-mance is generally superior in countries that completed their programs than in those that did not, although the inflation achievements of completers stand out. Tests for statistically significant differences in the data also failed to show anything even at 90 per cent confidence levels, with the sole excep-tion of the terms of trade – which may hint at a reason why programs break down. BOP improvements may therefore be less attributable to the programs themselves than to the greater concern with macroeconomic management that dealing with the IMF engenders. Where programs break down, coun-tries have to take alternative measures to try and salvage the BOP, and these rest heavily on compressing absorption and imports.

While the methodological weaknesses call into question how much reliance should be placed on one set of results in isolation, much greater confidence may be placed in results that are shared between studies using different methodologies. How do these results square with those found elsewhere?

Without undertaking a detailed review, we can make a number of important generalizations.[28] In terms of the key performance indicators, early before-and-after studies found no significant improvement in the current account BOP although both Mohsin Khan and Manuel Pastor dis-covered significant positive effects on the overall BOP in more recent research.[29] With–without tests tend to show stronger results for the current account.[30] For inflation a similar pattern emerges. Before-and-after tests reveal a record that is generally weak, with the inflation rate increasing as frequently as it declines. However, the results are almost always statistically insignificant. With–without tests and simulation studies suggest a better performance, although significance is at best low.

On economic growth, much the same picture of insignificance is found irrespective of the methodology used, although Morris Goldstein and Peter Montiel found IMF programs to have a significantly negative effect.[31] Simulation tests by Khan and Knight also predicted that demand manage-ment programs similar to those supported by the IMF will have negative short-run effects on growth, although subsequent research by them suggests that these effects can be ameliorated by incorporating supply-side measures to protect investment.[32]

Patrick Conway finds significant differences between the short-run and long-run effects of IMF programs on economic growth and investment, as contemporary reductions are followed by lagged increases.[33] In terms of target achievement, the general consensus is that only about a half of outcome targets are achieved.[34] A similar picture emerges in the case of policy targets. The weakest performance seems to be with respect to monetary restraint.[35] In terms of policy outcomes, the weakest performance is with respect to economic growth, at least in the short run. Sebastian Edwards, for example, records an average failure rate for economic growth of 72 per cent, and similarly discouraging results are discovered by P. S. Heller *et al.*, and by J. B. Zulu and S. M. Nsouli in the case of Africa.[36]

The overall picture is that while IMF-backed programs seem to nudge countries toward better overall BOP performance, their impact is rather muted. Moreover, they generally have rather insignificant effects on inflation and economic growth. This in turn implies that IMF-backed programs are unlikely to have strongly significant effects either on social and human variables or, therefore, on political stability. This is, again, generally what the evidence bears out.[37]

Where do we go from here? Policy conclusions

The IMF can fulfill a potentially useful role in developing countries by (1) offsetting sources of market failure that otherwise would severely limit their access to external finance and (2) providing support and advice with regard to economic policy. In an attempt to respond to this challenge, the IMF has evolved an array of lending facilities and developed and modified the conditionality under which it lends. However, evidence suggests that frequently it has been unable to provide large amounts of finance directly and that this has often forced countries to pursue BOP strategies that focus on short-term adjustment. The idea that the IMF has a strong indirect catalyzing effect on other public or private flows is also largely illusory, and this has further exposed the deficiencies of its direct lending role. For developing countries as a group, net lending from the Fund has been mostly negative since the mid-1980s, calling into question whether its performance is consistent with the role described in its Articles of Agreement. Article 1 sees the Fund as giving "confidence to members by making general resources...temporarily available to them under adequate safeguards, thus providing them with the opportunity to correct maladjustments in their balance of payments without resorting to measures destructive of national or international prosperity."

The changes to conditionality have also failed to alter the Fund's basic characteristics. Conditionality remains firmly founded on exchange rate devaluation and domestic demand restraint. However, reluctance to change these demand-side foundations cannot be based on the unrestrained success enjoyed by IMF-backed programs, most of which break down and fail to lead to significant macroeconomic improvements.

It is easy to see why some observers have suggested that the Fund should pull out of its involvement in developing countries. If it were to do so, however, problems of financing and adjustment would remain. More constructive, therefore, is to think about how the IMF might be reformed to become more effective.

To expect the Fund to demonstrate dramatic success in circumstances where for many years domestic governments have failed and where problems are deeply entrenched is not realistic. The scope for managing economies is frequently strictly limited. Examples of sustained and unambiguous economic success in the world are rare and should not be used as standards to assess the Fund's performance. The issue is not therefore whether the Fund should be associated with dramatic turnarounds in economic performance but rather whether its contribution toward securing improved economic performance might be raised.

I present the following proposals for change in this context. First, BOP problems are not always (or only) associated with economic mismanagement; external factors are also important. In these circumstances IMF-supported programs should de-emphasize the degree of conventional conditionality or aim to support policies that are more directly designed to reduce BOP vulnerability. The Fund should therefore continue to pay greater attention to supply-side factors – but not simply by incremental conditionality, which adds supply-side conditions to essentially demand-side programs, as has tended to happen in the past. Monetary restraint as the centerpiece of IMF-backed programs has doubtful theoretical legitimacy: monetary expansion does not appear to be a feature that distinguishes countries that turn to the IMF from those that do not, and Fund-backed programs exhibit little effect on the growth of monetary aggregates.

Negotiators who design the programs should pay more attention to the broad direction of policy and less to quantified performance criteria. Such a change could be accommodated in a way that would still allow the programs to be monitored. Again, the use of review missions has been a step in the right direction but should be taken further. Governments should be encouraged, in the first instance, to draft their own program for which they would then seek Fund support. The analysis would include an assessment of the nature and causes of BOP difficulties as well as an evaluation of policy alternatives. Countries that do not take this opportunity might then expect the Fund to draft a letter of intent, and those that did would make a precommitment to accept IMF-designed conditionality in the event of their own program failing. It is reasonable to presume that providing governments with the opportunity to design the program they will implement would significantly increase their sense of ownership. To the extent that lack of ownership adversely affects completion, a sense of ownership should positively affect it. The Fund could, however, serve as an arbitrator between factional interests within governments, inasmuch as inability to agree to a program domestically would result in heavier Fund involvement. Moreover, the degree of Fund input into the design of conditionality could be varied in the light of a country's track record. This would provide an additional incentive for governments not to abandon programs in midcourse and would help alleviate the moral hazard problem that arises where previous failure does not exert any adverse effect on future access to Fund resources.

Since the empirical evidence suggests that eventual disengagement from the Fund is helped by sustained economic growth, it is important that Fund-backed programs contain a strong growth orientation, both in design and presentation. Again the Fund has moved some distance in this direction over recent years but not far enough. Growth and structural adjustment need to replace conventional stabilization as the central focus of programs, since the two can be at odds if reductions in absorption fall heavily on investment, as has been shown to be the case. In a recently published internal review of conditionality relating to standby and EFF arrangements over 1988–92, the Fund acknowledges "the modest response of growth" and the weak investment response. Where growth did occur, the Fund again notes that, "apparently this resulted from improvements in efficiency of resource use, often as economies rebounded from unusually weak or negative growth." Significantly the review focuses on the need to shift to "distinctly faster growth tracks" and recognizes that this is related to the "influence of program design on investment."[38]

A major difficulty relates to the problems of constructing a model that captures the essence of the growth process and the interactions between financial and real sectors of the economy. This is a difficulty that the Fund should seek to overcome by undertaking more research into the causes of economic growth in developing countries; augmenting the financial programming model in a tangential fashion is not enough. Moreover, but also in the spirit of understanding the supply-side more fully, the Fund should move away from any inclination to assume that governmental failure is always a greater problem than market failure and should be exploring the synergy between the state and markets in the context of developing countries. What role can the state usefully perform, and how can the Fund encourage governments to take on this role?[39] A good deal of evidence has been accumulating over recent years to suggest that public investment crowds in rather than crowds out private investment in developing countries.[40] This in turn suggests that where fiscal deficits need to be corrected, attention should focus on increasing tax revenue by tax reform and improving the relative quality of public investment rather than simply by cutting it back overall.

A stronger growth-and-structural orientation carries its own consequences, since programs would have to be phased over a longer time span than has been conventional, certainly under standby arrangements. If BOP correction is to take longer, more supporting finance will be required, especially if the catalytic effect is insignificant. To the extent that additional finance enables an appropriate adjustment strategy to be supported – one that seeks to raise economic growth and induce a secular improvement in the BOP – the increased claims on the Fund will be temporary. Moreover, empirical evidence implies that lack of finance has sometimes impeded the success of programs and may have meant that governments have been less committed to them than would otherwise have been the case. A higher success rate among programs will strengthen their catalytic impact.

The success rate of programs may also be increased by providing additional supporting finance as and when needed to cover unforeseen contingencies. At present many programs are disrupted by exogenous shocks. Although the failure to meet performance criteria may be waived, the use of waivers is not transparent and is therefore uncertain, creating problems of moral hazard and confidence. The objective of contingency financing should be to protect programs against temporary outside shocks, and even against more permanent changes in outside factors, by allowing for more gradual modification to the initial program. Some of the financing for such "insurance" could come from developing countries themselves in the form of premiums. They would pay into an IMF-based scheme when external shocks are favorable and draw out, with additional financing supplied by the Fund, when they are unfavorable. The changes in design that greater and more secure financing would permit would make the Fund a more attractive source of finance and would increase the level of government commitment in borrowing countries. Agreeing to procedures for dealing with the problems that programs might encounter would also have benefits for the catalytic effect, as there would be greater confidence that the ultimate objectives would be achieved. The Fund already has acknowledged some of the logic of this change by introducing contingency elements to the compensatory facility, but again it has not carried the idea through fully.

Additional Fund financing would help developing countries escape from the vicious circle in which shortages of finance define strict short-term conditionality that, for a combination of economic and political reasons, is unsuccessful, leading to both greater demand for and less supply of external finance in the future. Reforms to conditionality could make the Fund more borrower-friendly and therefore might be assumed to encourage countries to turn to it at an earlier stage in the evolution of their BOP problems. Providing more time for negotiation might enable better thought-out programs that carry greater consensus to be adopted. This in turn could create those circumstances that the political economy literature has suggested are most conducive to reform. At present late referral leads to the type of strict conditionality that is itself a factor in discouraging countries from turning to the Fund earlier. The purpose of the exercise would be to encourage countries to seek IMF support before their BOP problems become acute. To some extent, policy conditionality could then be preventive rather than corrective.

According to analysis of the demand for IMF credit, these changes would increase claims on the Fund. Increased demand, along with longer-term programs, would place greater strains on the Fund's own financing capacity. Two solutions exist. The first would be to try to distinguish more clearly between governments that are serious about adjustment and those that are not. The Fund would undertake greater credit rationing. If it picked winners (and avoided losers) correctly it would clearly improve its success rate. The second solution would be to raise the lending capacity of the Fund by raising quotas so that it could carry out its modified role. However, while the changes proposed here would increase the use of Fund credit in the near term, to the extent that they made the Fund more effective, they could be expected to reduce claims on it in the longer term, as well as to increase the access to commercial finance of countries negotiating an IMF-backed program. The IMF's seal of approval would in effect gain a higher market value, and this itself would give the Fund greater leverage with developing countries.

It is possible, in principle, that the Fund could define two sets of criteria: one to determine access to borrowing from it and another to determine provision of subscriptions to it. At present countries have just one quota that determines both. This makes sense where the Fund is a form of credit union and all members are likely to draw on it at some time. However, the reality is completely different. Industrial countries provide most of the resources but do not themselves draw on the Fund. It may, therefore, be sensible to acknowledge reality by allowing access to Fund credit to be more formally related to the needs of members, with the provision of resources reflecting ability to pay.[41]

Some developing countries, of course, have further to come than others, and the IMF needs to be involved with low-income countries for a significant number of years. Rather than wishing that the situation were otherwise, it needs to address more specifically the needs of the poorest countries. This could be done, first, through flexibility in program design but could also involve the extended use of subsidies to cover all drawings by low-income countries on the Fund rather than just those under the ESAF. The Fund could also offer such countries greater assistance by allocating them SDRs.[42]

While the economic problems faced by low-income countries are severe and create a need for external financial assistance, their relatively small size means that the absolute amounts of finance are small. Significant additional financial support from the Fund would not therefore imply a large increase in the Fund's own resources.

Fund lending should also be streamlined by rationalizing the range of facilities under which members can draw. As shown earlier, the use of some facilities (particularly the EFF) has varied quite dramatically during the 1980s, while that of others has been persistently low. Rationalization does not necessarily mean reverting to one multipurpose facility. Much depends on how far the reform of conditionality is taken. If financial programming was to remain at its heart, it might be appropriate to retain three windows: standbys, extended arrangements, and compensatory and contingency lending. Standbys would rely on conventional stabilization measures. Extended arrangements would focus on longer-term structural adjustment but would still involve strict conditionality; whereas compensatory and contingency lending would revert to the principles underpinning the CFF but could involve a precommitment by borrowers. If conditionality was modified in the way outlined above to allow countries a greater input into its design, then the distinction between the different lending facilities would become much more blurred and their independence less justifiable.

The changes I am proposing in this chapter would require the support of the IMF's major shareholders. At least in the short run additional resources would need to be made available. The whole thrust of the reforms is to start from the notion of an optimal adjustment path and to work through to the amount of finance necessary to pursue it, rather than starting from a financing constraint and attempting to design an adjustment path that is consistent with it. Industrial countries could, however, do other things that would make the IMF more effective in its dealings with developing countries (although political realities may work against such change). First, they should resist the temptation to intervene for essentially short-term political reasons; this undermines the Fund's credibility and may be against their long-term political interests. Second, they could manage their own economies in ways that help create an international economic environment that facilitates adjustment in developing countries. The Fund could indeed assist developing countries, first, by exerting pressure on developed countries to pursue policies that create a conducive world economic environment, and, second, by identifying those policies in developed countries that have important implications for developing countries and then seeking to compensate developing countries for any adverse externalities suffered by them.

Having acquired much experience in dealing with developing countries, the IMF is now in a position to draw on this experience to modify its procedures in ways that will build on the somewhat modest effects that it has secured up to now. Developing countries might, however, have more confidence in the Fund if they believed that their interests were more fully represented in the institution's decision-making processes, especially as they account for a significant and growing share of world economic output.

Recent proposals made by the G-7 point in a very different direction.[43] While supporting the idea of a new EFM (paid for by extending the GAB) to provide finance in Mexico-type cases where private capital flows out even though IMF-approved policies are in place, and while encouraging the Fund to disclose more information to market participants in order to give early warning of economic problems, the G-7 does not back an increase in IMF quotas or additional SDR allocations but merely recommends that the Fund's financing capacity should be reviewed.

As far as IMF conditionality is concerned the G-7 wants this to be strong, encouraging the Fund to return to its core concern with macroeconomic policy. According to this view, it is the World Bank that should deal with structural and sectoral reform. Although the institutional division of labor between the IMF and the World Bank might certainly be reformed, the G-7 does not argue the case.[44] A stronger growth orientation for the Fund would clearly bring it into territory conventionally associated with the World Bank. However, this could be advantageous in terms of the compatibility of the adjustment advice coming from the two institutions. While it is easy to see the political forces that have motivated them, the current G-7 proposals relating to the Fund imply yet more emphasis on adjustment as opposed to financing – and, in relation to this, adjustment based on short-term demand management.[45] It is just such an emphasis that, according to the evidence presented here, has created problems for the Fund in its dealings with developing countries in the past. Returning to the Fund's core concern will indeed be a step backward – a step that demonstrates the failure to learn from the hard-earned experience that has been acquired over recent years.

Acknowledgements

This chapter draws freely on a research project undertaken jointly by Graham Bird and Tony Killick based at the Overseas Development Institute in London and financed by the U.K. Overseas Development Administration. The results of the research are reported more fully in two books, Graham Bird, 1995, *IMF Lending to Developing Countries: Issues and Evidence*, London: Routledge, and Tony Killick, 1995, *The Design and Effect of IMF Programs in Developing Countries*, London: Routledge. Thanks are due to David Bedford for research assistance and to Tony Killick for allowing me to make use of collaborative work. The comments of anonymous referees as well as the editor were also helpful in redrafting the chapter. The usual disclaimer applies.

References

Bird, Graham. 1987. *International financial policy and economic development*. London: Macmillan.

———. 1989. *Loan-loss provisions and Third World debt*. Essays in International Finance, no. 176. Princeton, N.J.: International Finance Section, Department of Economics, Princeton University.

———. 1990. The international financial regime and the developing world. In *The international financial regime*, edited by Graham Bird. London: Surrey University Press and Academic Press.

———. 1994a. Changing partners: Perspectives and policies of the Bretton Woods institutions. *Third World Quarterly* 15:483–502.

———. 1994b. *Economic assistance to low income countries: Should the link be resurrected?* Essays in International Finance, no. 193. Princeton, N.J.: International Finance Section, Department of Economics, Princeton University.

——. 1994c. The myths and realities of IMF lending. *The World Economy* 17:759–78.

——. 1995. *IMF lending to developing countries: Issues and evidence.* London: Routledge.

——. 1995. The G-7's plans for the IMF: Have the challenges of the twenty-first century been met? *Harvard Journal of World Affairs.*

Bird, Graham, and Tony Killick. 1995. *The Bretton Woods institutions: A Commonwealth perspective.* Commonwealth Economic Papers, no. 24. London: Commonwealth Secretariat.

Bird, Graham, and Timothy Orme. 1981. An analysis of drawings on the International Monetary Fund by developing countries. *World Development* 9:563–8.

Bleaney, Michael, and David Greenaway. 1993. Adjustment to external imbalance and investment slumps in developing countries. *European Economic Review* 37:577–85.

Bretton Woods Commission. 1995. Report and background papers to the Bretton Woods Commission. In *Bretton Woods: Looking to the Future.* Washington, D.C.: Bretton Woods Committee.

Cardoso, Eliana. 1993. Private investment in Latin America. *Economic Development and Cultural Change* 41:833–48.

Conway, Patrick. 1994. IMF lending programs: Participation and impact. *Journal of Development Economics* 45:365–91.

Corden, W. Max. 1993. Exchange rate policies for developing countries. *Economic Journal* 103:198–207.

Cornelius, Peter. 1987. The demand for IMF credits by sub-Saharan African countries. *Economic Letters* 23:99–102.

Cornia, Giovanni, R. Jolly, and Frances Stewart, eds. 1987. *Adjustment with a human face: Protecting the vulnerable and promoting growth.* Oxford: Clarendon.

Doroodian, Khosrow. 1993. Macroeconomic performance and adjustment under policies commonly supported by the International Monetary Fund. *Economic Development and Cultural Change* 41:849–64.

Edwards, Sebastian. 1989. *The IMF and the developing countries: A critical evaluation.* Carnegie–Rochester Conference Series on Public Policy, no. 31. Washington, D.C.: North Holland.

Finch, David C. 1989. *The IMF: The record and prospect.* Essays in International Finance, no. 175. Princeton, N.J.: International Finance Section, Department of Economics, Princeton University.

Goldstein, Morris, and Peter Montiel. 1986. Evaluating Fund stabilization programs with multicountry data: Some methodological pitfalls. *IMF Staff Papers* 33:304–44.

Grindle, Merilee S. 1994. Sustaining economic recovery in Latin America: State capacity, markets, and politics. In *Latin America's Economic Future?* edited by Graham Bird and Ann Helwege. London and San Diego: Academic Press.

Grindle, Merilee S., and John W. Thomas. 1991. *Public choices and policy change: The political economy of reform in developing countries.* Baltimore, Md.: Johns Hopkins University Press.

Gylfason, Thorvaldur. 1987. *Credit policy and economic activity in developing countries with IMF stabilization programs.* Studies in International Finance, no. 60. Princeton, N.J.: Princeton University.

Haggard, Stephan, and Robert Kaufman, eds. 1992. *The politics of economic adjustment.* Princeton, N.J.: Princeton University Press.

Haggard, Stephan, and Steven B. Webb. 1993. What do we know about the political economy of policy reform? *World Bank Research Observer* 8:143–68.

Heller, P. S., A. L. Bovenberg, T. Catsambas, K.-Y. Chu, and P. Shome. 1988. *The implications of fund-supported adjustment programs for poverty.* Occasional paper no. 58. Washington, D.C.: International Monetary Fund.

Joyce, Joseph. 1992. The economic characteristics of IMF program countries. *Economics Letters* 38:237–42.

Khan, Mohsin. 1990. The macroeconomic effects of Fund-supported adjustment programs. *IMF Staff Papers* 37:195–231.

Khan, Mohsin, and Malcolm Knight. 1982. Some theoretical and empirical issues relating to economic stabilization in developing countries. *World Development* 10:709–30.

———. 1985. *Fund-supported adjustment programs and economic growth.* Occasional paper no. 41. Washington, D.C.: International Monetary Fund.

Killick, Tony. 1989. *A reaction too far: Economic theory and the role of the state in developing countries.* London: Overseas Development Institute.

———. 1992. Continuity and change in IMF program design, 1982–92. Working paper no. 69. Overseas Development Institute, London.

———. 1993. Issues in the design of IMF programs. Working paper no. 71. Overseas Development Institute, London.

———. 1995. *The design and effect of IMF programs in developing countries.* London: Routledge.

Killick, Tony, with Moazzam Malik. 1992. Country experiences with IMF programs in the 1980s. *World Economy* 15:599–632.

Killick, Tony, Moazzam Malik, and Marcus Manuel. 1992. What can we know about the effects of IMF programs? *World Economy* 15:575–97.

Killick, T. 1995. *IMF Programmes in Developing Countries: Design and Impact.* Routledge London.

Knight, Malcolm, and Julio A. Santaella. 1994. Economic determinants of Fund financial arrangements. Working paper no. WP/94/36, Washington, D.C.: International Monetary Fund.

Nelson, Joan M., ed. 1990. *Economic crisis and policy change: The politics of adjustment in the Third World.* Princeton, N.J.: Princeton University Press.

Oxfam. 1993. *Africa make or break: The failure of IMF/World Bank policies.* Oxford: Oxfam.

Pastor, Manuel. 1987. The effects of IMF programs in the Third World: Debate and evidence from Latin America. *World Development* 15:249–62.

Sachs, Jeffrey D. 1989. Strengthening IMF programs in highly indebted countries. In *The International Monetary Fund in a multipolar world: Pulling together,* edited by Catherine Gwin and Richard E. Feinburg. Washington, D.C.: Overseas Development Council.

Salacuse, Jeswald W. 1994. *The art of advice.* New York: Times Books.

Santaella, Julio A. 1995. Four decades of Fund arrangements: Macroeconomic stylized facts before the adjustment programs. Working paper no. WP/95/74, Washington, D.C.: International Monetary Fund.

Schadler, Susan, Adam Bennett, Maria Carkovic, Louis Dicks-Mireaux, Maura Mecagni, James H. J. Morswik, and Miguel A. Salvastano. 1995. *IMF conditionality: Experience under stand-by and extended arrangements,* parts 1 and 2. Occasional papers nos. 128 and 129. Washington, D.C: International Monetary Fund.

Siddell, Scott R. 1988. *The IMF and Third World instability: Is there a connection?* London: Macmillan.

Stiles, Kendall W. 1990. IMF conditionality: Coercion or compromise? *World Development* 18:959–74.

Taylor, Lance. 1988. *Varieties of stabilization experience.* Oxford: Clarendon.

Williamson, John, ed. 1993. *The political economy of political reform.* Washington, D.C.: Institute for International Economics.

World Bank. 1989. *Adjustment lending: An evaluation of ten years of experience.* Washington, D.C.: World Bank.

Zulu, J. B., and S. M. Nsouli. 1985. *Adjustment programs in Africa: The recent experience.* Occasional paper no. 34. Washington, D.C.: International Monetary Fund.

8
Remodeling the Multilateral Financial Institutions

Graham Bird and Joseph P. Joyce

Since the International Monetary Fund (IMF) and the World Bank were first established in 1946, the world economy has changed in a number of important ways.[1] Not only have the volume, composition, and pattern of world trade changed, but capital flows have come to dominate the global balance of payments, as has been underlined by the financial crises of the 1990s (Europe in 1992–93, Mexico in 1994–95, and East Asia in 1997–98).

At the same time, the roles originally envisaged for the multilateral financial institutions have also changed. The IMF no longer oversees an adjustable peg exchange rate regime through which it effectively sought to coordinate macroeconomic policy globally, nor does it attempt to control the quantity of international reserves. Instead, it has taken on a new role in clearing up the debris from financial crises involving developing countries and countries in transition – a role for which it was not originally designed.

Meanwhile, the World Bank, which was established to fill the financing gaps left by private capital markets, has over the years found that in many instances these gaps are fewer than they used to be because private capital flows have increased; the Bank has therefore tended toward supporting softer areas of investment where it is still difficult to raise private money, and focusing, via its International Development Association, on the poorest developing countries.

The response of the multilaterals to a changing world economy has been to evolve in an incremental fashion rather than to embark upon fundamental reform. The reasons for this are easy to see. First, the problems that the world encountered up until the mid-1990s were not sufficiently pronounced or universal to warrant fundamental reform. In many respects, the world continued to perform satisfactorily in terms of conventional macroeconomic indicators. Second, crises, when they did occur, seemed to be temporary rather than prolonged, and primarily regional rather than global. Third, political economy considerations made piecemeal reform much easier to bring about, since not all members of the global community agreed on the need for fundamental reform or on what shape it should take.[2]

However, incrementalism has its dangers. Changes that may make sense when taken individually may make less sense when taken together. The whole may end up being less than the sum of the parts. The multilateral may have modified and, in some respects, extended their activities by means of a series of relatively small steps that perhaps would have appeared unacceptable if taken in one big step. On top of this, there is the question of whether the individual steps have all been in the same direction or whether we have been moving three steps forward and two (or even four) steps back!

The East Asian financial crisis brought about a sea change, or so it seemed. First, following hard on the heels of the Mexican peso crisis, and in turn being followed by the Russian and Brazilian crises, the question became, "At what point do crises become a global phenomenon?" Certainly, according to some observers, the crises represented a crisis of global capitalism.[3] Second, the East Asian crisis contained strong elements and even stronger threats of contagion, such that advanced economies worried that they would not escape the recessionary spillover effects. In these circumstances, calls for more fundamental reform rapidly started to appear on the global policy agenda. The Group of 7 (G-7) countries, for example, began to talk about a "new international financial architecture," with this phrase suggesting a broader and deeper perspective than had existed before.[4]

But, although this is an interesting catchphrase, what does "a new international financial architecture" mean, exactly? Broad phrases are frequently difficult to define precisely and the new international financial architecture is no exception. While it incorporates the dissemination of more information on policies and performance and increased recognition that the volatility of international capital flows needs to be addressed, these changes may be seen as merely a continuation of the previous evolutionary trend. The establishment of new lending windows in the IMF may be presented in a similar light. Moreover, strengthening IMF conditionality does not really sound like new architecture. Indeed, one of the least precise aspects of many of the new architecture proposals relates to the roles of the multilateral financing institutions in general and the role of the IMF in particular. When does tinkering with the existing international financial system become fundamental reform? Not simply by dint of being called a move toward a new international financial architecture.

This chapter, at least initially, tries to break away from ad hoc incrementalism. Instead, it adopts a zero-based approach to consider how the IMF should be reformed. By examining the deficiencies of private capital markets and analyzing how they might be rectified, we can design institutions to accomplish this aim and establish the best route for getting from where we are now to where we want to be. While a complete teardown and reconstruction may not be feasible, a blueprint can serve to guide future incremental reforms and ensure that changes are mutually reinforcing and consistent. Establishing an overall design seems to be what a new international financial architecture should be all about, but this seems to be precisely what is missing in much of the current "architecture debate."

In the second section of the chapter, we examine the deficiencies of private capital markets that in an important sense delineate a role for the multilateral financial institutions. Having discussed in general terms what this role should be, we go on in the third section to assess the institutions that we have (the IMF and the World Bank) and endeavor to isolate a number of areas where the existing institutions fall short. In addition, the experience of these institutions and their program countries allows a number of lessons to be learned. These need to be factored into the reform process. In the fourth section, we are more specific about ways in which the IMF and World Bank should be remodeled. And in conclusion, we offer some remarks about the political economy of the reform process and contrast our ideas about reform with some other proposals for reform that have been made.

What's wrong with private capital markets?

As a way of dealing with the need for short-term balance-of-payments finance and long-term development finance, there is a lot that is right with private capital markets. They mobilize huge amounts of finance and generally show an ability to adapt quickly to market opportunities by devising new instruments. While official, long-term resource flows to developing countries shrank during the 1990s, private flows grew from approximately $44 billion to over $200 billion (see Table 8.1). There can be little doubt that private capital markets have made a massive positive contribution to world economic welfare by intermediating globally between savers and spenders and by relieving financial constraints.

However, there is a downside, and in analytical terms it is a fairly conventional one. Reliance on markets in any situation opens up the possibility of "market failure." The principal sources of market failure include concentration among producers (monopoly, oligopoly), negative and positive externalities, the nonproduction of public goods, the overproduction of "bads" (such as addictive drugs), inadequate coordination, informational

Table 8.1 Net long-term resource flows to developing countries, 1990–98 (US$ in billions)

	1990	1991	1992	1993	1994	1995	1996	1997	1998[a]
Official flows	56.9	62.6	54.0	53.3	45.5	53.4	32.2	39.1	47.9
Private flows	43.9	60.5	98.3	167.0	178.1	201.5	275.9	299.0	227.1

Note: [a] Signifies provisional.

Source: World Bank, *Global Development and Finance: Analysis and Summary Tables* (Washington, D.C.: World Bank, 1999), p. 24.

deficiencies, instability, and inequality. Some of these failures, as well as others, can be shown to appear in the context of private capital markets.[5]

First, private markets will generally find it unattractive to lend to low-income countries when the lenders make decisions with a short-term horizon or the countries have not established a record of borrowing. Either because of their lack of resources or because of economic mismanagement of one sort or another, the poorest countries of the world lack creditworthiness. In one sense this may create an incentive for their governments to improve economic policies, but the world community has generally responded to this financing gap by providing foreign aid either bilaterally or via multilateral agencies, in particular the World Bank.

Second, lending decisions made by private lenders seeking a risk-adjusted commercial rate of return may be inappropriate where they are made with inaccurate or partial information. Because of asymmetric information, markets will never know for sure what the policy intentions of governments are. Moreover, it may be very expensive or simply not feasible for individual market operators to collect and interpret all the economic data that they might ideally wish to have before making lending and investment decisions. In any case, if they were to collect it individually, this would represent a tremendous waste of resources. Working on partial information, however, there are dangers of adverse selection. Should markets, for example, ration their lending exclusively on the basis of the rate of interest that borrowers are prepared to pay? Perhaps a willingness to sign loan contracts with relatively high interest rates is an indicator of a government's willingness to default. How do markets then assess the risks of repudiation when information is partial? Although they will have mechanisms for assessing country risk, experience shows that these are far from perfect.

Imagine that borrowing countries do encounter problems in meeting their outstanding debt obligations. How will markets respond? Individually, the best outcome for any single creditor is that all other creditors grant the borrower debt relief, thus ensuring that the borrower is able to meet its full obligations to the remaining creditor. But if all creditors pursue this strategy, no relief will be given and everyone will end up worse off. In this situation, debt relief may be Pareto-improving. But, at the same time, it is unlikely to be adopted by markets because each creditor will ideally prefer to get a free ride on the back of the debt relief provided by others. In principle, this free-rider problem may be overcome by coordination, but who within the context of private capital markets carries the responsibility for providing this function?

Similarly, in the midst of a financial crisis, where a borrowing country is experiencing extreme illiquidity, the incentive for each individual creditor will be to withdraw funds as quickly as possible. However, if all creditors do this, it will merely exacerbate illiquidity and make it more likely that everyone – creditors and debtors alike – will lose. The conventional analogy is with a fire in a building. An organized evacuation is likely to save more lives than a disorganized stampede by individuals in a state of panic. But who is responsible for organizing fire drills, identifying emergency exits, and so on? This is, in essence, a public good that will not be provided by individuals in isolation. Again, there is a coordination failure.

Financial crises flamed by investor panics may also have spillover and contagion effects, which individual creditors do not take into account when making their decisions. There can then be a domino pattern. In part, contagion may be an economic phenomenon, because recession, interest rate hikes, and currency depreciation in one country adversely affect export performance and the overall balance of payments elsewhere. But there may also be an important psychological or bandwagon effect as the predominant market sentiment changes. In other words, there will be externalities that are not internalized into the decisions made by private capital markets. Individual market operators will not see it as part of their role to deal with systemic risk, of which contagion is a part.

Even in dealing with individual country risk, private markets will be largely unable to enact measures that reduce risk other than by their own portfolio diversification. What measures might there be? An important risk-reducing mechanism is conditionality, by which loans are made contingent on a borrowing government pursuing an agreed range of economic policies designed to strengthen economic performance. Why will private markets find conditionality difficult to organize? First, and yet again, conditionality has to be a coordinated activity. Clearly, individual creditors cannot negotiate separate and possibly mutually inconsistent conditions. Apart from anything else, the transactions costs would, in all likelihood, be prohibitively high. Second, individual creditors have neither the information nor the expertise to devise appropriate conditions. They would have to start at the bottom of what would be a steep learning curve. Third, given the relatively poor data that creditors are likely to have, it would be difficult for them to monitor progress. Fourth, it would be equally difficult for private markets to enforce conditions and ensure that appropriate penalties were applied where countries lapsed.

Experience confirms the above. On the only occasion that private banks endeavored to put together a loan based on their own conditionality, they ended up saying never again. Creditors complained of at least as many problems dealing with each other as they did dealing with the borrowing government.[6]

In addition to the systemic risk discussed earlier, there will be systemic issues that lie outside the sphere of private capital markets on which decisions need to be made. These relate to the generalized exchange rate regime, international macroeconomic policy coordination, and the regulation of both domestic and international financial systems.

What would be the implications of leaving these various deficiencies of private capital markets unattended? In short, global economic welfare would be lower than it need be. Capital would be inefficiently allocated throughout the world. Capital movements would tend to be unstable and volatile, and there would be a high incidence of balance-of-payments crises. Governments might be effectively forced to pursue excessively strict deflationary (counterinflationary) policies in an attempt to impress private capital markets, so that while private capital markets might relax financing constraints in one way, they might impose an additional constraint in another. Because there would, in any event, be a high degree of contagion of financial crises, some governments would lose the ability to pursue macroeconomic policies based on domestic needs. Poor countries would find themselves starved of external finance, and living standards for many millions of people would therefore be adversely affected.

How can the deficiencies of private capital markets be overcome while retaining their undoubted advantages? To some extent, bilateral aid may help by providing external finance to low-income countries. But bilateral aid donors might be little better than private markets in collecting and interpreting data and in organizing conditionality.

The role of multilateral financial institutions

If there is a conventional list of market failures, there is also a conventional way of trying to deal with them. Market failure provides an analytical justification for government intervention, and domestic governments regulate domestic financial markets. But we do not have a global government. An alternative therefore has to be found in dealing with the failures of private capital markets, and this is where multilateral financial institutions fit in.

But just as markets may fail in certain ways, so too may governments. There are government failures, and costs associated with policy interventions, that need to be considered. These include poor information and slow decision and implementation processes. Partly as a consequence, there may be gaps between what policymaking governments intend and what actually happens. People may, for example, second-guess what policies governments will pursue and adjust their own behavior in such a way that the policies are no longer effective (the Lucas critique). Government intervention may encourage rent-seeking behavior, which wastes resources, and there may be little incentive for the public sector to be efficient (a common justification for privatization). Finally, governments are run by politicians and bureaucrats who, according to public choice theory, are likely to be self-serving.[7] Pursuing their own interests is unlikely to result in maximizing some social welfare function. In order to minimize these problems, governments need to be open, accountable, and democratic.

In designing multilateral financial institutions, it is therefore as important to bear in mind possible sources of government failure as it is to seek to overcome the sources of market failure. From the above analysis, the comparative advantage of multilateral financial institutions is likely to be in the areas of collecting information and interpreting it, negotiating policy conditionality, internalizing global externalities, coordinating behavior to offset free riding, dealing with systemic risk and other systemic issues, and providing finance (in appropriate circumstances) to countries that are shunned by private capital markets. However, they also need to ensure that their interventions are effective and efficient and that their organizational structures enable them to avoid the public choice critique. As part of this they need to discipline any bureaucratic tendency to grow in size and in sphere of activity. As a general guideline, the multilaterals should not seek to do things that private capital markets can do better.

How do the IMF and World Bank score?

While this section accentuates the negative in order to focus on areas where reform is necessary, this approach tends to misrepresent the contribution of the multilaterals to global economic welfare. One of the problems, however, is that it is difficult to measure their contribution with any great precision. To look at the flows of finance that they have provided and adjust these according to some "reasonable" rate of return gives one indication. Anne Krueger carries out such an exercise and concludes that World Bank lending alone has probably contributed to economic growth in the countries receiving its support by about 0.2 percent of GDP.[8] However, to the extent that the multilaterals have also exerted a positive effect on the quality of economic management via technical training and policy dialogue, their contribution overall is almost certainly very significantly greater than this.

Any cost-effectiveness study or cost-benefit study would, with little doubt, show that the IMF and the World Bank have played a useful and constructive role in the world economy.[9] This implies that draconian proposals to close them down are misplaced. However, to say that the multilaterals have played a constructive role is not to deny that they might be able to do better. Where have they fallen short?

The IMF may be assessed in terms of its adjustment role, its financing role, and its role in systemic management. As far as adjustment is concerned, the principal modality through which it has attempted to exercise this role has been conditionality. Incrementalism has witnessed an expansion in conditionality. Over the years, low conditionality finance (historically available via the Compensatory Financing Facility) has been abandoned and the number of conditions involved in Fund programs has increased.[10] Conditionality now covers not only demand-side instruments such as fiscal policy, monetary policy, and exchange rate policy, but often also detailed microeconomic and supply-side policies. Does the expansion in Fund conditionality reflect a track record of success that the Fund has been anxious to build upon? No; in many respects conditionality has become less effective, with the majority of

Fund programs remaining incomplete.[11] But why might governments fail to implement Fund programs? Clearly, there can be a range of reasons, including external shocks that blow programs off course and overambition in design. However, the Fund tends to blame a lack of commitment to reform by governments, although this is oversimplistic because it fails to go on to analyze why governments may be uncommitted and the complex political economy that underpins implementation.[12]

Assuming for a moment that conditionality is appropriately designed and identifies the right policies, it still appears to be a less than effective means of ensuring that these policies are adopted. Much the same can be said for World Bank conditionality in the context of policy-based structural adjustment lending.[13]

But has conditionality been well designed? There are concerns that by using conditionality, the multilaterals have encouraged governments to pursue policies about which there is legitimate debate.[14] These concerns cover the routine items of interest rate policy, fiscal policy, and exchange rate policy, as well as specific measures of economic liberalization and the speed and sequencing of liberalization in general. If there are things in economics that we know and things that we do not know, or at least are uncertain about, it may be sensible for conditionality to concentrate on the former and downplay the latter, allowing governments to retain more discretion in these areas.[15] This would limit the scope of conditionality. Moreover, given the uncertainties surrounding economic policy, it may be unjustifiable to be too precise quantitatively. While, because of the difficulties alluded to earlier, the multilaterals have a comparative advantage in conditionality as compared with private markets, it is a mistake to squander this by designing it in such a way as to make it relatively ineffective.

There is another point here that links the multilaterals' conditionality to private capital markets. In principle, conditionality should have a catalytic effect on private flows by signaling that governments are committed to economic policy reform. However, poor implementation and the rather weak overall effects of conditionality on economic performance undermine potential catalysis. Since countries turn to the Fund only when they are in severe economic distress and have no alternative source of finance, and since there are strong elements of recidivism in borrowing from the IMF and the World Bank, a program with the multilaterals may well be interpreted by the markets as an indicator of economic difficulties ahead. The evidence on catalysis suggests that overall the effect is weak, and in a sense this reflects the markets' judgment on conditionality.[16]

Another thing that may get in the way of the multilaterals maintaining a strong financial reputation is where their lending becomes influenced by external factors, with some major shareholding countries such as the United States putting pressure on the IMF and World Bank to make loans in circumstances where they would otherwise have said no. If multilateral lending

Table 8.2 Major borrowers from IMF

Year	Country	Total program commitment (US$ in billions)	Program commitment as % of all commitments in year
1995	Mexico	17.8	53
1996	Russia	10.1	58
1997	South Korea	21.0	53

Source: IMF, *Annual Reports*.

is allowed to become affected by politics, its part in overcoming the failures of markets will become constrained. Indeed, it is possible that the failures will be magnified.

Turning to the Fund's financing role, how much lending should it do? To take criticism to the extreme, an argument can be formulated that the Fund has lent too little to the many and too much to the few. In recent years there has been a large dispersion in the amount of funds committed to various countries. A few large countries have accounted for significant proportions of the total amount of IMF financing (see Table 8.2). What does this mean for the many smaller countries that divide up the remaining funds? Low-income countries that form the majority of the Fund's clients often encounter structural balance-of-payments problems that are likely to take a lengthy period of time to correct. Relatively slow adjustment implies relatively high financing in the short term (although lower financing in the long term). But what if external financing represents a binding constraint? Countries will have to change their adjustment strategies and opt for the quicker elimination of their current account balance-of-payments deficits. However, rapid adjustment will imply adjustment based on deflating domestic aggregate demand and, to the extent that the problems are structural, demand deflation will fail to correct them.

Although deflating aggregate demand will tend to reduce the current account deficit in the near term, the deficit will reemerge in the longer run when deflationary policies lapse. Indeed, to the extent that next period's aggregate supply is positively related to current period aggregate demand, deflationary policies will make the long-run situation worse.[17]

Inferior adjustment may therefore reflect inadequate financing. There is some evidence to suggest that the success of IMF programs is positively related to the amount of financing that is provided by them.[18] Moreover, countries will be keen to escape Fund conditionality as soon as possible, and this may help explain why so many programs break down.

But what about the idea of lending too much to the few? By this is implied the recent critique that the Fund has bailed out private capital markets and thereby created a moral hazard problem, in the sense that the prospect of bailouts encourages private markets to overlend. In a similar vein, the argument was made during the 1980s that the presence of the IMF and its unwillingness to lend to countries in arrears with private banks served to discourage banks from offering debt relief – the very relief required to provide a systemic solution to the debt crisis. The Fund was sometimes portrayed as a debt collector for the banks.

The general point is that intervention by the multilaterals designed to deal with a particular problem associated with private capital markets, such as the volatility of private capital flows, may itself have undesirable side effects. The solution is that the lending role of the multilaterals may need to be replaced by an enhanced coordinating role, with creditors being encouraged to share a larger proportion of the burden. Coordination is the mechanism through which private creditors can be prevented from attempting to secure a free ride. Excessive lending by the multilaterals may therefore reflect inadequate coordination.

What about systemic management? With the demise of the Bretton Woods system, much of the scope for systemic management disappeared. The world will not return to the 1950s and 1960s. To the extent that there is a systemic role for the Fund to play, it is not therefore in terms of managing a quasi–fixed exchange rate regime. Instead, it is in terms of the coordination role described above, and in terms of collecting, disseminating, and interpreting data and ensuring that countries comply with financial regulatory requirements. Although it may not immediately be apparent why the Fund needs to get involved in domestic banking standards, there is evidence to suggest that currency crises, in which the Fund has an unambiguous interest, often follow on domestic banking crises. This implies that the Fund needs to take an interest in domestic banking arrangements in its member countries just as much as it takes an interest in their domestic macroeconomic policies.[19]

Much of what has been said could also apply to policy-based lending by the World Bank. The Bank, however, focuses mainly on project lending, which it finances by mobilizing international capital either by its own direct borrowing, in which context it acts as a financial intermediary, or by contributions in the case of its soft loan arm, the International Development Association. The rationale for these activities again hangs on informational failures (with the Bank having better information than markets), monitoring and enforcement, public goods, and inequality. Private capital markets may fail to support worthy projects for reasons similar to those that mean domestic governments often have to take on the responsibility for public/infrastructural investment, such as the existence of public goods or the need for a longer time horizon to evaluate the benefits of the project. The principal area of criticism of the Bank tends to be in terms of whether it has defined this activity sufficiently narrowly, or whether it has carried on financing projects for which private capital would be directly available. To the extent that low-income countries continue to encounter a gap between the external finance they need for developmental projects and the finance they can raise on private capital markets, there will be a role for a multinational agency such as the World Bank.

The broad principle behind designing multilateral financial institutions must be the idea of filling gaps or making good deficiencies left by private provision but without creating additional problems as a consequence of their intervention.

An alternative way of approaching the task is to group member countries of the multilaterals into a range of classifications. Because of their unimpaired access to private capital markets, advanced countries are unlikely to need multilateral financial institutions. Middle-income developing countries and countries in transition usually have access to private capital markets but at other times may experience impaired access. Here the multilaterals need to support these countries and private capital markets – not in terms of providing a guaranteed and costless safety net, but by endeavoring to ensure that private lending decisions are well informed and that sound economic policies are pursued. This may imply occasional lending by the multilaterals, but the emphasis needs to be on helping to shift these economies across the margin of creditworthiness.

Low-income countries, by contrast, face longer-term financing problems, and here the lending role of the multilaterals is more important on an ongoing basis, or at least until these countries graduate into the category of better-off developing countries.

In both low- and middle-income developing countries, the multilaterals need to see external financing as part of a package of services they offer, with their adjustment input being an important part of the package. However, multilaterals need to ensure, as best they can, that they support appropriate policies and create an incentive for countries to pursue them. This almost certainly implies a flexible approach to conditionality.

To be effective, the multilaterals also need to carry the support of the world community as a whole. While quota-weighted voting systems may facilitate efficiency, the multilaterals need to avoid becoming dominated by their more powerful shareholders. This may be difficult to achieve if they rely heavily on subscriptions, reviewed by a political process, to finance their activities.

In the next section, we go on to examine some more specific proposals for remodeling the IMF and World Bank to comply with the blueprint laid out earlier. Our conclusion is that these institutions do not need to be rebuilt from scratch. Demolition is unnecessary.

Remodeling: design features

In terms of a new international financial architecture, the IMF will continue to be the premier multilateral financial institution. The role of the

World Bank, however, should not be overlooked. It will continue to be important as a source of development finance for low-income countries. As far as its policy-based lending is concerned, many of the comments made below about IMF conditionality could also be applied to that of the Bank.

While some observers have seen reform of the Fund as a relatively small component of the new international financial architecture, we present it as much more central. After all, the very word *architecture* suggests some over-all plan, and it is unwise to assume that this will somehow satisfactorily emerge from private capital markets. Taking the design lead is precisely what the Fund should be doing. But what items should be on the IMF remodeler's checklist?

First, and fundamental, is the reform of conditionality. The aim should be for consensus and commitment. This will require more flexibility than in the past. The Fund should adopt as light a touch as possible and seek to mini-mize its interventions. There should be a greater distinction between low- and high-conditionality lending, reflecting the distinction between liquidity and solvency problems. The Fund should also distinguish between balance-of-payments crises that are the product of poor domestic macroeconomic management and those due to volatile capital markets. Conditionality might be reformed to follow a sliding scale; governments with a good track record of economic policy and in possession of their own economic reform agenda might expect to receive light conditionality, with this becoming heavier only in cases where governments are reluctant to formulate their own programs or where past promises have not been kept. The Fund in the future needs to work harder to avoid the accusations of excessive and misdirected interven-tion, a classic source of "government failure," and arrest and reverse the trend toward more conditionality.

Second, reforming conditionality would be an important element in improving program implementation and success, which is a function of "ownership." Countries would then be encouraged to turn to the Fund earlier, when their economic situations were not so dire. At the same time, slippage should be more heavily penalized. There should be sticks as well as carrots. Countries that have failed to keep their policy promises would find that it becomes harder to negotiate a new program, not least because the degree of conditionality would be greater. At this stage, the Fund would become more hands on than hands off.

It is important, however, that the Fund recognizes more fully that eco-nomic growth may be a constraint *on* the balance of payments and not simply constrained *by* the balance of payments. For low-income countries this almost certainly means that the Fund needs to increase the amount of finance it provides to such countries. This in turn would further encourage countries to design and implement sensible programs of economic reform. Moreover, given the absolute volume of finance involved, it would not have a significant effect on the Fund's resource position.

Of course, improving the track record of conditionality and strengthening the commitment to economic reform would also have the benefit of reinforcing the Fund's catalytic effect on other capital flows, such that an increased proportion of the financing could be met from private sources. Low-income countries could also be assisted by means of a special allocation of special drawing rights (SDRs) to them, an idea that has been around for some time.[20]

In the case of better-off developing countries and countries in transition, the Fund needs to avoid, as far as possible, getting into the situation where it is making large loans in crisis conditions. This is what puts pressure on the Fund's resource base and threatens to perpetrate a moral hazard problem. Even if it were to be politically feasible, the Fund should resist invitations to develop in the direction of becoming a formal international lender of last resort; it lacks many of the characteristics of an international central bank and could become exposed to moral hazard problems. It should attempt to play down its crisis lending role and play up its crisis management role. The emphasis should be on coordinating creditors at a time of crisis in a way that ensures that they are unable to pass the cost of the crisis on to the Fund. This will almost certainly impair the willingness of private capital markets to lend, but currency crises often reflect excessive lending in the past more than deficient lending in the present. The details of strengthening the Fund's coordinating role are complex but not insurmountable.

In terms of dealing with capital volatility, the logic of proposals that the Fund should collect and disseminate fuller amounts of data almost goes without saying. To the extent that there are informational failures of one sort or another, these need to be corrected. However, more doubts exist about what should be expected from the Fund in terms of interpreting data and drawing appropriate policy conclusions. Like other institutions, the Fund's forecasting record has not always been strong.

In the context of capital volatility, it is perhaps more important that the Fund should not make countries liberalize their capital accounts as part of conditionality. There are strong arguments that if anything should be open, it should be the Fund's mind about capital account liberalization. In order to help avoid their destabilizing effects, many developing countries may need to retain the option of imposing some sort of tax on capital movements. The Fund often likes to see itself as a doctor diagnosing country illnesses and prescribing appropriate medicines (which, of course, may be unpleasant to take). The Fund also needs to recall that the doctor's first objective is to do no harm. Premature capital account liberalization may harm developing countries.[21]

While attempting to minimize its role as a crisis lender to better-off developing countries, the Fund also needs to avoid becoming itself resource constrained. The use of IMF credit has more than doubled in the years 1994–98 (see Table 8.3). It therefore needs to break away from the system of periodic

Table 8.3 Total use of IMF credit
(US$ in millions)

Year	Credit
1994	44,144
1995	61,101
1996	60,106
1997	70,798
1998	95,459

Source: World Bank, *Global Development and Finance: Country Tables* (Washington, D.C.: World Bank, 1999), p. 14.

quota reviews by which its resource base is increased at discrete moments in time. Instead, its resources need to be determined with a higher degree of automaticity by, for example, maintaining a ratio between Fund quotas and world trade within a specified range. A formula could be devised that also endeavored to capture the importance of the capital account in causing overall balance-of-payments difficulties, which will remain the primary focus of the Fund. An automatic formula-based approach would also overcome some of the accusations that have been made against the Fund's management – including, that it engages in hurry-up lending prior to a quota review.[22] It would also serve to protect the Fund from direct political influences over its lending capacity. More radical proposals to use additional SDR allocations as a way of financing the Fund would, however, probably encounter substantial resistance from the Fund's principal shareholders, who may wish to keep the institution on a short leash.

This may also rule out the option of the Fund following the lead of the Bank and financing itself by borrowing directly from private capital markets. However, in many ways this is an attractive option, because by using this mechanism the Fund would be able to directly catalyze private capital.[23] To private capital markets, lending to the Fund could be an appealing complement to direct country lending since, while it might offer a lower return, it would also carry less risk. In this way the Fund would be able to offer a safety net to private capital markets. The Fund would, of course, need to continue to receive subscriptions and other contributions to finance its concessionary activities. Where the Fund's major shareholders insist on the short-leash approach, however, the task is to ensure that the leash is not so short as to cause strangulation.

Insulating Fund decisions from political considerations represents a substantial challenge, since it is in many ways a fundamentally political institution. But its remodeling needs to take into account that it will lose an important part of its financial reputation if its decisions become too heavily influenced by the political preferences of its major shareholders. There is a case for allowing the Fund's own staff more executive discretion. But then, who checks up on them? The Fund often comes over as a rather closed, opaque, and self-defensive institution. If Fund staff are to be granted more decisionmaking power, this has to be accompanied by greater openness and accountability. Either the Fund has to become more self-critical or expose itself formally to the criticisms of others.[24] At the same time, depoliticizing the Fund should not exclude the borrowing countries from the sense of partnership with the Fund, which they require if they are to undertake fundamental policy reforms.

The final "design feature" strongly follows on from a zero-based strategy. The Fund now possesses a mind-boggling array of lending facilities, including standbys and the Extended Fund Facility (EFF), the Poverty Reduction and Growth Facility (PRGF), formerly known as the Enhanced Structural Adjustment Facility (ESAF), the Compensatory Financing Facility (CFF), and the Supplemental Reserve Facility (SRF). The Fund's response to the East Asian crisis was to add to this an extra swift disbursement window. There is considerable scope for rationalizing this range of lending facilities and concentrating on may be two that emphasize the analytical distinctions that were made earlier.[25] One could involve short-term loans where the principal problem is a lack of liquidity. The second could be longer term and would deal with problems of insolvency and structural adjustment. The degree of concessionality could be determined by the per capita income of the borrowing country. To some extent, this would be a matter of regularizing the current situation, since in reality some of the Fund's existing lending windows are little used. There is little chance that if the Fund were being built from scratch it would be designed with as many windows as it currently has.

Conclusion

The East Asian financial crisis has led to claims that a new international architecture is needed. But what does this mean? Most accounts of it are rather imprecise. It is usually seen as involving only limited reforms to the IMF, the world's premier international financial institution. The accent, where reform to the Fund is envisaged, is placed on either expanding its role in providing information and in "strengthening" conditionality or abandoning conditionality altogether in favor of preconditions. The Fund itself has favored increasing its jurisdiction to cover capital account liberalization, while others have suggested an increased supervisory role as important, particularly in terms of domestic financial systems. To us, some of these ideas are good and largely uncontroversial, although perhaps of more limited benefit than is sometimes assumed; others, however, are bad and potentially damaging.

In any case, our view is that the Fund is central to the concept of a new international financial architecture and therefore requires much closer fundamental examination. The Fund should be designed to make good the deficiencies of private capital markets, while bearing in mind the potential dangers of intervention. Following on from this analytical approach is a "job specification" that delineates a clear role for the Fund. Reform of the Fund should cover its adjustment role, its financing role, and its role in systemic management. At the same time, the World Bank needs to adopt a similar orientation in dealing with the deficiencies of private capital markets.

Is this a task that can be achieved? It can if there is sufficient political will. Failure to agree on and implement a program of reform will indeed, in this case, reflect a lack of political will (irony intended). In previous years, and even at the time of the fiftieth anniversary of the Bretton Woods institutions, there was little enthusiasm for fundamental reform. But the severity of the East Asian crisis along with its contagion effects may have created a global environment that is conducive to reform. The hope is that political leaders grasp the opportunity to undertake the necessary institutional remodeling and refurbishment. The worry is that as the global economy recovers and memories of the crisis fade (until the next one), the temptation will be to settle for marginal incremental reform. As a consequence, the reality will lag behind the rhetoric and the new international financial architecture will end up becoming just another empty phrase.

9
How Important is Sound Domestic Macroeconomics in Attracting Capital Inflows to Developing Countries?

Graham Bird

Introduction

Developing countries tend to run current account balance of payments deficits on their trade in goods and services. Decumulating international reserves as a means of financing such deficits is not a long-term option, and may not even be a short-term option where reserves are already meagre. Inflows of capital in the form of either foreign aid or private capital offer a potential alternative. Failing to attract capital inflows implies that national income and domestic living standards will have to decline. An imbalance where domestic saving falls short of domestic investment either calls for foreign financing or for corrective domestic action which reduces consumption or investment. Given the related adjustment costs, developing countries will be anxious to make themselves attractive to foreign creditors. But how can they do this?

All creditors, whether official or private, stress the importance of 'sound' domestic macroeconomic performance and policy in potential capital-importers, and have often sought to guarantee this by making loans conditional on the involvement of the International Monetary Fund (IMF) in domestic policy-making.

But to what extent can developing countries expect to increase their attractiveness to foreign capital by modifying macroeconomic policy, whether under the auspices of the IMF or not? Is there some continuous and increasing relationship between the quality of domestic macroeconomic performance and policy on the one hand, and capital inflows on the other. Or is there simply a discrete distinction between sound and unsound macroeconomics?

Foreign investors and aid donors will have an interest in the future economic performance of countries in which they are 'investing'. In the case

141

of aid donors a principal purpose of aid is to foster economic development, and although this does not exclusively depend on economic growth, it is reasonable to assume that economic growth in the recipient country is a relevant consideration to donors. Providers of private capital, whether in the form of bank loans, bonds, portfolio equity investment, or direct investment, will also be concerned about the future economic performance of capital-importing countries. Sound macroeconomic policy and performance might be seen as reducing the degree of uncertainty surrounding their investment decisions. Where the borrower is the domestic government, there is the additional dimension of sovereign risk. The performance of the economy will directly affect a government's ability to service its obligations. But even the return on portfolio and direct investment will be influenced by overall macroeconomic performance.

Reducing uncertainty in this way presupposes that there is a consensus on what is 'sound macroeconomics'. In practice the situation is somewhat paradoxical. For while there probably is broad agreement on what constitutes 'unsound' macroeconomic policy and performance, there is significant disagreement about many of the fundamental macroeconomic relationships that underpin it. Given these uncertainties is it likely that investors will place great weight on macroeconomic details? For similar reasons it might be anticipated that Fund involvement in developing countries will, in practice, be of little significance in determining capital flows to them.

The purpose of this chapter is to examine how macroeconomic policy and performance will influence the attractiveness of potential capital-importing countries to capital exporters. The analysis suggests that, apart from being penalized for severe macroeconomic mismanagement, developing countries cannot necessarily expect to be rewarded for avoiding it or for seeking to strengthen macroeconomic performance from period to period. The chapter does not specifically examine other aspects of economic policy, such as trade and financial liberalization, or privatization, although much the same conclusions reached about macroeconomic policy and performance probably apply to them as well, for similar reasons.[1]

The chapter has the following layout. The next section reviews existing theoretical models of private capital flows to developing countries and describes some of their shortcomings, particularly in terms of their treatment of the domestic macroeconomics of capital-importing countries. The third section reviews some of the key areas of macroeconomic uncertainty which imply that 'sound macroeconomics' is a definitionally weak concept. In this context it discusses not only the ambiguities in standard macroeconomic theory, but also the question of whether developing country macroeconomics differ from developed country macroeconomics. The section on macroeconomic policy goes on to ponder why a reasonable degree of consensus relating to macroeconomic policy coexists alongside disagreements over theory, and what the implications are for the relationship between domestic macroeconomics and capital inflows to developing countries, disaggregating across these. The next section examines the extent to which international financial institutions (IFIs) can be expected to influence capital inflows in the light of the foregoing analysis. The section on conditionality examines whether different ideas apply to different forms of capital flow. The next section examines empirical evidence relating to private capital flows to see whether it is consistent with the *a priori* expectations that have been formed. It also provides additional evidence to suggest that developing countries should not anticipate that 'sound' domestic macroeconomics will have a powerful, immediate, and continuing effect on capital inflows. In relation to attracting foreign capital, whereas fulfilling certain macroeconomic criteria may be a necessary condition, it is unlikely to be sufficient; unsound macroeconomic policy will deter private capital inflows, while sound policy may not necessarily encourage them. The final section offers some concluding remarks concerning international policy. The chapter provides a cautionary message concerning the extent to which individual countries can expect to attract foreign capital via the macroeconomic policies they pursue and the macroeconomic performance which they achieve.

Pull and push factors in explaining private capital flows: a theoretical background

Table 9.1 provides data on the surge of capital flows to developing countries, as a group, during the 1990s. Although this is only the latest phase in what has been a story of 'feast' and 'famine', with a rapid increase in bank lending in the 1970s being followed by a dearth of private lending in the years

Table 9.1 Aggregate net private capital flows to developing countries, 1990–96 (billions of U.S. dollars)

Type of flow	1990	1991	1992	1993	1994	1995	1996[a]
Total private flows	44.4	56.9	90.6	157.1	161.3	184.2	243.8
Portfolio flows	5.5	17.3	20.9	80.9	62.0	60.6	91.8
Bonds	2.3	10.1	9.9	35.9	29.3	28.5	46.1
Equity	3.2	7.2	11.0	45.0	32.7	32.1	45.7
Foreign direct investment	24.5	33.5	43.6	67.2	83.7	95.5	109.5
Commercial banks	3.0	2.8	12.5	−0.3	11.0	26.5	34.2
Others	11.3	3.3	13.5	9.2	4.6	1.7	8.3
Memo items							
Aggregate net resource flows	100.6	122.5	146.0	212.0	207.0	237.2	284.6
Private flows' share (per cent)	44.1	46.4	62.1	74.1	77.9	77.7	85.7

[a] Preliminary.

Source: World Bank Debtor Reporting System.

Table 9.2 Net private capital flows to developing countries by country group, 1990–96 (billions of U.S. dollars)

Country group or country	1990	1991	1992	1993	1994	1995	1996[a]
All developing countries	44.4	56.9	90.6	157.1	161.3	184.2	243.8
Sub-Saharan Africa	0.3	0.8	−0.3	−0.5	5.2	9.1	11.8
East Asia and the Pacific	19.3	20.8	36.9	62.4	71.0	84.1	108.7
South Asia	2.2	1.9	2.9	6.0	8.5	5.2	10.7
Europe and Central Asia	9.5	7.9	21.8	25.6	17.2	30.1	31.2
Latin America and the Caribbean	12.5	22.9	28.7	59.8	53.6	54.3	74.3
Middle East and North Africa	0.6	2.2	0.5	3.9	5.8	1.4	6.9
Income group							
Low-income countries	11.4	12.1	25.4	50.0	57.1	53.4	67.1
Middle-income countries	32.0	44.0	64.8	107.1	104.2	130.7	176.7
Top country destinations[b]							
China	8.1	7.5	21.3	39.6	44.4	44.3	52.0
Mexico	8.2	12.0	9.2	21.2	20.7	13.1	28.1
Brazil	0.5	3.6	9.8	16.1	12.2	19.1	14.7
Malaysia	1.8	4.2	6.0	11.3	8.9	11.9	16.0
Indonesia	3.2	3.4	4.6	1.1	7.7	11.6	17.9
Thailand	4.5	5.0	4.3	6.8	4.8	9.1	13.3
Argentina	−0.2	2.9	4.2	13.8	7.6	7.2	11.3
India	1.9	1.6	1.7	4.6	6.4	3.6	8.0
Russia	5.6	0.2	10.8	3.1	0.3	1.1	3.6
Turkey	1.7	1.1	4.5	7.6	1.6	2.0	4.7
Chile	2.1	1.2	1.6	2.2	4.3	4.2	4.6
Hungary	−0.3	1.0	1.2	4.7	2.8	7.8	2.5
Percentage share of top twelve countries	83.6	76.8	87.4	84.1	75.4	73.3	72.5

Notes: Private flows include commercial bank lending guaranteed by export credit agencies.
[a] Preliminary.
[b] Country ranking is based on cumulative 1990–95 private capital flows received. Private flows include commercial bank loans guaranteed by export credit agencies.
Source: World Bank Debtor Reporting System and staff estimates.

following the Latin American debt crisis in the 1980s, it has led to a related surge in the literature which attempts to identify the causes and implications of capital flows.[2] However Table 9.2 shows that private capital flows have been highly concentrated in a relatively small number of Latin American and Asian economies. The idea of a surge of private capital to developing countries therefore needs to be put into perspective.

It has become conventional to divide the causes of the surge into 'pull' and 'push' factors, and to distinguish between permanent and temporary elements.[3] This last distinction has led to attempts to disentangle the extent to which contemporary flows represent a process of stock adjustment, implying that they will be temporary and will decline as equilibrium is approached, assuming no further disequilibriating shocks occur. Here the speed of adjustment varies inversely with the costs of adjustment, which are generally assumed to increase with the size of adjustment.

Some models also decompose the domestic return on assets into a project-expected return and a country creditworthiness factor (Fernandez-Arias and Montiel, 1996).

Models based on the notion of risk minimization through portfolio diversification view as the fundamental determinants of international capital flows the global investment opportunity set, the covariances between the expected returns on investment projects, the preferences of investors as between present and future consumption, and the degree of risk aversity of investors.[4] However, difficulties in capturing these influences, as well as the fact that capital flows, which are the mechanism through which the arbitrage equilibrium condition is attained, may be disrupted by regulation and capital market imperfection, has focused attention on more measurable proximate determinants.

A representative model of recent capital flows to developing countries is that offered by Fernandez-Arias and Montiel (1996),

$$F = F(d, c, w, s) \tag{1}$$

where F is the vector of net flows of all types, d captures changes in domestic factors at the project level, c covers changes in country creditworthiness, w shows changes in the opportunity cost of funds in the world economy, and s represents the inherited stock of liabilities from the previous period. According to this model, increases in d and c, or decreases in w will tend to generate a sustained surge in inflows.

Within this theoretical framework, 'improved domestic macroeconomic policies' are interpreted to have a positive pull effect on capital inflows by increasing the long-run expected rate of return, reducing perceived risk, and driving up short-run interest rates. A further implication of the model is that further 'improvements' in domestic macroeconomic policies will result in further capital inflows.

Policies that reduce domestic absorption relative to income (a further pull factor), are presented as increasing country creditworthiness, which is assumed to depend on the expected present value of resources available for external payments relative to a country's liabilities. Thus,

$$c = Y/(R - g) \tag{2}$$

where Y is a measure of available resources, g is the assumed growth rate of these resources, and R is the claimholders' discount rate, determined by returns available elsewhere in the world. According to this model, c will increase as Y and g increase, and decrease as R increases. Equation (2) suggests that a country's creditworthiness, c, increases as g rises relative to R. Macroeconomic policy may affect c by influencing economic growth – to the extent that economic growth is not purely a supply side phenomenon – and by influencing uncertainty about the future and therefore the risk component of the discount rate, R. Where unsound contemporary macroeconomic policy reduces g and increases R, it will reduce c and, other things being constant, this will reduce F. In the context of this model governments can influence capital flows via their conduct of domestic macroeconomic policy. There will therefore in principle be a role for pull factors.

Exogenous, or push, factors affecting w include foreign interest rates and levels of economic activity, bandwagon effects, either based on changing economic fundamentals or speculative bubbles, and the easing of access to capital markets in creditor countries.

Other variants on the above model have sought to capture domestic 'pull' factors (broadly defined) by means of the black market foreign exchange premium, credit ratings, or the secondary market price of external debt. Again however, the implication is that capital inflows will be an increasing function of the determinants that underlie these proxy measures. Domestic macroeconomic policy and performance are assumed to be reflected by them.

A feature of the models summarized above is that capital-importing countries can continue to make themselves increasingly attractive by continuously improving economic policy and performance, even if this is by a process of period-by-period stock adjustment.

But is it feasible to detect marginal policy and performance improvements? Is there sufficient consensus on what represents sound macroeconomics? The next section argues that there is not, and that, while macroeconomic performance and policy will exert an influence over capital flows, the influence does not take the form implied by the above analysis.

An alternative theoretical background is to use the concept of macroeconomic and, in particular, current account balance of payments sustainability (Milesi-Ferretti and Razin, 1996). At first glance this implies that there is a discrete distinction between macroeconomic situations that are either 'sustainable' or 'unsustainable'.

The concept of sustainability is, however, problematic. It clearly incorporates a solvency component, which involves a present value budget constraint. Solvency considerations can be applied to the current account balance of payments, domestic and public finance, and external debt. Indeed to some extent equation (2) above says something about solvency, in terms of the relative values of g and R. The situation is solvent for as long as $g \geqslant R$.

However, even where insolvency is not a problem in the above sense, the situation may be unsustainable because of short-term illiquidity or cash flow constraints. Moreover, the extent to which crises of illiquidity occur depends on the ability and willingness of governments to change policies. The literature on debt sustainability has, for example, drawn a sharp distinction between forecasts built on the assumption that the 'best' policies are pursued, as compared with those that assume that 'current' policies continue. In this context the superficial discreteness of the sustainability concept disappears, since sustainability depends on the probabilities attached to different policy combinations.

From the point of view of capital flows there is also a simultaneity problem in as much as sustainability is simultaneously both a function of and a determinant of capital inflows.

In trying to find operational indicators of the concept of current account sustainability, Milesi-Ferretti and Razin (1996) use similar indicators to those used in some of the country risk literature (Bird, 1989). They distinguish between structural features (investment/savings, economic growth, openness, the composition of external liabilities and financial structure), macroeconomic policy stance (exchange rate policy, fiscal policy, trade policy and capital account policy regime), and political economy factors.

They argue that current account deficits become more sustainable in terms of structural features as investment and savings increase, the rate of economic growth increases, economies become more open and diversified, equity instruments become more important, and the quality of financial supervision improves. In terms of macroeconomic policy they focus on the need to avoid currency overvaluation and budget deficits, and to pursue trade liberalization and open capital account policies. Political economy factors, they argue, point to the importance of political stability, as well as a range of factors which help determine the degree of policy flexibility.

Without pursuing the idea of sustainability any further, enough has been said to show that sustainability models include domestic macroeconomic policy as a key element. This not only appears directly via exchange rate policy and fiscal policy, but also more indirectly in terms of its capacity to influence 'structural features' and the probability of implementation in the context of political economy factors.

However, in terms of moving from a broad theoretical framework to an operational model, the idea of sustainability is less helpful. It still implies, as do the push/pull models, that there will be a graduation of sustainability and that improving macroeconomic policy may be expected to have a positive effect on capital inflows at the margin by means of increasing the probability of, for example, current account and debt sustainability.

The upcoming analysis in this chapter suggests that the relationship between domestic macroeconomic policy is rather different from this. While the notion of sound macroeconomics is significant, its importance is less subtle than some push/pull and probabilistic sustainability models imply because of the degree of uncertainty surrounding it.

'Sound' macroeconomics: what does it mean?

Whatever form capital inflows take, foreign investors will prefer to see good rather than bad macroeconomic policy and performance in capital-importing countries. The link between domestic macroeconomics and expected returns to foreign investors may be direct in the case of sovereign debt, or indirect in the case of portfolio and direct investment. It may be difficult for firms in the private sector to appear significantly more creditworthy that the countries in which they are based. Generally speaking, a country generating a rapid rate of non-inflationary economic growth, with prospects that this will continue, will appear more attractive to foreign investors than one where the domestic economy is stagnating, irrespective of whether the investments are in the public or private sector. Certainly the managers of mutual funds in the 1990s, as did commercial bank loan officers before them in the 1970s and early 1980s, claim to look for 'sound' macroeconomic policy and for good macroeconomic prospects at the country level.

But, in rigorously assessing macroeconomic performance and prospects, is it not useful to know how the economy in question works so that reasoned judgements may be made? What is the appropriate macroeconomic model, and what determines key macroeconomic variables such as domestic saving, investment, economic growth, and the balance of payments. Moreover, what impact should individual policy instruments be expected to have?

Lack of precision in these areas unavoidably makes judgements on the macroeconomy very difficult, and this surely implies that they will carry less weight when foreign investors make lending and investment decisions. On all of the above there is substantial uncertainty. New classical macroeconomics paints a very different picture of how an economy works than does new Keynesian macroeconomics, and leads to sharply conflicting conclusions about macroeconomic policy. Neo-structural analysis suggests that developing countries need a separate macroeconomic model altogether. Within this, prices are determined on a cost-plus as opposed to a market-clearing basis, and inflation reflects structural weaknesses and not just excess aggregate demand. Contractionary demand-side policies lead to falling output, employment and real income, rather than a declining rate of inflation. Exchange rate devaluation is stagflationary, as a consequence of its contractionary effect on aggregate domestic demand combined with the cost-push effects of rising import prices. Reductions in public investment lead to falling private investment with 'crowding in' being a stronger force than 'crowding out'. Reducing domestic absorption has a negative effect on exports, since the domestic market acts as a springboard from which to raise exports. And the stagflationary effects of rising interest rates swamp efficiency gains. Furthermore, according to the neo-structuralist model, capital formation has a high import content, and there is little scope for substituting domestic resources for imported capital goods.

While neo-structuralism encounters its own problems, not least in terms of dealing with exchange rate overvaluation and macroeconomic instability, its raises enough doubts about the relevance of 'conventional' macroeconomic analysis and policy tools in developing countries to generate uncertainties for foreign investors.

The uncertainties surrounding underlying macroeconomic models is echoed in assessing the wisdom of individual policy tools. With respect to fiscal policy there is disagreement over the extent to which fiscal deficits create problems. Even within the context of specific models, fiscal deficits may or may not be a cause for concern. In a neo-Keynesian model, a fiscal deficit will tend to be inappropriate where the private sector is also in deficit, government expenditure has low marginal productivity, the economy is at or close to full productive potential, and there is crowding out. But in a different set of circumstances it may become a sensible policy choice. Moving across theories, ideas based on notions of Ricardian equivalence maintain that changes in fiscal policy simply induce offsetting changes in the behaviour of the private sector which have a neutralizing effect; but will such forward-looking agents exist in developing countries?

Using a simple *IS-LM-BP* model, Figure 9.1 illustrates that an increasing fiscal deficit may have different effects on the overall balance of payments in a 'typical' developing country where response elasticities are low (giving steep schedules), than in a 'typical' developed country where they are relatively high, and capital is highly interest rate elastic. The differences are reinforced if it is further assumed that, as a consequence of thin financial markets, developing economies will be forced to monetize fiscal deficits. As drawn, Figure 9.1 presupposes that developing countries carry high risk premia such that foreign capital inflows are relatively inelastic with respect to the domestic rate of interest. Sound macroeconomic policy and performance may be presented as

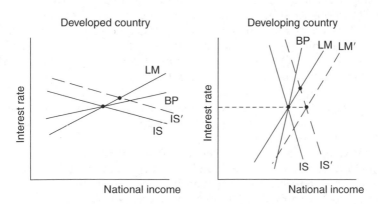

Figure 9.1 The effect of fiscal expansion

a way of reducing such premia, thereby flattening the *BP* schedule, with financial deepening flattening the *LM* schedule. However a problem may still remain if, as neo-structuralists claim, fiscal deficits in developing countries are particularly vulnerable to exogenous shocks, since they then stand as a highly imperfect proxy for fiscal policy (Fanelli *et al.*, 1994).

Monetary policy based on a money supply rule will only make sense where the demand for money is stable, and where the authorities are able to define and control the money supply. Yet these requirements may be elusive in many developing countries (Killick, 1995). The wisdom of interest rate targeting depends, *inter alia*, on the sensitivity of savings to interest rates and on the degree of international capital mobility. But saving has frequently proved unresponsive to changes in interest rates in developing countries, and assessing the degree of capital mobility requires potential foreign investors to calculate the responsiveness of other foreign investors to interest rate changes; when these other foreign investors are making similar calculations about them.

Expectations will also be central to evaluating the wisdom of exchange rate policy. Will devaluation correct currency misalignment, and eliminate current account deficits? Will it raise confidence and have a positive effect on capital inflows? Or will it fail to strengthen the current account and be taken as a lead indicator of future economic problems, and further devaluations? The debate over exchange rate policy has focused on the alternatives of first, the 'nominal anchor approach' which favours exchange rate pegging as a means of reducing inflationary expectations and second, the 'real targets approach' which maintains that nominal targets lead to currency misalignment, balance of payments deficits, and the expectation of eventual devaluation, and therefore inflation. Although the Mexican peso and East Asian crises have probably tipped the balance against the nominal anchor approach (Bird, 1998), empirical surveys carried out before the crises were generally ambivalent about the relative superiority of the two approaches (Corden, 1993). There are, once more, considerable areas of uncertainty.

Even if it were possible to identify a set of policies about which there was scientific agreement, there is no guarantee that they will be implemented by governments in developing countries. While less scientific ambiguity might help, there will still be costs and benefits associated with any policy stance; there will be gainers and losers from any set of policies. Moreover, costs and benefits are likely to have different inter-temporal patterns. Where costs are imposed in the short run on a powerful group in society, they may be able to effectively resist change in spite of the prospect that there will be net national gains in the long run (Rodrik, 1996). Furthermore, the size and distribution of the costs and benefits of particular policies may not be known with certainty at the time that the policies need to be implemented. It is therefore feasible that different decisions will be made by different policy-makers for no reason other than that they differ in their beliefs about how the policies will be perceived. Assessing the probability of policy implementation therefore creates yet another layer of uncertainty. The *effects* of capital inflows will also be unknown to foreign investors. Is imported capital to be used to finance domestic investment or consumption? Using foreign capital inflows to sustain consumption in the short run may form part of a coherent longer-term development strategy, or may represent a desire to avoid painful changes in domestic policy. Meanwhile using it to finance speculative investment may fail to generate an adequate rate of return.

However used, capital inflows may cause macroeconomic instability in recipient countries (Calvo *et al.*, 1996; Corbo and Hernandez, 1996). Other things being constant, they will either cause the nominal exchange rate to appreciate or the domestic money supply to expand. In either event the effects on the real exchange rate may lead to open economy crowding out, as domestic production is replaced by foreign production. Capital inflows may, by this mechanism, create the current account deficits that then have to be financed by further capital inflows. At the same time, attempts to sterilize the effects of capital inflows on the domestic money supply will tend to push up interest rates and create further incentives for capital to flow inwards. Rising interest rates may also have adverse consequences for levels of domestic economic activity. It is possible via these linkages to envisage dynamic models of speculative bubbles and volatility within which capital inflows themselves contribute to circumstances which, although initially attracting further capital, ultimately repel it. Should foreign investors take such possibilities into account when making their original decisions? The problem yet again is that economic forces will pull in different directions in different countries, and the domestic policy responses may also be different. How do investors judge whether policy-makers will make the right policy judgements?[5] Model uncertainty, combined with uncertainty surrounding the political economy of policy reform appear to leave potential foreign investors with few clues.

On top of this, a feature of developing countries is their vulnerability to outside shocks either via changes in their income terms of trade or via changes in global interest rates. It is now well recognized that contractionary monetary policy in OECD countries contributed to the Latin American debt crisis of the early 1980s by causing recession, and therefore a reduced demand for Latin American exports, and by exerting upward pressure on interest rates (Alien *et al.*, 1992). While investors may consider the sensitivity of countries' performance to different scenarios, it is, by definition, impossible to forecast on the basis of 'predictable shocks'. And yet while it is impossible to predict precisely what shocks will occur, experience suggests that the future will not be surprise free. Shocks in this sense are predictable.[6] Things become no clearer in terms of the determinants of economic growth, where uncertainty surrounds its causal connection with investment (Blomstrom *et al.*, 1996), and its relation to natural resources (Sachs and Warner, 1995), and savings, as well as the contribution of exogenous growth theory.[7] A detailed review of the theory and empirical evidence on the savings function concluded that, 'saving is an enormously complex issue and many aspects of the process are still not well understood' (IMF, 1995).

The conclusion emerges that claims that foreign investors look for sound macroeconomics in capital-importing countries cannot reflect certainty about how developing economies function or about what their detailed macroeconomic prospects are. Scientifically, it is not yet possible to form such judgements with any degree of certainty. The idea of sound macroeconomics must therefore mean something significantly different and less ambitious.

Consensus on macroeconomic policy: a satisficing approach

Although there is considerable disagreement about the ways in which economies function, there is a significant measure of consensus about key sources of macroeconomic failure. Uncontrolled and excessive monetary growth leads to inflation and balance of payments problems. While there is disagreement about the precise costs of inflation, and, as discussed in the previous section, the extent to which current account deficits are sustainable (Milesi-Ferretti and Razin, 1996), there is agreement that rapid inflation is undesirable and that current account deficits can become unsustainable. It is generally conceded that large fiscal deficits have adverse consequences one way or another, and that currency overvaluation damages the current account of the balance of payments as well as the domestic economy. Foreign investors will be influenced by these factors and will be unwilling to lend to countries performing unsatisfactorily. In this sense macroeconomic management and performance may still be expected to influence capital flows. But there will be a satisficing, as opposed to a maximizing approach to evaluating macroeconomic policy. Poor policies and performance will filter countries out as recipients of foreign private capital. Allowing macroeconomic policy and performance to slip below a specific satisfactory threshold may be expected to have a discernibly negative effect on capital inflows. Failing to achieve satisfactory levels of performance will significantly impair a country's access to private capital. However, the analysis contained here suggests that improving macroeconomic policy and performance *beyond* the threshold of satisfaction will have little beneficial effect on capital inflows. In this sense sound macroeconomics will not be deterministic.

But at what levels will thresholds of satisfaction be set? At what point does monetary growth become 'excessive', or fiscal deficits become 'too large'. Far below the threshold there may be little debate, but around the threshold it is harder to say. While reducing inflation from three to two digits indicates a degree of economic success, real exchange rates are still likely to appreciate and this will have adverse consequences for the current account balance of payments. There again, is it better in such circumstances to peg the value of a currency, in an attempt to gain anti-inflation credibility, but at the cost of failing to correct incipient balance of payments deficits, or to devalue the exchange rate and run the risk of creating additional inflation? It is most improbable that foreign investors will be able to answer these questions: hence capital outflows rarely occur before a crisis is well advanced and indicators of performance have moved clearly and unambiguously below the 'satisfactory' threshold.

In large measure the attractiveness of developing countries to foreign investors may depend on the confidence created by governments that they will make sensible macroeconomic decisions as things evolve, rather than on the basis of certain knowledge as to what is sensible in any given set of circumstances. This may well explain the surge of capital flows to Latin America in the early 1990s. Policies had shifted from somewhere significantly below, to somewhere significantly above a threshold of satisfaction and governments thereby created confidence that *future* policies would be well-chosen. Even so it is surprising that in isolation, such policy shifts would have an immediate effect on capital flows. In countries with a poor record of macroeconomic management and performance, governments will surely encounter a credibility problem. Foreign investors will 'wait and see' before responding to shifts in policy in order to minimize the uncertainty surrounding the permanence of policy changes. There may not be an immediate pay-off from adopting satisfactory macroeconomic policy.[8]

The interpretation of 'sound' macroeconomics offered in this section is much less demanding than that discussed in the previous one. According to the satisficing approach foreign investors attempt to reduce uncertainty by ruling out of consideration countries with clearly unsatisfactory macroeconomic performance and policy. High inflation, low economic growth, large fiscal deficits and monetary expansion, severely over-valued exchange rates and the related current account deficits and reserve losses will make countries unattractive to foreign capital. Correcting such macroeconomic shortcomings will be a precondition for access to private foreign capital in whatever form it takes. At the same time, however, the satisficing approach implies that attaining a threshold of satisfaction does not guarantee countries access to private capital.

Moreover, going beyond the threshold does not mean that there will be increasing capital inflows. Domestic macroeconomic policy and performance will be a significant discrete variable determining whether private flows are zero or positive, but it will be insignificant in determining the actual volume of positive inflows.

The satisficing approach to macroeconomic policy and performance relates closely to the concept of sustainability, discussed in the section on private capital flows, which itself is proxied to some extent by features such as currency overvaluation and fiscal deficits. Developing countries which are pursuing macroeconomic policies deemed by private capital markets to be unsustainable will generally be unattractive locations in which to invest. The switch from unsustainable to sustainable policies is the strategically significant change.[9]

Does disaggregation make a difference?

As shown by Table 9.1, a feature of private lending to developing countries since the 1970s has been the shift away from bank lending and towards bonds and, more particularly, direct and equity portfolio investment. Banks based their decisions on rather rudimentary considerations of country risk, with risk matrices incorporating a limited number of macroeconomic variables. However, the underlying analysis frequently made little attempt to be scientific; macroeconomic indicators were aggregated in a fairly haphazard way to provide an overall 'measure' of risk. To a significant degree, the imprecision of the banks' country risk analysis reflected the macroeconomic uncertainties discussed earlier. Banks assembled data on various aspects of a country's macroeconomy without being confident about how the data should be interpreted. Broad judgements tended to be made about what constituted poor performance, but the analysis of country risk was insufficiently subtle to pick up marginal changes (Bird, 1989). As a consequence bank lending was strongly influenced by internal organizational factors and by the psychology of disaster myopia (Guttentag and Herring, 1986). Given the lack of a strong scientific basis for judgement, herd behaviour and contagion effects became common aspects of bank lending. Banks viewed country risk analysis as an 'art' rather than a 'science'.

It might initially be thought that other forms of lending would differ in significant ways. Does, for example, the purchase of bonds not reveal a longer-term horizon than that underlying bank lending? Can the same not be said of direct investment which may also surely be much more microeconomic in orientation focusing on particular sectors or industries and on labour costs and other costs of production? Does equity portfolio investment similarly reflect a microeconomic assessment more than a macroeconomic one, with investors attempting to identify strong sectors of the economy and therefore enterprises that will enjoy increasing stock market value?[10]

Analyses of specific types of capital inflow confirm that different motivations may exist. In a recent survey of foreign direct investment Graham (1995) concludes that, 'most analysts agree that explanations for foreign direct investment based on the organisational theory of the firm have more power than other genres of theory', p. 126. Indeed, in his review of the determinants of FDI, he does not even mention the macroeconomics of the host country.[11] Given the significance of multinational enterprises in

FDI this may be relatively unsurprising. It may also be anticipated that FDI will be more stable than portfolio investment, as the data in Table 9.1 confirms. Explaining equity portfolio investment in terms of expected stock market performance could be helpful if there was an agreed basis upon which to formulate expectations about future stock market prices. But, in general, studies suggest that sophisticated models perform little, if at all, better than simple extrapolation. Stock prices appear to follow a fairly random walk (Malkiel, 1990). Rather than seeking to identify stocks that have particularly strong growth prospects investors may simply be seeking to diversify their portfolio of assets in order to reduce overall risk, as discussed in the section on private capital flows and here, it is the co-variance between stocks which is important.

While differences in investor motivation do exist between the various types of capital flow, the differences as they relate to the macroeconomics of potential recipients may be less pronounced. New forms of lending have exhibited many of the features formerly associated with bank lending. Volatility has been just as much a cause for concern in the case of portfolio investment as it was in the case of bank lending. Emerging stock markets not only facilitate the inflow of portfolio capital but also ease its exit. By the same token, purchasing bonds does not necessarily reflect a long-term commitment when there is a secondary bond market in which they may be sold.

While the new forms of lending do not have the direct implications that bank lending did for borrowing countries' short-term external indebtedness, it is difficult to see how they would be either significantly more or significantly less influenced by the macroeconomic policy and performance of recipient countries. In discussing their investment decisions managers of mutual funds talk in general and informal terms of taking a view about countries' economic prospects. To a substantial degree the process of 'taking a view' appears to rest on the implicit use of a country risk matrix similar to that used by the banks fifteen years earlier, with this incorporating a loose and ill-defined array of macroeconomic variables.

In the case of foreign direct investment the prospects of individual enterprises will be influenced by the economic prospects of the countries in which they are located. Even if direct investment and purchasing bonds were to involve a longer-term perspective, this merely implies that greater weight will be attached to economic growth than to other macroeconomic variables. However, given the uncertainties surrounding both the growth process and the relationship between short-term macroeconomic stability and long-run economic growth, it is hard to see that a longer-term orientation will do anything to reduce the uncertainties that were presented earlier as lying at the heart of private international capital flows: indeed a lengthening of the time horizon may increase the degree of uncertainty still further. The conclusion therefore emerges that the change in the type of private capital flow has done little to affect the relationship between capital flows in aggregate and the macroeconomics of potential capital-importing countries.

Can IFI conditionality help?

If governments are seeking to build up the confidence of foreign investors by maintaining sound macroeconomic policy and performance and thereby gain access to private capital, is there anything that they can do to more rapidly establish a good reputation and shorten the lag before confidence is established? What is the scope for importing the reputation of the IMF in the design of macroeconomic policy?

Certainly the IMF claims that, through its conditionality, it exerts a significant catalytic effect on other financial flows, including private capital flows. If this were to be the case, developing countries anxious to attract foreign capital should seek its endorsement.

However, there are severe deficiencies with this line of reasoning. Perhaps the principal problem is that countries tend to turn to the IMF only when they are in economic distress. Those that have been economically successful do not borrow from the Fund. The involvement of the IMF in a country's economic affairs may therefore be interpreted by foreign investors as a sign of economic weakness rather than strength.

Moreover, the idea that the IMF can assist in the design of macroeconomic policy presupposes that it is well equipped to identify the correct policies. But, by definition it cannot know more than there is to know, its knowledge is constrained by the underlying uncertainties. The policy instruments supported by the IMF, including the control of monetary aggregates, raising interest rates, fiscal retrenchment, and exchange rate devaluation will have beneficial economic effects in the context of some models but not others. In terms of their direct impact on capital flows they may have both positive and negative implications. Increasing interest rates and devaluing the exchange rate will be associated with capital inflows where there is a high degree of capital mobility, risk premia are low, and where devaluation is seen as correcting currency misalignment. But, where higher interest rates are viewed as likely to lead to recession, and devaluation is seen as a precursor of inflation and further devaluation, foreign capital is more likely to exit than enter.

Add to this the facts that the majority of Fund-supported programmes break down, that even where fully implemented the policies favoured by the Fund have little statistically significant effect on the main macroeconomic variables, and that countries, having once borrowed from the IMF, are likely to return to it in the short term, and there is little reason to anticipate that foreign investors will view the involvement of the IMF in a confidence-building and uncertainty-reducing way. Not surprisingly econometric studies have failed to find a connection between Fund involvement and private capital inflows (Bird, 1994; Bird and Rowlands, 1997).

Empirical evidence

Many studies of the surge of capital flows to developing countries during the 1990s attribute them to a combination of 'push' and 'pull' factors. Chuhan *et al.* (1993) find that equity flows are more sensitive than bond flows to global factors, whereas bond flows are more sensitive to country-specific ones. Montiel (1995) provides evidence to support a 'pull' explanation of capital flows, by noting that case studies of individual countries receiving large capital inflows almost invariably identify substantial changes in policy regimes immediately preceding the inflow episode, a claim endorsed by Krugman (1995). However, a survey of the formal evidence suggests that, overall, the weight of evidence favours a push interpretation based on changing US interest rates (Fernandez-Arias and Montiel, 1996).

In a recent study using cointegration and error correction models to distinguish between long-run and short-run determinants, Taylor and Sarno (1997) claim that their results provide 'unequivocal' evidence that long-run equity and bond flows from the US to Latin American and Asian countries are about equally sensitive to global factors (largely US interest rates) and country-specific factors (as measured by credit ratings and black market exchange rate premia) and that both sets of determinants are significant. As far as the short-term dynamics are concerned, they find that push and pull factors are about equally important in determining portfolio flows for both Asian and Latin American countries, but that, in the case of bond flows, push factors are relatively much more important. US interest rates are found to be a particularly important determinant of short-run portfolio, and especially bond flows to developing countries.

Related research has focused on trying to identify the economic determinants of developing country credit-worthiness (Haque *et al.*, 1996). Based on a study of sixty developing countries over 1980–93, Haque *et al.* claim that credit ratings are significantly influenced by economic fundamentals: the ratio of non-gold foreign exchange reserves to imports, the ratio of the current account balance to GNP, economic growth, and inflation. They also discover that all developing country ratings were adversely affected by increases in global interest rates, independent of the domestic economic fundamentals. Regional location and export structure (whether countries were primary product or manufactured good exporters) were also found to be important.

To the extent that pull factors, as proxied by credit ratings, are themselves determined in part by push factors (global interest rates) the research hints at multi-collinearity problems, but it also confirms that crossing thresholds of performance may be more important than changes in performance within thresholds. Haque *et al.*, find, for example, that it is more important to reduce inflation from high rates, than to continue to reduce it beyond a point at which it is only moderate. A similar observation can be made about reserve holdings which Haque *et al.* find to be the single most significant influence over credit ratings. Can countries raise their creditworthiness in perpetuity by accumulating foreign exchange reserves; which will, in any case, reduce their need to borrow. If there is a threshold for reserve adequacy, going beyond it may do little to raise creditworthiness further. In as much as reserve accumulation results from the pursuit of restrictionary domestic demand management policies, there may be internal consistency between this component of credit rating, reduced current account deficits, and reduced inflation. But if such policies also reduce economic growth rates, there is a potential inconsistency in the markets' approach to judging sound macroeconomics which suggests theoretically unsound foundations.

Haque *et al.*, also discover considerable persistence in the ratings. It is difficult for countries to alter them unless 'significant developments' (positive or negative) occur.[12] This finding is again consistent with the basic theme of this chapter. Beyond establishing basic satisfactory standards, developing countries cannot expect to make themselves progressively more attractive by improvements in macroeconomic policy and performance. The results found by Haque *et al.*, generally reflect the deficiencies of the county risk analyses undertaken by credit rating agencies. For the most part these continue to display the shortcomings of the country risk analysis undertaken by the international banks during the 1970s and 1980s, with little analysis of what constitutes sound macroeconomics.

In a study of contagion effects, Calvo and Reinhart (1996) confirm the importance of push factors in explaining capital movements. However, they go on to show that in addition to global factors, which tend to affect all capital-importing countries in a similar way, there are additional regional contagion effects which can work in both a positive and a negative direction. They also find that following the Mexican peso crisis in 1994–95 it was difficult to discover a link between the extent of contagion and economic fundamentals.[13] Colombia, with a large current account balance of payments deficit, was unaffected, while Brazil, with a smaller one, was affected. Some countries with fixed exchange rates (Argentina and Brazil), were affected, while others (Hong Kong and Thailand), were not, except for a very short time. Chile and Colombia escaped serious adverse consequences in spite of the fact that, like Mexico, they had experienced sharp real exchange rate appreciation. The Philippines, in spite of a managed floating exchange rate was hardest hit amongst Asian economies. In relation to the discussion in this chapter it is relevant that an apparently unifying theme across the countries which were most seriously affected by the Mexican crisis was their track record of poor macroeconomic management. It may take time to build enduring reputation.

Broadly speaking the evidence reported above is consistent with the claim that for as long as countries exhibit severely unsatisfactory macroeconomic policy and performance they will find themselves, in effect, ineligible to tap private international capital markets, and they may experience difficulties when international financial crises occur even for a time after macroeconomic policy and performance have improved: hence the effect of regime changes discovered by Montiel (1995) and Krugman (1995) and the distribution of contagion effects discovered by Calvo and Reinhart (1996). However, beyond this threshold of satisfaction, capital movements are not adequately explained by changes in domestic macroeconomics: assuming that these are captured by the proxies used in empirical studies such as country credit ratings. Indeed, global factors appear to be at least, if not usually more important, and, by definition, there is little that individual developing countries can do about these. In seeking to attract foreign capital, developing countries might reasonably conclude that they will be penalized for getting their domestic macroeconomics 'wrong' but may not be rewarded for getting it 'right'.

However, while the evidence is consistent with the idea that there will be no strong continuous relationship between a country's contemporary macroeconomic situation and capital flows, available empirical studies have not disaggregated between various components of macroeconomic policy and performance. Rather than testing the relationships in a formal way, Table 9.3 provides evidence relating to key macroeconomic indicators for six individual developing countries, Mexico, Brazil, Argentina, Malaysia, Indonesia and Thailand. Portfolio investment is used as a proxy for capital flows.

In Mexico portfolio investment rose sharply over 1989–93. Early in this period the rise occurred in spite of accelerating inflation. Later in the period it occurred in spite of a rapidly declining rate of economic growth and sharply deteriorating fiscal and current account balance of payments positions. It is difficult to account for the substantial increase in portfolio investment in 1993 in terms of key macroeconomic variables, although international reserves were being accumulated and this might have had a positive impact on perceived creditworthiness. In the Mexican case, the threshold of satisfaction seems to have been crossed at the beginning of the 1990s. Macroeconomic policy and performance were no longer deemed to be unsatisfactory, and capital inflows were no longer ruled out on these grounds. However, beyond this, changes in portfolio investment appear to have been little influenced by underlying contemporary macroeconomics. Portfolio flows increased when many aspects of macroeconomic performance were deteriorating. With the benefit of hindsight the basic macroeconomic data in 1993 foretold the Mexican peso crisis in 1994, although the data are not consistent with any obvious lag structure.

In Brazil, portfolio investment rose very rapidly in 1994 but fell back in 1995. But if it was the large reduction in inflation, rapid economic growth and improved fiscal position which encouraged capital inflows in 1994, why did the inflows decline in 1995 when inflation and economic growth performance were still good? A ready explanation is, of course, Brazil's exposure to a contagion effect from Mexico, and perhaps also the rapidly increasing

Table 9.3 Capital inflows and economic performance

	1985	1986	1987	1988	1989	1990	1991	1992	1993	1994	1995	1996
Mexico												
Inflation	57.7%	86.2%	131.8%	114.2%	20.0%	26.7%	22.7%	15.5%	9.8%	7.0%	35.0%	34.4%
Economic growth	2.2%	-3.1%	1.7%	1.3%	4.2%	5.1%	4.2%	3.6%	2.0%	4.5%	-6.2%	5.1%
Government finance	-3581	-10,341	-27,466	-37,843	-25,589	-19,436	-1900	15959	4156	-9927	-10,562	—
Deficit or surplus as per cent of current GDP	7.6%	-13.1%	-14.2%	-9.6%	-5.0%	-2.8%	-0.2%	1.5%	0.3%	-0.7%	-0.6%	—
Current account balance of payments	-1184.0	-2951.0	2328.0	-4629.0	-8368.0	-11,426.0	-17,634.0	-27,827.0	-27,040.0	-33,430.3	-4616.0	—
Exchange rate regime	MF	MF	MF	MF	MF	MF	MF	MF	MF	MF	IF	IF
Portfolio investment	-595.00	-517.00	-1,002.00	1,001.00	354.00	3,361.00	12,741.00	18,041.00	28,111.00	8,185.00	-10,140.00	—
Foreign direct investment	1984.00	2036.00	1184.00	2011.00	2785.00	2549.00	4742.00	4393.00	4389.00	10,972.00	6963.00	—
IMF programme in place	EA	SB	SB	SB	EA	EA	EA	EA			SB	SB
Brazil												
Inflation	226.9%	145.2%	221.7%	682.3%	1287.0%	2937.8%	440.9%	1008.7%	2148.4%	2668.5%	84.4%	18.2%
Economic growth	7.8%	7.5%	3.5%	-0.1%	3.2%	-4.6%	0.3%	-0.8%	4.2%	5.7%	—	—
Government finance	0.00	0.00	0.00	0.00	-0.07	-0.67	-0.26	-24.39	-1314.98	—	—	—
Deficit or surplus as per cent of current GDP	-11.1%	-13.3%	-12.0%	-15.2%	-18.6%	-6.2%	-0.4%	-3.9%	-9.3%	—	—	—
Current account balance of payments	-428.00	-5391.00	-1520.00	4065.00	781.00	-4622.00	-2964.00	3900.00	-1583.00	-3576.00	-21,757.00	—
Exchange rate regime	AI	AI	MF	AI	AI	IF	IF	IF	IF	IF	MF	MF
Portfolio investment	-234.00	-451.00	-428.00	-498.00	-391.00	579.00	3808.00	7366.00	12,928.00	47,784.00	10,171.00	—
Foreign direct investment	1441.00	345.00	1169.00	2804.00	1131.00	989.00	1103.00	2061.00	1292.00	3072.00	4,859.00	—
IMF programme in place	EA	SB	SB	SB	SB	EA	EA	SB			SB	SB
Argentina												
Inflation	672.1%	90.1%	131.3%	343.0%	3079.8%	2314.0%	171.7%	24.9%	10.6%	4.2%	3.4%	0.2%
Economic growth	-7.0%	7.1%	2.5%	-2.0%	-7.0%	-1.3%	10.5%	10.3%	6.3%	8.5%	-4.6%	4.4%
Government finance	-0.28	-0.24	-0.63	-1.49	-21.46	-226.06	-963.02	-73.00	-1574.00	-1885.70	—	—
Deficit or surplus as per cent of current GDP	-5.3%	-2.4%	-2.7%	-1.3%	-0.7%	-0.3%	-0.5%	0.0%	-0.6%	-0.7%	—	—
Current account balance of payments	-952.00	-2861.00	-4227.00	-1572.00	-1313.00	3554.00	-1440.00	-6076.00	-7925.00	-10,296.00	-2,878.00	-4347.00

Exchange rate regime	MF	MF	MF	MF	MF	IF	P$	P$	P$	P$	P$	P$
Portfolio investment	−617.00	−542.00	−572.00	−718.00	−1098.00	−1105.00	8227.00	1060.00	22,345.00	4772.00	5069.00	11,808.00
Foreign direct investment	919.00	574.00	−19.00	1147.00	1028.00	1836.00	2439.00	4045.00	2555.00	3068.00	4181.00	4285.00
IMF programme in place	SB	SB	SB	SB	SB	SB	SB	EA	EA	EA	EA	SB
Indonesia												
Inflation	4.7%	5.8%	9.3%	8.0%	6.4%	7.8%	9.4%	7.5%	9.7%	8.5%	9.4%	7.9%
Economic growth	2.5%	5.9%	4.9%	5.8%	7.5%	7.2%	7.0%	6.5%	6.5%	7.7%	8.2%	7.8%
Government finance	−948	−3621	−1037	−4388	−3362	798	982	−1096	2018	3580	10,084	—
Deficit or surplus as per cent of current GDP	−1.0%	−3.5%	−0.8%	−3.1%	−2.0%	0.4%	0.4%	−0.4%	0.6%	0.9%	2.2%	—
Current account balance of payments	−2011.00	−4170.00	−2355.00	−1651.00	−1447.00	−3406.00	−4522.00	−3351.00	−2643.00	−3411.00	−7862.00	—
Exchange rate regime	MF	MF	MF	MF	MF	MF	MF	MF	MF	MF	MF	MF
Portfolio investment	−35.00	268.00	−88.00	−98.00	−173.00	−93.00	−12.00	−88.00	1805.00	3877.00	4100.00	—
Foreign direct investment	310.00	258.00	385.00	576.00	682.00	1093.00	1482.00	1777.00	2004.00	2109.00	4348.00	—
IMF programme in place												
Malaysia												
Inflation	0.3%	0.7%	0.3%	2.6%	2.8%	2.6%	4.4%	4.8%	3.5%	3.7%	5.3%	3.5%
Economic growth	−1.0%	1.0%	5.4%	8.9%	9.2%	9.7%	8.4%	7.8%	8.3%	9.2%	9.5%	
Government finance	−5708	−7506	−6153	−3891	−5260	−5515	−5640	−6243	354	4408	1860	
Deficit or surplus as per cent of current GDP	−7.4%	−10.5%	−7.7%	−4.3%	−5.1%	−4.8%	−4.4%	−4.2%	0.2%	2.4%	—	
Current account balance of payments	−607.32	−159.99	2497.98	1658.79	176.83	−971.95	−4271.17	−2339.26	−3278.43	−4749.54	−7509.97	
Exchange rate regime	CC	CC	CC	CC	CC	CC	CC	CC	CC	MF	MF	
Portfolio investment	1941.57	29.83	139.70	−447.92	−107.06	−254.73	170.18	−1122.33	−708.60	−1649.23	−439.63	
Foreign direct investment	694.71	488.87	422.68	719.42	1667.87	2332.46	3998.45	5183.36	5005.64	4341.80	4131.52	
IMF programme in place												
Thailand												
Inflation	2.4%	1.8%	2.5%	3.8%	5.4%	6.0%	5.7%	4.1%	3.4%	5.2%	5.7%	5 8%
Economic growth	4.6%	5.5%	9.5%	13.3%	12.2%	11.6%	8.4%	7.8%	8.3%	8.8%	8.6%	
Government finance	−55	−48	−29	11	55	99	118	80	66	67	123	—

Table 9.3 (Contd.)

	1985	1986	1987	1988	1989	1990	1991	1992	1993	1994	1995	1996
Deficit or surplus as per cent of current GDP	-5.2%	-4.2%	-2.2%	0.7%	2.9%	4.5%	4.7%	2.8%	2.1%	1.9%	3.0%	—
Current account balance of payments	-1702.57	22.30	-590.25	-1890.65	-2744.20	-7494.43	-7832.39	-6949.04	-7113.26	-9212.98	-14040.53	—
Exchange rate regime	CC	CC	CC	CC	CC	CC	CC	CC	CC	CC	CC	CC
Portfolio investment	894.98	-29.49	345.86	530.07	1486.23	-38.09	-81.06	924.36	5455.36	2486.24	4082.95	
Foreign direct investment	163.20	262.51	351.93	1105.38	1775.46	2443.56	2014.00	2113.03	1804.09	1366.45	2067.99	
IMF programme in place	SB	SB										—

Inflation: per cent changes in the CPI
Economic growth: per cent change in real GDP
Government finance: deficit (−) or surplus in billions of national currency
Current account balance of payments: trade, service and income in millions of US dollars
Portfolio investment: portfolio liabilities in millions of US dollars
Foreign direct investment: direct investment into the country in millions of US dollars
Exchange rate regime:
 MF: Managed float
 AI: Adjusted according to a set of indicators
 IF: Independently floating
 CC: Pegged to a composite currency
 P$: Pegged to the US dollar
IMF programme in place:
 SB: Stand-by arrangement
 EA: Extended arrangement
 ESA: Enhanced structural adjustment arrangement
Exchange rate regime as of September of that year, except '85 and '86 as of November of that year
IMF programmes as of November of that year.

Source: International Financial Statistics, IMF.

current account balance of payments deficit. Certainly, the Brazilian example illustrates that good inflation and growth performance does not guarantee capital inflows in the form of portfolio investment.

The sharp increase in portfolio investment in Argentina in 1993 is difficult to explain given the weak fiscal situation, but may have represented a response to a perceived commitment by the government to economic reform. For some reason macroeconomic policy remained credible in spite of a growing fiscal deficit. Indeed it was in 1994, at the same time as there was a significant fiscal improvement, that portfolio investment fell. Economic growth remained rapid, and it again seems that a contagion effect from Mexico was probably at work. Portfolio investment picked up a little in 1995, even though economic growth was significantly negative.

In Indonesia an eye-catching feature of macroeconomic performance over 1985–95 was the rapid rate of economic growth. However, it was only after the fiscal deficit was eliminated in 1992 that portfolio investment became positive for any sustained length of time.

Malaysia also reveals strong macroeconomic performance over a protracted time period, with low inflation and rapid economic growth. However, even the elimination of fiscal deficits after 1991 failed to generate portfolio investment. The only year over the period 1988–95 when portfolio investment was positive was 1991 and this coincided with a sharp acceleration in inflation, a declining rate of economic growth (albeit still at 8.6 per cent), an increasing fiscal deficit, and a big increase in the current account balance of payments deficit.

In Thailand, it is similarly difficult to explain changes in portfolio investment purely in terms of changes in conventional macroeconomic indicators. These suggest that macroeconomic performance was strong throughout the post-1988 period. However low inflation, rapid economic growth and fiscal rectitude did not result in portfolio investment until 1993. Apart from an increasing current account deficit, there is again little in the data in Table 9.3 that explains the decline in portfolio investment in 1994. Perhaps Thailand also experienced some early contagion from Mexico but this, itself, is difficult to explain in terms of economic fundamentals.[14]

This empirical exercise is interesting more for what it does not show than for what it does. Across a range of randomly selected developing countries it does not show any clear connection between key macroeconomic indicators and private capital inflows in the form of portfolio investment. Changes in portfolio investment do not seem to be easily reconciled to changes in key macroeconomic variables. Even reducing fiscal deficits, which may be taken to reflect the stance of government macroeconomic policy, seems to be relevant in some cases but not all of them.

Variations in the response to changing fiscal deficits could either imply that investors are unsure how to interpret them, or that they recognize that the fiscal position is only one part of the macroeconomic picture. Changing fiscal balances may themselves have a range of causes, not all of which have equivalent implications for the future. A fiscal deficit may, for example, be reduced by state divestiture, while leaving government expenditure and tax revenue unaffected, or by broadening the tax base and by improving rates of collection. Furthermore, the effects of fiscal deficits depend on the macroeconomic circumstances within which they occur. While there is evidence that fiscal deficits are frequently a central cause of macroeconomic disequilibria in developing countries (Easterly and Schmidt-Hebbel, 1993) this need not, in principle, always be the case.[15]

The evidence presented here is therefore consistent with the findings of econometric studies which emphasize the importance of 'push' factors and contagion effects, as well as other studies which suggest that regime changes may be important in spite of the fact that they have not filtered through into any discernible improvement in overall macroeconomic performance.

Moreover, across the range of countries examined, the involvement of the IMF does not emerge as a significant factor. There is little indication here that private capital markets put much credence on it.[16]

The notion that while private capital markets remain uncertain as to how to interpret a nuanced economic picture, 'they know a bad one when they see one', finds some support in the markets' attitude towards the countries in transition (CITs). In general these economies exhibited poor economic performance throughout the early 1990s with very rapid rates of inflation, negative rates of economic growth and weakening current accounts in the balance of payments. This, combined with doubts about the sustainability of economic policy reform within such an economic environment, provided a strong disincentive to private capital inflows. In the context of these economies, the involvement of the IMF again seems to have failed to generate a positive catalytic effect.

While the adoption of policies based on the 'Washington consensus' which includes stricter macroeconomic policy, was associated with a surge of private capital into Latin America, a similar policy commitment apparently lacked credibility in the context of many CITs.

The empirical evidence presented here appears to be consistent with the idea that private capital markets will penalize countries that allow severe macroeconomic instability to arise. In this respect countries seeking private capital inflows need to avoid getting the macroeconomics wrong.[17] However, given the ambiguities over what is good macroeconomics, it is much more difficult to exert a positive effect on capital flows simply through macroeconomic policy and performance. There is an underlying asymmetry. Avoiding severe macroeconomic mismanagement and instability may be a necessary condition in order to attract private capital from abroad but it is not a sufficient condition, at least in the short run.

To some extent individual investors may defer their judgement to the credit rating agencies. But the same fundamental problems associated with assessing macroeconomic performance, policy and prospects are encountered by them as well.

The data in Table 9.3 also confirm the suspicion that foreign direct investment will be influenced by different factors than portfolio investment, since the trends in the two types of investment do not match; an observation reinforced by the aggregate data in Table 9.1. Changing macroeconomic policy and performance should not therefore be expected to have uniform implications for all forms of capital flows.

Empirical evidence does not suggest any straightforward winning formula by which developing countries may set out to attract foreign capital. Whereas allowing severe and unsustainable macroeconomic disequilibria to arise, as reflected by rapid inflation and by large fiscal imbalances, will be unattractive and will generally have negative effects, correcting them does not guarantee attractiveness. The empirical evidence confirms the *a priori* reasoning that beyond a threshold additional efforts to strengthen macroeconomic policy and performance may not yield a high rate of return in terms of attracting capital inflows.

Concluding remarks

Many developing countries face deficiencies of domestic saving and foreign exchange. With foreign aid declining in real terms it becomes increasingly important to ask what they can do to attract private capital. Without capital inflows, shortages of external financing are likely to constitute an effective constraint on economic development. Within this context a key question is 'how important is it to get the macroeconomics right?'. Can developing countries expect to be rewarded for improved macroeconomic performance by capital inflows? Clearly if they can, there is an additional incentive to seek such improvement.

However, the analysis in this chapter suggests that there will be no short-run pay-off to improved macroeconomics, beyond a point at which severe macroeconomic disequilibria are eliminated. Whereas there are predictable penalties for getting the macroeconomics badly wrong, there are no equivalently predictable rewards for getting it 'right'. In large measure this is the consequence of the ambiguities surrounding what is sound macroeconomics. Macroeconomics is simply too uncertain to encourage investors to attach deterministic weights to indicators of macroeconomic policy and performance. For as long as these uncertainties remain, it is difficult to see how domestic macroeconomics will become a dominant factor in explaining capital flows. Where individual investors attach a heavy weight to macroeconomic variables they do so in the absence of strong scientific justification.[18] Herd behaviour among investors does not therefore reflect universal agreement on the underlying macroeconomics. Instead it reflects just the opposite; uncertainty and a reluctance to be isolated or left behind.

Similarly, contagion effects often confirm the absence of informed scientific judgement, which opens the door to waves of optimism and pessimism and to speculative crises.

In these circumstances it is unrealistic to expect that the better provision of macroeconomic data by countries or the more open interpretation of such data by the IFIs will have a strong impact on international capital flows. Volatility is likely to remain a key feature of international capital markets which are driven by unstable short-term expectations and by outside global factors. The added twist is, of course, that such volatility is itself destabilizing.

Apart from working towards gaining a better understanding of macro-economic relationships, international public policy needs to cater for the intrinsic instability of private capital flows, and this delineates a role for international financial institutions. In part this role should be to assist countries in avoiding severe macroeconomic disequilibria. However, the problem here is that countries usually turn to the IFIs in conditions of macroeconomic crisis when private capital is already making its exit. Ways need to be found for the IFIs to monitor performance, and to increase their direct involvement before crises have developed. By averting crises and by increasing the commitment of governments to avoid future macroeconomic mismanagement, the IFIs could have a beneficial effect on private capital flows.

By the same token, however, it is unreasonable to expect too much from detailed policy conditionality which also lacks secure scientific credentials. Its apparent failures undermine rather than strengthen the catalytic effect.

A final policy conclusion is that even where policy and performance in developing countries avoid severe macroeconomic disequilibria, international financial institutions will continue to have a role to play in providing external finance. Indeed, given the nature of recent financial crises, the (potential) lending role of IFIs (in particular the IMF) needs to be expanded. Downsizing their lending role will have the effect of further exposing developing countries to the unavoidable instabilities associated with private capital markets and of weakening the incentive for governments to persist in their efforts to strengthen domestic macroeconomic fundamentals.

References

Allen, C., Currie, D., Srinivasan, T. and Vines, D. (1992). 'Policy interactions between OECD countries and Latin America in the 1980', *The Manchester School*, **60**, 1–20.

Bird, G. (1989). *Commercial Bank Lending and Third World Debt*. London: Macmillan, ch. 1 and 2.

Bird, G. (1994). 'The myths and reality of IMF lending', *The World Economy*, **17**(5), 759–78.

Bird, G. (1998). 'Exchange rate policy in developing countries: what is left of the nominal anchor approach?', *Third World Quarterly*, **19**(2), 255–76.

Bird, G. and Rowlands, D. (1997). 'The catalytic effect of lending by the international financial institutions', *The World Economy*, **20**(7), 967–92.

Blomstrom, M., Lipsey, R. E. and Zejan, M. (1996). 'Is fixed investment the key to economic growth', *Quarterly Journal of Economics*, **CXI**(1), 209–16.

Calvo, G. A. (1996). 'Capital flows and macroeconomic management: tequila lessons', *International Journal of Finance and Economics*, **1**(3), 207–24.

Calvo, G. A., Leiderman, L. and Reinhart, C. M. (1993). 'Capital inflows and real exchange rate appreciation in Latin America: the role of external factors', *IMF Staff Chapters*, **40**(1), 108–51.

Calvo, G. A., Leiderman, L. and Reinhart, C. M. (1996). 'Inflows of capital to developing countries in the 1990s', *Journal of Economic Perspectives*, **10**(2), 125–39.

Calvo, S. and Reinhart, C. (1996). 'Capital flows in Latin America: is there evidence of contagion effects?', *Policy Research Working Papers*, 1619. Washington, DC: The World Bank.

Cardoso, E. A. and Dornbusch, R. (1989). 'Foreign private capital flows'. In Chenery, H. and Srinivasan, T. N. (eds), *Handbook of Development Economics*, **11**.

Chuhan, P., Claessens, S. and Mamingi, N. (1993). 'Equity and bond flows to Asia and Latin America'. *Policy Research Working Papers*, No. 1160. Washington, DC: The World Bank.

Claessens, S., Dooley, M. and Warner, A. (1995). 'Portfolio capital flows: hot or cold?', *The World Bank Economic Review*, **9**.

Corbo, V. and Hernandez, L. (1996). 'Macroeconomic adjustment to capital inflows: lessons from recent Latin American and East Asian Experience', *World Bank Research Observer*, **11**(1), 61–85.

Corden, M. (1993). 'Exchange rate policies for developing countries', *Economic Journal*, **105**(423), 198–207.

Daveri, F. (1995). 'Costs of entry and exit from financial markets and capital flows to developing countries', *World Development*, **23**, 1375–85.

Dornbusch, R. (1992). 'The case for trade liberalisation in developing countries', *Journal of Economic Perspectives*, **6**(1), 69–85.

Easterly, W., Kremer, M., Pritchett, L. and Summers, L. H. (1993). 'Good policy or good luck? Country growth performance and temporary shocks', *Journal of Monetary Economics*, **32**, 459–83.

Easterly, W. and Schmidt-Hebbel, K. (1993). 'Fiscal deficits and macroeconomic performance in developing countries', *World Bank Research Observer*, **8**(2), 211–38.

Fanneli, J., Frenkel, M. R. and Taylor, L. (1994). 'Is the market-friendly approach friendly to development: a critical assessment'. In Bird, G. and Helwege, A. (eds), *Latin America's Economic Future*. New York: Academic Press.

Fernandez-Arias, E. (1996), 'The new wave of capital inflows: push or pull?', *Journal of Development Economics*, **48**(2), 389–418.

Fernandez-Arias, E. and Montiel, P. J. (1996). 'The surge in capital inflows to developing countries: an analytical overview', *The World Bank Economic Review*, **10**, 51–77.

Garber, P. M. (1996). 'Managing risks to financial markets from volatile capital flows: the role of prudential regulation', *International Journal of Finance and Economics*, **1**(3), 183–96.

Goldstein, M., Mathieson, D. J. and Lane, T. (1991). 'Determinants and systemic consequences of international capital flows'. In *Determinants and Systemic Consequence of International Capital Flows*, March, Occasional Paper No. 77. Washington, DC: International Monetary Fund.

Graham, E. M. (1995). 'Foreign direct investment in the world economy'. In *Staff Studies for the World Economic Outlook*, Washington, DC: IMF.

Greene, J. and Villaneuva, D. (1991). 'Private investment in developing countries: an empirical analysis', *IMF Staff Papers*, **38**(1), 33–58.

Guttentag, J. M. and Herring, R. J. (1986). 'Disaster myopia in international banking', *Essays in International Finance*, No. 164, Princeton.

Haque, N. ul, Kumar, M. S., Mark, N. and Matthiesen, D. J. (1996). 'The economic content of indicators of developing country creditworthiness', *IMF Staff Papers*, **43**(4), 68–723.

IMF, (1995). 'Saving in a growing world economy'. In *World Economic Outlook*. Washington, DC: IMF.

Killick, T. (1995). *IMF Programmes in Developing Countries: Design and Impact*. London: Routledge.

Krugman, P. (1994). *Peddling Prosperity: Economic Sense and Nonsense in the Age of Diminished Expectations*. New York: W. W. Norton.

Krugman, P. (1995). 'Dutch tulips and emerging markets', *Foreign Affairs*, **28**(4), 28–44.

Krugman, P. (1998). 'What happened to Asia?', mimeographed, January.

Malkiel, B. G. (1990). *A Random Walk Down Wall Street*. New York: W. W. Norton.

Mankiw, N. G. (1995), 'The growth of nations', *Brookings Papers on Economic Activity*, No. 1.

Milesi-Ferretti, M. G. and Razin, A. (1996). Current account sustainability, *Princeton Studies in International Finance*, No. 81.

Montiel, P. J. (1995). 'The new wave of capital inflows: country policy chronologies', mimeographed, Oberlin College, Department of Economics, Oberlin, Ohio.

Obstfeld, M. (1995). 'International capital mobility in the 1990s'. In Kenen, P. B. (ed.) *Understanding Interdependence: The Macroeconomics of the Open Economy*. Princeton: Princeton University Press.

Radelet, S. and Sachs, J. (1998). 'The East Asian financial crisis: diagnosis, remedies, prospects, mimeographed', *Brookings Papers on Economic Activity*, **1**, 1–75.

Rodrik, D. (1992). 'The limits of trade policy reform in developing countries', *Journal of Economic Perspectives*, **6**(1), 87–105.

Rodrik, D. (1996). 'Understanding economic policy reform', *Journal of Economic Literature*, **XXXIV**(1), 9–41.

Sachs, J. D., Tornell, A. and Velasco, A. (1995). 'The collapse of the Mexican peso: what have we learned?', *NBER Working Paper*, No. 5142, June.

Sachs, J. D. and Warner, A. M. (1995a). 'Natural resource abundance and economic growth', Harvard Institute for International Development, mimeographed, December.

Schadler, S., Carkovic, M., Bennett, A. and Kahn, R. (1993). 'Recent experiences with surges in capital inflows', *IMF Occasional Paper*, **108**, December.

Taylor, M. P. and Sarno, L. (1997). 'Capital flows to developing countries: long term and short term determinants', *World Bank Economic Review*, **11**(3).

Williamson, J. (1993). 'Issues posed by portfolio investment in developing countries'. In Claessens, S. and Gooptu, S. (eds), Portfolio Investment in Developing Countries, *World Bank Discussion Papers*, Washington, DC: The World Bank.

World Bank (1991). *World Development Report*, Washington, DC: World Bank.

Young, A. (1995). 'The tyranny of numbers: confronting the statistical realities of the East Asian growth experience', *Quarterly Journal of Economics*, 641–80.

10
Convertibility and Volatility: The Pros and Cons of Liberalising the Capital Account

Graham Bird

The late 1990s have seen an interesting juxtaposition between international financial crises in Latin America and East Asia involving a high degree of capital volatility, on the one hand, and the pursuit of capital account liberalisation by the International Monetary Fund on the other. A natural question is whether it makes sense to encourage capital account liberalisation at a time when capital movements seem either to have created or at least to have contributed to financial crises. The logic behind free capital convertibility in such circumstances is not immediately obvious; indeed intuition points in the opposite direction.

The purpose of this chapter is to present succinctly and assess briefly both the arguments for and against capital convertibility in order to evaluate the wisdom of the IMF's policy initiative on liberalising the capital account.

The chapter is organised in the following way. The section on capital flows provides a summary of recent capital flows to developing countries identifying key features. The next section analyses the principal arguments for and against capital convertibility. The section titled 'Assessing the arguments', assesses these arguments in the light of recent experience. The next section examines various mechanisms for regulating capital flows, while the final section offers a few concluding remarks on the political economy of capital account liberalisation.

Capital flows to developing countries

Table 10.1, taken from the World Bank's *Global Development Finance 1998* (GDF, 1998), provides data on net long-term resource flows to developing countries over the period 1990–97. Over the period as a whole, and while official development finance (foreign aid) declined from $56.4 billion in 1990 to $44.2 billion in 1997, total private flows rose sharply by more than 500 per cent from $41.9 billion to $256.0 billion. Clearly private capital became an increasingly important source of international finance for developing

Table 10.1   Net long-term resource flows to developing countries (billion U.S. dollars)

Type of flow	1990	1991	1992	1993	1994	1995	1996	1997[a]
All developing countries	98.3	116.3	143.9	208.1	206.2	243.1	281.6	300.3
Official development finance	56.4	62.7	53.8	53.6	45.5	54.0	34.7	44.2
Grants	29.2	35.1	30.5	28.4	32.7	32.6	29.2	25.1
Loans	27.2	27.6	23.3	25.1	12.9	21.4	5.4	19.2
Bilateral	11.6	13.3	11.1	10.0	2.5	10.0	−7.2	1.8
Multilateral	15.6	14.4	12.2	15.2	10.4	11.3	12.6	17.4
Total private flows	41.9	53.6	90.1	154.6	160.6	189.1	246.9	256.0
Debt flows	15.0	13.5	33.8	44.0	41.1	55.1	82.2	103.2
Commercial blank loans	3.8	3.4	13.1	2.8	8.9	29.3	34.2	41.1
Bonds	0.1	7.4	8.3	31.8	27.5	23.8	45.7	53.8
Other	11.1	2.7	12.4	9.4	4.7	2.0	2.3	8.3
Foreign direct investment	23.7	32.9	45.3	65.6	86.9	101.5	119.0	120.4
Portfolio equity flows	3.2	7.2	11.0	45.0	32.6	32.5	45.8	32.5

Note: Developing countries are defined as low- and middle-income countries with 1995 per capita incomes of less than $765 (low) and $9385 (middle).
[a] Preliminary.
Source: *Global Development Finance 1998*.

countries. By 1997 it was more than five times as important as foreign aid as a source of funds for them.

However, when the data are decomposed, what also emerges from the table is that certain types of private capital flow are very unstable, even on an annualised basis which understates the extent of instability. Commercial bank loans that rose strongly from $3.4 billion in 1991 to $13.1 billion in 1992 fell away even more quickly to a mere $2.8 billion in 1993. Portfolio equity flows that rose rapidly in 1993, fell in 1994 and (much less so) in 1995, but then increased by more than $13 billion between 1995 and 1996, rising from $32.5 billion to $45.8 billion, only to fall back again by exactly the same amount in 1997.

Instability is also a feature within individual years. As *GDF 1998* graphically reports, for emerging markets with access to private capital flows, 1997 was a 'rollercoaster year' (*IMF Survey*, Vol. 27, No. 7, April 6, 1998, p. 103).

Bonds are no exception to the general rule of volatility and show a similarly unstable path, rising up until 1993, falling back in 1994 and 1995 and then rising again in 1996 and 1997. The only component of private lending that shows stable growth throughout the period is foreign direct investment, which rose from $23.7 billion in 1990 to $120.4 billion in 1997.

While indicating the instability of private capital flows to developing countries, Table 10.1 does not show the extent to which these flows are concentrated in a small group of countries. In fact, throughout the 1990–97 period, the share of the top twelve countries never fell below 72.5 per cent and sometimes (in 1992) rose to as much as 87.4 per cent of total private flows. For sub-Saharan African economies there were *net outflows* of private capital in 1992 and 1993, and only relatively modest inflows for the rest of the period. The data therefore broadly show the following pattern; a strong upward trend in private capital flows to developing countries, considerable instability about that trend, and a wide dispersion in the distribution of private capital between developing countries.

Free capital mobility: arguments for and against

Arguments for

There are a number of arguments that may be assembled favouring free capital mobility. First, there is the claim that it allows capital to be allocated in a globally efficient way by flowing towards countries which offer the highest rate of return. World output and economic growth will be maximised if capital goes to where its marginal productivity is greatest. Controls that interfere with the free movement of capital will therefore constrain global economic growth.

Second, controls will, in any case, not work, as efforts will be made to circumvent them. In part these efforts may involve corruption. At the very least capital controls will encourage unproductive rent-seeking activity. Furthermore, to the extent that controls are motivated by a desire to protect a weak domestic financial sector, or to defend unsound domestic economic policies, any 'success' that they have will in fact represent a failure.

A third argument advanced for free capital mobility is that capital movements will effectively police domestic economic policy by rewarding good policy and penalising bad policy. Taken to extremes this argument could be presented as an argument for closing down the IMF. Relying on private international capital markets involves 'hidden conditionality' since potential borrowers will know the sorts of policies that will attract or repel international capital, and in these circumstances the Fund's involvement will simply distort the efficient global allocation of a capital, by providing resources to countries that private capital markets have deemed uncreditworthy.

Fourth, while attempting to avoid macroeconomic disequilibria, developing and emerging economies may rationally choose to smooth consumption over time. Access to international capital enables them to do this. Moreover, to the extent that economic development is constrained by shortages of foreign exchange, free capital mobility relaxes the constraint and facilitates faster economic growth and development.

Finally, from the lenders' perspective, free capital mobility confers on them the right to choose where they will place their funds. This allows them to minimise risks through portfolio diversification, as well as to maximise the return on their portfolio.

Arguments against

Liberalising the capital account might be appropriate in a 'first best' world. Arguments against it hinge largely on the claim that this world does not exist. Distortions are to be found in a number of areas. Private international capital markets are subject to market failure. Capital mobility in the presence of trade distortions, differential tax treatment across countries, and differences in prudential regulation can lead to the global misallocation of capital. Trade protection may distort the estimated rate of return to domestic investment in an upward direction which encourages excess capital inflows. These in turn may mean that there is an inefficient use of domestic resources as capital intensity is favoured over labour-intensity. A similar upward bias may be created by relatively lax taxation or regulation. The efficiency argument for free capital mobility therefore presupposes that these distortions have been harmonised. In the absence of harmonisation, the second-best solution may be that controls over capital markets are used to neutralise the effects of other distortions.

Even where no trade, tax, or regulatory distortions exist, there can be no presumption that capital will be globally allocated to where it yields the highest rate of return. While it depends somewhat on the type of capital involved, there is no generally adequate theoretical basis for explaining capital flows. The empirical evidence is that bank lending, bonds and portfolio investment are influenced by a combination of 'pull' and 'push' factors. Relative interest rates that are dictated by the international stance of short-run monetary policies, levels of economic activity, and expected exchange rate changes, all have a part to play. But these influences do not guarantee that capital will be allocated efficiently.[1] With imperfect capital markets, interest rates will not necessarily reflect the marginal productivity of capital. Capital flows may be influenced by speculation more than by economic fundamentals. The fact that fundamentals normally change relatively slowly, whereas the pattern of capital flows is unstable, suggests that fundamentals are not the driving force, and that capital markets are myopic.

Big swings in international capital flows suggest that investors are influenced more by cosmetic factors and by what others are doing. In this way, speculative bubbles build up and then burst as the mood of the market changes. Creditors make lending decisions not on the basis of a scientific analysis of expected relative rates of return but rather on the basis of a desire not to be out of step with everyone else. International lending may therefore be as much psychological as it is economic; but psychology does not guarantee an efficient allocation of global savings. The tendency for creditors' views to cluster in this way eliminates the broader distribution of opinion that would otherwise stabilise international lending. Even where fundamentals are significant in determining capital flows, the outcome will tend to be pro-cyclical and therefore destabilising. Countries with high domestic savings rates and strong economic growth will, for example, be more attractive than those with low savings rates and slow economic growth. Private markets will therefore direct resources to countries at times when their need is less, and away from them when their need is greater. A loss of liquidity consequent on (say) a shortfall in export revenue will result in capital outflows, and a further loss of liquidity which then makes the economic situation weaker.

Next, there are pronounced 'externalities' in international lending. There are positive and negative contagion effects. These exist, for example, where troubles in one country make lenders less willing to lend to other countries that are geographically proximate; even where there are no strong economic inter-linkages between them.

Contagion effects again challenge the whole idea that private international capital markets allocate global savings efficiently. Furthermore, waves of optimism and pessimism in capital markets may be self-fulfilling. With flexible exchange rates, expectations of exchange rate depreciation may lead to heavy selling which then drives down the value of the currency and creates fundamental problems in terms of inflation, which retrospectively justifies the depreciation, and in terms of recession, which may be induced by the high interest rates adopted in an attempt to stabilise the value of the currency.

To the extent that capital movements affect as well as reflect economic fundamentals, capital convertibility may be interpreted as being incompatible with flexible exchange rates.

But is this not all too negative? Is capital account liberalisation not simply a natural extension to trade liberalisation which few deny enhances global economic welfare? In fact, of course, there is some debate about exactly how great the benefits are from trade liberalisation (Dornbusch, 1992; Rodrik, 1992). More importantly there are significant differences between the current account and the capital account of the balance of payments. For a start, capital flows are much larger than trade flows. Capital movements are heavily influenced by changes in expectations which are themselves elastic and narrowly distributed amongst creditors. Financial assets within a specific group of countries tend to be highly substitutable, so that arbitrage is encouraged. The bottom line is that, whereas we rarely experience international trade crises, we do experience international financial crises. Liberalising the capital account is not therefore simply a natural extension of current account liberalisation.

Finally, free capital mobility may have distributional consequences if enhanced private capital flows are seen as meeting the systemic needs of developing countries for external financing. Where private capital markets accurately assess risk, countries without access to private capital will be those that are uncreditworthy. Capital account liberalisation may then have incentivising effects as countries are encouraged to pursue policies which increase their creditworthiness. But where private capital markets miscalculate risks a sub-optimal distribution of capital will result, and the incentive effects will not necessarily encourage appropriate policies.

Moreover, is it always desirable that countries deemed uncreditworthy by private capital markets have no access to external financing? This is, in principle, where foreign aid fills a gap left by private international capital markets. But what if increased private capital flows, facilitated by capital account liberalisation, are perceived by donors as meeting the external financing needs of developing countries as a whole? Certainly, increasing private capital flows during the 1990s coincided with falling aid flows. Now if private capital goes to one group of countries (the better-off developing countries), whereas aid goes to another (the poorest developing countries), the changing composition of resource flows will have important distributional consequences that disadvantage low income countries. Furthermore, low income countries will be adversely affected alongside other developing and emerging economies where international financial crises, which are in part caused by capital volatility, lead to global economic recession.

Assessing the arguments

At present it is not possible to provide a full and measured assessment of all the issues raised in the debate about capital account liberalisation. In the absence of a first best solution, it is difficult to say which is the best of the second best solutions. Which is the preferable set of distortions? Moreover, the regulation of capital flows can take on various forms, and again it is not clear as to which form is preferable. However, there is some evidence relating to free capital mobility and capital controls upon which to draw.

Casual empiricism during the 1990s reveals a number of features of private capital flows. First, they are unstable; this implies that they are not strongly related to economic fundamentals or to underlying productivities. Flows of private capital to Latin America in the early 1990s were as much to do with interest rates and economic activity in the United States as they were to do with the economic fundamentals in Latin America (Calvo, Leiderman and Reinhart, 1993). In many respects the move out of recession in the U.S. strengthened the economic fundamentals in Latin America, and yet it led to a capital outflow from the region. Similarly, it is unreasonable to try and explain the rapid turnaround in private capital flows to East Asia in 1996–97 in terms of economic fundamentals. Rather than fulfilling a stabilising role, capital flows are often destabilising, with excessive inflows causing as many problems as excessive outflows.

Evidence from the Mexican peso crisis and East Asian crisis is inconsistent with the argument that markets are forward-looking, basing lending decisions on rational expectations. Instead, there is much more casual support for the claim that markets are poor at assessing long-term risks, and that they take a short-term view based on current market sentiment which leads to herd behaviour. Spreads have been found not to increase in advance of crises, and rating agencies do not downgrade countries until crises have already begun.

The behaviour of international capital markets can, however, affect economic fundamentals in a way that makes short-term expectations self-fulfilling in the long run. There are therefore 'multiple equilibria', and expectations influence which of these is forthcoming.

The Mexican and East Asian crises also provide evidence for the existence of contagion effects that are not fully explained in terms of economic fundamentals (Calvo and Reinhart, 1996). There are bandwagon effects based on psychological regionalisation. This is again inconsistent with the claim that markets are efficient. Psychological contagion does not lead to an efficient global allocation of capital.

Furthermore, it is difficult to find any convincing evidence that free capital mobility both rewards 'good' and penalises 'bad' policy behaviour and economic performance. This is unsurprising given the ambiguities relating to these concepts.[2] While 'really bad' policies and performance may be self-evident, it is difficult to make more nuanced judgements outside this range. While capital markets may, therefore, penalise really bad economic policies, they may not penalise less bad ones, and certainly may fail to reward good ones (and increasingly good ones). Reflecting this, capital flowed into Mexico when its fiscal deficit was significantly larger (relative to GDP) than that in most East Asian economies at a time when capital was flowing away from them. Of course the size of the fiscal deficit is a poor indicator when examined in isolation. At the very least, it needs to be assessed relative to the balance between private sector saving and investment.

Another conventional economic indicator is the exchange rate. But it is notoriously difficult to calculate fundamental equilibrium exchange rates and therefore the *extent* of currency misalignments. Private capital continued to flow into Mexico and Thailand over a period when, retrospectively, their currencies were almost certainly overvalued. Capital flows did little to police exchange rate policy, and, if anything, contributed to fundamental disequilibrium, especially given that the capital tended to move out as quickly as it moved in, leading to exchange rate overshooting.

Evidence from the 1990s, therefore, provides little optimism that free capital mobility will have the consequences that advocates claim. There can be little presumption that capital account liberalisation will contribute to resolving the sorts of international financial problems encountered during the 1990s.

But what about the evidence on the use of capital controls? On the basis of a survey of the available literature on the effects of capital controls, Dooley (1996) concludes that they generally appear to have little power to influence variables such as the volume and composition of private capital flows, changes in international reserves, and the exchange rate. 'In particular', he claims, 'there is little evidence that controls have proved capable of heading off successful speculative attacks on inconsistent policy regimes' (p. 680). However, these conclusions may be interpreted in different ways. Almost by definition controls will not head off 'successful' speculative attacks, otherwise they would not be successful. Moreover, a concern associated with free capital mobility is that it may threaten consistent policy regimes. Finally, the observation that controls 'generally' have 'little power' does not rule out the possibility that they may be useful in some specific circumstances. There is evidence, for example, that Chile was to some extent able to insulate itself from the contagion effects of the Mexican peso crisis through its use of capital controls, and that the East Asian economies most exposed to contagion were those that had liberalised their capital accounts.[3] Even the suggestion that controls have little power suggests that their *adverse* consequences will be insignificant. If advocates of capital account liberalisation are to argue that it will have significant beneficial effects, they must also claim that capital controls have significant adverse effects; the evidence is not consistent with this. Rodrik (1998) examines the relationship between the degree of capital account liberalisation and three indicators of economic performance: per capita GNP growth, the investment rate, and inflation. In short he concludes that, 'capital controls are essentially uncorrelated with long-term economic performance once we control for other determinants' (p. 61).

The evidence might be interpreted as meaning that capital account liberalisation is an irrelevance; it will not be of much benefit, but it will do little harm. However, the available empirical evidence on the effects capital controls covers the period prior to the 1990s. Given that capital volatility, contagion, and myopic behaviour by private capital markets have characterised the 1990s, it may be legitimate to assume that data from the 1990s will be less neutral about the effects of capital account liberalisation.

Broadly speaking, the evidence offers little support for the idea that full capital account convertibility should be imposed on all countries. The theoretical arguments for this are only imprecisely defined, and the empirical evidence in favour of capital account liberalisation is uncompelling. Although capital controls have disadvantages and limitations they may represent a useful policy instrument in some circumstances.

It is difficult to sustain the argument that capital account liberalisation will reduce the incidence of international financial crises such as those experienced in Mexico in 1994–95 and East Asia in 1997–98. Indeed the evidence is more consistent with the claim that the potency of these crises was enhanced by capital liberalisation.

Handling volatility and regulating capital flows

How can countries avoid the sorts of financial crises that have been seen in Mexico and in East Asia? The short answer is 'with difficulty'.

While capital inflows may help to fill domestic savings gaps and facilitate economic growth that then provides the resources to service and pay back the loans, things are rarely this straightforward. If the capital-importing country is trying to keep a pegged exchange rate – perhaps as a way of reducing inertial inflation – capital inflows will lead to an increase in the domestic money supply, as the central bank buys foreign exchange, and inflation will accelerate. If the government then tries to sterilise the effects of the foreign exchange intervention by issuing bonds, this will keep interest rates high and perpetuate the capital inflows. If it unpegs the exchange rate, the value of the currency will rise and this will weaken the current account of the balance of payments and exert a deflationary effect on the domestic economy. This, of course, may then lead to capital outflows. Governments may be anxious to neutralise the contractionary effects of capital outflows, and decide to increase domestic credit creation to offset them. However, not only will this lower interest rates and lead to further capital outflows, but it will also result in a loss of international reserves if the government intervenes to prop up the exchange rate. The decline in reserves then leads to a loss of creditor confidence and the possibility of a speculative crisis.

For many years economists have been aware of the 'impossible triad' comprising a fixed exchange rate, independent monetary policy, and free capital mobility. Countries can opt for any two of these, but not all three. Seen in this context, how high a priority should be placed on free capital mobility as opposed to pegged exchange rates and independent monetary policy. Macroeconomic management is difficult enough in most developing economies without being exposed to instability in capital flows which may then destabilise exchange rates (with economically fundamental repercussions), or narrowly constrained domestic monetary policy. Unstable capital flows create another layer of difficulty for policy-makers struggling to stabilise the domestic economy. Just as too little foreign capital can thwart aspirations regarding economic growth, too much can be destabilising and threaten a sudden reversal, which then adversely affects economic growth. The destabilising effects of unregulated capital flows may swamp any efficiency gains. But how might private international capital flows be regulated? A desirable part of any system must be to distinguish between flows that are related to trade and long-term direct investment, and flows that are short-term and speculative.

In principle, the options are fairly clear. Either capital flows can be directly controlled so that the wishes of capital importers and capital exporters are frustrated, or market-based solutions can be used to change their wishes. Most famously (or notoriously) the latter genre includes the idea of a tax on international currency transactions, otherwise known as the Tobin tax (named after its initial proponent James Tobin).[4]

Welfare economics suggests that market-based measures are generally superior to controls. But in the context of capital flows, a Tobin tax, at the sort of rates that might be politically feasible, would be least effective at precisely the times at which it is most needed. In the midst of a currency crisis speculation would offer an attractive expected rate of return, even with a Tobin tax. Moreover, claims that the tax would discriminate against speculative round tripping as against long-term investment have been overplayed. In fact, the tax could have exactly the opposite effect (Davidson, 1997).

So what is the answer? The IMF's answer is that countries should run their economies so impeccably that capital volatility is eradicated. We seem to be back to that first best perfect world in which governments do everything right and markets are all-knowing. Clearly no one would advocate that countries should pursue 'unsound' economic policies, but it is wishful thinking to imagine that shocks will never occur and that all policy mistakes will be avoided.

What is left? As far as capital instability is concerned perhaps capital controls, appropriately used, are the least imperfect way of dealing with an imperfect world. But what use is 'appropriate' and what use is 'inappropriate'? There is no well defined formula. After all the world is an uncertain place. Qualitatively, capital controls need to be used to moderate excessive inflows and sudden outflows which would otherwise be macroeconomically destabilising. They should be used as a way of protecting sound domestic policies rather than as a way of offsetting the effects of over-expansionary domestic fiscal policy and misplaced exchange rate policy. In some cases, controls might not need to be implemented at all. Even the threat of them might be expected to discipline private international capital markets. In the East Asian case there is an argument that it was the probability of an IMF bail out, should a crisis occur, that encouraged foreign investors to downgrade the risks and to over-lend, which then actually contributed to causing the crisis (Feldstein, 1998). In other words, the incentive structure was at fault. The threat of capital controls would increase the perceived risk of foreign lending and would avoid excesses, thereby stabilising capital flows and reducing the possibility of crises. Perhaps East Asian economies liberalised their capital accounts too early.

As a short-term device capital controls may be helpful in moderating capital flows and averting crises, even though they are not effective at allowing countries to drive a permanent wedge between domestic and foreign interest rates. In other words, they may be a potentially useful additional policy instrument if used in a selective and sophisticated way. Should developing countries be encouraged to abandon a potentially useful policy instrument?

The political economy of capital account liberalisation

Recent international financial crises have shown just how susceptible a world of capital mobility is to extreme instability. Capital instability imposes severe costs. The literature on the sequencing of economic reform has generally put capital account liberalisation at the end of the process, precisely because of its potentially destabilising effects.

Why at a time when the Fund is emphasising the pressing need to find a solution to the problem of capital volatility is it also pressing ahead with the drive towards capital account liberalisation?

One explanation is that the very nature of the IMF bureaucracy means that once started on a campaign for reform it is difficult institutionally to halt it. There are elements of 'cognitive dissonance', where new contradictory evidence is de-emphasised or ignored. It is of course difficult to ignore the East Asian crisis, and it is noticeable that IMF statements became more moderate and nuanced as the crisis progressed. Thus, in March 1998 Stanley Fischer, the Fund's First Deputy Managing Director was saying that 'liberalisation without a necessary set of preconditions in place is extremely risky' (*IMF Survey*, Vol. 27, No. 6, March 23, 1998, p. 82). Countries, it seems, need to be allowed 'more time' to strengthen their financial systems before capital markets are opened.

Another explanation also draws on the theory of bureaucracy. Jagdish Bhagwati (1998) has argued that there is a U.S. Treasury-Wall Street complex in favour of free capital mobility. U.S. financial institutions want to have the option of being able to invest world-wide and do not want to be constrained by capital controls. They want to be able to take full advantage of investment opportunities in developing countries. Other financial markets, such as London, might be expected to have a similar point of view. It would be surprising if the influence of these powerful lobbyists was not felt in the IMF, given the Fund's reliance on the industrialised economies to provide its own resources.

The rapid expansion of private lending to developing countries can also be used by developed countries' governments as a justification for reduced foreign aid. If private capital is meeting their financing needs, it will meet them even better with capital account liberalisation? Of course, the answer is that many of the world's poorest developing countries do not have access to private capital.

Finally, since the beginning of the 1980s, there has been a trend towards greater conditionality. Extending the jurisdiction the IMF to include the capital account would allow this trend to be continued, even though there are serious doubts as to whether conditionality is the best way of encouraging economic reform because it relies on coercion rather than commitment (Bird, 1998).

Clearly capital controls are not the complete answer to the instability of international capital markets. But as a part of a package of policies they remain useful, and may for a time help to insulate countries from the destabilising effects of capital volatility while other reforms are pursued. Hard evidence in favour of free and fully liberalised capital mobility is difficult to find, whereas evidence concerning the effects of capital instability is difficult to avoid.

The *IMF Survey* reports Stanley Fischer as saying that 'there is no established body of analysis on capital controls – what works and what does not – and a host of questions needs to be examined'. While the Fund argues that a capital account amendment to its Articles of Agreement would provide an appropriate context in which to conduct such analysis, it might be thought more appropriate to undertake the analysis first. This is not a propitious time to be vigorously pursuing capital account liberalisation. It is a propitious time to be thinking about the imperfections of international capital markets and how these can be overcome.

References

J. Bhagwati (1998), 'The Capital Myth', *Foreign Affairs*, May–June.

G. Bird (1998), 'The Effectiveness of Conditionality and the Political Economy of Policy Reform: Is it Simply a Matter of Political Will?', *Journal of Policy Reform*, Vol. 1.

G. Bird (1999), 'How Important is Sound Macroeconomics in Attracting Capital Flows to Developing Countries', *Journal of International Development*, Vol. 9, pp. 1–26.

G. Calvo, L. Leiderman and C. Reinhart (1996), 'Inflows of Capital to Developing Countries in the 1990s', *Journal of Economic Perspectives*, No. 10.

S. Calvo and C. Reinhart (1996), 'Capital Flows to Latin America: Is there Evidence of Contagion Effects?', *Policy Research Working Paper*, 1619, World Bank, June.

P. Davidson (1997), 'Are Grains of Sand in the Wheels of International Finance Sufficient to do the Job when Boulders are Often Required', *Economic Journal*, 107, May.

M. P. Dooley (1996), 'A Survey of Literature on Controls over International Capital Transactions', *IMF Staff Papers*, Vol. 43, No. 4, December.

R. Dornbusch (1992), 'The Case for Trade Liberalisation in Developing Countries', *Journal of Economic Perspectives*, Winter.

M. Feldstein (1998), 'Refocusing the IMF', *Foreign Affairs*, March–April.

S. Fischer *et al.* (1998), 'Should the IMF Pursue Capital Account Convertibility?', *Essays in International Finance*, No. 207, May.

M. Haq, I. Kaul and I. Grundberg (eds) (1996), *The Tobin Tax: Coping with Financial Volatility*, Oxford, Oxford University Press.

C. Massad (1998), 'The Liberalisation of the Capital Account: Chile in the 1990s', in Fischer *et al.*, *op. cit.*

D. Rodrik (1992), 'The Limits of Trade Policy Reform in Developing Countries', *Journal of Economic Perspectives*, Winter.

D. Rodrik (1998), 'Who Needs Capital Account Convertibility', in Fischer *et al.*, *op. cit.*

11
Coping with, and Cashing in on, International Capital Volatility

Graham Bird and Ramkishen S. Rajan

Introduction

The volatility of international capital flows and the incidence of international financial crises have led to calls for the existing international financial architecture to be reformed. But how? One idea that has been around since the 1970s is that a tax should be levied on international currency transactions. Would such a tax reduce capital volatility and help avoid currency crises, or would it prove ineffective and infeasible? The political economy of currency taxation suggests that the idea will receive more support if it can be shown to make a significant contribution to offsetting the perceived inefficiencies of private international capital markets.

This chapter explores what can be expected from a currency tax in this respect. It shows that there are simple but neglected analytical issues that make such a tax an attractive idea. If the tax is relatively ineffective in helping to avoid financial crises and calming markets, it will be relatively effective at providing the resources necessary to mitigate the aftermath of such events. The chapter offers new proposals for using the revenue from currency taxation to finance the operations of the International Monetary Fund (IMF).

The layout of the chapter is as follows: the following section provides a statistical summary of resource flows to developing countries between 1990 and 1997 (i.e. prior to the acute market turmoil in emerging economies in 1998), and analyses the implications of what is shown. The next section provides an anatomy of capital flows and of a financial crisis (i.e. a typical 'boom–bust' cycle). The section on capital volatility examines the nature of capital volatility and goes on to discuss various ways of attempting to engender greater stability in the flow of private international capital, following in particular on the idea of taxing international currency transactions. The following section explores the revenue-generating properties of currency taxation and examines the extent to which an apparent weakness of the tax may in fact be a strength. The section on using the revenue from currency taxation explores various ways in which the revenue from the tax may be used. Having briefly examined some existing ideas, particularly in the context of enhancing foreign aid flows, the section goes on to analyse two new ideas: financing an international lender of last resort, and (co-financing) the IMF. The final section offers a few concluding remarks by way of summary.

Resource flows to developing countries

Table 11.1 provides World Bank (1997) data on net resource flows to developing countries over 1990–97. Overall, these tripled from $98.3 billion in 1990 to $300.3 billion in 1997. However, while private flows increased more than six-fold (from $41.9 billion in 1990 to $256 billion in 1997), official development finance (ODF) was lower in 1997 than it had been in 1990. Indeed, in 1996, ODF was only $34.7 billion as compared with $56.4 billion in 1990 and $62.7 billion in 1991. Accordingly, the share of ODF in total capital flows to developing countries fell dramatically from 57 per cent in 1990 to about 15 per cent in 1997, slightly higher than the trough of 12 per cent in 1996 (Table 11.2). There is therefore *prima facie* evidence of 'aid fatigue' or 'aid weariness' among donor countries. Data from donor countries fortifies this point. OECD donors have cut back significantly on foreign aid, and in 1997, this component was only 0.22 per cent of the OECD's GNP,

Table 11.1　Net long-term resource flows to developing countries ($ billion), 1990–97

	1990	1991	1992	1993	1994	1995	1996	1997	Average
Official development finance	56.4	62.7	53.8	53.6	45.5	54.0	34.7	44.2	50.6
Grants	29.2	35.1	30.5	28.4	32.7	32.6	29.2	25.1	30.4
Loans	27.2	27.6	23.3	25.1	12.9	21.4	5.4	19.2	20.3
Bilateral	11.6	13.3	11.1	10.0	2.5	10.0	−7.2	1.8	6.6
Multilateral	15.6	14.4	12.2	15.2	10.4	11.3	12.6	17.4	13.6
Private flows	41.9	53.6	90.1	54.6	160.6	189.1	246.9	256.0	149.1
Debt	15.0	13.5	33.8	44.0	41.1	55.1	82.2	103.2	48.5
Commercial banks	3.8	3.4	13.1	2.8	8.9	29.3	34.2	4.1	17.1
Bonds	0.1	7.4	8.3	31.8	27.5	23.8	45.7	53.8	24.8
Others	11.1	2.7	12.4	9.4	4.7	2.0	2.3	8.3	6.6
Foreign direct investment	23.7	32.9	45.3	65.6	86.9	101.5	119.0	120.4	74.4
Portfolio equity	3.2	7.2	11.0	45.0	32.6	32.5	45.8	32.5	26.2
Total	98.3	116.3	143.9	208.1	206.2	243.1	281.6	300.3	199.7

Notes: Developing countries are defined as low- and middle-income countries with 1995 per capita incomes of less than $765 (low) and $9835 (middle).

Source: World Bank (1997).

Table 11.2   Relative shares of net long-term resource flows to developing countries, 1990–97

	1990	1991	1992	1993	1994	1995	1996	1997	Average
ODF/total	0.57	0.54	0.38	0.26	0.22	0.22	0.12	0.15	0.31
PF/total	0.43	0.46	0.63	0.74	0.78	0.78	0.88	0.85	0.69
Debt/PF	0.36	0.25	0.38	0.28	0.26	0.29	0.33	0.40	0.31
CBL/PF	0.09	0.06	0.15	0.02	0.06	0.15	0.14	0.16	0.10
Bond/PF	0.00	0.14	0.09	0.21	0.17	0.13	0.19	0.21	0.13
FDI/PF	0.57	0.61	0.50	0.42	0.54	0.54	0.48	0.47	0.52
Port/PF	0.08	0.13	0.12	0.29	0.20	0.17	0.19	0.13	0.17

Notes: ODF – Official development finance; PF – Private flows; CBL – Commercial bank lending; FDI – Foreign direct investment; Port – Portfolio flows.

Source: Computed from data in Table 11.1.

Table 11.3   Relative variability of various components of private flows to developing countries, 1990–97

	Private flows	Debt	Commercial bank lending	Bonds	FDI	Portfolio equity
Var	6692.6	972.8	238.5	360.0	1459.0	282.7
CV	44.9	20.01	14.0	14.5	19.6	10.8

Notes: Var – variance; CV – coefficient of variation.

Source: Calculated from data in Table 11.1.

the smallest share since comparable statistics began in the 1950s (World Bank, 1998).[1]

The reasons for this almost certainly involve a combination of changes. These include the global political environment, in particular the end of the Cold War which blurred ideological differences and removed much of the political motivation for aid;[2] a general perception that aid has been ineffective at encouraging economic growth and reducing poverty (due to, for instance, the possibility that aid substitutes for, rather than supplements domestic resources); and the desire on the part of donors to reduce their own fiscal deficits (World Bank, 1998; White and Woestman, 1994).

While the World Bank provides only annual data on capital flows, an indication of the instability of the various forms of private capital flows may be seen from computations of coefficient of variation, or CVs (Table 11.3). Interestingly, FDI flows have the highest CV, while portfolio flows have the lowest, suggesting that FDI flows are the most variable and portfolio flows the least variable. This conclusion is, however, misleading, as CVs do not consider the trend. Thus, while the CV is larger for FDI than for other capital flows, there is also a consistent (and predictable) upward trend for FDI.

Strictly speaking, what is needed is a measure of variation around this *trend* rather than around the *average*. With insufficient data points to identify a definite trend, perhaps a more useful indicator is the number of consecutive years over which there are positive or negative changes, without a change in direction.

For commercial bank loans, there were consecutive annual directional changes in each year between 1990 and 1993 inclusive. Although bank lending then increased persistently between 1993 and 1997 with no further directional changes, the rate of change varied, with rapid expansions in 1993–94 and 1994–95 being followed by much more modest increases in 1995–96 and 1996–97 (in both percentage and absolute terms). The pattern for bonds is a little different, with directional changes occurring only in 1992–93 and 1995–96. Bond flows increased sharply in 1992–93 when commercial bank lending was declining, and fell in 1997–94 when bank lending increased. 'Other debt flows' show four changes of direction, with these being fairly evenly spread over 1990–97.

Portfolio equity flows exhibit three directional changes over 1990–97, although these all occurred in the period between 1993 and 1997 when bank lending increased persistently. Over the earlier period 1990–93 portfolio investment persistently increased, although again the rate of increase varied, with a particularly rapid increase occurring between 1992 and 1993. While not shown by the data in Table 11.3, it should be noted that portfolio investment comprises some relatively stable elements, such as investments by life insurance companies and pension funds, along with highly unstable investments like country funds and mutual funds. Only FDI showed no directional change throughout the entire 1990–97 period. Moreover, as noted, the rise in FDI took place at a fairly persistent rate, and on average, constituted about half of all private flows. This stability of FDI flows is consistent with the statistical study by Frankel and Rose (1996), who found that a low ratio of FDI to debt is consistently associated with a high probability of a currency crash; while Chuhan *et al.* (1996) and World Bank (1999) have also found FDI to be a more reliable source of financing.[3]

The World Bank data referred to above excludes short-term flows (especially debt) or asset transactions (such as changes in foreign deposits held by developing country residents). In light of this, Table 11.4 provides IMF data on capital flows. While the FDI and portfolio data are in line with those of the World Bank, of significance is the component termed 'other net investment'. Broadly, this category includes short- and long-term credits (including use of IMF credit) as well as currency and deposits and other accounts receivable and payable. Unsurprisingly, it is this component that shows the greatest degree of variability, whether measured by the CVs or the directional changes discussed (Table 11.5). It may also be seen that this component turned negative in 1994 and 1997–98, periods corresponding to the Mexican Tequila crisis and the turmoil in East Asia, respectively. Note also

Table 11.4 Net capital flows to developing countries ($ billion), 1984–97

	1984–89[a]	1990–96[a]	1994	1995	1996	1997	Average
Private capital flows	17.8	129.4	133.8	148.2	190.4	139.0	117.8
Foreign direct investment	12.2	57.9	86.5	86.5	108.5	126.5	82.3
Portfolio investment	4.9	51.1	22.2	22.2	52.7	55.5	43.6
Other investment[b]	0.6	20.4	39.5	39.5	29.3	−43.0	11.6
Official flows	27.2	16.8	32.1	32.1	3.2	−3.3	32.9
Change in reserves[c]	5.1	−54.8	−67.1	−67.1	−95.2	−57.8	−22.6

[a] Annual averages.
[b] May include official flows.
[c] Implies an increase.

Source: IMF (1998).

Table 11.5 Relative variability of various components of private flows to developing countries, 1990–97

	Total private flows	Other investment	FDI	Portfolio equity	Reserves
Var	3289.8	3509.5	1477.7	701.9	4681.5
CV	27.9	303.7	18.0	16.1	207.4[a]

Notes: Var – variance; CV – coefficient of variation.
[a] Absolute value.

Source: Calculated from data in Table 11.4.

the sharp instability of net official reserves, suggesting that these act as a buffer to the variability in short-term private flows. Moreover, use of *net* data almost certainly serves to understate the degree of capital volatility.

The general points made above about the volatility of private capital flows are reinforced by Table 11.6 which provides data from the Institute of International Finance (IIF) for the five East Asian economies most afflicted by the regional financial crisis (namely, Indonesia, Korea, Malaysia, Philippines and Thailand). While net private flows saw a sharp reversal (net outflow) of over $100 billion between 1996 and 1997 and another net outflow of $30 billion between 1997 and 1998, this was primarily due to net (short term) lending by commercial banks, which averaged about $60 billion in 1995 and 1996, but became negative at about – $26 billion in the next two years. Similarly, official reserves varied sharply: from an increase of about $19 billion in 1996, to a decrease of $32.5 billion in 1997, and then

Table 11.6 Net capital flows to East Asia (Indonesia, Korea, Malaysia, Thailand and Philippines) ($ billion), 1995–99

Type of capital flow	1995	1996	1997	1998[a]	1999[b]
External financing	81.5	100.6	28.8	−0.5	−1.2
Private flows	79.0	103.2	−1.1	−28.3	−4.8
Equity investment	15.9	19.7	3.6	8.5	18.7
Direct	4.9	5.8	6.8	6.4	14.2
Portfolio	11.0	13.9	−3.2	2.1	4.5
Private creditors	63.1	83.5	−4.7	−36.8	−23.4
Commercial banks	53.2	65.3	−25.6	−35.0	−18.8
Nonbanks	9.9	18.2	21.0	−1.7	−4.6
Official flows	2.5	−2.6	29.9	27.8	3.5
Financial institutions	−0.3	−2.0	22.1	21.6	−2.0
Bilateral creditors	2.9	−0.6	7.4	6.1	5.5
Resident lending/others	−26.5	−26.8	−35.0	−16.9	−14.9
Reserves (excl. gold)	−14.0	−19.3	32.5	−41.1	−27.0

[a] Estimates.
[b] Forecast.

Source: IIF (1999).

to a rise of about $41 billion in 1998. To a lesser extent, portfolio flows have also been variable while, in sharp contrast, FDI flows have remained extremely stable.[4]

Not shown in any of the tables is the fact that private capital flows are very unevenly spread between developing countries. Between 1990 and 1997, the five largest recipients of capital inflows have accounted for over 50 per cent of total inflows to developing countries and the top twelve have accounted for about 75 per cent of that total (Lopez-Mejia, 1999; World Bank, 1998).[5] While the share of private capital flows has risen substantially in Asia and Latin America, accounting for well over 80 per cent of total flows, ODF has remained a significant source of external finance for highly indebted poor countries, often located in Africa, and has amounted to about 7–8 per cent of GNP for a typical low income country (World Bank, 1998).

Anatomy of capital inflows and a financial crisis

Having observed the extent of variability of net private capital flows to developing countries (debt obligations in particular), it is useful to consider a typical boom–bust episode associated with such instability in capital flows. Financial crises have been recognized as sharing broadly similar empirical regularities. Domestic and international financial deregulation in the reforming economy leads to an initial surge in capital inflows. This occurs as there is general euphoria about prospects for the economy, and investors try to arbitrage differences in *ex-ante* interest rate differentials.[6] Commercial banks and other financial institutions in the country find it relatively easy to borrow from international capital markets and concomitantly lend to domestic customers rather freely. Flush with liquidity, and given relatively lax prudential supervision of banks and other financial institutions along with inadequate disclosure, some of the funds are channeled towards 'excess' consumption of both tradables and nontradables. To the extent that it is generally more difficult to discriminate between good and bad risks during a boom, resources are also inefficiently allocated to relatively unproductive investment projects, including real estate. Non-residents also move funds into the country's stock exchange, hence further fuelling asset price inflation.

Since the domestic currency is invariably pegged (usually to the US$), there is an inevitable overvaluation of the currency in real terms (i.e. real exchange rate appreciation), as wages, other costs and the prices of nontradables in general all rise. Consequently, the export competitiveness of the economy is eroded, with resources being reallocated to the nontradables sector[7] in which the marginal productivity of capital may be relatively low. These factors work in tandem to lead to a deterioration in the trade/current account balance.[8] Eventually, a sudden turnaround in market sentiment – from euphoria to panic – causes a massive selling of the currency, leading a generalised and rapid reversal of net flows. A currency crisis thus ensues, culminating in banking and financial crisis[9] – because of high loan concentrations and other microeconomic distortions such as deposit insurance (explicit or implicit) – with potentially calamitous consequences for the real economy.[10] But how can this boom–bust scenario be avoided?

Capital volatility and currency taxation

Broadly speaking there are two ways of approaching the problem of excessive capital volatility. The first is to frustrate the wishes of market participants by directly controlling market movements. The second is to use a market-based mechanism to modify the structure of price incentives that face market participants, thereby inducing them to modify their behaviour; this is where the idea of currency taxation comes in. Capital controls may or may not work in the sense of reducing volatility, but they do not generally generate revenue.[11] In contrast, a currency tax – like all taxes – may be expected to raise revenue. But will it reduce forex volatility? There are various layers to answering this question. A fundamental issue relates to the causes of volatility, and this in turn raises issues relating to the way in which forex markets function.

Functioning of the forex market

Krause (1991) has very neatly documented that the issue of forex market volatility is not something new.[12] For instance, in response to Keynes, Milton Friedman and James Meade in the early 1950s argued that 'rational, profit-seeking speculation' in the forex market had to be stabilizing. While this was the prevailing orthodoxy by the end of the Bretton Woods era, the events in the forex markets that followed led to an about-turn in the views of most informed observers of international financial markets. In fact, William Baumol in 1957 illustrated that in the presence of uncertainty about the turning points of exchange rates (assuming they follow a cyclical pattern), an optimal short-term strategy was one of buying when the market is rising and selling when it is falling. This was in sharp contrast to the seeming commonsensical 'buy low–sell high' Friedman–Meade strategy. The Baumol strategy was also consistent with the Keynes 'beauty contest' view of international finance, and seems to be in concurrence with the views of the market participants.

Kaldor (1987) attempted to reconcile the two preceding views – that is, the Friedman–Meade view that speculation and financial markets are stabilizing versus the Keynes–Baumol view that free markets are destabilizing. He put forward the thesis that traders follow the Baumol strategy but only for a while. Once the exchange rate is over a certain 'threshold' and seems grossly overvalued (on the basis of fundamentals), the market will reverse itself, resulting in an eventual movement towards the long-run equilibrium. Hence, while the market may temporarily overshoot the long-run equilibrium (leading to 'rational bubbles', whereby the price becomes increasingly removed from the economic value of the underlier), the long-run tendency is towards equilibrium. Kaldor's other important contribution to furthering the debate was to suggest the existence of heterogeneous agents in the currency markets. In particular, he argued that financial market participants at any point in time could be divided into two broad groups, viz. the 'speculators', who followed the Baumol–Keynes strategy, and – for want of a better term – 'fundamentalists', who focused on the trend of 'non-speculative elements' or market fundamentals. Intuitively, the greater the proportion of speculators to fundamentalists, the more destabilizing is unfettered forex market trading in the short to medium term.

The Kaldorian thesis has been confirmed by three recent survey studies of forex market participants worldwide (see Bird and Rajan, 2001; and references cited within). Motivated by these findings, Flood and Taylor (1996, p. 286) have concluded that:

> the finding that a high proportion of foreign exchange market participants deliberately use analytical techniques that ignore macro fundamentals (i.e. 'technical' or 'chartist' analysis), especially over shorter horizons ... underscores the importance of allowing for the interaction of diverse forces in the short run determination of exchange rates.

Referring to the same issue, Frankel and Rose (1995, pp. 1713–4) note that:

(this) area of research is quite small. However, it is potentially important, since it is part of the market microstructure work that is concerned with some of the most central issues of international finance, such as excess volatility and exchange rate determination. We hope for further developments.

Frankel (1996) has himself recently specified a model which presents a realistic structure for the forex market, and which takes into account the heterogeneity of and interaction between the two groups of agents.[13] We introduce a simple formalization of forex instability which extends the original Frankel model in the appendix. For the purpose at hand though, the main conclusions from the model may be summarized as follows:

(a) The benefit of a flexible exchange rate for any country is the ability to undertake independent macroeconomic policy (and thus experience dif-fering inflation rates), though the drawback is its greater bilateral exchange rate variability.
(b) The greater the proportion of 'long-term investors' or 'fundamentalists' in the market, the less variable the exchange rate.
(c) Where 'chartists' dominate the market, we would expect that the exchange rate will be very variable in the short term, with this vari-ability falling over time, in the absence of random shocks. In other words, 'fundamental things apply as time goes by' (Flood and Taylor, 1996, p. 283).
(d) The model also explains the growing variability of exchange rates over time. The more variable is the exchange rate, the less certain are parti-cipants about the fundamentals driving the market, with the result that the proportion of speculators rises. In other words, there may be a vicious cycle or self-fulfilling prophecy, in which speculation and variability feed on each other in the short term (De Long *et al.*, 1989; Schleifer and Summers, 1990).
(e) The importance of a cost-based levy in reducing exchange rate volatility also becomes apparent. An aim of international currency taxation is to reduce the volatility of spot exchange rates by lessening the speculative element in the market (Tobin, 1996).[14]

How does currency taxation fit in?

The above simple model makes apparent how a tax on currency transactions can, in principle, reduce exchange rate volatility. Specifically, one of the aims of such a tax is to reduce the volatility of spot exchange rates by lessening the speculative element (i.e. agents with extrapolative expectations) in the market. The aim is to discourage short-term speculative capital movements.

James Tobin in 1972 (Tobin, 1978, 1996) originally proposed such a currency tax. The so-called Tobin tax (TT) is essentially a permanent, uniform, ad-valorem transaction tax on international forex flows. Since the tax can be amortized over a longer period, the burden of a TT is claimed to be inversely proportional to the length of the transaction, that is, the shorter the holding period, the heavier the burden of tax. For instance, a TT of 0.25 per cent implies that a twice-daily round trip carries an annualized rate of 365 per cent; while in contrast, a round trip made twice a year, carries a rate of 1 per cent. Accordingly, and considering that 80 per cent of forex turnover in 1995 involved round trips of a week or less (BIS, 1996), the TT ought to help reduce exchange rate volatility, and curtail the intensity of boom–bust cycles. Intuitively, the tax will reduce the expected gains from speculation and could, therefore, reduce the incentive to speculate.

Various aspects of the Tobin tax are explored in the papers collected in a United Nations Development Program-sponsored book (ul Haq *et al*., (eds) 1996), by papers in the *Economic Journal Policy Forum* (**105**, 1995), and in Davidson (1997), Felix (1996), Spahn (1996) and Stotsky (1996). Cornford (1996), De Simone (1998), and Raffer (1998) provide fairly detailed reviews of the ul Haq *et al*., book, while Bird (1998) provides a more succinct review. Apart from the fundamental and possibly intractable political economy issues raised by the tax (will countries go along with the idea?), what are the main analytical issues that emerge from the research that has been done?

First, currency taxation will probably be far more successful in – and ought to be aimed at – moderating (short-term) capital *inflows* (especially debt financing), rather than *outflows*. In other words the aim should be to prevent excessive booms from occurring in the first instance, rather than attempting to eliminate the busts that invariably follow (i.e. the tax ought to be applied counter-cyclically). This is also consistent with other empirical studies on capital restraints in general which indicate that they are more effective at preventing 'excessive' capital inflows than at stemming capital flight.[15]

Second, the tax cannot be applied unilaterally, as this will merely lead to a migration of forex transactions to untaxed countries (i.e. there will be geographical substitution towards tax havens). In the light of this, it has been noted that the geographical coverage of the tax must be universal in the sense of including most, if not all countries in the world.[16]

Third, if the tax is limited to spot transactions (as per Tobin's original suggestion), this will lead to a tax-saving reallocation of financial transactions from traditional spot transactions to derivative instruments. As such, it ought to be applied to all derivative products such as forwards, futures, options and swaps.

Fourth, while further research needs to be done in order to determine issues such as the optimal tax rate and coverage, there is broad consensus that the tax must be levied at a rate that minimizes the incentive to undertake synthetic transactions to evade it (asset substitution), and avoids creating incentives to centralize the structure of forex markets (Frankel, 1996). Suggestions of the 'most appropriate' rate of taxation have generally ranged between 0.1 and 0.25 per cent (see next section).

In assessing the effects of a Tobin tax, much of the existing literature has focused on the elasticity of speculative capital movements with respect to currency taxation. In seeking to deter speculative capital movements and to reduce exchange rate volatility, what matters is the expected gain from speculation relative to the costs defined to include payment of the tax. In circumstances where expectations of currency devaluation strengthen, a flat rate tax will become progressively less effective. Indeed, it will be in the midst of a currency crisis, when its stabilizing properties are most needed, that a currency tax will be at its least effective because of the large expected gains from speculation. Davidson (1997) formally illustrates this point;[17] while more graphically, Dornbusch (1998) points out that, 'anyone who contemplates 30 per cent depreciation will happily pay 0.1 per cent Tobin tax'. This observation has led to suggestions that, if the prime interest is to reduce volatility, the tax may have to be applied at different rates depending on market conditions (Spahn, 1995, 1996).

But does the potential insensitivity of speculative capital movements to the relatively low rates of currency taxation dictated by political feasibility eliminate any appeal that the Tobin tax may have?

Cashing in on capital volatility

The low elasticity of capital movements with respect to currency taxation reduces the effectiveness of the Tobin tax as an instrument for stabilizing capital flows.[18] But, at the same time, it raises its effectiveness as a generator of revenue. This important but neglected analytical point is particularly appropriate at a time when reform of the international monetary system is focusing not only on measures that will reduce the incidence of international financial crises, but also measures that will help to deal with them when they do occur.[19] The Tobin tax has been conventionally presented as a preventive measure directed at reducing volatility, stabilizing capital movements and avoiding financial crises. However, more appropriately, it should be seen as an instrument for helping to deal with financial crises once they have happened. In this context, many of the criticisms that have been made of the tax disappear. While the low elasticity of capital movements with respect to currency taxation is a disadvantage, from the viewpoint of calming markets and avoiding crises, it is an advantage in terms of generating revenue.

Rather than reducing capital volatility, the strength of the argument for currency taxation therefore lies in cashing in on it. From this perspective, the low elasticity is exactly what is needed. Indeed, we have a win–win situation. After all, governments tax many activities that have negative externalities, such as smoking. If cigarette taxes are effective in stopping people from smoking that is good news. If they are ineffective, that is also good news in as much as the tax will generate revenue, part of which may be used to finance the cost of providing health care for smokers. Can the analogy be applied to currency taxation? The key point is that the case for the Tobin tax does not depend centrally on sophisticated and complex calculations of tax rates and elasticities. Should the elasticity with respect to the tax turn out to be relatively high, the effect will be to stabilize forex markets, and its preventive role will be significant. Should the elasticity turn out to be relatively low, as many calculations suggest, then, although the preventive role is insignificant, the relatively large amount of revenue generated may be used to help mitigate the effects of international financial crises. But in ballpark terms, what revenue would be raised by taxing currency transactions?

Estimating the revenue from currency taxation is a complicated methodological exercise since much depends on the rate and coverage of the tax; the level of transactions costs; the elasticity of capital movements with respect to the effective increase in transaction costs associated with the tax; as well as the extent to which it is avoided. Early estimates which put the annual revenue as high as $1,500 billion or even $3,650 billion were calculated incorrectly with a strong upward bias. Using an alternative methodology and a range of assumptions about pre-tax transactions costs and elasticities, Felix and Sau (1996) come up with a range of estimates. For a 0.25 per cent tax, they suggest that revenue of about $300 billion would have been generated, using 1995 figures of forex turnover. The revenue would have been $200 billion using 1992 forex volume. For a 0.1 per cent tax using 1995 forex volumes, they calculate that the revenue would have been either $148 billion (with 0.5 per cent transactions costs) or $180 billion (with 1.0 per cent transactions costs). Making the assumption that a Tobin tax of 0.1 per cent would double transactions costs, and that an elasticity of 0.32 'might not be a bad guess', Frankel (1996) estimates revenue of about $166 billion. D'Orville and Najman (1995) calculate that a 0.25 per cent tax would raise about $140 billion per year.

Given these studies, it may not be unreasonable to assume that a transactions tax of 0.25 per cent will generate annual revenue of about $150 billion. What is certainly true is that a Tobin tax may be expected to raise a lot of money. The key point here remains that the amount of revenue generated will be negatively related to the elasticity of financial flows with respect to the tax.

Using the revenue from currency taxation

How might the revenue from currency taxation be used? Kaul and Langmore (1996) make the assumption that high-income countries would have to be allowed to retain 80 per cent of the revenue to encourage their participation, whereas poorer countries would be allowed to retain more. They then go on to discuss a range of national and international uses for the proceeds of the tax. Of course, it is not difficult to construct a list of worthy uses including foreign aid, international peacekeeping and security, enhancing the global environment, improving world health, and so on. Kaul and Langmore suggest that the revenue from a Tobin tax could be used in an internationally co-operative way to overcome the sources of previous inaction on these issues arising from the free rider problem and the prisoner's dilemma. Basically, they suggest that the revenue from a global Tobin tax could be used to finance global public goods. Given their assumptions about how the proceeds from a 0.1 per cent Tobin tax would be shared, they suggest that $27 billion could be available for 'international purposes', although their idea of capping international contributions at $2 billion reduces this figure.

Clearly, there is plenty of room for debate about the numbers used by Kaul and Langmore and the priorities amongst global public goods. Different assumptions lead to different estimations of the amount of revenue that could be used for international purposes. Why not assume that a larger proportion of the revenue (say) 50 per cent, could be used for international purposes if these were perceived as being of direct benefit to the principal financial centres thereby incentivising them to participate? This would give an annual resource flow of about $75 billion.

The analytical point here is that the more compelling financial centres find the uses to which the revenue from an international currency tax will be put, the more prepared they will be to retain a smaller proportion of the proceeds. With this in mind, an alternative to the 'global public good' approach is to focus on the deficiencies of global capital markets, and to consider ways in which the revenue from international currency taxation could be used to mitigate them.

We have already established that the stabilizing properties of currency taxation may be significantly reduced if financial flows have a low elasticity, but that this will in turn increase revenue generation from the tax. Can the revenue generated be used to help deal with the ramifications of international financial crises and the boom and bust pattern of financial flows? Furthermore, can the revenue help to offset the degree of concentration of private capital flows? In short, can revenue from currency taxation enhance the efficiency and equity of the international financial system? In the remainder of this chapter, we focus on two alternatives that have not been examined in the existing literature. These are: the creation of an international lender of last resort (ILLR) facility, and increased financing for the IMF. A third alternative which has received some scrutiny is to use the revenue in order to supplement conventional foreign aid flows, and we briefly examine this first.[20]

Augmenting foreign aid flows

As the numbers in Table 11.1 reveal, revenue from a currency transaction tax, even if one were to take the $24 billion figure suggested by Kaul and Langmore (1996), would be large relative to other resource flows. It would have been about the same size as official grants in 1997 and would have been about a third more than loans from the multilateral institutions. The revenue from a currency tax could help deal with a foreign aid 'crisis', and help reverse a downward trend in aid flows.

But if donor countries have chosen to cut conventional forms of foreign aid, why should they favour introducing a currency tax designed to raise revenue to finance aid flows via an alternative route? Much depends on whether the fall in foreign aid has reflected a budgetary constraint in donors or a perception amongst them that aid is ineffective. A currency tax would remove the domestic budgetary constraint, but it would do little for aid effectiveness, except in as much as aid channelled through multilateral institutions has generally been more effective than bilateral aid. Moreover, with growing evidence that foreign aid *is* effective when combined with good domestic economic policy, the global political environment may become less hostile to using global taxation as a way of bringing about global income redistribution aimed at poverty reduction (Burnside and Dollar, 1997; Mosley and Hudson, 1997; World Bank, 1998).

Much foreign aid has thus far gone to middle-income developing countries (World Bank, 1998). But perhaps it is the poorer countries which, while attempting to introduce 'appropriate' economic reforms, have often remained trapped in a 'low investment equilibrium' (Huang and Shirai, 1994) and need it more. This is not to say that impoverished countries with inappropriate/distortive policies should be overlooked. As noted by the World Bank (1998, p. 6), 'aid agencies need to find alternative approaches to helping highly distortive countries, since traditional methods have failed in these cases'. To use the revenue from a currency transaction tax to augment multilateral aid flows would, in these circumstances, have the appeal of assisting countries that are largely by-passed by private international capital markets. Thus a policy directed towards offsetting the inefficiencies of markets could also be used to mitigate inequity.

However, the idea of currency taxation which, after all, has been around for some time, could perhaps be made more attractive to the international community if it were to be presented as a way of dealing with a new global problem rather than merely a new way of dealing with an old one. Extreme international capital and forex instability is, of course, just such a new global problem. How might the revenue from international currency taxation be used to help in this context?

An international lender of last resort

The clearest statement to date regarding the need for a *national* lender of last resort (NLLR) is probably by Mann (1999), who has noted that a NLLR exists 'because distress at a single financial institution could spill over to sound financial institutions, thus impairing the conduct of the whole system ... Because the economic benefit of the financial system as a whole exceeds that created by individual firms, there is a rationale for very occasional intervention by a lender of last resort to prevent contagious spillovers'. Just as central banks conventionally fulfil a NLLR function in order to stabilize national monetary systems in circumstances where confidence ebbs, so it has often been suggested that an ILLR should be established to fulfil a similar function internationally.

There are however a number of well-rehearsed difficulties with such a lender of last resort proposal, particularly at the international level. These range from the moral hazard problem, which may lead to overborrowing and overlending,[21] through to the costs of international institution building. Do we need another international agency? On top of these, there is the perennial question of whether an ILLR would have sufficient resources to create confidence that its operations will be successful. There is after all a fundamental difference between national and international lenders of last resort, since the NLLR has the capacity to create money and is, therefore, not exposed to a liquidity constraint. Uncertainties over the liquidity of an ILLR would undoubtedly undermine its credibility and its powers of stabilization.

Although international currency taxation would generate large amounts of finance according to most estimates and comparators, the amount of finance would still be small relative to the size of private international capital markets. The data in Table 11.6, for example, show a turn round of almost $100 billion between 1996 and 1997 in five East Asian economies. This needs to be contrasted with the (albeit annual) $24 billion that Kaul and Langmore claim might be available for international purposes from the revenue generated by a Tobin tax. It is, therefore, a reasonable presumption that at least at the outset, the revenue from such a tax would fall some way short of the level required to create an effective ILLR. Could the revenue be put to better use in another way?

Financing the IMF

While there are significant arguments against using Tobin tax revenue to finance a new ILLR, another option is to use it to help finance the operations of the IMF by augmenting or replacing other sources of finance.[22] There are a number of reasons that make this an attractive idea.

The lending operations of the IMF have increased sharply in the mid-to-late 1990s. At the end of October, 1998, the Fund had standby, EFF or ESAF arrangements with sixty-one countries amounting to approved lending of nearly 49 billion SDRs (about $68 billion). Fund lending more than doubled between 1990 and 1998. What is more, the Fund has been called upon to make loans that are individually large, notably to Korea, Brazil and Russia. The new Supplemental Reserve Facility (SRF) introduced at the end of 1997, enables countries to far exceed the conventional quota based limits on borrowing from the Fund. Its increased lending activity has created liquidity problems for the institution. The ratio of the Fund's uncommitted and adjusted liquid resources to its liquid liabilities (the liquidity ratio) fell from 120.5 per cent in April 1997 to only 44.8 per cent in April 1998. With the increased demand for its financial assistance, the Fund has been forced to extend its General Arrangements to Borrow (GAB) in order to supplement its quota-based subscriptions, and in January, 1997, the Executive Board approved the New Arrangements to Borrow (NAB) under which potentially twenty-five participating countries stand ready to lend the IMF up to SDR 34 billion (about $45 billion) if needed to forestall or cope with an impairment of the international monetary system or to deal with an exceptional situation that 'threatens the stability of the system'.

There are many weaknesses with the way in which the IMF is currently financed (Bird, 1987). The quota-based subscription system permits the Fund's resources to be only at best indirectly linked to the global need for IMF loans, and the generally five yearly reviews of quotas involve a methodology which is exposed to political influence and delay as the Eleventh General Review has aptly illustrated. Arrangements such as the NAB are essentially *ad hoc* and crisis-driven. In March 1998, the Fund assessed its own liquidity position as being 'vulnerable' and 'under considerable strain'. And this surely undermines confidence and credibility in the Fund's role as an international financial institution designed to engender stability.

A proposal for using SDR allocations to finance the Fund's operations (Polak, 1996) has garnered little support since it would increase overall global liquidity and is perceived as having potentially inflationary consequences. In contrast, using Tobin tax revenue to finance or co-finance the Fund's operations would represent an application of redistributive international fiscal policy as opposed to expansionary monetary policy. However, it would also help avoid the globally recessionary consequences of an illiquid IMF. It would provide the Fund with a year-on-year *flow* increase in resources (as opposed to the current system of occasional stock adjustments) and these increases would in one sense, be indexed against the likely needs of the international monetary system for Fund lending, since the Fund's resources would be linked to the volume of currency transactions which might be expected to rise as an international financial crisis developed. There would, therefore, be an automatic counter-cyclical component in the availability of IMF resources. Moreover, since Fund lending is temporary and revolves, the resource base of the IMF would increase over time, and beyond a point at which its resources were deemed adequate, the revenue from the Tobin tax could be more heavily directed towards other uses.

A second reason why the idea of using Tobin tax revenue to help finance the Fund is attractive, is that evidence suggests that the success of Fund-backed programmes is positively related to the amount of finance that the

Fund itself lends (Killick, 1995). At present, the availability of Fund finance is frequently a binding constraint on the design of adjustment and this means that countries are forced to adopt quick-acting adjustment policies which concentrate on reducing domestic aggregate demand rather than on increasing aggregate supply (Bird, 1997). This may be a particular problem for poorer countries that require structural adjustment.

Using Tobin tax revenue to help finance the IMF therefore has the appeal that it would confer benefits on low-income countries to a much greater extent than would be the case if the revenue were; used to establish an ILLR; the latter would be of principal advantage to those better-off developing countries and countries in transition that had attracted private capital in the first place. In the case of an ILLR, the benefits to poorer developing countries would primarily be in the sense of releasing resources elsewhere in the system, to the extent that this occurred. Without providing sufficient resources to finance a credible ILLR, the revenue from an international currency tax could provide sufficient resources to strengthen the IMF's position in calming international financial crises. Additional financing would also provide an extra incentive for countries to involve the Fund at an earlier stage in the evolution of a crisis and this could help to avoid the worst excesses. Moreover, with more finance at its own command, there would be fewer delays in putting together financial assistance packages.

By carrying a more substantial proportion of the financial obligations itself, the Fund could also be more effective in helping to organize an orderly workout from a financial crisis, by encouraging private creditors to reschedule loans. Many authors have made a strong case for an international agency to fulfil this kind of role (Cohen, 1989; Sachs, 1989; Radelet and Sachs, 1998); revenue from international currency taxation would enable the Fund to carry out this function more effectively by allowing it to take a significant share in the related financial commitments. Furthermore, other things being equal, and as noted above, additional finance from the IMF would enable borrowing countries to adopt longer-term policies that might reduce the social, political and economic costs often associated with short-run adjustment based on contracting domestic aggregate demand. This could make IMF-backed programmes more acceptable to governments and increase the commitment to and success of such programmes. At present, the clear majority of Fund-backed programmes remain uncompleted (Killick, 1995).

If additional financing were to have this effect then what may initially appear as a weakness of the proposal to use Tobin tax revenue to help finance the Fund becomes a strength. An objection to the proposal may come from those who claim that the Fund's operations are ill-designed and counter-productive (Feldstein, 1998). If this claim is justified, why provide it with additional resources? As the existing literature shows, there is potentially plenty of scope for improving the design of IMF-backed programmes with a view to making them more effective. Arguing that the Fund should be provided with extra resources is certainly not to argue that it should cease to try and improve its policy advice. Indeed, to the extent that the design of IMF-backed programmes is constrained by its available resources, the Fund may be prevented from supporting superior long-term economic strategies.

Bird (1997) argues that the emphasis on structural adjustment in the late 1980s and early 1990s was less successful than it might have been because the necessary short run financial assistance was inadequate. With increased resources from Tobin tax revenue, the Fund would be able to increase the size of its loans where longer-term structural adjustment was required. If, as a consequence, IMF programmes were to become more successful, the demand for loans from low income countries might be expected to decline over time, and this again would serve to alleviate the Fund's own liquidity problems, reinforcing the idea that a substantial proportion of the revenue from a Tobin tax would only need to be directed to the Fund in the short to medium term. Griffith-Jones (1996) has already suggested that the IMF's Articles of Agreement should be modified to allow it to collect the Tobin tax. An extension of this idea is that the Fund should then (in the short to medium term at least) use the revenue it collects to finance its own operations.

Concluding remarks

Following evidence from East Asia and Latin America that international capital volatility continues to be an important global problem, and with related claims that reforms to the international financial architecture are needed both to reduce the incidence of international financial crises and to help deal with them when they do occur, this chapter has explored the relevance of taxing international currency transactions (the Tobin tax).

Although, in principle, a currency tax should reduce foreign exchange volatility by reducing the speculative element in forex flows, there is no guarantee that in practice it will have this effect. However, if a properly designed Tobin tax is unsuccessful in this regard, it must be because international capital flows are relatively inelastic with respect to such taxes. The low elasticity that limits the effectiveness of the tax in reducing capital volatility increases its power to raise revenue. This revenue may then be used to counteract the deficiencies of private international capital markets both in terms of their inefficiencies and inequities. It is in this sense that currency taxation may be an appropriate policy for dealing with the international financial problems that have been experienced in the 1990s and that lie ahead in a world of more fully liberalized capital accounts.

Of the two alternatives explored in this chapter, a more compelling case is made for using the revenue from a Tobin tax to supplement the resources of the IMF than to attempt to establish a new international lender of last resort. The revenue would alleviate the Fund's illiquidity and would, as a consequence, allow it to support longer-term structural adjustment in low income countries (where necessary) and play a pivotal stabilizing role in the context of international financial crises.

Acknowledgements

Comments by an anonymous referee of this journal and Mukul Asher are appreciated. The usual disclaimer applies.

Appendix: a more specific model on exchange rate volatility

Given the predominance of the US dollar in forex transactions, we consider only bilateral exchange rates and assume the other (focus) currency to be the baht (b). All variables are in log form.

$$s = m - d + u \qquad (1)$$

where s is the spot exchange rate (baht per \$); m is the supply of domestic (Thai) assets relative to US assets; d is the relative demand for domestic assets; and u is a stochastic term.

$$d = wd_i + (1 - w)d_s \qquad (2)$$

where w is the fraction of long-term participants or 'fundamentalists'; $(1 - w)$ is the fraction of short-term participants (speculators) or chartists; d_i is the relative domestic asset demand by the fundamentalists; and d_s is the relative asset demand by the chartists. Chartists are assumed to have extrapolative (or momentum) forecasts, i.e. they expect the exchange rate to diverge from equilibrium (hence creating a 'bubble'), while fundamentalists expect convergence. Accordingly, we rewrite the relative demand for domestic assets (d) as follows

$$d = [wf_i q(s - \mathbf{s}) - (1 - w)f_s v(s - \mathbf{s})] \qquad (3)$$

where f_i and f_s denote the demand elasticities of the fundamentalists and chartists for foreign assets with respect to their corresponding expectations; and q and v are the rates of expected convergence (by the fundamentalists) and divergence (by the chartists) of the spot rate from the long-run 'equilibrium level', which is denoted by $\mathbf{s}$.

Thus, the fundamentalists' behaviour is stabilizing or regressive in that if the spot rate is higher than the equilibrium rate, a depreciation is expected and vice versa (i.e. exchange rate reversion). On the other hand, the 'chartists', who make use of analytical techniques or trading rules ('momentum models') to forecast exchange rates (all of which essentially extrapolate past trends), tend to have a destabilizing effect.

As an extension of Frankel's model, assume that the equilibrium exchange rate ($\mathbf{s}$) is based on the purchasing power parity theorem (PPP).

$$\mathbf{s} = p_h - p_u \qquad (4)$$

where p_h and p_u refer to home and US (foreign) price levels respectively.

Substituting (4) into (3) and placing the result in (1), we obtain:

$$s = \frac{\left\{ m + [wf_iq - (1 - w)f_sv](p_h - p_u) + u \right\}}{[1 + wf_iq - (1 - w)f_sv]}$$

$$\begin{aligned}
\text{Var}(s) = (1/A^2)\{&\text{Var}(m) + (1 - A)^2[\text{Var}(p_h) + \text{Var}(p_u)] \\
&- 2(1 - A)[\text{Cov}(m, p_u) - \text{Cov}(m, p_h) + (1 - A)\text{Cov}(p_h, p_u)] \\
&+ \text{Var}(u)\}
\end{aligned} \tag{5}$$

where Var is the variance, Cov is the covariance and $A = [1 + wf_iq - (1 - w)f_sv]$. We assume that $\text{Cov}(u, m) = \text{Cov}(u, P_u) = \text{Cov}(u, p_h) = 0$. With the maintained assumption of $A > 1$, it can be shown that $\partial\text{Var}(s)/\partial w < 0$, i.e. the greater the proportion of long-term investors or fundamentalists in the market, the less variable the exchange rate; or, conversely, the greater the proportion of speculators, the more destabilizing the effect on the exchange rate. Further, $\partial\text{Var}(s)/\partial(f_i\, q) < 0$ and $\partial\text{Var}(s)/\partial(f_s\, v)0 > 0$, i.e. the more sensitive or responsive are the speculators to the expected divergence between the spot and equilibrium exchange rate relative to the fundamentalists, the more variable will be the spot exchange rate. For a given w, this in turn is less likely the larger is (f_iq) and the lower is (f_sv); or conversely, for a given (f_iq), the lower is (f_sv) and the larger is w.

References

Bank of International Settlements (BIS). 1996. Central Bank Survey of Foreign Exchange and Derivatives Market Activity. May.

Bank of International Settlements (BIS). 1998. Press Release on Central Bank Survey of Foreign Exchange and Derivatives Market Activity in April 1998: Preliminary Global Data. October 19.

Bird G. 1987. Financing the Fund and reforming quotas. In *International Financial Policy and Economic Development*, Bird G (ed.). Macmillan: London.

Bird G. 1996. The International Monetary Fund and developing countries: a review of the evidence and policy options. *International Organization* 50: 477–511.

Bird G. 1997. External financing and balance of payments adjustment in developing countries: getting a better policy mix. *World Development* 25: 1409–20.

Bird G. 1998. The Tobin tax: coping with financial volatility. *Review of International Economics* 6: 706–8.

Bird G. 1999. Crisis averter, crisis lender, crisis manager: the IMF in search of a systemic role. *The World Economy* 22: 975–95.

Bird G, Rajan R. 2001. International currency taxation and currency stabilisation in developing countries. *Journal of Development Studies* February 37(3): 21–39.

Burnside C, Dollar D. 1997. Aid, policies and growth. *World Bank Policy Research Working Paper No. 1777*.

Calvo G, Leiderman L, Reinhart C. 1995. Capital inflows to Latin America with reference to the Asian experience. In *Capital Controls, Exchange Rates and Monetary Policy in the World Economy*, Edwards S (ed.). Cambridge University Press: Cambridge.

Chuhan P, Perez-Quiros G, Popper H. 1996. International capital flows: do short-term investment and direct investment differ? *World Bank Policy Research Working Paper No. 1507*.

Cohen B. 1989. Developing country debt: a middle way. *Essays in International Finance.* Princeton, May 173.

Cornford A. 1996. The Tobin tax: silver bullet for financial volatility, global cash cow or both? *UNCTAD Review* 105–20.

D'Orville H, Najman D. 1995. *Towards a New Multilateralism: Funding Global Priorities.* United Nations: New York.

Davidson P. 1997. Are grains in the wheels of international finance sufficient to do the job when boulders are often required? *Economic Journal* 107: 671–86.

Davidson P. 1998. Volatile financial markets and the speculator. Paper presented to the Royal Economic Society Annual Conference, Warwick, England, April.

DeGrauwe P, Dewachter H, Embrechts M. 1993. *Exchange Rate Theory: Chaotic Models of Foreign Exchange Markets.* Blackwell: Oxford, UK.

De Long B, Shleifer A, Summers L, Waldmann R. 1989. Positive feedback investment strategies and destabilizing rational speculation. *Working Paper No. 2880*, NBER.

De Simone F. 1998. The Tobin tax: coping with financial volatility: a review article. *Singapore Economic Review* 42: 32–49.

Dooley M. 1995. A survey of academic literature on controls over international capital transactions. *IMF Working Paper WP/95/127.*

Dornbusch R. 1998. Capital controls: an idea whose time is gone. mimeo, March.

Edwards S. 1998. Capital inflows into Latin America: a stop-go story. *NBER Working Paper No. 6441.*

Eichengreen B. 1996. The Tobin tax: what have we learned? In *The Tobin Tax: Coping with Financial Viability*, ul Haq M, Kaul I, Grunberg I (eds). Oxford University Press: Oxford.

Eichengreen B, Wyplosz C. 1996. Taxing international financial transactions to enhance the operation of the International Monetary System. In *The Tobin Tax: Coping with Financial Viability*, ul Haq M, Kaul I, Grunberg I (eds). Oxford University Press: Oxford.

Feldstein M. 1998. Refocusing the IMF. *Foreign Affairs.* March/April.

Felix D. 1996. Financial globalization versus free trade: the case for the Tobin tax. *UNCTAD Review* 63–104.

Felix D, Sau R. 1996. On the revenue potential and phasing in of the Tobin tax. In *The Tobin Tax: Coping with Financial Viability*, ul Haq M, Kaul I, Grunberg I (eds). Oxford University Press: Oxford.

Fischer S. 1999. On the need for an international lender of last resort. mimeo, IMF, January.

Fisher B. 1993. Impediments in the domestic banking sector to financial opening. In *Financial Opening: Policy Issues and Experiences in Developing Countries*, Reisen H, Fisher B (eds). OECD: Paris.

Flood R, Taylor M. 1996. Exchange rate economics: what's wrong with the conventional macro approach. In *The Microstructure of Foreign Exchange Markets*, Frankel J, Galli G, Giovannini A (eds). The University of Chicago Press: Chicago.

Frankel J. 1996. How well do markets work: might a Tobin tax help? In *The Tobin Tax: Coping with Financial Viability*, ul Haq M, Kaul I, Grunberg I (eds). Oxford University Press: Oxford.

Frankel J, Rose A. 1995. Empirical research on nominal exchange rates. In *Handbook of International Economics*, Vol. III, Grossman G, Rogoff K (eds). Elsevier Press: The Netherlands.

Frankel J, Rose A. 1996. Currency crisis in emerging markets: empirical indicators. *Journal of International Economics* 41: 351–68.

Glick R, Moreno R. 1994. Capital flows and monetary policy in East Asia. *Working Paper 9408*. Center for Pacific Basin Monetary and Economics Studies, Federal Reserve of San Francisco.

Griffith-Jones S. 1996. Institutional arrangements for a tax on international currency transactions. In *The Tobin Tax: Coping with Financial Viability*, ul Haq M, Kaul I, Grunberg I (eds). Oxford University Press: Oxford.

ul Haq M, Kaul I, Grunberg I (eds). 1996. *The Tobin Tax: Coping with Financial Viability*. Oxford University Press: Oxford.

Huang D, Shirai S. 1994. Information externalities affecting the dynamic pattern of foreign direct investment: the case of China. *IMF Working Paper WP/94/44*.

IMF. 1998. *World Economic Outlook*. IMF: Washington, DC.

IMF. 1999. The IMF's response to the Asian crisis. January 17.

Institute of International Finance (IIF). 1999. Capital flows to emerging market economies. January 27.

Kaldor N. 1987. Limits of growth. *Oxford Economic Papers* 38: 187–98.

Kaminsky G, Reinhart C. 1996. The twin crises: the causes of banking and balance of payments crises, board of governors of the federal reserve system. mimeo, September.

Kaul I, Langmore J. 1996. Potential uses of the revenue from a Tobin tax. In *The Tobin Tax: Coping with Financial Viability*, ul Haq M, Kaul I, Grunberg I (eds). Oxford University Press: Oxford.

Killick T. 1995. *IMF Programmes in Developing Countries: Design and Impact*. Routledge: London.

Krause L. 1991. *Speculation and the Dollar: The Political Economy of Exchange Rates*. Westview Press: Boulder.

Krugman P. 1998. Saving Asia: it's time to get radical. *Fortune* September 7: 33–8.

Lensink R, White H. 1998. Does the revival of international private capital flows mean the end of aid?: an analysis of developing countries access to private capital. *World Development* 27: 1221–34.

Lopez-Mejia A. 1999. Large capital flows: a survey of the causes, consequences, and policy responses. *IMF Working Paper No. 99/17*.

Lundborg P. 1998. Foreign aid and international support as a gift exchange. *Economics and Politics* 10: 127–41.

Mann C. 1999. Market mechanism to reduce the need for IMF bailouts. *International Economic Policy Briefs 99–4*. Institute for International Economics.

Mathieson D, Rojas-Suarez L. 1993. Liberalization of the capital account: experiences and issues. *Occasional Paper No. 103*.

Mosley P, Hudson J. 1997. Has aid effectiveness increased? (mimeo).

Ostry J. 1997. Current account imbalances in ASEAN countries: are they a problem? *IMF Working Paper No. 51*.

Polak J. J. 1996. Should the SDR become the sole financing technique for the IMF? In *The Future of the SDR in the Light of Changes in the International Monetary System*, Mussa M, Boughton JM, Isard P (eds). IMF: Washington DC.

Radelet S, Sachs J. 1998. The East Asian crisis: diagnosis, remedies and prospects. *Brookings Papers on Economic Activity* 1: 1–74.

Raffer K. 1998. The Tobin tax: reviving a discussion. *World Development* 26: 529–38.

Rajan R. 1999a. Economic collapse in Southeast Asia. *Policy Study*. The Lowe Institute of Political Economy: Claremont, CA.

Rajan R. 1999b. Banks, financial liberalization and the interest rate premium puzzle in East Asia. *Discussion Paper No. 99/12*; Centre for International Economic Studies.

Reinhart C, Todd-Smith R. 1997. Temporary capital controls. mimeo, August.

Sachs J. 1989. New approaches to the Latin American debt crisis. *Essays in International Finance*. Princeton **174**.

Schadler S, Carkovic M, Bennett A, Kahn R. 1993. Recent experiences with surges in capital inflows. *IMF Occasional Paper No. 108*.

Schleifer A, Summers L. 1990. The noise trader approach to finance. *Journal of Economic Perspectives* **4**: 19–33.

Spahn P. 1995. International financial flows and transactions taxes: survey and options. *IMF Fiscal Affairs Working Paper, 60*; IMF, Washington DC.

Spahn P. 1996. The Tobin tax and exchange rate stability. *Finance and Development*. (June) **33**.

Stotsky J. 1996. Why a two-tier Tobin tax won't work. *Finance and Development*. (June) **33**.

Tanzi V. 1998. The impact of economic globalization on taxation. International Bureau of Fiscal Documentation (August/September) 338–43.

Tinbergen J. 1990. The optimum amount of development assistance. In *Towards Economic Recovery in Sub-Saharan Africa: Essays in Honour of Robert Gardiner*, Pickett J, Singer H (eds). Routledge: London.

Tobin J. 1978. Proposal for international monetary reform. *Eastern Economic Journal* **4**: 153–9.

Tobin J. 1996. Prologue. In *The Tobin Tax: Coping with Financial Viability*, ul Haq M, Kaul I, Grunberg I (eds). Oxford University Press: Oxford.

White H, Woestman L. 1994. The quality of aid: measuring trends in donor performance. *Development and Change* **25**: 527–54.

World Bank. 1997. *Global Development Finance 1997: Analysis and Summary Tables*. Oxford University Press: New York.

World Bank. 1998. *Assessing Aid: What Works, What Doesn't, and Why?* Oxford University Press: New York.

World Bank. 1999. *Global Economic Prospects 1998/99 and the Developing Countries: Beyond Financial Crisis*. Oxford University Press: New York.

12
The Catalytic Effect of Lending by the International Financial Institutions

Graham Bird and Dane Rowlands

Introduction

For many less developed countries (LDCs) and countries in transition (CITs) external financing is frequently an effective constraint on economic growth and development. Capital inflows may be used to overcome shortages of domestic saving, thereby permitting higher levels of investment, as well as shortages of foreign exchange, thereby permitting larger quantities of imports.

But from where do LDCs and CITs attract foreign capital? In essence it may come from public sources in the form of bi-lateral and multi-lateral assistance, or from private sources in the form of bank lending, bonds, and portfolio and direct foreign investment. The 1990s have experienced a rapid decline in the relative importance of official financing and a corresponding increase in the relative importance of private lending, and this has created additional problems for capital importing countries. Aid donors are becoming increasingly selective and have been inclined to make aid more and more conditional, while the pattern of private capital flows is sometimes difficult to explain, exhibiting a high degree of volatility. In such circumstances how do capital importing countries make themselves appear more attractive to potential foreign lenders?

The international financial institutions (IFIs) can play a potentially key role in this context not only as a direct source of multi-lateral assistance, but also by indirectly influencing flows from other public and from private sources. Indeed the International Monetary Fund (IMF) has emphasised the importance of its catalysing role, maintaining that its overall influence on international financial flows is much greater than would be suggested by its direct provision of finance alone. Clearly, at a time when the value and pattern of financial flows to LDCs and CITs are undergoing substantial change, it is particularly relevant to examine the contribution that can be made by the IFIs. Do they have the ability to mobilise and stabilise large quantities of finance, even in circumstances where their own capacity to provide finance is limited? It is, of course, quite possible that the answer to this question will be nuanced. The IFIs can themselves lend under a range of facilities and it may be that not all of them have an equivalent catalytic effect, especially as the degree and nature of conditionality vary across individual facilities. Moreover, other financial flows can come from a range of sources and the ability of the IFIs to exert an influence may vary depending on the source of funds. IMF conditionality might, for example, be expected to have a greater impact on short-term bank lending than longer term direct investment. Finally, the catalytic effect may be more pronounced in some countries than in others depending upon individual country characteristics such as the perceived commitment of the government to economic reform.

In a recent review of its conditionality, the IMF notes that only about half the countries studied 'benefited from capital inflows'. It acknowledges that 'there were disappointments', with capital inflows failing to materialise as projected in some countries, particularly in sub-Saharan Africa and Central Europe (Schadler *et al.*, 1995). It is interesting that in such an apparently comprehensive and wide-ranging study of conditionality, there is no analytical evaluation of the Fund's catalysing role. The catalytic effect almost seems to be taken for granted, even in the face of contrary evidence, which is then viewed as a 'disappointment' rather than something which theoretical analysis might explain.

Another Fund-based study emphasises the role that IMF conditionality performs in signalling policy credibility (Dhonte, 1997). Latin America's renewed access to financial markets is claimed to be a response to changed policies which 'Fund programmes have been instrumental in stimulating', p. 10.

This chapter sets out to investigate various aspects of the catalytic effect in greater detail than has been done up until now. The next section discusses its general theoretical foundations, essentially trying to establish whether, in principle, it should be expected that IFIs will have a positive catalytic effect on other financial flows. The section on empirical evidence on catalytic effect reviews the evidence that is currently available, and the following section presents new estimations which illustrate the complexity of the catalytic effect, and shed light on how past evidence may be reconciled. The section on policy implications then makes some policy suggestions that lead on from this empirical work as to how the catalytic effect might be enhanced. The final section offers a few concluding remarks.

The catalytic effect: some theoretical foundations

The involvement of the IFIs in a country's economic affairs may be expected to have a catalytic effect on other financial flows when the credibility of domestic economic policy is increased as a consequence. Governments often turn to the IFIs in the belief that the related endorsement of economic policy has a positive capital market value. The IFIs are frequently presented as gatekeepers that can unlock the door to private capital and other financial flows.[1]

But why might the credibility of a country's economic policies be improved by involving the IFIs? A first dimension relates to the design of economic policy. For IFI involvement to have a positive catalytic effect there must be a presumption that economic policy will be better designed and more appropriate to a country's existing economic situation and needs. The implication is that it is possible to perceive of an optimal mix of policies and that involving the IFIs results in a mix that is closer to this optimum than where governments are left to design policy on their own.

In the case of the IMF the relevant focus will tend to be on the design of policies aimed at stabilising the economy and managing aggregate demand, and will straddle fiscal policy, monetary policy and exchange rate policy. In the case of the World Bank the focus will be more on structural policies aimed at influencing aggregate supply and longer term development, and will incorporate policies designed to eliminate economic distortions and encourage greater reliance on free markets. In practice the institutional focus may be a little blurred as the IMF has become more involved in structural adjustment and as the World Bank has used elements of policy conditionality that encroach into areas, such as the exchange rate, which have traditionally been regarded as the territory of the Fund.

Taking, as an example, the nature of the conditionality conventionally favoured by the IMF, it may be presumed that Fund involvement in the design of macroeconomic policy will be associated with an increase in the domestic rate of interest (due to restrictive monetary policies) and a fall in the value of the domestic currency (typically an explicit devaluation). However, it is not at all clear that these policy changes should in theory be expected to be associated with additional capital inflows.

In the context of the asset market model of the balance of payments an increase in domestic interest rates should, other things being equal, certainly have a positive effect on capital inflows. But, rising interest rates may also increase the likelihood of default to such an extent that the expected rate of return to capital falls and this will have a negative effect. Moreover, in as much as higher interest rates are expected to lead to economic recession, capital inflows in the form of direct and portfolio investment may be adversely affected.

A further complication arises from the general use of foreign currency denominated debt bearing interest rates based on the London Interbank Offer Rate (LIBOR). In this case, IMF conditions on domestic monetary policy and interest rates will have a negligible direct effect on inducing capital flows through traditional asset market mechanisms. On the contrary, the indirect effects of tight monetary policy may repel new capital flows by reducing economic growth and the associated repayment prospects. The asset market model also identifies the importance of expected exchange rate changes in influencing capital flows. Where a current devaluation reduces the expected incidence of future devaluations it will have a positive effect on the capital account. But where current devaluation is seen as a lead indicator of future devaluation, it will have a negative effect. Furthermore, devaluations raise the domestic currency costs of servicing foreign currency denominated debt. Even in the narrow context of the asset market model, therefore, the *a priori* effects of IMF conditionality on capital flows are ambiguous.

Extending the analysis beyond the asset market approach also leads to analytical difficulties. Consider the simple balance of payments approach. Countries generally turn to the IMF when they face severe balance of payments difficulties. These difficulties are usually associated with current account problems, which IMF conditions such as devaluation and deflation are clearly designed to address. If effective, however, the movement of the current account towards a surplus must be matched by one or both of an accumulation of foreign reserves and a capital account moving towards deficit. Effective IMF programmes, therefore, may well be associated with observed reductions in net capital inflows, though the timing of these events will vary depending on such factors as the duration of any *J*-curve effect (which illustrates how the current account typically reacts to an exchange rate depreciation).

The theoretical basis for the proposition of a catalytic effect based on IMF conditionality, therefore, is unclear. There may be a general consensus that policies designed to reduce fiscal deficits, rates of monetary expansion, and exchange rate overvaluation are generally useful in correcting a severe balance of payments deficit, as will be the case for most countries turning to the Fund. However, there remain doubts about the use of interest rate hikes and currency devaluation, both in terms of their efficacy in achieving their stated policy objectives and in terms of their consequences for subsequent capital flows.

The design of structural adjustment programmes under the auspices of the World Bank is also open to debate, with an argument sometimes being made that market-friendly policies are not always friendly towards economic development (Fanelli, Frenkel and Taylor, 1994). Financial liberalisation may, for example, create problems for domestic banking systems and may adversely affect economic growth, and trade liberalisation may reduce tax revenues and create additional fiscal problems. In reviewing the economic performance of developing countries over the last thirty years, Rodrik (1996) argues that success depends more significantly on appropriate macroeconomic stabilisation than on policies of economic liberalisation such as those favoured by the World Bank. There is certainly enough debate surrounding the question to imply that foreign lenders will not always assume that IFI-supported programmes are appropriately designed.

But doubts about the effects of IFI involvement on the credibility of economic policy go beyond the issue of policy design. Does the negotiation of an agreement with the IFIs act as a reliable signal that the related policies will actually be implemented, or is there a time consistency problem? Both theory and evidence suggests that it would be unwise for potential investors to assume that governments will always, or even more often than not, fully implement agreed policy programmes. There are various reasons why slippage may occur. Some of these may lie outside the control of governments and involve, for example, a decline in a country's income terms of trade or an increase in world interest rates. In these circumstances governments are anxious to implement programmes but find it impossible to do so. In other cases, however, governments may make discrete decisions to opt out of agreed programmes. Where the benefits of signing an agreement, in terms of anticipated additional capital inflows, outweigh the perceived costs in terms (say) of the loss of national sovereignty, but the benefits from implementation fall short of the costs, it will be rational for governments to sign agreements with no *ex ante* intention of carrying them through. In other circumstances the initial intention may be to implement the programme, but as events unfold the actual costs of implementation turn out to be higher and/or the actual benefits turn out to be lower than expected, leading governments to reassess their initial choice (Bird, 1998). Since the effects of IFI-supported programmes are uncertain, it is quite probable that outcomes will not match expectations and that governments will renege on agreements. Herein lies the possibility of a two-way causal relationship as the degree of implementation depends on the extent of the catalytic effect, and the extent of the catalytic effect depends on the degree of implementation. Foreign lenders may not lend if they believe that countries only pursue policies to impress capital markets, and governments may not implement IFI programmes if they believe that capital markets will be unimpressed.

Even where outcomes *exceed* expectations, governments may choose to abandon agreed programmes since the very improvement in economic performance will eliminate the circumstances in which referral to the IFIs originally occurred. It is, for example, the increasing effectiveness of the balance of payments constraint which drives countries towards the IMF. Countries that can circumvent balance of payments difficulties also tend to circumvent the Fund. If balance of payments difficulties ameliorate during the course of a Fund-backed programme, countries may opt not to carry the programme through to completion since the balance of payments constraint has been relaxed. Theoretical considerations are therefore quite consistent with the notion that IFI-supported programmes will not be fully implemented.

The empirical evidence shows that, in the case of the IMF, non-completion is common, with more than fifty per cent of programmes remaining incomplete (Killick, 1995).[2] Studies of the World Bank's policy-based lending have also identified a significant degree of slippage (Mosley, Harrigan and Toye, 1991). Poor implementation challenges the idea that there will be credibility gains from IFI-conditionality.[3]

Indeed, a counter argument can be made that conditionality will have a negative effect on credibility. The reasoning is as follows. Conditionality effectively coerces governments into pursuing policies which they would otherwise have rejected. It is therefore fundamental to IFI conditionality that governments feel a lack of ownership of the programme, and this will imply less commitment to it.[4] Ownership and conditionality are, in this basic sense, inconsistent. Policies which are home-grown will carry more credibility than those that are designed by the IFIs. Conditionality therefore reduces credibility, and the impact on capital flows will therefore tend to be negative and not positive as claimed by the catalytic effect. At the very least, conditionality will cloud the degree of commitment of a government to an IFI-approved programme, and it then becomes difficult for foreign lenders to determine the extent to which a programme has been adopted voluntarily. Conditionality therefore gets in the way of governments establishing their own reputation for economic management.

Moreover, considerable empirical evidence suggests that a significant determinant of IFI-backed programmes is the existence of recent past IFI programmes (Conway, 1994; Rowlands, 1994a; Knight and Santaella, 1994; Bird, 1995; and Killick, 1995). If countries only turn to the IFIs in times of economic distress, this implies that current agreements with the IFIs indicate future economic distress, and this again suggests that there will be a negative catalytic effect, with the negotiation of an IFI-backed programme sending out pessimistic signals about future economic performance which then lead to capital outflows rather than inflows.

Evidence on the impact of programmes supported by the IMF and the World Bank suggests that their effects are at best muted (Khan, 1990; Conway, 1994; Killick, 1995; and Santaella, 1995). As far as the Fund is concerned there appear to be significant but small positive effects on the current account of the balance of payments, but not significant effects on inflation and economic growth. Some studies discover a negative short-term effect on economic growth, with a general consensus being that both IMF and World Bank supported programmes have a negative effect on investment. The reduced investment could be received favourably by lenders if it implies that the savings gap has also been reduced, with corresponding improvements in the country's ability to service and repay external debt. For such a positive impact, however, the savings rate cannot deteriorate significantly; where a fall in investment is matched by an equivalent increase in consumption, no such implication may be drawn. On the negative side, foreign investors will prefer to see increasing investment and savings rates because of the probable beneficial effects on economic growth. Moreover, where most of the contraction initially occurs in public sector investment as a consequence of fiscal tightness, this may have implications for private investment because of the 'crowding in' effects of public investment (Greene and Villaneuva, 1991; and Bleaney and Greenaway, 1993).

Consequently, there can be no expectation based on empirical evidence that the negotiation of a programme supported by the IMF or the World Bank will lead to a significant improvement in economic performance as judged by conventional macroeconomic indicators. Studies of IFI-supported programmes also reveal a poor record of success in terms of influencing intermediate policy variables such as monetary expansion (Killick, 1995; and Santaella, 1995). Why, therefore, should foreign lenders regard the negotiation of an agreement as relevant and why should there be a catalytic effect? At best the effects of IFI conditionality appear either irrelevant or unpredictable with respect to the sorts of factors which should influence capital flows.

Disaggregation may, however, be important due to the heterogeneity of capital flows. While an expectation that a balance of payments deficit will be reduced may, in principle, have a positive effect on short-term financing, an expectation that economic growth will be adversely affected may have a negative effect on long-term direct investment. Similarly, official bilateral or multilateral financing may also react quite differently from the various suppliers of private capital.

Official lenders may be concerned to find some objective indicator of 'effort' and 'intent' whereas private lenders will be looking for 'achievement'. Governmental aid agencies may merely have to persuade their domestic finance ministries that recipients are serious about economic reform; the negotiation of a programme with the IFIs may be taken by them as a reasonable proxy for seriousness. Aid donors will not be looking for commercial rates of return, and this implies that official lending has to fulfill less searching criteria (at least from an economic viewpoint). The negotiation of an IFI-backed programme may therefore be sufficient to generate extra official lending, whereas it will only generate private flows if it is then implemented and proves effective. The test for catalysis is therefore stricter for private flows.

A slightly different approach to understanding the theoretical foundations of the catalytic effect would start by asking what factors influence capital inflows and then examine the extent to which the involvement of the IFIs may be expected to influence these.[5] Do the IFIs effectively act as agents for private foreign lenders and aid donors? Subject to the reservations discussed earlier, IFI conditionality may be seen as standing as a proxy for the disciplined domestic economic policy that foreign investors wish to see, thereby enhancing the expected rate of return on capital inflows. However, the preferences of the IFIs are unlikely to mirror those of either private lenders or aid donors. Conditionality designed by the IFIs will be based on their own institutional utility functions and, in these circumstances, will not necessarily be perceived as raising the welfare of foreign suppliers of finance. Indeed if it were to be argued that aid flows are by definition non-commercial and that aid donors have a welfare function that is diametrically opposed to that of commercial lenders, it would then be expected that, were IFI conditionality to have a positive catalytic effect on private flows, it would have a negative effect on public flows, and *vice versa*. This suggests that a simplistic and uni-dimensional approach to the catalytic effect will be analytically misplaced.

In this context it makes little theoretical sense to present IFI finance as either universally a substitute for or a complement to other forms of finance since at a disaggregated level it may simultaneously be both. Take, for example, a country in severe economic distress lacking creditworthiness. Such an economy is heavily reliant on aid flows, but aid donors may seek to make aid programme-tied via IFI conditionality which may, as a result, have a positive effect on public flows. From the demand side, governments might prefer to borrow commercially where this option is available to them, regarding the IFIs as lenders of last resort. Here increased borrowing from the IFIs would be determined by falling access to private finance and the two sources of finance would be substitutes (not complements as implied by the catalytic effect). Bureaucratic theories of the IFIs contend that they modify conditionality depending on the availability of private external capital. Here again it is IFI conditionality and IFI lending which depend on the availability and price of commercial lending. The causal relationship runs in exactly the opposite direction to the one implied by the catalytic effect. If most aid is conditional in some way, recipients may be largely indifferent as to its source. However, borrowing countries may not be indifferent between unconditional commercial finance and conditional IFI finance unless the latter were to be provided on concessional financial terms. This reasoning suggests that while there will be a positive relationship between IFI lending and other public flows, there will be a negative relationship between IFI lending and private flows. The catalytic effect might exist for other public flows but not exist (or even appear negative) in the case of private flows.

What does our discussion of the theoretical foundations of the catalytic effect lead us to expect? First, the catalytic effect will be as strong or as weak as the perceived impact of IFIs on the credibility of a government's economic policy. However, given disagreements over the design of policy, the poor record of implementation, and the muted effects of IFI programmes on both policy variables and economic variables, there is little reason to expect a strong catalytic effect as a consequence of enhanced credibility. Second, since different financial flows may be influenced by different factors, or by the same factors but to different extents, the catalytic effect is unlikely to be the same across all financial flows. Indeed, there are some reasons to believe that while it may appear to be positive for aid flows it will appear to be negative for commercial flows. Certainly the theoretical analysis does not provide as compelling a justification for the catalytic effect as the IFIs seem to believe exists. But what does the empirical evidence show?

Past empirical evidence on the catalytic effect

Although it is difficult to identify exactly when the catalytic effect was first described, its widespread currency was clearly facilitated by numerous anecdotal accounts of IFI (primarily IMF) agreements being followed by fresh capital inflows (Kenen, 1986; McCauley, 1986; de Vries, 1986; Buira, 1987; and Pool and Starnos, 1987). The 'gatekeeper' role of the IMF was subsequently formalised in institutional settings such as the Paris Club (Milivojevic, 1985). The catalytic effect, however, cannot be proved definitively on the basis of these anecdotal observations since there was no way of testing the counterfactual. More systematic evidence is required.

Most of the existing systematic empirical evidence on the catalytic effect has been coincidental to work that has had a different focus. Attempts to estimate the demand function for IMF credit and to explain the economic characteristics of user and non-user countries have, for example, often included a variable designed to capture the significance of alternative (usually private) sources of finance (Bird and Orme, 1981; Cornelius, 1987; Joyce, 1989; and Bird, 1994, 1995). The results of such studies have generally suggested the absence of any significant relationship, or at best only a weak relationship which is as likely to be negative as positive. A negative coefficient implies that IMF lending and private lending are substitutes, rather than the complements that the catalytic effect predicts.

With a focus on aspects of external debt, other research has also raised doubts about the complementarity hypothesis. Using a sophisticated econometric model, Hajivassiliou (1987) attempts to explain in detail the pattern of debt servicing problems in LDCs between 1970 and 1982. His results reveal a significant negative relationship between IMF involvement and both the supply of new loans and the level of arrears deemed 'acceptable' by a country's creditors. Unfortunately the model is not designed specifically to test the catalytic effect, and the results may be biased by the use of IMF agreements as part of a proxy for debt servicing problems. The absence of complementarity between IMF support and other forms of new lending, however, provides no support for the catalytic effect.

In a study of the impact of structural adjustment under the sponsorship of the IMF and the World Bank over the period 1982–86, Faini *et al.* (1991) also find a significant negative correlation between IFI lending and net private credit. A similar result is discovered by Killick (1995), who finds that IMF agreements are generally associated with a net deterioration in the capital account of the balance of payments of the countries involved, with loans from the Fund in effect being used to pay off previous commercial loans rather than encourage new ones. A review of case study evidence undertaken by the same author fails to provide any compelling support for the catalytic effect. In the isolated cases where any positive effect appears to be at work, it applies only to other public flows and not to private capital. Earlier case study research had found a similar pattern, concluding that IMF involvement was neither a necessary nor a sufficient condition for private capital inflows (Bird, 1978).

The need to distinguish between the effects on private and public flows is highlighted by Rowlands (1994b) who, on the basis of aggregate econometric investigation, discovers a catalytic effect of Fund lending on other public flows but not on private flows. Rowlands also shows that the catalytic effect, to the extent that it exists, is not time invariant.

Further evidence against the idea of a catalytic effect of IMF lending on private capital flows comes from Ozler (1993) who sets out to explain the determinants of interest rate spreads on commercial loans to developing countries over 1968 to 1981. He finds that countries that had had IMF standby agreements seem to have been charged higher interest rates than those that had not, suggesting that IMF involvement is taken to indicate higher risks and providing no support for a positive impact on credibility.

Most of the studies cited have concentrated on the IMF, where the claims for a catalytic effect have been strongest. Research that has examined the effects of World Bank structural adjustment lending has also discovered a generally neutral effect on private flows even when a range of methodologies have been used (Mosley, Harrigan and Toye, 1991). Thus the overall assessment must be that neither of the key multilateral IFIs have been shown to have a particularly strong catalytic effect on lending.

In summary a large portion of the available empirical evidence fails to provide support for the claim that the IFIs have an important catalysing role. Although this is broadly consistent with theoretical expectations, a number of doubts still remain. First, as noted earlier, most of the studies quoted have not set out directly to test for the catalytic effect and have been designed accordingly. The evidence on it has therefore often been the by-product of research with a different focus. Second, the existing research has usually been conducted at a high level of aggregation, and relationships that exist may therefore have been concealed. Case study evidence, on the other hand, has probably been too partial and piecemeal to allow firm generalisations to be drawn. The next section presents some new empirical evidence about IMF agreements that helps to explain some of the anomalies in the debate on the catalytic effect.

New empirical evidence

The models

As indicated previously, a major obstacle to the investigation of the catalytic effect is the absence of a well-defined theoretical model of capital flows.

Four distinct problems arise from this deficiency. First of all, the choice of the dependent variable is not obvious. Second, the selection of explanatory variables is largely arbitrary. Selecting the form of the equation to be estimated is the third problem, while the lag structure imbedded in the model represents the fourth source of uncertainty. We do not claim to solve these problems in the results presented here. Rather we focus on how the choice of dependent variable may explain some of the discrepancies between previous investigations regarding the catalytic effect, as well as on the sensitivity of the results to sample disaggregation.

The results presented here are based on a series of new ordinary least-squares regressions which were run on a panel data set of 90 LDCs from 1974–89.[6] The sample was restricted to IMF members only, though tests indicate that this restriction has no significant effect on the estimation results. The focus of the study is on IMF high-conditionality agreements, which should have relatively strong effects according to proponents of the catalytic theory.

As indicated, there is no reliable theory to which we can appeal in order to identify the 'best' dependent variable. The dependent variables used in this chapter are all based on the level of new lending commitments to a country. Direct foreign investment is not included. The incorporation of commitments (rather than disbursements) in the dependent variable is innovative. This choice is motivated by the expectation that lending commitments are more immediately sensitive to changes in the borrowing country, while disbursement measures may have a lag structure arising from previous commitments. It should also be recognised that commitment-based variables have potential deficiencies, the most obvious being the potential for disbursement horizons (i.e. the number of years over which the commitments will be disbursed) to change. The three different versions of the dependent variable used here are, new lending commitments net of principal repayments (unscaled), net new lending commitments as a percentage of GNP, and net new lending commitments as a percentage of exports. Since the importance of capital flows depends on their magnitude relative to the size of the economy, rather than their absolute level, the estimations using the scaled versions of the dependent variable should yield more relevant results. The use of gross lending commitments (i.e. unadjusted for principal repayments) did not significantly alter the qualitative results of the estimations.

The independent variables were chosen primarily on the basis of the estimating models used by Hajivassiliou (1987), Savvides (1990) and Rowlands (1994b). The key difference with Hajivassiliou's original model is the separation of the IMF variable from the arrears and rescheduling indicators. In addition, those explanatory variables most pertinent to direct foreign investment were not included in the present estimations.

The first four explanatory variables measure *domestic characteristics* of the economy. The first of these is per capita income. While both Savvides and Rowlands found the effect to be largely positive in the reduced form equation (due to supply effects), Hajivassiliou finds only a negative influence through the demand side. This empirical discrepancy can be explained in part by Rowlands' use of squared per capita income in addition to the linear term, which he found to have a negative coefficient. The square of per capita income is the second explanatory variable in this analysis as well. The third and fourth variables are the GDP growth rate and the investment-to-GDP ratio. Growth had an insignificant effect in Hajivassiliou's study, where it was included as a determinant of both the demand and supply of new loans. Investment may be expected to have a positive effect on new flows, since it raises the current demand for financing at the same time as leading to improved future repayment ability, thereby encouraging supply. Growth rates, being backward looking, may have a weaker effect, although a positive effect should occur for supply reasons if lenders forecast future performance partly on the basis of past growth.[7]

The next four explanatory variables focus on the *external characteristics* of countries. The first of these is the debt-service ratio, which Hajivassiliou uses as a determinant of loan demand with an expected and estimated positive coefficient. The next variable is the exports-to-GNP ratio, which had a positive effect in Savvides's study of capital flows, but an insignificant effect in Hajivassiliou's. The approximately equivalent variable used by Rowlands (the ratio of imports plus exports to GNP) was found to have a negative effect in some circumstances. The reserves-to-imports ratio was used by Hajivassiliou in the equation for the supply of new loans and found to have no significant effect. As a demand variable, relatively high reserves may be expected to reduce the demand for loans by LDC governments to the extent that they provide a substitute channel for financing current account balance of payments deficits. However, private lenders may take higher international reserves as signalling enhanced creditworthiness and, in these circumstances governments may build up reserves in order to improve their access to private capital markets; indeed private capital inflows may be used to help accumulate international reserves. The fourth variable capturing an external characteristic is the international interest rate, represented by the LIBOR rate.

To reflect information delays, the previous eight variables were all lagged in the estimation equations. Regressions on the unlagged data, however, were not qualitatively different from those reported here.

The final two variables are binary, and are not lagged in the estimations since they would be observable events.[8] The first of these indicates repayment difficulties, and takes the value of 1 when a country is either in arrears or has rescheduled some of its debt in either the current or preceding year. Typically problems signalled by such an event should be negatively associated with new lending for supply reasons. However, the positive effect on demand, plus the potential for defensive lending by creditors, may generate a positive correlation between repayment difficulties and loan commitments. Previous studies have generally found the corresponding rescheduling variable to have a negative influence on new loans. The second binary variable indicates whether or not a country has an IMF stand-by or Extended Fund Facility agreement, and is thus the key variable for analysing the catalytic effect.

The results

The results of the full-sample estimations are provided in Table 12.1 with the definitions of terms and sources of data being reported in the Appendix. Although the magnitudes of the coefficients are not strictly comparable due to the differences in scaling, the general effects of different variables can be compared. In general, the domestic characteristic variables had the same coefficient signs in all three models, though in many cases their estimated coefficients were insignificant. With regard to external characteristics the

Table 12.1 The full-sample estimation results

Independent variables	Dependent variables		
	Net commitments	Commitments/ GNP	Commitments/ exports
Domestic characteristics			
Constant	***263.1 (3.6)	***8.70 (14.3)	**5.20 (17.0)
GDP per capita	−170.4 (0.4)	***−29.20 (7.5)	***−18.40 (9.2)
[GDP p.c.]^2	−364.2 (0.5)	***26.30 (4.3)	***18.30 (5.8)
GDP growth	***−8.8 (2.5)	0.040 (1.4)	**0.03 (2.0)
Investment/GDP	3.5 (1.2)	***0.063 (2.7)	***0.04 (3.0)
External characteristics			
Debt service ratio	***1734 (7.4)	2.80 (1.5)	***2.93 (3.0)
Exports/GNP	***−294.0 (2.7)	***4.23 (5.0)	***−3.65 (8.4)
Liquidity	−143.3 (1.6)	***−3.27 (4.4)	0.27 (0.7)
LIBOR	***−40.5 (4.6)	***−0.39 (5.5)	***−0.11 (3.1)
Difficulties	***−153.9 (3.1)	**0.91 (2.2)	*** 0.76 (3.5)
IMF agreement	49.2 (1.0)	−0.41 (1.1)	***−0.68 (3.4)
Summary statistics			
No. of observations	1865	1862	1854
Durbin Watson	0.69	1.02	0.82
Adjusted R^2	0.31	0.096	0.15
F-test	***78.0	**19.7	***34.5

Notes: To facilitate the reporting of the results, the coefficients for the GNP-scaled model were multiplied by 100, while those of the export model were multiplied by 10. This rescaling does not affect the *t*-statistics, which appear in parentheses. Variables marked ***, ** or * are significant at the 1%, 2.5% and 5% levels of significance, respectively.

effect of the debt service ratio, international reserves, and international interest rates tended to be consistent across all the models estimated. When the signs of the estimated coefficients for these variables did differ, the outlier was insignificant. The exports-to-GNP ratio and the binary variable for repayment difficulties all had significant coefficients, but the sign varied across the models. Thus the estimation results are clearly sensitive to the choice of the dependent variable used to measure new loan commitments. Of specific interest in the context of this chapter are the estimated coefficients for the IMF agreement indicator. In the unscaled model the coefficient was positive, but insignificant. In the model in which net commitments were scaled by GNP, the effect was negative, but also insignificant. It is only in the third model, where new loan commitments are scaled by exports, that a negative and significant coefficient is found. Because of its use of exports to scale the new loan commitments, this last model most closely resembles Hajivassiliou's study which, as noted earlier, raised doubts about the catalytic effect. In summary the evidence presented in Table 12.1 calls into serious question the existence of a positive catalytic effect, and even indicates that the effect may actually be negative.

In addition to the full sample results, however, a number of disaggregated estimations were performed in order to check for the consistency of the results across various sub-samples of the data. All three models were estimated again discriminating between official and private lending commitments. These two additional estimations, plus the original total lending commitment estimations, were then run for the separate time periods of 1973–81 and 1982–89, and on the different recipient groups of relatively better off and poor LDCs. The coefficient estimates vary across the sub-samples, as would be expected, although most retain their sign and degree of significance.[9] The results for the IMF indicator variable are provided in Table 12.2.

In only three cases did the IMF agreement indicator have the positive and significant estimated coefficient as predicted by the catalytic effect. These were for unscaled official lending commitments. The positive effect appears to be largely associated with the earlier period and with poorer countries, which may be a primary target for official lending. The positive influence of the IMF found here could account for early anecdotal observations about a positive catalytic effect. The effect largely evaporates for private lending, for better off countries, and for the 1982–89 sub-period, following the debt crisis. Furthermore, the observed increases in lending were not evaluated in the context of a country's size, that is, the observation was of absolute, not relative, new lending. The use of unscaled lending commitments, and the limited sample in which the effect is observed, raises serious questions about the relevance and generality of a catalytic effect.

The version of the model in which new loan commitments are scaled by GNP reveals that in two cases IMF agreements appear to have a systematic *negative* effect on new lending. The effect is concentrated in the later

Table 12.2   Disaggregated estimation results for the IMF indicator

Sample	IMF indicator coefficient (*t*-statistic)		
	Net commitments	Net commitments GNP	Net commitments exports
Total, full sample	49.2 (1.0)	−0.41 (1.1)	*** −0.68 (3.4)
Total, 1973–81	9.1 (0.2)	−0.27 (0.5)	−0.27 (1.1)
Total, 1982–89	−10.7 (0.2)	*** −0.15 (2.6)	*** −1.29 (4.8)
Total, poorer LDCs	53.9 (1.5)	−0.66 (1.2)	*** −9.71 (3.2)
Total, richer LDCs	−75.0 (0.7)	0.47 (1.0)	0.02 (0.1)
Official, full sample	*** 66.9 (2.8)	0.41 (1.2)	*** −0.65 (3.4)
Official, 1973–81	*** 76.8 (3.0)	0.05 (0.1)	−0.08 (0.4)
Official, 1982–89	40.6 (1.0)	** −1.19 (2.3)	*** −1.23 (4.0)
Official, poorer LDCs	* 45.7 (1.7)	−0.43 (0.9)	*** −0.88 (3.0)
Official, richer LDCs	24.9 (0.6)	0.20 (0.7)	−0.02 (0.2)
Private, full sample	−17.6 (0.5)	−0.001 (0.0)	−0.03 (0.5)
Private, 1973–81	−67.6 (1.6)	−0.32 (1.0)	* −0.19 (1.8)
Private, 1982–89	−51.4 (0.9)	−0.27 (1.5)	−0.06 (1.1)
Private, poorer LDCs	8.2 (0.3)	−0.23 (1.0)	−0.10 (1.3)
Private, richer LDCs	−99.8 (1.1)	0.26 (0.9)	0.04 (0.4)

Notes: To facilitate the reporting of the results, the coefficients for the GNP-scaled model were multiplied by 100, while those of the export scaled model were multiplied by 10. This re-scaling does not affect the *t*-statistics, which appear in parentheses. Variables marked ***, ** or * are significant at the 1%, 2.5% and 5% levels of significance, respectively.

(post-1981) period and appears to be particularly pronounced for official lending, an unexpected result. These results are corroborated in the third set of estimations in which new loan commitments are scaled to exports. In these estimations a negative coefficient for the IMF agreement indicator is estimated in seven out of fifteen cases. The negative effect is particularly pronounced in the later period and for poorer LDCs. The primary category of lending adversely affected is official commitments. In only the case of the scaled model for the earlier period did the commitment of private loans appear to be significantly negatively affected by IMF agreements.

The conclusions from these estimations do not generally support the notion of a positive catalytic effect. Some important qualifications, however, should be pointed out. The strongest evidence against the catalytic effect has come from models in which the new loans have been scaled by exports. Since IMF conditions frequently stipulate exchange rate devaluation, the observed negative coefficient might reflect export expansion rather than loan contraction. However, an attempt to capture this explanation by using the previous year's export levels in the regressions led to no substantive differences in the coefficient estimates. Nonetheless the far weaker negative effects in the model where loans are instead scaled by GNP (a more slowly evolving variable than exports and one that evidence suggests is largely unaffected by IMF-backed programmes) implies that some of the observed effect of the IMF indicator may be due to changes in the export scaling variable rather than loan commitments.

Further caution must be exercised in interpreting the results. The absence of a formal model to explain international lending is a serious constraint, since the estimating equations may be mis-specified as a consequence. The sensitivity of the results to the specification of the dependent variable highlights this problem. We have already noted one potential deficiency of the measure used here, and if disbursement horizons do indeed decline when IMF agreements are negotiated, then the results here would understate any positive catalytic effect. Finally, the estimation technique is simple ordinary least squares. This technique is sufficient for the illustrative purposes of this chapter, but caution must be exercised in drawing firm and precise conclusions.

The most important lesson from the estimations provided here and elsewhere in the literature is that it may not be sensible to speak about a catalytic effect at all. The overall evidence indicates that the effect of the international financial institutions on other lenders varies across time and location. Therefore, we need more sophisticated theoretical and empirical research which concentrates on explaining the nuances of any IFI catalysis.

Policy implications

The policy implications of the results reported in this chapter are clear and unambiguous at one level, but nuanced, multifaceted, and ill-defined at another. To the extent that IFIs determine their lending policies on the assumption that negotiating a programme will lead to significant extra capital inflows for the borrower from other sources, these policies are likely to be sub-optimal. Furthermore, since the design of adjustment policy reflects assumptions about the supply of external financing, overestimating capital inflows will result in inappropriately designed adjustment strategies which are therefore likely to fail. The shift by the IMF towards medium-term structural adjustment during the mid-to-late 1980s and away from the almost exclusive emphasis that had previously been placed on managing domestic aggregate demand brought with it additional external financing needs. Structural adjustment is unlikely to succeed if starved of finance. The Fund appears to have assumed, perhaps on the basis of partial and, in the event, unrepresentative evidence, that finance would come from elsewhere, catalysed by its own involvement. In practice the catalytic effect was largely unforthcoming and IMF-backed programmes showed an increasing tendency to break down. Significantly the likelihood of breakdown appears to vary inversely with the amount of finance provided by the Fund.

The policy implications that follow on from the existence of little or no catalysis may be represented as a range of options. First, if structural adjustment requires additional external financing, the Fund (and Bank) will, in the short run, have to take on greater responsibility for providing it; they should not assume that it will materialise from other sources, at least until confidence has been established over time. Second, without the willingness to provide larger amounts of supporting finance, the Fund will have to revert to encouraging older-style short-term demand-side adjustment. The potential Catch-22 here is that private capital markets may favour this type of adjustment over structural adjustment and be more prepared to support it financially (even though it requires less such support). Scepticism about structural adjustment may have prevented private capital markets, or indeed official lenders, from providing the amounts of finance upon which its success depends. Third, a commitment by the IFIs to structural adjustment in circumstances where the catalytic effect does not exist and where the institutions' own lending capacity is constrained, implies that they may have to be more selective in terms of the countries they support. However, a final policy option is for the IFIs to create or strengthen the catalysing role in the future. How might they set about doing this?

It is in this context that policy becomes nuanced and less well-defined. The IFIs need to be able to identify the circumstances in which their involvement has had positive, neutral and negative consequences for other capital flows, and then seek to create the circumstances that are associated with a positive effect. However, Fund conditionality has historically been largely invariant in terms of its fundamentals (even during the era of structural adjustment), and this suggests that it is 'other factors', outside the design of programmes, that determine the sign and size of the catalytic effect. This could imply that the Fund is essentially impotent in enhancing the catalytic effect.[10] Alternatively it may mean that it needs to influence the 'other factors', including perhaps the perceived degree of government commitment to policy reform and therefore the credibility of IFI-backed programmes, or, indeed that it needs to be more flexible in its design of conditionality, varying programmes to reflect individual country differences.

However, research has yet to establish, in any detail, the circumstances which favour a significant and positive catalysing impact by the IFIs. Does the strength of the effect depend on small variations in programme design and, if so, how; or on the extent to which countries implement programmes, and if so to what extent; does the catalytic effect take longer to materialise than has been assumed, and if so, how long does it take; does it depend on other economic and political characteristics, and if so which ones? Until these questions can be answered with some measure of confidence the IFIs need to focus more generally on improving the effectiveness of their conditionality, and on increasing their own contingent lending capacity.

More concretely the analysis in this chapter suggests that some recent policy initiatives are ill-conceived. The idea of a 'three-pronged' approach to programme design comprising, first, reining in domestic demand through fiscal and credit constraint, second, adopting structural reforms to promote a desirable supply response in the domestic economy and to improve the efficiency of resource use, and third, mobilising external financing to support adjustment programmes (*IMF Survey*, 31 July 1995), makes little sense when the third prong is often absent and certainly unpredictable. Moreover, the notion that the Fund can defuse Mexico-type financial crises by calming market fears, and can stabilise private capital flows by providing more information on country-specific macroeconomic performance assumes that the institution exerts an influence over international capital flows that the evidence fails to find. The direct implication of this is that policies to stabilise capital markets need to be sought elsewhere. Evidence presented here suggests that the IMF perhaps exerted its strongest influence over private international lending at a time when it was directly coercing the private international banks to lend to developing countries in the aftermath of the debt crisis. IMF support became conditional on private capital market lending. While the circumstances under which coercion is a viable option have probably passed, a more permanent lesson is that official co-ordination can on occasions, and in particular at a time of crisis, overcome free riding by private lenders. The Fund and Bank therefore need to examine ways of designing an institutional framework, other than coercion, that will help to co-ordinate private lending. Certainly the IFIs need to acknowledge that up to now their conditionality has not inspired confidence amongst private lenders. The IMF's seal of approval has not had a high or significant market value. The signalling role of the IMF and the World Bank – the most frequently cited source of a near-term catalytic effect – has clearly not operated as intended, and this raises serious and fundamental questions about the whole *modus operandi* and rationale of conditionality.

There are stronger empirical reasons for defending IFI conditionality as a means of catalysing official lending. But as a feature upon which to build, this rationale is uncompelling when official lending has been declining and is likely to continue to do so. Besides, this will only be relevant for the poorest countries and not those middle income countries which look to the IFIs' endorsement as a way of accelerating their access to private capital markets. Countries will be under a less strong incentive to turn to the IMF at an early stage of balance of payments difficulty, or to agree and then fully implement programmes of policies, if there is little likelihood that they will be rewarded by additional private inflows. A vicious circle can easily become established under which the poor record of conditionality fails to inspire confidence amongst private lenders, while simultaneously inadequate private financing undermines the effectiveness of conditionality. Repetition of this circle of events only serves to strengthen negative catalysis. Co-ordination problems imply that breaking out of this vicious circle is an issue for international public policy. At present the image of the Fund as a lender of last resort only to be used at times of balance of payments crisis when no other alternatives exist is hardly consistent with a strongly positive signal, particularly where commercial considerations are paramount.

Conclusions

The catalytic effect of international financial institutions is an important policy issue. The ability to leverage additional funds from private and official lenders (as well as investors) would be a valuable tool for multilateral institutions seeking to improve conditions in developing countries. Recent events, such as the Mexican peso crisis, also illustrate how important it is to be able to galvanise rapidly substantial financial resources. Unfortunately the previously accepted 'stylised fact' about the IFI's catalytic effect appears to be too stylised and insufficiently grounded in fact.

The theoretical reasons as to why the IFIs should have a catalytic effect are inconclusive at best. Meanwhile the actual effects of IFI conditionality do little to instil investor confidence. In conjunction with the enforcement and compliance problems, the basis for assuming complementarity between multilateral lending and other capital flows is, therefore, very tenuous. Furthermore, the theory makes it clear that any catalytic effect depends crucially on the goals and perceptions of other lenders and investors, whose views are unlikely to be identical or constant. Thus it makes little theoretical sense to suggest that the IFIs will induce a stable and symmetric reaction from a set of heterogeneous lenders, or to assume that such reactions are insensitive to the characteristics of the borrowing country.

The empirical evidence generally supports these conclusions. In the absence of a strong theoretical model of capital flows, empirical analyses must be interpreted with caution. The results of previous empirical studies have been at least partially contradictory. The estimations presented in this chapter set out more directly to test for the existence of a catalytic effect but find little evidence to support it. They do, however, indicate that the effect of the IFIs is sensitive to how capital flows are measured. Furthermore any catalytic effect on lending, positive or negative, varies across time, lenders and recipients.

For this reason it is legitimate to ask whether the catalytic effect may have become stronger since the end of the 1980s, beyond the period covered by this study. Certainly there are those who claim that the surge of capital flows into Latin America was in part associated with the IMF's involvement. Such loose empiricism is, however, over-casual. Our evidence suggests that the catalytic effect on private flows was at its strongest when IFIs were coercing private markets into lending and this was no longer the case in the 1990s. Moreover, the Mexican peso crisis, as well as econometric evidence

(Chuhan, Claessens and Mamingi, 1993; Claessens, Dooley and Warner, 1995; Fernandez-Arias, 1996; and Fernandez-Arias and Montiel, 1996), illustrates how short-term capital flows are dominated by things other than IFI involvement.[11] The shift to new forms of private international lending provides no justification for believing that the IFIs' catalysing role will be enhanced. As far as official lending is concerned, and at an overall level, an increasing spread of country involvement by the IMF has coincided with a declining trend in aid flows.

The results reported in this chapter have important policy implications. Finance from IFIs may substitute for rather than complement other flows. The premise of a universally positive catalytic effect will lead to inappropriate conditionality and will have adverse consequences for its effectiveness. A positive catalytic effect could certainly be important, particularly where is applies to private capital flows and since official lending is on a downward trend, but the IFIs will have to rethink their relationships with private lenders and capital markets if this potential role is to become generally significant. To the extent that a catalytic role exists, it is likely to be a long-run phenomenon and to depend on the extent to which the IFIs make a significant contribution to improving the economic fundamentals in the countries in which they are involved. There is no quick fix. As of now the IFIs need to acknowledge that their involvement is as likely to have negative effects on other financial flows. The IFIs catalysing role has been misrepresented in the past. It has been too frequently taken for granted with insufficient attention being paid to its theoretical and empirical foundations. This chapter has attempted to enhance our understanding, but it also identifies an agenda for future research into what is an important element of IFI reform.

Appendix

Data definitions and sources

Commitments are the new credit commitments made to a country by official lenders (i.e. bilateral or multilateral) or private lenders (i.e. commercial banks, bond markets and other private sources). Source: World Bank: *World Tables* (computerised).

Debt service ratio is the ratio of interest and principle payments on debt as a proportion of a country's exports of goods and services. Source: World Bank: *World Tables* (computerised).

Difficulties is a dummy variable taking on the value of 1 if the country's government was in arrears on its external payment obligations, or had rescheduled its debts to either its official or private lenders, in either the current or previous year. Sources: IMF: *Exchange Arrangements and Exchange Restrictions* Annual Reports; IMF: *Balance of Payments Yearbook*; IMF: *International Capital Markets Developments and Prospects* and World Bank: *World Tables* (computerised).

Exports-to-GNP ratio is the ratio of a country's exports of goods and services to its GNP. Source: World Bank: *World Tables* (computerised).

GDP per capita is the ratio of a country's per capita GDP to the per capita GDP of the United States. The calculation used primarily the Penn World Tables data for the comparison. On occasion it was necessary to supplement these data with World Bank data to either extend the Penn World Tables or construct an approximate series. Sources: Penn World Tables (computerised); World Bank: *World Tables* (printed and computerised).

GDP growth is the annual percentage increase in real GDP. Source: World Bank: *World Tables* (printed and computerised).

IMF agreement is a dummy variable which takes the value of 1 if an IMF stand-by or EFF arrangement was available to a country for at least part of a given year, and takes the value 0 otherwise. Source: *IMF Annual Report*, 1970–94.

Investment/GDP is the percentage of GDP devoted to investment. The primary source was the Penn World Tables (computerised). Supplemented by the World Bank: *World Tables* (printed and computerised).

LIBOR is the London Interbank Offer Rate on US government 6 month treasury bills less the rate of US consumer price inflation. Source: IMF: *International Financial Statistics*.

Liquidity is the ratio of a country's official foreign reserves (excluding gold) to its imports. Source: IMF: *International Financial Statistics* (computerised), World Bank: *World Tables* (computerised).

References

Bird, G. (1978), *The International Monetary System and the Less Developed Countries* (Macmillan, 1978, second edition, 1982).

Bird, G. (1994), 'The Myths and Realities of IMF Lending', *The World Economy*, **17**, 759–78.

Bird, G. (1995), *IMF Lending to Developing Countries: Issues and Evidence* (London, Routledge).

Bird, G. (1996), 'The International Monetary Fund and Developing Countries: A Review of the Evidence and Policy Options', *International Organization*, **50**, 477–511.

Bird, G. (1998), 'The Effectiveness of Conditionality and the Political Economy of Policy Reform: Is it Simply a Matter of Political Will?', *Journal of Policy Reform*, **1**, 89–113.

Bird, G. and T. Orme (1981), 'An Analysis of Drawings on the International Monetary Fund by Developing Countries', *World Development*, **9**, 563–8.

Bleaney, M. and D. Greenaway (1993), 'Adjustment to External Imbalances and Investment Slumps in Developing Countries', *European Economic Review*, **37** (April), 577–85.

Buira, A. (1987), 'Adjustment with Growth and the Role of the IMF in the 1980s', in S. Dell, (ed.), *The International Monetary System and its Reform: Papers Prepared for the Group of Twenty-four* (The Netherlands; Elsevier Science Publishers), 729–49.

Chuhan, P., S. Claessens and N. Mamingi (1993), 'Equity and Bond Flows to Asia and Latin America', *Policy Research Working Papers*, No 1160 (The World Bank, Washington, DC).

Claessens, S., M. Dooley and A. Warner (1995), 'Portfolio Capital Flows: Hot or Cold?', *The World Bank Economic Review*, 9, 153–74.

Conway, P. (1994), 'IMF Lending Programs: Participation and Impact', *Journal of Development Economics*, 45, 365–91.

Cornelius, P. (1987), 'The Demand for IMF Credits by Sub-Saharan African Countries', *Economics Letters*, 23, 99–102.

de Vries, M. (1986), 'The Role of the International Monetary Fund in the World Debt Problem', in M. Claudon (ed.), *World Debt Crisis: International Lending on Trial* (Cambridge, Mass, Ballinger Publishing Company), 111–22.

Dhonte, P. (1997), 'Conditionality as an Instrument of Borrower Credibility', *IMF Working Paper on Policy Analysis and Assessment*, 97/2 (IMF, Washington, DC).

Fernandez-Arias, E. (1996), 'The New Wave of Capital Inflows: Push or Pull?', *Journal of Development Economics*, 48, 389–418.

Fernandez-Arias, E. and P. Montiel (1996), 'The Surge of Capital Inflows to Developing Countries: An Analytical Overview', *The World Bank Economic Review*, 10, 51–77.

Faini, R., J. de Melo, A. Senhadji-Semlali and J. Stanton (1991), 'Macro Performance Under Adjustment Lending', in V. Thomas, A. Chhibber, M. Dailami, and J. de Melo (eds.), *Restructuring Economies in Distress. Policy Reform and the World Bank* (Washington DC, The World Bank), 222–42.

Fanelli, J. M., R. Frenkel and L. Taylor (1994), 'Is the Market-Friendly Approach Friendly to Development: A Critical Review', in G. Bird and A. Helwege (eds.), *Latin America's Economic Future* (Academic Press, London and San Diego).

Greene, J. and D. Villanueva (1991), 'Private Investment in Developing Countries: An Empirical Analysis', *IMF Staff Papers*, 38, 33–58.

Hajivassiliou, V. (1987), 'The External Debt Repayment Problems of LDCs: An Econometric Model Based on Panel Data', *Journal of Econometrics*, 36, 205–30.

Joyce, J. (1989), 'The Economic Characteristics of IMF Program Countries', *Economics Letters*, 38, 237–42.

Kenen, P. (1986), *Financing, Adjustment and the International Monetary Fund* (Washington DC, The Brookings Institution).

Killick, T. (1995), *IMF Programmes in Developing Countries: Design and Impact* (Routledge/ODI, London).

Knight, M. and J. Santaella (1994), 'Economic Determinants of Fund Financial Arrangements', *IMF Working Paper*, WP/94/36 (Washington DC, IMF).

McCauley, R. (1986), 'IMF: Managed Lending', in M. Claudon (ed.), *World Debt Crisis: International Lending on Trial* (Cambridge, Mass, Ballinger Publishing Company), 123–46.

Milivojevic, M. (1985), *The Debt Rescheduling Process* (New York, St Martin's Press).

Mosley, P., J. Harrigan and J. Toye (1991), *Aid and Power: The World Bank and Policy-Based Lending*, 2 Vols (London, Routledge).

Ozler, U. (1993), 'Have Commercial Banks Ignored History?', *American Economic Review*, 83, 608–20.

Pool, J. C. and S. Stamos (1987), *The ABCs of International Finance* (Lexington, Mass, Lexington Books).

Rodrik, D. (1996), 'Understanding Economic Policy Reform', *Journal of Economic Literature* (March), 9–41.

Rowlands, D. (1994a), 'Political and Economic Determinants of IMF Conditional Credit Agreements, 1973–1989' (The Norman Paterson School of International Affairs Development Studies Working Paper 6).

Rowlands, D. (1994b), 'The Response of New Lending to the IMF' (The Norman Paterson School of International Affairs Development Studies Working Paper 7).

Santaella, J. A. (1995), 'Four Decades of Fund Arrangements: Macroeconomic Stylized Facts Before the Adjustment Programme', *IMF Working Paper*, WP/95/94 (IMF, Washington DC).

Savvides, A. (1991), 'LDC Creditworthiness and Foreign Capital Inflows, 1980–86', *Journal of Development Economics*, **34**, 309–27.

Schadler, S., A. Bennett, M. Carkovic, L. Dicks-Mireaux, M. Mecagni, J. H. J. Morsink and M. A. Savastano (1995), *IMF Conditionality: Experience Under Stand-By and Extended Arrangements: Part I: Key Issues and Findings, and Part II: Background Papers*, Occasional Papers, Nos 128 and 129 (IMF, Washington, September).

Treasury Committee (1997), *International Monetary Fund, Fourth Report* (together with Proceedings, Minutes of Evidence and Appendices), House of Commons, London Stationery Office.

Ul Haque, N. *et al.* (1996), 'The Economic Content of Indicators of Developing Country Creditworthiness', *IMF Staff Papers* (December), 688–723.

Ul Haque, N., D. Mathieson and S. Sharma (1997), 'Causes of Capital Inflows and Policy Responses to them', *Finance and Development* (March) 3–9.

13
The Political Economy of Foreign Aid: Fatigue or Regeneration?

Graham Bird

Introduction

Since the early 1990s there has been a pronounced fall in the real amount of foreign aid provided by donors for developing countries. Over the same period, while progress has been made in some parts of the developing world, Africa, a region which has relied heavily on aid flows, has witnessed little if any reduction in poverty. Indeed, the number of people living in poverty world-wide is likely to rise in the remaining years of the twentieth century. On the face of it aid is being withdrawn when it is still desperately needed.

But is foreign aid effective in alleviating poverty? If not, reducing it may be the sensible thing to do. If there are no developmental returns, why incur the cost?

Foreign aid: the empirical picture

A number of significant trends in foreign aid may be gleaned from the Tables provided in this Section, all of which are drawn from the OECD's *Development Co-operation Report*, 1996, the IMF's *Official Financing for Developing Countries*, 1998, and *Global Development Finance* 1998, published by the World Bank. Table 13.1 shows that Official Development Assistance (ODA) fell from US$62.7 billion in 1991 to US$34.7 billion in 1996. Bilateral ODA, which represents two-thirds of all official flows, dropped 7 per cent in real terms and 10 per cent in nominal terms in 1996. A 16 per cent increase in multilateral aid in real terms only partially offset the decline in bilateral assistance. Not surprisingly, given the positive growth performance amongst OECD countries, aid as a percentage of donors' GNPs fell to an average of 0.25 per cent in 1996, the lowest for thirty years. Data in Table 13.2 provide a breakdown by donor over the period 1980–95. During the 1980s, the aid/GNP ratio had been roughly constant at about 0.34 or 0.33 per cent; economic growth in donor countries implied a related growth in real aid over this period.

Table 13.1 Net resource flows to developing countries

	Current $ billion									Per cent of total		
	1987	1988	1989	1990	1991	1992	1993	1994	1995	1987	1989	1995
I Official development finance (ODF)	56.7	61.4	61.1	69.8	69.7	69.8	70.1	71.6	69.4	66.1	52.7	28.3
1. Official development assistance (ODA)[a]	43.9	47.9	49.0	52.9	58.6	58.9	56.4	60.5	60.1	51.2	42.2	24.7
of which: Bilateral disbursements	34.0	36.8	36.6	39.4	42.4	41.4	39.6	41.3	40.6	39.6	31.6	16.0
Multilateral disbursements	9.9	11.1	12.4	13.5	16.2	17.5	16.8	19.2	19.5	11.5	10.7	8.7
2. Other ODF	12.8	13.5	12.1	16.9	11.1	10.9	13.7	11.1	9.3	14.9	10.4	3.6
of which: Bilateral disbursements	6.2	7.0	5.3	6.7	4.4	7.4	6.4	7.5	5.0	7.2	4.6	2.0
Multilateral disbursements	6.6	6.5	6.8	10.2	6.7	3.5	7.3	3.6	4.3	7.7	5.9	1.6
II Total export credits	-1.6	-2.2	9.4	4.7	1.8	1.3	-0.6	9.3	11.0	-1.9	8.1	4.3
of which: Short-term	4.1	2.0	4.8	4.5	-0.8	0.5	-1.5	0.2	0.8	4.8	4.1	0.3
III Private flows	30.7	39.1	45.5	51.8	50.8	76.8	86.4	134.1	158.9	35.8	39.2	67.4
1. Direct investment (DAC)	19.4	21.8	26.5	26.4	22.6	27.3	38.6	48.5	53.6	22.6	22.8	23.7
of which: to offshore centres	10.9	8.9	6.5	7.1	6.5	9.5	9.5	9.1	9.0	12.7	5.6	3.6

2. International bank lending[b]	7.0	7.8	10.5	15.0	11.0	31.0	9.0	42.6	70.0	8.2	9.1	29.6
of which: Short-term	5.0	4.0	8.0	7.0	12.0	25.0	7.0	44.0	50.0	5.8	6.9	27.7
3. Total bond lending	−1.0	1.6	2.2	0.9	6.5	11.1	29.0	29.0	19.3	−1.2	1.9	7.6
4. Other private[c]	1.3	3.7	2.3	4.4	5.3	1.4	4.0	8.0	10.0	1.5	2.0	4.0
5. Grants by non-governmental organisations	4.0	4.2	4.0	5.1	5.4	6.0	5.8	6.0	6.0	4.7	3.4	2.4
Total net resource flows (I + II + III)	85.8	98.3	116.0	126.3	122.3	147.8	155.9	215.0	239.3	100.0	100.0	100.0
At 1994 prices and exchange rates:												
Total net resource flows	114.3	121.5	144.8	141.4	132.2	150.8	162.5	215.0	218.5			
Total official development finance	75.5	75.9	76.3	78.1	75.4	71.2	73.1	71.6	63.4			
Total ODA receipts	58.5	59.2	61.2	59.2	63.4	60.1	58.8	60.5	54.9			
Total DAC ODA (bilateral and multilateral)	54.1	58.2	57.1	59.3	61.3	62.1	58.9	59.2	53.6			

[a] Excluding forgiveness of non-ODA debt for the years 1990 to 1992.
[b] Excluding bond lending by banks (item III.3), and guaranteed financial credits (included in 11).
[c] No reporting has been received from DAC Members on portfolio investment.

Table 13.2 ODA performance of DAC countries in 1995 and recent years

	$ millions			Per cent of GNP						Change in percentage 1995/94			Annual average % change in volume[b]
	1995 actual[a]	1994 actual[a]	1995 volume[b]	1980/84 average	1985/89 average	1994/95 average	1993	1994	1995	In national currency	In $	In volume terms[b]	1989/90–1994/95
Australia	1194	1091	1148	0.48	0.42	0.35	0.35	0.34	0.36	7.9	9.4	5.2	2.5
Austria	767	655	663	0.29	0.23	0.33	0.30	0.33	0.33	3.3	17.0	1.2	9.3
Belgium	1034	726	894	0.56	0.46	0.35	0.39	0.32	0.38	25.5	42.4	23.1	-3.9
Canada	2067	2250	2042	0.45	0.47	0.40	0.45	0.43	0.38	-7.7	-8.1	-9.2	-0.6
Denmark	1623	1446	1409	0.76	0.89	0.99	1.03	1.03	0.96	-1.1	12.2	-2.6	3.3
Finland	388	290	314	0.29	0.54	0.32	0.45	0.31	0.32	11.9	33.9	8.1	-14.5
France	8443	8466	7437	0.53	0.59	0.59	0.63	0.64	0.55	-10.4	-0.3	-12.2	0.8
Germany	7524	6818	6509	0.46	0.41	0.32	0.36	0.34	0.31	-2.5	10.3	-4.5	-0.9
Ireland	153	109	141	0.20	0.21	0.27	0.20	0.25	0.29	31.3	40.8	29.7	17.4
Italy	1623	2705	1554	0.20	0.37	0.21	0.31	0.27	0.15	-39.4	-40.0	-42.6	-9.7
Japan	14489	13239	13396	0.31	0.31	0.28	0.27	0.29	0.28	0.8	9.4	1.2	0.2
Luxembourg	65	59	56	0.20	0.18	0.38	0.35	0.40	0.36	-2.9	10.1	-5.9	14.4
Netherlands	3226	2517	2789	1.01	0.97	0.79	0.82	0.76	0.81	13.1	28.2	10.8	-0.8
New Zealand	123	110	109	0.28	0.26	0.23	0.25	0.24	0.23	1.2	12.0	-1.2	2.7
Norway	1244	1137	1087	0.97	1.09	0.95	1.01	1.05	0.87	-1.7	9.5	-4.4	1.1
Portugal	271	308	231	0.03	0.16	0.31	0.29	0.35	0.27	-20.7	-12.2	-25.0	8.3
Spain	1348	1305	1198	0.09	0.10	0.26	0.28	0.28	0.24	-3.8	3.3	-8.2	10.1
Sweden	1704	1819	1513	0.85	0.89	0.86	0.99	0.96	0.77	-13.4	-6.3	-16.8	-1.8
Switzerland	1084	982	924	0.27	0.31	0.35	0.33	0.36	0.34	-4.6	10.3	-5.9	3.0
United Kingdom	3157	3197	2990	0.37	0.31	0.29	0.31	0.31	0.28	-4.2	-1.3	-6.5	1.8
United States	7367	9927	7187	0.24	0.20	0.12	0.15	0.14	0.10	-25.8	-25.8	-27.6	-4.4
Total DAC	58894	59156	53590	0.34	0.33	0.28	0.30	0.30	0.27	-7.8	-0.4	-9.4	-0.9
of which EU Members	31478	30420	27697	0.44	0.45	0.40	0.44	0.42	0.38	-6.2	3.5	-9.0	-0.6

[a] At current prices and exchange rates.
[b] At 1994 exchange rates and prices.

Declining foreign aid in the 1990s has not been replaced by grants by non-governmental organisations (NGOs). These had risen quite sharply between 1987 and 1992 but levelled off thereafter, falling in real terms. By 1995 such grants stood at slightly less than 10 per cent of ODA. Was anything taking the place of declining aid and charitable giving? Private flows have been the principal source of growth in net financial flows to developing countries during the 1990s. This represented a dramatic reversal from the 1980s, when, in the aftermath of the Third World debt crisis, private flows fell significantly, failing to recover to even their 1980 level by 1990; over this period, aid had been of increasing relative importance. Private flows that had represented a modest 39 per cent of total net resource flows to developing countries in 1989, accounted for about 88 per cent in 1996. In terms of the external financing of developing countries, the 1990s have witnessed a massive overall move to the market caused by a combination of increasing private lending and declining aid flows.

Overall figures can, of course, be misleading and this is true of the aid data presented above. As revealed by Table 13.2, not all DAC countries have allowed their aid-to-GNP ratios to decline during the 1990s; but either the increases have been small, such as in the UK's case, or the countries are insignificant donors in absolute terms. The dominant absolute change has been the sharp decline in US aid, although significant falls have also occurred in Canada, Germany, Italy, Japan, the Netherlands, Norway and Sweden. In 1992 the US provided US$11,709 million of ODA, placing it as the largest single aid donor. By 1995 US aid had fallen to US$7,367 million in current prices, below the aid disbursements of Japan, France and Germany. Aid fatigue is exemplified by the US.[1]

At the same time, and re-enforcing these trends, aid flows from non-DAC countries had become almost completely insignificant by the mid-1990s accounting for only about US$1,000 million in 1995. Saudi Arabian aid, for example, fell from US$1,700 million in 1991 to US$192 million in 1995.

But has the decline in ODA been accompanied by any change in its distribution? Table 13.3 provides data on this, showing that over 1984/85–1994/95 there was indeed a redistribution of aid away from Asia and the Middle East and North Africa, and towards Sub-Saharan Africa; the redistribution towards SSA is part of a longer run trend which has been in place since the mid-1970s. The share of aid going to Latin America and the Caribbean has remained fairly constant. At the same time even the regions that have benefited most from the redistribution of aid have received less aid as a percentage of their GNPs since the beginning of the 1990s. Aid-reliance in SSA, for example, fell from 22.4 per cent in 1989–90 to 7.8 per cent in 1994–95. However, the reliance of most of SSA (as well as other low-income developing countries), on aid as compared to private flows, remains undiminished. In large measure private capital flows have by-passed the poorest countries and have been heavily skewed to a relatively small group

Table 13.3 Total net receipts of ODA by region and selected developing countries

	Per cent of total ODA			Per cent of DAC bil. ODA	Share in total population	ODA receipts		ODA as a percentage of LDCs' 1994 GNP		GNP per capita[a] ($) 1994
	1984–85	1989–90	1994–95	1995	(%) 1995	$ billion 1995	Annual real % change 1985–95	1989–90	1994–95	
Sub-Saharan Africa	29.6	35.9	36.7	37.2	13.0	18.2	0.0	22.4	7.8	..
of which:										
Côte d'Ivoire	0.4	1.2	2.8	2.4	0.3	1.2	18.0	11.7	25.7	610
Zambia	1.0	0.9	2.7	4.1	0.2	2.0	12.3	26.8	42.6	350
Mozambique	1.1	2.1	2.3	2.2	0.4	1.1	4.4	156.7	95.7	90
Ethiopia	2.2	2.0	1.9	1.8	1.2	0.9	−5.9	30.7	20.9	100
Tanzania	1.8	2.3	1.8	1.8	0.7	0.9	−1.1	69.3	—	140
Uganda	0.6	1.2	1.5	1.6	0.4	0.8	8.4	—	19.8	190
Rwanda	0.6	0.6	1.4	1.4	0.2	0.7	7.1	24.5	123.1	80
Kenya	1.4	2.4	1.4	1.4	0.6	0.7	−1.7	25.7	10.7	250
Ghana	0.7	1.4	1.2	1.3	0.4	0.6	5.5	22.5	11.2	410
Cameroon	0.6	1.0	1.2	0.9	0.3	0.4	4.1	7.9	8.6	680
Zimbabwe	0.9	0.7	1.0	1.0	0.2	0.5	0.2	9.9	10.3	500
Somalia	1.2	1.0	0.7	0.4	0.2	0.2	−12.1	—	—	..
Sudan	3.0	1.7	0.6	0.5	0.6	0.2	−20.5	14.7	—	..
Madagascar	0.6	0.8	0.6	0.6	0.3	0.3	−2.3	29.2	16.1	200
Congo	0.3	0.3	0.5	0.3	0.1	0.1	0.7	14.9	21.0	620
Zaire	1.0	1.7	0.4	0.4	1.0	0.2	−10.8	19.5	—	..
Nigeria	0.1	0.6	0.4	0.4	2.4	0.2	12.7	1.9	0.6	280
Eritrea	—	—	0.3	0.3	0.1	0.1	—	—	—	..
Asia	32.1	31.7	30.7	30.4	68.9	14.9	−2.3	2.2	0.7	..
of which:										
China	2.9	4.5	6.7	7.2	27.0	3.5	6.8	1.0	0.7	530
India	5.6	3.4	4.0	3.5	29.7	1.7	5.0	1.1	0.7	320

	(1)	(2)	(3)	(4)	(5)	(6)	(7)	(8)	(9)	[a]
(name cut off)	1.0	1.2	3.0	2.0	2.7	1.3	3.3	17.3	3.0	220
Pakistan	2.3	2.5	2.4	1.6	2.9	0.8	−4.7	5.6	2.3	430
Philippines	1.4	2.2	1.9	1.8	1.5	0.9	−0.1	4.8	1.5	950
Thailand	1.6	1.6	1.4	1.8	1.3	0.9	−0.3	2.1	0.5	2410
Sri Lanka	1.6	1.4	1.1	1.1	0.4	0.6	−4.9	17.7	5.0	640
Oceania	2.6	2.7	3.0	3.3	0.1	1.6	1.1	47.6	19.8	..
North Africa and Middle East	21.3	16.9	13.3	11.3	5.7	5.5	−8.1	2.5	1.3	..
of which:										
Egypt	5.7	7.5	4.6	4.1	1.3	2.0	−4.8	21.8	5.6	720
Israel	5.5	2.7	1.6	0.7	0.1	0.3	−21.6	5.3	1.0	14530
Morocco	1.9	1.6	1.1	1.0	0.6	0.5	−10.5	6.6	1.9	1140
Syria	2.7	0.8	1.1	0.7	0.3	0.3	−12.8	5.6	—	..
Jordan	2.1	1.2	0.9	1.1	0.1	0.5	−6.5	25.4	7.8	1440
Yemen	1.6	0.8	0.3	0.4	0.3	0.2	−15.1	10.3	4.7	280
Tunisia	0.6	0.7	0.2	0.1	0.2	0.1	−13.9	6.2	0.6	1790
Latin America	13.1	10.9	12.0	13.2	10.7	6.5	−2.0	1.2	0.4	..
of which:										
Bolivia	0.6	1.1	1.3	1.4	0.2	0.7	6.1	23.5	11.9	770
Peru	1.0	0.8	0.8	0.9	0.5	0.4	−3.6	3.2	0.9	2110
Mexico	0.4	0.3	0.8	0.8	2.1	0.4	3.0	0.1	0.1	4180
El Salvador	0.9	0.8	0.7	0.8	0.1	0.4	−2.4	17.9	12.2	600
Honduras	1.0	0.8	0.6	0.6	0.1	0.3	−7.6	14.6	3.8	1360
Costa Rica	0.8	0.5	0.1	0.1	0.1	0.0	−26.5	9.0	0.6	2400
Southern Europe	1.3	1.8	4.4	4.6	1.5	2.3	12.1	1.1	1.7	..
of which:										
Turkey	0.7	1.4	0.5	0.6	1.4	0.3	−0.6	1.6	0.2	2500
Cyprus	0.1	0.1	0.1	0.0	0.0	0.0	−10.7	1.4	—	..
Overall total	100.0	100.0	100.0	100.0	100.0	49.0	−2.0	3.0	0.9	..

Note: Net ODA from DAC Members and DAC Member-financed multilateral organisations. Excluding amounts not allocated by country.

[a] World Bank Atlas basis.

Table 13.4 Population living below US$1 a day in developing and transitional economies, 1987–93

Regions	Population covered by at least one survey (per cent)	Number of poor (millions)			Headcount index (per cent)			Poverty gap (per cent)		
		1987	1990	1993	1987	1990	1993	1987	1990	1993
East Asia and the Pacific	88.0	464.0	468.2	445.8	28.2	28.5	26.0	8.3	8.0	7.8
(excluding China)	(61.5)	(109.2)	(73.5)	(73.5)	(23.2)	(17.6)	(13.7)	(3.8)	(3.1)	(3.1)
Eastern Europe and Central Asia	85.9	2.2	n.a	14.5	0.6	n.a	3.5	0.2	n.a	1.1
Latin America and the Caribbean	83.9	91.2	101.0	109.6	22.0	23.0	23.5	8.2	9.0	9.1
Middle East and North Africa	46.7	10.3	10.4	10.7	4.7	4.3	4.1	0.9	0.7	0.6
South Asia	98.4	479.9	480.4	514.7	45.4	43.0	43.1	14.1	12.3	12.6
Sub-Saharan Africa	65.9	179.6	201.2	218.6	38.5	39.3	39.1	14.4	14.5	15.3
Total	85.0	1227.1	n.a	1313.9	30.1	n.a	29.4	9.5	n.a	9.2
Total (excluding ECA)	85.0	1224.9	1261.2	1299.3	33.3	32.9	31.8	10.8	10.3	10.5

Note: These estimates revise and update those in *Implementing the World Bank's Strategy to Reduce Poverty* (World Bank 1933b). There are a number of differences between these numbers and previous estimates, including those in *World Development Report 1990*. New household surveys have become available; a total of 122 surveys for sixty-seven countries were used in constructing the above estimates. They also incorporate new estimates of PPP exchange rates for converting US$1 per day (in 1985 prices) into local currencies. And the numbers are estimated from those countries in each region for which at least one survey was available during the period 1985–94. The proportion of the population covered by such surveys is given in column 1. Survey dates often do not coincide with the dates in the above table. To line up with the above dates, the survey estimates were adjusted using the closest available survey for each country and applying the consumption growth rate from national accounts. Using the assumption that the sample of countries covered by surveys is representative of the region as a whole, the numbers of poor are then estimated by region. This assumption is obviously less robust in the Middle East and African regions. The headcount index is the percentage of the population below the poverty line. The poverty gap index is the mean distance below the poverty line (zero to the nonpoor) expressed as a percentage of the poverty line.

n.a.: Not available.

of better-off Latin American and Asian developing countries. For these countries private capital has not replaced foreign aid.

Relevant in the context of the redistribution of foreign aid is the fact that the so-called CEEC and NIS countries (Central and Eastern European Countries and New Independent States of the former Soviet Union) now form a new category of aid recipients. In 1995 they received aid flows of over US$9,000 million that is about 0.04 per cent of the GNP of DAC countries and about 15 per cent of total aid to developing countries. The largely unjustified concern that countries in transition would 'crowd out' developing countries from private capital markets (Collins, 1993), should perhaps have been more appropriately directed towards aid, where there apparently has been a significant degree of crowding out. US aid is somewhat replenished when flows to CEEC/NIS countries are included, but even so the US aid budget declined sharply, and still showed 'aid fatigue'.

But why have donors suffered from aid fatigue? Is it born out of frustration that aid has not delivered its promises? Perhaps the benefits as perceived by donors have not outweighed the costs, with the result that aid is increasingly seen as an inefficient use of donors' resources. What has caused these changed perceptions?

Before moving on to examine these questions, a prior question is whether the decline in foreign aid shown above reflects aid's success in reducing world-wide poverty. Is aid no longer needed? The data in Table 13.4 show that this is not the case. While the incidence of poverty throughout the world fell slightly over 1987–93, the number of people living in poverty has increased. In its recent report on *Poverty Reduction*, from which the table is taken, the World Bank tellingly describes the situation in the following terms, 'poverty reduction is the most urgent task facing humanity today' (p. vii). But if poverty reduction remains 'urgent' why have donors been *reducing* their aid flows?

The economics of aid and its effectiveness: fatigue sets in

Early economic analysis of aid was built on the premise that development and poverty-reduction ultimately depend on economic growth. In principle, therefore, the main focus of foreign aid was placed on its role in encouraging economic growth in developing countries. In seeking to explain economic growth development economics took as its starting point the Harrod–Domar growth model. This may be summarised briefly by the fundamental growth equation $g = s/v$, where g is the rate of economic growth, s is the domestic savings ratio, and v is the incremental capital-output ratio (ICOR), reflecting the marginal productivity of capital. The model says that in order to achieve a specific or targeted rate of economic growth at a given and constant marginal productivity of capital a country needs a specific amount of investment and therefore a specific amount of savings to finance the investment. To the extent that domestic savings fall short of this level, foreign aid can help by filling the savings gap.

An extension to the analysis introduced the idea that problems could still exist and economic growth could still be frustrated, even where a country generated sufficient domestic savings, if it proved impossible to convert excess savings into the foreign exchange earnings necessary to finance development-related imports (often capital goods). As well as the savings gap there was also, therefore, a foreign exchange gap measuring the gap between the foreign exchange needed to finance imports and the foreign exchange earned through exports. There were, in other words, two gaps; hence 'dual gap' analysis (Chenery and Strout, 1966). Foreign aid played a twin role in helping to close both gaps. Where it was shortfalls in domestic savings and foreign exchange earnings that were the effective constraints on economic growth, the conclusion was drawn that foreign aid would relax these constraints and foster economic growth. Much of the theoretical justification for foreign aid has remained loosely based on dual gap analysis ever since.

However, the dual gap model provides a less than perfect basis for analysing foreign aid. First, it has become accepted that economic growth is not synonymous with economic, social and human development. Countries may grow according to economic measures, but still fail to develop. The view that economic growth alone ensures that more widely defined developmental objectives will be attained has been rejected. Economic growth remains important, even necessary, but not sufficient.

Second, dual gap analysis rests on a number of restrictive assumptions which have been shown to be unrealistic in many developing countries. Early criticism of the model had identified its implicit rigidities that tended to understate the role that developing countries themselves had in fostering economic development and to overstate the role of foreign aid. Over time these deficiencies have become more apparent. Clearly to the extent that there is scope for increasing domestic savings and increasing the productivity of investment, the need for foreign aid can be reduced. At the same time foreign aid (imported saving) may 'crowd out' domestic saving and be used to finance investment projects which have a lower than average productivity. Where, in practice, foreign aid induces a fall in the domestic savings ratio and an increase in the incremental capital-output ratio (ICOR), it will fail to have the anticipated positive effect on the rate of economic growth.

Inflexibility also seemed to exist in the context of the foreign exchange constraint, where dual gap analysis downplayed the scope for using exports as a way of substituting domestic resources into imports. Export growth offers a potential way of closing the foreign exchange gap, and critics of dual gap analysis claimed that it was through this route that excess domestic labour supply could be substituted into scarce foreign capital goods without the need for foreign aid. Essentially the criticism was that dual gap analysis was unduly pessimistic about the prospects for export expansion in developing countries, which could be enhanced by policies aimed at diversification and the exchange rate.

Subsequent economic analysis has tended to concentrate, in some detail, on the behavioural responses of recipients to foreign aid inflows. A compelling critique of foreign aid can be assembled if it can be shown that it finances current consumption rather than investment, it finances unproductive government expenditure which then crowds out private investment with a higher productivity, it is 'fungible' and is used to replace the domestic development budget and to finance government fiscal deficits associated with increased current expenditure, it results in appreciating real exchange rates, which discourage exports and encourage imports (Dutch disease), worsening current account balance of payments deficits, and it generally creates the wrong set of incentives, not only in relation to relative prices, exchange rates and interest rates, but also by creating a moral hazard in terms of encouraging governments to postpone necessary, but politically costly, adjustment. Over the years there has been accumulating evidence to suggest that these are real rather than purely hypothetical problems.[2]

Moreover, to the extent that the dangers are real, they suggest that foreign aid will fail to have a significant positive impact on economic growth; this is indeed what, until recently, the available macroeconomic evidence has shown. Numerous studies have failed to discover any statistically significant causal relationship between aid and economic growth, in spite of the fact that studies of aid-effectiveness at the micro level have, again until recently, shown a generally satisfactory rate of return.[3] Typical of the mid-1990s consensus on aid-effectiveness, Boone (1996) argues that the empirical evidence supports the claim that aid neither fosters economic growth, nor benefits the poor as measured by improvements in human development indicators. It does not increase investment, but, in effect, is simply used to finance increased current consumption. While it is possible that the methodologies of measurement are deficient, over-estimating the micro returns and under-estimating the macroeconomic returns (White, 1992), the inconsistency between the micro and macro evidence on aid-effectiveness can also clearly be explained by the fact that micro effectiveness studies hold 'other things' constant. The existence of the micro-macro paradox therefore itself implies that aid has adverse effects in terms of reducing domestic savings and investment, fungibility, Dutch disease, and moral hazard.

Evidence that foreign aid fails to foster economic growth in developing countries also undermines, at source, the argument that it is to the mutual advantage of recipients and donors (Brandt, 1980). The essence of this argument is that, via its effects on economic growth in recipients, foreign aid increases the demand for exports from the donors that then benefit from export-led growth and the related increases in output and decreases in unemployment. Leaving to one side the fact that the 'mutuality doctrine' rests strongly on a somewhat unfashionable neo-Keynesian view of how the world economy works, it loses credibility almost totally if aid is found to be ineffective at generating economic growth in aid-recipients.

Aid which finances current consumption rather than investment may of course alleviate short-term poverty; aid has an humanitarian role. Even if ineffective in raising economic growth, aid could have been successful in reducing poverty. Again there are methodological problems here associated with the counter-factual; what would have happened had aid not been provided? However, the weight of evidence on the poverty-reducing effects of aid is not strongly supportive of it either. Most studies that have examined the subject conclude that aid does not seem to help the poorest people in aid-receiving countries.[4] Moreover, the data in Table 13.3 show that poverty in Africa, a region that has received large and increasing amounts of aid, remains endemic,[5] and, as reported earlier, Boone (1996) finds no statistical link between aid and human development indicators. If aid was promulgated in the belief that it would significantly reduce poverty, frustration with its apparent inability to do so could clearly be a source of aid fatigue.

Another important element in the evolving economics of foreign aid also helps to explain why aid fatigue set in. In the context of dual gap analysis the case for aid rests on the twin assumptions that first, financing gaps exist, and second, they will not be filled by private international capital markets. It is not coincidental therefore that aid flows fell in the first half of the 1990s at the same time as private flows were rising. At the aggregate level much of the task of financing economic development appeared (misleadingly) to have been taken over by private capital markets, suggesting that foreign aid was no longer needed (Lal, 1996).

Based on a model that is theoretically deficient, surrounded by empirical evidence that suggests that it is ineffective in achieving its economic and humanitarian objectives, and with its financing role apparently having been taken over by private capital markets, it is easy to see why the economic case for aid has been seen to become weaker, and why donors have suffered from aid fatigue. But is the perception accurate? Have things changed? It would be ironic if aid donors started to cut aid budgets at precisely the same time as evidence is beginning to emerge that aid has become more effective. Does such evidence exist? Before going on to examine this question, aid fatigue in the mid-1990s needs to be investigated from a political perspective.

The politics of foreign aid fatigue

Attempts to explain the distribution of aid have frequently distinguished between 'recipient needs' and 'donor interests' (Grilli and Reiss, 1992, Burnside and Dollar, 1997). The consensus emerging from econometric studies confirms what an eye-balling of the data linking individual donors with individual recipients suggests, namely that donor interests have dominated.[6] These may be commercial, although the historical evidence is that political and military factors have generally been more prominent. In substantial part, foreign aid has been a political phenomenon. If so, it is reasonable to assume that changing politics lie at the heart of changing aid flows. It is also reasonable to assume that the politics of aid may have undermined its effectiveness in terms of economic growth and poverty reduction (Boone, 1996; Burnside and Dollar, 1996).

But has foreign aid been any more effective at achieving its political objectives? The empirical evidence suggests not (Mosley, 1987). Aid has been an inefficient way of buying political influence, and this provides another explanation of aid fatigue.

Probably more significant, however, have been the huge global political changes which there have been during the 1990s. First, the ties of colonialism have loosened. However, the evidence does not suggest that this is an important factor. Former colonial powers such as the UK and France remain quantitatively significant aid donors, and much of their aid still goes to former colonies.[7]

Second, and much more importantly, there has been the fall of Communism and the end of the Cold War. This explanation appears to fit the fact that the discrete shift in the size of foreign aid happened in 1992. The Cold War explanation of changing aid flows has a number of dimensions. First, Western countries have no longer felt the need to provide aid as a means of discouraging the spread of Communism. There is no longer a 'foreign aid war' in which the East and West attempt to outbid each other in buying influence. Second, COMECON has ceased to be an aid donor. Third, and at the same time as the CEEC/NIS have stopped being donors they have started being recipients. The thawing of the Cold War has therefore had a double-edged effect on the size and pattern of aid flows, by eliminating donors and creating a new group of recipients.

Combined with the Cold War effect, the changing political economy of OECD countries, along with changing economic priorities, has made them less willing to give aid. Although predating the fall in aid, there has been a general and downward reassessment of what governments can achieve. A more recent development has been the strong desire to reduce fiscal deficits. This was an acute political issue in the US in the mid-1990s where a Democratic President vied with a Republican-dominated Congress to eliminate the US fiscal deficit. But similar pressures have been experienced within Europe, especially where members of the European Union have been anxious to guarantee their eligibility to participate in a single currency as part of Economic and Monetary Union. With the Maastricht convergence criteria stipulating a maximum fiscal deficit of 3 per cent of GDP, and maximum government debt of 60 per cent of GDP, European countries have been forced to reassess all aspects of government expenditure.

Foreign aid constitutes a lower political priority than health, social security, state pensions, and unemployment benefit. High levels of unemployment in Europe, along with demographic changes which have put increasing pressure on domestic elements of government expenditure have therefore made the political climate much less conducive to aid, which has been perceived to carry a higher opportunity cost. It is difficult for governments that are cutting politically sensitive domestic expenditure to leave the foreign aid budget intact.

In as much as aid is still politically motivated, the politics has shown itself in the form of an interest in human rights, civil liberties, and corruption in aid recipients. But these represent weak motivational forces for aid as compared with strategic political or military objectives. While in the long run a lack of human rights in aid-receiving countries may be a source of political instability, and this could affect a donor's strategic self-interests, such matters are difficult to calculate with precision. Indeed donors have in the past sometimes acted as if they favour strong authoritarian regimes. With the associated uncertainty, and given the long-term time frame, donors probably discount quite heavily the destabilising effects of human rights abuse, although such abuses provide a ready and convenient way of justifying aid reductions.

If donors have perceived the political opportunity cost of aid to rise, and the benefits to decline, it is not difficult to see why aid fatigue has crept in. Since the perceived benefits of aid, in terms of humanitarian and economic returns, will be approximately shared by all donors, differences in donor behaviour can be ascribed primarily to differences in the underlying politics. In this context it is not surprising that with the thawing of the Cold War, with less generous welfare programmes than in Europe, and a culture which is less supportive of state intervention, the cut in aid budgets has been particularly sharp in the United States.

In a political environment that is generally unfavourable to aid, the misgivings about its economic and humanitarian effectiveness provide further public legitimisation. Moreover, the humanitarian arguments for aid can be countered by governments referring to its poor record in terms of poverty alleviation, and by focusing more heavily on the role of NGOs as the appropriate means for providing humanitarian assistance. On top of this, there is always the argument that aid is globally regressive, taxes paid by relatively poor people in relatively rich countries finance aid which goes to relatively rich people in relatively poor countries. Given the degree of income inequality in many developing countries, as well as the evidence that aid tends not to reach the poorest sectors in society, this remains a compelling point.

But does all this mean that the politics are stacked against any regeneration of foreign aid? If so, why did the UK Government in 1997 produce a White Paper setting itself ambitious aid targets? Perhaps the politics as well as the economics are changing.

From fatigue to regeneration

So far this chapter has provided an explanation of the decline in foreign aid flows in the first half on the 1990s based on a combination of economics and politics. But how long will fatigue last? And are there forces at work that may regenerate foreign aid?

Aid regeneration: the economics

As noted earlier economic growth is a necessary condition for sustained improvement in human development. In the past, however, foreign aid has been analysed within the context of a very rudimentary growth model. During the last ten years or so growth theory has itself been a growth industry and, albeit gradually, a better understanding of the determinants of economic growth is emerging. With this, it will become clearer where aid can make a positive contribution.

New growth theory, for example, suggests that aid should be directed at increasing productivity (partly by enhancing technology transfer), and at improving the stock of human capital through education, training and health; areas where private capital markets may be inefficient. New research claims to have identified robust connections between the nature of economic systems and economic growth, implying that liberalisation, particularly in the form of open trading relationships, have a beneficial long run effect on economic growth (Sachs and Warner, 1995, 1997; and Edwards, 1998). This clearly carries lessons with it for the design of aid policies.

More directly two recent studies have identified a significantly positive effect of foreign aid on economic growth as well as on other indicators of human development. One of these studies has been published by the World Bank (Burnside and Dollar, 1997) which suggests that previous evidence failed to pick up a positive effect because it included all aid recipients together. Burnside and Dollar distinguish between those aid recipients that have pursued sound macroeconomic policies as proxied by open trade regimes, fiscal discipline, and the avoidance of high inflation and those that have not. Although aid is shown to be ineffective in the countries where domestic policy has been unsound, it has been effective in those with good domestic policies, raising economic growth above (and reducing infant mortality below) levels that would previously have been expected. The beneficial effect of aid is particularly marked for low-income countries. Over the period 1970–93, Burnside and Dollar find that amongst low income countries with good policies those with large amounts of aid enjoyed annual per capita income growth of 3.5 per cent as compared with 2.0 per cent growth for those with only small amounts of aid. Foreign aid significantly increased the rate of return (by about 30 per cent) to good domestic economic policies. Thus Burnside and Dollar report, 'a robust finding that aid has a positive impact on growth in a good policy environment' (p. 33).[8]

The second study by Mosley and Hudson (1997) is compelling particularly as it comes from researchers who have previously discovered no significant effect of aid on growth (Mosley, 1987). Indeed even in this study they only find a significantly positive effect when they divide their sample into two sub-periods. It is only since the early 1980s that aid seems to have been effective in stimulating economic growth. But why? Mosley and Hudson offer an explanation that is consistent with Burnside and Dollar's finding. They claim that the relationship between aid and growth underwent a structural change in the early 1980s. Essentially, the factors that had previously accounted for the micro-macro paradox (with the exception of the negative effect of aid on domestic savings) have become less significant since then. In particular, the decline in domestic development budgets has made foreign aid much less fungible; aid recipients have been less able to substitute foreign aid for domestic expenditure on development. They also point out that the increased effectiveness of aid coincided with the shift to conditional policy-based lending by the World Bank, and an increasing policy dialogue. Where the policies favoured by the Bank have been implemented there is a reasonable presumption that the recipient will have been pursuing sound policies as measured by Burnside and Dollar.[9]

It is also interesting that they find a positive coefficient of aid on economic growth over a period of time when the data in section 2 show that aid was being more heavily directed to low income developing countries where growth prospects might have been expected to be relatively poor.

For the poorest developing countries, private capital flows have not replaced foreign aid. Evidence on the determinants of capital flows does not give a sanguine view of the chances for these countries to gain access to international capital markets in the short to medium term. Furthermore, much of the investment required in low income countries is of the type conventionally eschewed by the private sector. Foreign aid will therefore remain important for low income countries.

The above analysis paints an increasingly positive picture. But what about the politics?

Aid regeneration: the politics

While the ending of the Cold War has removed the strategic military and political motives for giving foreign aid, this type of bi-lateral aid was, in any case, ineffective in economic, humanitarian, and probably even in political terms. Aid was frequently allocated to recipients simply because of their strategic significance. It was often associated with poor economic policies and therefore never had much chance of being successful. Recipients did not have to concern themselves with hard policy choices since they could in effect trade on their strategic importance.

The thawing of the Cold War creates an opportunity for donors to re-focus aid on countries where sound policies are being pursued, and where there is a reasonable presumption that it will show a high economic and social rate of return. To the extent that some developing countries have access to private capital markets to meet their financial needs, foreign aid can be concentrated on the rest, and in particular the low income countries.

Other political factors towards the end of the 1990s are also conducive to a regeneration of foreign aid. As the industrial economies have moved out of recession the sizes of their fiscal deficits have fallen and this reduces the domestic political opportunity cost of foreign aid from the donors' perspective. It is perhaps relevant that a regeneration of interest in aid, as reflected in 1997 by the publication of a new governmental White Paper, happened in the UK where macroeconomic performance was generally stronger than elsewhere in Europe. Furthermore, the new Labour Government elected in 1997 might be thought likely to give a higher priority to reducing income inequality both at a national and an international level. The election of a new government could also be reflective of a changing public mood. Given the media attention paid to global poverty in the run-up to the G7/G8 summit in England in 1998, there is also some additional evidence of an increasing degree of public support for policies directed towards reducing global poverty. Evidence that aid is effective in encouraging economic growth and reducing infant mortality can only help to strengthen an incipient increase in such support.

A recent analysis of public attitudes towards foreign aid across OECD countries is helpful in identifying trends, differences between donors, and factors which influence public support for aid. The study shows that except in a few donors, public support for aid did not generally decline during 1985–95. However, the exceptions included the United States and Canada, where the opposition to aid grew strongly in the mid-1990s. When assessed against other foreign policy objectives foreign aid is generally ranked towards the bottom. Out of the ten foreign policy goals only 16 per cent of Americans placed development assistance as their top priority, and overall aid was ranked ninth. Public attitudes in OECD countries favour aid to the needy as opposed to strategic allies, aid to countries that are geographically more proximate, aid channelled through multilateral institutions, and aid focused on health, basic needs, disaster relief and the environment.

While younger generations are more supportive of aid, there is a widespread scepticism about aid-effectiveness and in particular the effects of waste and corruption.

What determines public opinion concerning aid? It does not seem to depend on economic conditions in donors, even though high domestic unemployment is often cited as a reason for opposing aid. Moreover, it does not seem to depend on the donor's degree of openness; although liberal immigration policies are sometimes seen as a substitute for aid. Ethical and moral considerations, along with perceptions of the effectiveness of aid appear to exert an important influence over public opinion.

Survey data therefore suggests that public support for aid can be increased by evidence that it is more effective in raising economic growth and more particularly improving human development. Reforms that seek to strengthen aid's effectiveness are therefore likely to receive public support. Aid fatigue amongst the general public is not a widespread phenomenon across all donors and there is still a basis of public support upon which regeneration can take place.

Reforming foreign aid: the role of conditionality

The reform of foreign aid raises both relatively uncontentious and contentious issues. Relatively uncontentious is that the global political environment in the second half of the 1990s better allows foreign aid to be allocated to where it is most needed. This argues for a shift from bi-lateral aid, which has always been more political, to multi-lateral aid which can focus more strongly on recipient needs. It also argues for a further reduction of aid to countries that do not have access to private international capital markets.[10] By redirecting aid away from where it is ineffective to where it is effective, its overall effectiveness can be increased with no necessary increase in the total amount of aid.

Also fairly uncontentious is the claim that the quality of foreign aid for recipients may be increased by making it simultaneously both more micro and small scale, perhaps by being more heavily channelled through NGOs, and more macro, supporting programmes of macroeconomic policies. Aid should continue to shift away from focusing inappropriately on large scale capital projects. In relation to this, the quality of aid would be increased by reducing the extent to which it is tied to projects and procurement; this would allow aid recipients to develop in ways that most effectively exploit the availability of domestic resources.

It is also uncontentious that recipients will benefit more from foreign aid if they pursue sound economic policies. Furthermore, there is probably reasonable consensus about what these policies are? More contentious is how to ensure that aid recipients pursue such policies.

What does the evidence show about the connection between aid and domestic policy reform? Does aid facilitate poor policies or encourage good ones? The answer is rather inconclusive. Good and bad policies have historically been pursued with and without aid. Burnside and Dollar (1997a) conclude that

> there is no systematic relationship between the amount of aid that countries get and policy reform (or the lack of it) [...] policy reform is largely driven by domestic social and political forces. (p. 6)

On the other hand, Mosley and Hudson (1997) attribute the increased effectiveness of aid since the early 1980s in part to the conditionality of the World Bank. So what is the role of conditionality in raising the effectiveness of aid? Can it be used to persuade reluctant governments to adopt sound policies and thereby link aid to policy reform?

The emerging evidence on the political economy of policy reform is fairly clear that conditionality does not induce reform unless governments are fully committed to it (Bird, 1998, Killick 1998). Where 'ownership' is low, they tend to back-slide and fail to implement agreed programmes (Johnson and Wasty, 1993). Multilateral aid agencies and the IFIs should therefore focus on trying to maximise the commitment of aid recipients to reform.[11] In one way or another governments need to be empowered to design their own programmes for development and poverty alleviation and then be judged on their efforts to carry them through, allowing for factors beyond their control such as adverse terms of trade shocks.[12] On the twin bases of evaluating domestically designed *ex ante* programmes and *ex post* performance, donors should adjust their allocation of aid in order to establish an appropriate set of incentives. Developing countries pursuing poor policies should not generally receive large amounts of aid. Those pursuing good policies should be supported. As noted earlier, foreign aid raises the rate of return to good policies and it can in this way incentivise governments to adopt sound economic policies. Greater selectivity by donors in the allocation of aid will therefore create the appropriate incentive structure.

Conditionality is not an effective mechanism for inducing policy reform. Indeed Collier *et al.* (1997) argue that there are fundamental inconsistencies between the inducement function of conditionality and its other functions such as selectivity and signalling. They propose that aid allocation should reflect *ex post* growth performance and human development rather than *ex ante* policy conditionality. Such a change taken to extreme would probably be politically unacceptable to donors. However, it may be feasible to re-focus conditionality on eliminating a narrower range of key distortions, thereby leaving as much policy discretion as possible in the hands of governments, that will then be judged on the basis of *ex post* economic performance, modified to allow for external factors beyond the control of the country concerned.[13]

The above analysis suggests that reform of foreign aid should focus first, on moving away from bi-lateral aid towards multi-lateral aid, and second, on reforming the conditionality of the multi-lateral aid agencies, in particular the World Bank, in a way that minimises conditionality and concentrates more narrowly on key areas of economic policy and performance.

Clearly there will be occasions when emergency relief has to provide an exception to the above rule, but if aid is to have positive effects on development and poverty reduction it has to be perceived as an *instrument* for achieving these objectives rather than the simple outcome of underdevelopment and poverty.

Concluding remarks

Frustration with its apparently poor record in achieving its developmental and poverty-reducing objectives, combined with political changes in the world, brought about a sharp decline in foreign aid in the mid-1990s. This was the era of aid fatigue. Some commentators saw declining aid as an entirely good thing – emphasising the ineffectiveness of aid – while others saw the situation as critical, condemning many millions of people to poverty.

On the basis of recent analysis and evidence the conclusion may be reached that, when combined with sound domestic economic policies, foreign aid has a discernibly positive impact on both economic growth and other indicators of human development. It may also be concluded that, as there has been an increasing global consensus upon what these policies are, so aid has in turn become more effective. The decline in foreign aid in the first half of the 1990s has therefore been a lagged response to its earlier poor record.

As there is a greater recognition of what aid can achieve, there is a reasonable presumption that foreign aid will be re-generated. This presumption is re-enforced by global political changes which initially led to declining aid flows but may subsequently lead to a re-direction of aid to countries where it is likely to be effective in economic and humanitarian terms. Such a re-direction of aid will create a set of incentives that encourages developing countries to pursue policies that will assist their future development.

This having been said, it would be unwise to expect too much from foreign aid. Research undertaken at the Harvard Institute for International Development, and briefly reported by Sachs (1997), shows that many of the poorest regions of the world suffer from geographical impediments that aid will find it difficult to overcome. In a way, however, this makes it even more important to ensure that foreign aid plays as positive a role as it can. With increasing evidence that aid can make a difference, and with a more conducive political environment, the era of aid fatigue in the mid-1990s may be followed by one of aid regeneration. Indeed with the publication of the UK Government's White Paper in 1997 and preliminary evidence to suggest an upturn in the flow of foreign aid in 1997 (see Table 13.1), there is reason to believe that regeneration may have already begun.

References

Bird, G., (1983), 'Low Income Countries and International Financial Reform', *Journal of Developing Areas*, October.

Bird, G., (1994), 'Economic Assistance to Low Income Countries: Should the Link be Resurrected?', *Essays in International Finance*, No 193, Princeton, July.

Bird, G., (1998), 'The Effectiveness of Conditionality and the Political Economy of Policy Reform: Is it Simply a Matter of Political Will?', *Journal of Policy Reform*, Vol. 1.

Boone, P., (1994), 'The Impact of Foreign Aid on Savings and Growth', London School of Economics, mimeographed.

Boone, P., (1996), 'Politics and the Effectiveness of Foreign Aid', *European Economic Review*, Vol. 40, No. 2, pp. 289–330.

Brandt, W. *et al.*, (1980), *North-South: A Programme for Survival* (The Brandt Report), London, Pan Books.

Brewster, H., Yeboah, D., (1994), 'Aid and the Growth of Income in Aid-Favoured Developing Countries: Policy Issues', *Cambridge Journal of Economics*, 18, pp. 145–62.

Burnside, C., Dollar, D. R., (1997), 'Aid, Policies and Growth', *World Bank Working Paper*, No. 1777, Washington, June.

Burnside, C., Dollar, D., (1997a), 'Aid Spurs Growth in a Sound Policy Environment', *Finance and Development*, December.

Cassen, R., *et al.*, (1994), *Does Aid Work?*, (London: Oxford University Press). II. ed.

Chenery, H. B., Strout, A. M., (1996), 'Foreign Assistance and Economic Development', *American Economic Review*, 54 (4) pp. 679–733.

Collier, P., Guillaumant, P., Guillamant, S., Gunning, J. W., (1997), 'Redesigning Conditionality', *World Development*, Vol. 25, No. 9.

Collins, S. M., (1993), 'Capital Flows to Developing Countries: Implications for the Economies in Transition', *Proceedings of the World Bank Annual Conferences on Development Economics*. 1992.

Development Assistance Committee (DAC), (1997), Development Co-operation, 1996 Report, (Paris: OECD).

Edwards, S., (1998), 'Openness, Productivity and Growth: What Do We Really Know?' *Economic Journal*, 108, March.

Feyzioglu, T., Swaroop, V., Zhu, M., (1996), 'Foreign Aid's Impact on Public Spending', *Policy Research Working Paper*, 1610, (Washington: The World Bank), May.

Grilli, E., Reiss, M., (1992), 'EC Aid to Associated Countries: Distribution and Determinants', *Weltwirtschaftliches Archiv*, Heft 2, pp. 202–20.

Heller. P. S., (1975), 'A model of Public Fiscal Behaviour in Developing Countries: Aid, Investment and Taxation', *American Economic Review*, Vol. 65, No. 3, June, pp. 429–45.

Hyden, G., (1995), 'Reforming Foreign Aid to African Development', *Development Dialogue*, 1995-2, pp. 34–52.

Jayawardena, L., (1993), *The Potential of Development Contracts*, (Helsinki: UNU-WIDER).

Johnson, J. H., Wasty, S. S., (1993), 'Borrower Ownership of Adjustment Programs and the Political Economy of Reform', *World Bank Discussion Paper*, 199, (Washington: The World Bank).

Katada, S. N., (1997), 'Two Aid Hegemons: Japanese–US Interaction and Aid Allocation to Latin America and the Caribbean', *World Development*, Vol. 25. No. 6, pp. 931–45.

Killick, T., (1991), 'The Development Effectiveness of Aid to Africa', in I Hussain and J Underwood (eds.), *African External Finances in the 1990s*, (Washington: The World Bank).

Killick, T., (1998), *Conditionality of Aid: Political Economy of Policy Change*, (London: Routledge).

Lal, D., (1996), 'Foreign Aid: An Idea Whose Time Has Gone', *Economic Affairs*, Vol. 10, No. 4, Autumn, pp. 9–13.

Mosley, P., (1987), *Overseas Aid: Its Defence and Reform*, (Brighton: Wheatsheaf).
Mosley, P., Hudson, J., (1997), 'Has Aid Effectiveness Increased?', mimeographed.
Ofstad, A., Tostensen, A., Vraalsen, T., (1991), *Towards a Development Contract: A New Model for International Agreements with African Countries*, Bergen Chr Michelsen Institute: DERAP, December.
Pack, H., Pack, J. R., (1990), 'Is Foreign Aid Fungible? The Case of Indonesia', *Economic Journal*, 100, pp. 188–94.
Pack, H., Pack, J. R., (1993), 'Foreign Aid and the Question of Fungibility', *Review of Economics and Statistics*, pp. 258–65.
Riddell, R., (1987), *Foreign Aid Reconsidered*, London ODI and James Curry.
Rodrik, D., (1996), 'Why Is There Multilaterial Lending?' *Annual World Bank Conference on Development Economics*, 1995.
Sachs, J., (1997), 'The Limits of Convergence: Nature, Nuture and Growth', The Economist, 14 June.
Sachs, J., Warner, A., (1995), 'Economic Reform and the Process of Global Integration', *Brookings Papers in Economic Activity*, No. 1, pp. 1–95.
Sachs, J. D., Warner, A. M., (1997), 'Fundamental Sources of Long Run Growth', *American Economic Review*, Vol. 87, No. 2, May.
Snyder, D. W., (1996), 'Foreign Aid and Private Investment in Developing Countries', *Journal of International Development*, Vol. 8, No. 6, November–December, pp. 735–46.
Stokke, O., (ed.), (1996), *Foreign Aid Towards the Year 2000: Experiences and Challenges*, (London: Frank Cass).
van Wijnbergen, S., (1986), 'Macroeconomic Aspects of the Effectiveness of Foreign Aid: The Two Gap Model Home Goods Disequilibrium and Real Exchange Rate Misalignment', *Journal of International Economics*, Vol. 21, August, pp. 123–36.
White, H., (1992), 'The Macroeconomic Impact of Development Aid: A Critical Survey', *Journal of Development Studies*, Vol. 28, No. 2, January, pp. 241–63.
White, H., (1998), *Aid and Macroeconomic Performance*, (London: Macmillan).
White, H., Wignaraja, G., (1991), 'Real and Nominal Revaluation during Trade Liberalisation in Sri Lanka: A Case of Aid Induced Dutch Disease', *Centro Studi Luca d'Agliano/QEH Development Studies Working Paper 37*, Oxford.
World Bank, (1989), Annual Review of Evaluation Results, OECD Report, No. 8614, October.
Younger, S. D., (1992), 'Aid and the Dutch Disease: Macroeconomic Management When Everyone Loves You', *World Development*, Vol. 20. No. 11, November, pp. 1587–97.

14
Economic Assistance to Low-Income Countries: Should the Link be Resurrected?

Graham Bird

Introduction

The Special Drawing Right (SDR) was established at the beginning of the 1970s for the purpose of acquiring greater control over the amount of international liquidity in the international monetary system. It was believed that there was an optimum quantity of international reserves. If this quantity were exceeded, there would be global inflation; if it were not reached, there would be recession and unemployment. The late 1960s had been perceived as a period during which international liquidity was inadequate. Moreover, the way in which international reserves were created under the Bretton Woods system relied heavily on the state of the U.S. balance of payments, and this was generally perceived to be unsatisfactory. SDRs seemed to offer a more centralized and controllable mechanism. It was intended that the SDR would eventually take over as the principal reserve asset in the international monetary system.

SDRs were allocated to participants – essentially the member countries of the International Monetary Fund (IMF) – in relation to their IMF quotas. The theoretical basis for this was the assumption that the resultant pattern of supply would match the pattern of long-term demand for reserves. As a consequence, no long-term unrequited resource transfers were envisaged, and the scheme was intended to be neutral with respect to permanent resource flows, thereby ensuring that all participants would gain a liquidity yield by enjoying an increase in their owned reserves, an increase they were not obliged to earn by giving up resources or by borrowing. This demand-based method of allocating SDRs was not, however, the only one possible. SDRs could be allocated with other objectives in mind, just as seigniorage from money creation could be used by national governments for varied purposes (Hawkins and Rangarajan, 1970; Grubel, 1972).

Developing-country representatives quickly suggested that the SDR offered a chance to change the distribution of benefits associated with the older methods of reserve creation, benefits they felt had been distributed mainly to industrialized and relatively rich countries. They argued that there should be a "link" between SDR allocations and the provision of financial assistance to developing countries.

There were various versions of the link proposal. The "inorganic" link envisaged voluntary contributions by developed countries in the form of currencies or SDRs either to development agencies or directly to developing countries at the time of each SDR allocation. Under some circumstances, these contributions would be tied to expenditure in donor countries. A central advantage of the inorganic link was that it required no change in the IMF's Articles of Agreement.

The "organic" link, by contrast, involved changing the distribution formula for SDRs so as to increase the proportion of any given allocation going to developing countries, either directly or through the intermediation of development agencies. A key argument for an organic link was that, whereas quotas were taken to reflect the demand for reserves to hold, developing countries should be expected to spend the SDRs they received. Per capita income, balance-of-payments instability, and adjustment costs were put forward in this context as more relevant criteria on which to distribute SDRs to developing countries.

Variations on the basic theme included proposals to use newly created SDRs, either directly or through contributions from developed-country recipients, to finance a subsidy account that would then redirect those SDRs to developing countries. The account might make grants, in which case contributors would pay the charges on using SDRs, or provide interest-bearing credit lines, in which case the ultimate recipients would pay the charges. An extension of this idea was to use SDRs to finance a special account that would then support stabilization and adjustment programs approved by the IMF. In effect, developing countries that successfully negotiated a program with the IMF would receive additional resources in the form of SDRs. Such a scheme, however, would change the nature of SDRs in that the receipt of the SDRs would depend on the acceptance of IMF conditionality.

The basic link proposal led to much official and academic debate (summarized, for example, in Park, 1973, and Bird, 1982c). Those opposed to the proposal prevailed, however, and the link was not introduced. The deciding factor seems to have been the antagonists' claim that the link would be inflationary, because it represented a net increase in world aggregate monetary demand with no matching increase in real aggregate supply. But there was also the related concern that recipients would be allowed to squander unconditional SDRs.

When the developing countries did not get the link, they took some consolation in the addition of the Extended Fund Facility (EFF) to the array of IMF lending windows in 1974. The EFF was intended to be of particular relevance to developing countries, because it provided financial assistance in support of longer-term and structural balance-of-payments adjustment.

Moreover, even under the existing SDR scheme, developing countries took advantage of an "informal" link, for they were heavy net users of the new reserve asset, which carried only a nominal charge and only limited reconstitution provisions requiring participants to maintain over a five-year period an average balance of SDRs of at least 30 percent of their net cumulative allocations (Helleiner, 1974; Bird, 1976, 1979). The abrogation of this reconstitution requirement in 1981 would, other things being constant, have increased the value of the informal link, but other things did not stay constant. The interest rate and charge on SDRs were simultaneously raised to a market-equivalent rate, and the effect was to increase the cost of net use of SDRs (as well as to increase the return to net acquisition).[1] The developing countries, as net users, undoubtedly lost out.

Of course, the developing countries stood to gain most from the link if the SDR became a widely accepted (if not the principal) international reserve asset and an important source of reserve growth. To the extent that an increase in the interest rate on SDRs was needed to achieve this objective, it might have been seen as a price worth paying. Moreover, many developing countries were deemed uncreditworthy by private international capital markets and either encountered an effective availability constraint or could borrow only at a rate significantly above average market rates; in these circumstances, SDRs continued to confer benefits on developing countries. Indeed, the combined short-term effect of dropping the reconstitution requirement and raising the interest rate was to raise the benefits of SDRs to developing countries (Bird, 1981, 1982b). The general view, however, was that the increase in the charge on using SDRs destroyed the benefits of the link, and so the proposal, which had already been downplayed by the developing countries in order to win support for other reforms such as the EFF, now practically disappeared from the reform agenda.

The increase in the interest rate on the SDR was intended to make it a more attractive asset to hold and thereby to assist in establishing it as the system's principal reserve asset, but it did not have this effect. The system moved away from SDRs altogether and toward multiple reserve currencies. No new allocations of SDRs have been made since 1981, and they have come to be viewed by some as largely irrelevant (Chrystal, 1978, 1990b).

It is not difficult to see how the attractiveness of the SDR could be enhanced by improving its properties as an international medium of exchange and financial asset, (Bird, 1985; Coats, 1990), and some authors have continued to argue that moving toward the SDR would represent a systemic improvement (Coats, 1990). Periodically, a call comes for a new allocation of SDRs (Williamson, 1984), and the IMF's managing director, Michel Camdessus, has argued strongly for a new allocation as well as for a voluntary redistribution of SDRs from industrial countries to low-income countries (LICs) and to the countries of the former Soviet Union (FSU) and the Council for Mutual Economic Assistance (CMEA).[2]

At a press conference held on April 20, 1993, to launch the new Systemic Transformation Facility (STF) for economies in transition, Camdessus is quoted as saying:

> How is an SDR allocation relevant to the problem of these countries? Are there grounds for an SDR allocation now in the membership? My answer is yes, with a personal conviction I try to have shared by the membership. Why? Because to allocate SDRs you need to demonstrate that there is a long-term global need for reserve supplementation. And this need is there. At present, 40 percent of our membership has reserves accounting to less than ten weeks of imports.
>
> Second, for the small low-income countries, the situation is one of true catastrophe...the case for the SDR allocation is very strong. It would allow us to correct a factor that for me is embarrassing – the fact that 37 of our members, particularly the countries of the former Soviet Union, have never been allocated SDRs, while other members of the IMF have allocated to themselves, in much less pressing circumstances, a significant amount. So I think an allocation would help us to correct some of this imbalance.
>
> I encourage the membership to consider voluntary schemes for a redistribution of SDRs, particularly the SDRs that would be allocated to industrial countries that do not need them. Then you would have extraordinary positive leverage to help industrial countries do more, not only for Russia but for all countries where the problem of external financing comes with a severe acuity. (*IMF Survey*, May 3, 1993)

Is Camdessus' "personal conviction" well founded?

This essay asks whether, in the circumstances of the early 1990s, there is a case for a limited allocation of SDRs specifically and exclusively to low-income countries. Undeniably, such countries face acute financing problems, and it is worth examining the extent to which these might be overcome by receiving SDRs. From the viewpoint of international political economy, a proposal of this type might encounter fewer objections than one that confers benefits on poor countries merely as a coincidental feature of a more general SDR allocation. Moreover, it will emerge that the effectiveness and efficiency of a limited allocation of SDRs to low-income countries can be enhanced if one is not at the same time too concerned about the SDR's systemic role within the international financial regime. In this regard, the irrelevance of the SDR as an international reserve asset may be an advantage.

The layout of the chapter is as follows. The next section briefly reviews the balance-of-payments problems that are encountered by LICs. The section on benefits for low-income countries enumerates the benefits that an allocation of SDRs to LICs would confer on them and makes some approximate quantitative estimates of those benefits. The following section looks at the potential costs for other countries not receiving SDRs and examines the implications for the international monetary role of the SDR. The section on international political economy discusses the international political economy of a limited allocation of SDRs to LICs and investigates whether such a proposal would receive the international-community support (or acquiescence) necessary for its adoption. The final section offers brief conclusions.

The financing problems of low-income countries

Apart from domestic economic mismanagement, balance-of-payments difficulties emanate from a number of sources. First, there may be secular changes in exports, imports, and long-term capital flows. For example, a country producing and exporting goods that have a low income elasticity of demand and importing goods that have a higher elasticity of demand will tend to encounter balance-of-payments problems. Such factors reflect payments deficits and surpluses as essentially structural phenomena. In addition, when demand and supply are themselves unstable, low price elasticities of demand and supply will tend to result in instability in the terms of trade. This instability in part reflects vulnerability to exogenous shocks. Both of these factors influence the incidence of payments deficits and surpluses.

Other important aspects of the balance of payments relate to the speed and efficiency with which deficits may be financed or corrected. The capacity of a country to finance a payments deficit depends on the level of its international reserve holdings and the availability of finance from the private international banks and the Bretton Woods (and other) institutions. The capacity for adjustment within the economy depends, in turn, on a number of factors. These include the extent to which domestic consumption goods may be switched into exports, and, more generally, the scope for short-term export expansion and efficient import substitution, the degree of money illusion, the flexibility of domestic economic policy, the level of infrastructural investment, and, related to these, the values of the price elasticities of export supply and import and export demand.

With low elasticities and a high degree of real-wage resistance, the scope for balance-of-payments adjustment will be strictly constrained. To the extent that the adaptability of an economy is positively related to its level of economic development, it is likely that developing countries will encounter more difficulty in coping with balance-of-payments problems than do developed countries. An important feature of the 1970s, 1980s, and 1990s, however, has been the growing irrelevance of grouping all developing countries together. Disaggregation is vitally important. This may be based on various economic indicators including per capita income, the degree of export diversification, the nature and pattern of trade, and geographical location. Against this background, a number of indicators may be assembled to reflect the size and nature of a country's or countries' payments problem. Examination of such indicators suggests that the balance-of-payments problems of low-income countries are particularly pronounced.

Data presented in Table 14.1 show that, although many developing countries (with the exception of the newly industrializing Asian economies) experienced quite persistent current-account deficits, the size of the deficits expressed as a percentage of exports of goods and services was significantly greater for LICs than for other groups. From 1984 to 1993, for example, the deficit measured this way was on average more than seven times greater for LICs than for developing countries. Declines in trade, and particularly in import volumes, have also been more common in LICs, and such reductions in volume may be a useful indicator of underlying balance-of-payments constraints; these constraints may, through economic policy, be transformed into declines in trade. For developing countries as a group, import volumes have risen persistently since 1987, with summed annual percentage increases amounting to 60 percent. For LICs, summed import volume growth was only just over 11 percent, with import volumes falling in 1987, 1990, and 1991 (IMF, 1992, table 25A, p. 119).

The statistical state of the current-account balance of payments is, however, an imperfect guide to the size of payments problems. Disequilibria may be temporary and self-reversing, capital flows may allow a current-account deficit to be sustained, but, at the same time, *ex post* payments data may conceal the extent to which other macroeconomic policy objectives have been subjugated. Overall, however, there appears to be evidence of a secular deterioration in the balance of payments of LICs.

To some extent, this deterioration is associated with the downward trend in the price of primary commodities relative to manufactures. For the countries of Sub-Saharan Africa, the sum of annual percentage declines in terms of trade over the 1985–92 period was 38.5 percent; for the small low-income countries as a group, it was 29 percent. This compares with a decline of only 20 percent for all developing countries taken together.

The fall in the relative price of primary products is particularly relevant for LICs because they have a relatively high degree of export concentration on such products. Data from the United Nations Conference on Trade and Development (UNCTAD) from 1982 to 1984 reveal that, whereas primary products made up more than 50 percent of total exports for 58 percent of developing countries, 71 percent of low-income countries experienced this degree of concentration.

The problems created by such secular deteriorations are exaggerated by short-term instability around this trend. Although better-off developing countries are not exempt from such instability (Love, 1990), the least-developed countries appear to experience the greatest instability in their terms of trade as well as in the purchasing power of their exports and in their import volume (Helleiner, 1983b).

Table 14.1 Developing countries' balance of payments on current account

	1984	1985	1986	1987	1988	1989	1990	1991	1992	1993	1994
In billions of U.S. dollars											
All developing countries	-33.6	-27.5	-46.9	-4.7	-24.9	-16.9	-11.6	-87.9	-67.1	-104.6	-106.2
Africa	-7.9	-0.5	-10.2	-4.5	-9.8	-7.3	-3.0	-4.6	-7.5	-8.3	-4.1
Asia	-3.6	-13.8	4.0	22.1	9.6	0.8	-2.7	-2.7	-4.5	-25.1	-28.3
Middle East and Europe	-19.9	-9.1	-24.3	-11.9	-12.9	-1.8	—	-61.1	-20.3	-27.8	-27.1
Western Hemisphere	-2.1	-4.1	-16.4	-10.4	-11.7	-8.6	-6.0	-19.6	-34.8	-43.3	-46.6
Sub-Saharan Africa	-3.1	-3.5	-6.0	-6.5	-7.9	-6.7	-8.6	-8.3	-8.8	-8.4	-7.0
Four newly industrializing Asian economies	7.2	10.4	23.2	30.9	28.3	24.4	14.3	9.7	10.0	4.5	0.8
Small low-income countries	-7.2	-7.4	-7.4	-8.3	-9.8	-9.9	-11.1	-10.0	-10.5	-10.9	-10.0
In percent of exports of goods and services											
All developing countries	-5.2	-4.5	-8.1	-0.7	-3.1	-1.9	-1.1	-8.1	-5.7	-8.3	-7.7
Africa	-10.1	-0.7	-14.8	-5.7	-12.0	-8.3	-3.0	-4.7	-7.6	-8.6	-4.2
Asia	-1.5	-5.7	1.5	6.5	2.3	0.2	-0.5	-0.4	-0.7	-3.3	-3.4
Middle East and Europe	-10.7	-5.4	-18.3	-7.9	-8.2	-1.0	—	-29.5	-9.2	-12.7	-11.8
Western Hemisphere	-1.6	-3.3	-14.9	-8.4	-8.4	-5.6	-3.5	-11.5	-19.5	-23.1	-23.1
Sub-Saharan Africa	-12.0	-13.4	-23.3	-22.9	-26.9	-21.2	-25.3	-25.1	-27.3	-26.0	-20.9
Four newly industrializing Asian economies	5.3	7.7	14.5	14.5	10.6	8.1	4.4	2.6	2.4	1.0	0.2
Small low-income countries	-31.8	-33.0	-32.2	-33.2	-35.9	-34.5	-35.5	-30.8	-31.3	-30.5	-25.4

Note: Includes official transfers.

Sources: IMF, World Economic Outlook, 1992, 1993, 1994.

What all this implies is that LICs are more likely than other countries to encounter balance-of-payments deficits. How can they respond? A first possibility is that they can run down their international reserves. But are their reserves adequate?

One, albeit imperfect, indicator of reserve adequacy is the ratio between reserves and imports, with a very approximate "rule of thumb" being that reserves are inadequate if they stand below 25 percent of imports or, in other words, are insufficient to finance imports for more than three months.[3] Data on reserve ratios are presented in Table 14.2, where it may be seen that low-income countries persistently fail this test. The theory of the demand for reserves suggests that demand is a positive function of the incidence of balance-of-payments deficits, the costs of adjustment, and national income, and a negative function of the degree of access to international credit, the degree of exchange-rate flexibility, and the opportunity cost of holding reserves.[4] On balance, these factors suggest that LICs will have a relatively strong demand for reserves and that low reserve ratios are indicative of reserve inadequacy rather than of a low need for reserves.

With inadequate reserves, countries may be forced to adjust. It is reasonable to presume that most poor countries possess a relatively low degree of structural flexibility. Markets may often be ill-developed and price elasticities low, with the result that the scope for switching resources rapidly into the production of traded goods will be strictly limited. In a global economic environment that is hostile to export expansion, developing-country governments frequently possess few alternatives to a deflationary program of balance-of-payments stabilization. The cost of such programs on economic growth, at least in the short term, and on future export growth may also be significant. In addition, such economic costs have been shown to put considerable strain on fragile democratic political systems, and it is therefore important not to lose sight of the political costs of adjustment.[5] The capacity for short-term adjustment is likely to be particularly constrained in LICs, where economies are inflexible, per capita income is low, technical competence is limited, and political support for the government is often tenuous.

Low structural flexibility and low response elasticities will also weaken the impact of exchange-rate changes; for this reason, it is in the context of LICs that most resistance to devaluation has been encountered. At the same time, pegging exchange rates to a major currency, as have thirteen Sub-Saharan African countries belonging to the franc zone, runs the danger of encountering the "third-currency phenomenon," under which inappropriate exchange-rate changes associated with changes in the world value of the major currency impose additional balance-of-payments problems on the countries tying their currencies to it. It is not surprising to find that researchers claim that the adoption of generalized flexible exchange rates actually raised the demand for reserves in such countries (Heller and Khan, 1978; Aghevli, Khan, and Montiel, 1991).

Table 14.2 Developing countries' reserves

	1984	1985	1986	1987	1988	1989	1990	1991	1992	1993	1994
	In billions of U.S. dollars										
All developing countries	164.6	188.2	195.8	255.2	249.6	271.5	319.9	388.0	408.6	448.1	446.6
Africa	7.2	9.7	9.3	11.0	10.8	12.7	17.5	21.2	18.3	19.3	21.7
Asia	67.4	79.4	104.6	148.4	158.6	168.5	194.2	237.5	236.8	246.9	241.2
Middle East and Europe	49.4	57.8	48.3	57.5	49.1	57.0	59.9	63.4	64.8	71.8	69.3
Western Hemisphere	40.5	41.2	33.7	38.3	31.1	33.3	48.3	65.9	88.7	110.0	114.4
Sub-Saharan Africa	3.1	4.1	5.1	6.0	6.5	7.2	8.5	9.8	9.8	10.2	11.1
Four newly industrializing Asian countries	29.0	43.5	67.8	102.8	111.4	117.7	126.3	143.6	152.7	161.8	161.1
Small low-income countries	4.6	4.9	5.4	5.5	5.7	5.7	6.2	7.3	7.2	8.0	8.6
	Ratio of reserves to imports of goods and services										
All developed countries	23.8	28.5	30.1	35.1	29.3	28.7	30.2	33.1	31.7	32.1	29.5
Africa	7.9	11.4	10.5	11.8	10.5	11.9	14.9	18.4	15.3	16.3	18.9
Asia	25.8	29.7	37.8	45.0	37.4	34.9	35.6	38.3	33.6	31.3	27.3
Middle East and Europe	24.1	32.7	30.6	34.7	28.7	30.2	28.0	26.8	27.0	29.0	26.9
Western Hemisphere	30.2	31.4	26.0	27.8	20.0	19.8	26.5	33.2	39.7	45.9	44.5
Sub-Saharan Africa											
Four newly industrializing Asian countries	22.6	35.1	49.2	56.3	46.7	43.2	40.5	39.7	37.5	36.1	32.0
Small low-income countries	11.9	12.3	13.0	12.2	11.5	11.1	11.4	13.1	12.5	13.3	13.8

Note: Official holdings of gold are valued at SDR 35 an ounce. This convention results in a marked underestimate of reserves for countries that have substantial holdings of gold. Valuing gold at the market price would further accentuate the *relatively* weak reserve position of low-income countries because they hold little gold.

Sources: IMF, *World Economic Outlook*, 1992, 1993, 1994.

Faced with adjustment difficulties and high adjustment costs, it may be tempting for LICs to borrow from international capital markets to finance balance-of-payments deficits, but in this they encounter a problem in the form of credit rationing and the existence of an availability constraint. Moreover, no risk premium that they would be prepared to meet would help unlock commercial finance, because commercial lenders, aware of the problem of adverse selection, would accurately conclude that the LICs could not afford to pay such high rates and that the higher default risk would more than offset any expected profits from an increase in the interest rate. It is not surprising to find that only very small amounts of short-term commercial lending have been directed to LICs, the access of which to bond finance is yet more impeded.

Notwithstanding their low level of commercial borrowing, LICs have failed to avoid debt problems and the need to renegotiate their debts through the Paris Club. Although many simple debt indicators can be misleading, and although, in the main, LICs have acquired official debt, their debt-service ratio was nevertheless more than ten percentage points higher than the average ratio for developing countries in 1992. Indeed, for low-income countries such as those in Sub-Saharan Africa, the debt problem has become progressively more pronounced. By 1990, the ratio of total external debt to exports for Sub-Saharan Africa was 370 percent, compared with 255 percent for developing countries in the Western Hemisphere. The ratio of total debt to GDP in the Sub-Saharan countries was more than twice that in the Western Hemisphere developing countries. LICs therefore encounter the problem of "debt overhang," with its negative adjustment incentives, that Latin American debtors experienced in the 1980s. Moreover, large debt-service ratios and low adjustment incentives will do nothing to enhance future creditworthiness.

All of the above evidence suggests that LICs have experienced structural weakening in their balance of payments, instability associated with export concentration, low levels of both reserves and access to finance, and severe adjustment difficulties. But their problems do not end with these.

LICs have frequently been compelled to turn to the IMF for financial assistance. Some analyses suggest, however, that the IMF's conventional wisdom of devaluing the national currency in question, and of deflating domestic demand is at its least relevant in the context of LICs. This is reflected in the high failure rate for IMF-supported programs in LICs and the fact that LICs account for almost all cases of arrears within the IMF.[6] Faced with an *ex ante* financing gap, LICs have had to close it *ex post* by lowering growth and by accepting a significant fall in living standards.

There is clearly no easy solution to the complex economic problems of LICs, but could it be that an appropriately sized allocation of SDRs to them would at least help?

The benefits of a link for low-income countries

An allocation of SDRs to LICs would surely help to correct the problem of reserve inadequacy. The benefit may be represented by the costs of reserve acquisition that would thereby be avoided. Reserves may, in principle, be acquired by borrowing or by sacrificing the consumption of real resources by running a balance-of-payments surplus. Low-income countries have low creditworthiness, are credit rationed, and are unable to borrow from private capital markets at any interest rate. Under these circumstances, the benefits of receiving SDRs are perhaps more appropriately viewed in terms of the interest rate the countries would have been *willing* to pay in private capital markets. They can, however, borrow from the IMF, but this would involve them in having to accept and implement a range of conditions, therefore incurring a "cost" in terms of loss of sovereignty. The reluctance of countries to borrow from the IMF unless unavoidable and to use it only as a lender of last resort (which may also be the *only* resort in the case of LICs) suggests that this cost is perceived as being high; as a cost avoided, however, it would be a benefit conferred by SDR allocation.

The cost of sacrificing real resources may in one sense be interpreted as the value of the goods that are exported rather than consumed domestically and the value of the imports that are foregone. But it is also instructive to consider the means by which imports are reduced. Taking the simplest of import functions, $M = mY$, where M equals the total value of imports, m is the propensity to import, and Y is national income, it may be seen that reducing imports will involve a sacrifice in terms of income that varies inversely with the value of m. If imports are further assumed to be made up of capital goods with a high marginal productivity, it follows that the long-term sacrifice will substantially exceed the short-term sacrifice. If, in addition, income is assumed to be subject to diminishing marginal utility, it follows that the receipt of SDRs will confer significant benefits.

It has to be recognized, however, that LICs may perceive the benefits of receiving SDRs as being rather less than the above discussion would suggest. Prior to receiving SDRs, LICs had the opportunity to increase reserves by pursuing appropriate policies, such as deflating domestic demand. The fact that they did not reveals something about their preferences. Assuming rationality, they would have been expected to substitute reserves for income for as long as the benefits of additional reserves appeared to exceed the costs of lost income. The benefits of receiving additional SDRs *gratis* would therefore be perceived by LICs as having a value that is less than the resource cost of acquiring reserves; moreover, the benefit per SDR would decline at the margin.

Viewing the benefits of SDRs purely in terms of the liquidity yield on additional international reserves is theoretically legitimate, but it may be unrealistic. Given the instability of their payments balances, their high adjustment costs, and their lack of access to other forms of international credit, LICs may need the additional insurance that would be provided by a larger inventory of reserves. But insurance is a luxury good, and LICs may not be able to afford it. If they were to receive a windfall in the form of additional SDRs, there might be other uses that would generate greater marginal utility for them than would be associated with using SDRs to increase reserve holdings. In short, LICs might be expected to spend any additional SDRs. Not only is this what would be expected, it is what has happened. Poor countries have been the heaviest net users of SDRs.

For some observers, this heavy net use has called into question the whole rationale of the SDR as a *reserve* asset. But it clearly means that we need to modify our analysis of the benefits of SDRs to recipients. Furthermore, it becomes necessary to establish a sharp distinction between the short-term and the long-term benefits, as well as between benefits and resource transfers. The benefits will tend to exceed the value of the real resource transfers that are financed by spending SDRs.

SDRs may be spent on imported consumer goods or imported capital goods. Alternatively, they may be used to service outstanding debt obligations. In a neoclassical general-equilibrium world, the marginal benefits of any of these forms of expenditure will be equal. It needs to be recognized, however, that, whereas buying imports of consumer goods confers short-term benefits, cancelling or reducing debt, or purchasing capital imports, generates benefits over the longer term. As soon as we pass into the long term, we need to start discounting in order to come up with a present-value estimate of benefits. We also need to estimate the marginal productivity of imported real resources. Assuming, however, that the marginal productivity exceeds the rate of discount (and this would be the rationale behind using SDRs this way in the first place), the long-term benefits will exceed both the short-term benefits and the value of the initial resource transfers associated with spending SDRs.

Up to now, the discussion implies that LICs will receive substantial benefits from an allocation of SDRs; but there is some overestimation. Net use of SDRs also currently carries a rate of interest (or more accurately in a technical sense, and as noted earlier, a rate of charge). The benefits of net use vary inversely with the rate of interest. Including the interest rate in the analysis again means that the time profile of benefits will vary; instantaneous use of SDRs will result in short-term and long-term benefits depending on how the SDRs are used, but it will also carry with it interest obligations that will move forward in time. For long-term benefits to be positive, the marginal rate of productivity net of the interest rate must exceed the rate of discount.

Furthermore, if SDRs were to be allocated on a regular basis, the time could eventually arrive when the interest payments associated with previous net use of SDRs would exceed new allocations, and the related resource transfers associated with the scheme would at that point turn negative for net users (Bird, 1982b). If the intention is to maximize the benefit of SDRs for net users, an easy way of doing this is to reduce (or eliminate) the rate of charge on using them; this issue is discussed further in the section titled "Considerations of international political economy."

There are, however, other ways in which LICs might benefit or perceive themselves to benefit from receiving SDRs. First, to the extent that SDRs are added to international reserve holdings or are spent in such a way that the future performance of the economy can be expected to be improved, the SDRs can raise the recipient's credit worthiness. Credit rationing will then be relaxed and the interest rate at which the country can borrow from international capital markets will fall. In fact, most LICs are so far from enjoying access to capital markets that it is difficult to see this as a practical benefit for them. It would be much more relevant for developing countries just on the wrong side of the margin of creditworthiness.

More pertinent in the case of some LICs would be the potential use of SDRs to clear arrears with the IMF. As mentioned earlier, arrears have become a significant problem for a number of LICs, for they remain ineligible to draw resources from the IMF while in arrears. Thus, although receiving SDRs would not relax the availability constraint that applies to commercial borrowing, it would relax the constraint that applies to borrowing from the IMF.

Another factor relating to the quality of SDRs as perceived by recipients is that, in contrast to drawings from the IMF through standbys and extended arrangements or through structural-adjustment facilities, the net use of SDRs carries no conditionality. It is reasonable to assume that the objective function of an LIC government in its dealings with the IMF has utility positively related to the volume of resources and negatively related to the degree of policy conditionality. Presenting LICs with additional and zero-conditionality financial resources would, in these circumstances, unambiguously raise their utility. Whether LICs can *actually* gain from being able to escape IMF conditionality depends on its net effectiveness.

Whereas recipients will view the lack of conditionality as an advantage, the IMF's major shareholders may be expected to view it as a serious weakness. To them, conditionality represents a means of encouraging countries receiving IMF support to modify policy both macroeconomically in terms of the management of aggregate demand and microeconomically in terms of establishing price incentives that, by increasing aggregate supply, will alleviate the underlying macroeconomic disequilibrium. In circumstances in which economic adjustment is badly needed, unconditional SDRs will be seen as enabling low-income countries to avoid adjustment and to substitute external financing that may itself allow the disequilibrium to worsen. For these reasons, the trend has been to make aid more conditional rather than less conditional.

Furthermore, a public-choice analysis of IMF lending predicts hostility from the IMF's management as well, because it is conditionality that confers on the managers their power and influence. Their utility according to such models will be a positive function of both lending *and* conditionality.

Camdessus' position apart, why would they support expanding unconditional finance in the form of SDRs?

A more measured approach seeks to assess the effectiveness and efficiency
of IMF conditionality. Where it works and works well, allowing LICs to avoid
it may be seen as a weakness of SDR allocation. Where it does not work or
works badly, allowing LICs to sidestep it should not be cause for concern.
Indeed, when IMF conditionality has a negative effect on the countries that
accept it, avoidance can be seen as a benefit. There is now a large literature
dealing with the design and effects of IMF-supported programs. Studies
differ in terms of the methodology used and the detailed results discovered,
but generally they suggest that, although there may be a small positive effect
on the current account of the balance of payments, there are no significant
effects on very much else.[7] Thus, Mohsin Khan (1990, p. 222) concludes that
"one would be hard-pressed to extract from existing studies strong inferences
about the effects of Fund programs on the principal macro economic targets."

Empirical evidence suggests that it is quite frequently external shocks
(and not economic mismanagement alone) that force countries to turn to
the IMF in the first place, and additional shocks that then blow adjustment
programs off course. Lack of commitment by governments may clearly be
a factor in causing programs to remain uncompleted, but most studies suggest that it makes little difference whether or not the negotiated program is
fully implemented. Furthermore, commitment may be encouraged by adequate financial support. Significantly, the completion rate of IMF-supported
programs tends to increase as the amount of finance provided by the IMF
(relative to the country's balance-of-payments deficit) rises.

There is also a (perhaps growing) view that a greater commitment
to adjustment can be induced if governments feel a stronger degree of
"ownership" of the program they are implementing. This might suggest that
less emphasis should be placed on conditionality imposed from outside
and more emphasis on policy designed by the country itself. If structural
economic adjustment takes a relatively long time to achieve, increasing the
amount of external financing through SDR allocation will enable more
appropriate adjustment policies to be pursued in preference to those that
focus on the short-term deflation of domestic aggregate demand. Macroeconomic stabilization is clearly important, but there is the danger that
excessive reliance on deflating domestic demand will squeeze out strategic
developmental imports and compress investment, with adverse long-
term consequences for aggregate supply. To the extent that the optimal
speed of adjustment tends to be lower in LICs than elsewhere, an additional
allocation of SDRs will help provide the international finance that is the
counterpoint to longer-term and more gradual adjustment.

A residual concern for LICs is that additional allocations of SDRs will
merely crowd out other financial aid, as well as nonfinancial aid that has
a monetary value. To the extent that crowding-out occurs and SDRs fail to

provide *additional* finance, the benefits from receiving SDRs will be reduced. The calculation will, however, need to be a little more subtle than this, for different types of aid are seen by recipients as being of different qualities. If high-quality assistance associated with SDR allocation were to crowd out an exactly equivalent value of other lower-quality financial aid, recipients would retain positive net benefits. Again, however, if the objective were to maximize the benefit from an allocation of SDRs to LICs, the solution would be to ensure that it had no adverse effect on other aid flows.

Can we more formally use the variables above to estimate the welfare benefits of SDRs to recipients? Much depends on how the SDRs are used and on the values assumed for the marginal productivity of resources, the interest rate on net use, the social discount rate, and the marginal propensity to import.

As noted, the benefit from holding SDRs may be seen as the associated liquidity that is thereby derived. This may be measured either by the opportunity cost of acquiring a similar quantity of reserves by alternative means or by the opportunity cost of the adjustment that is avoided. These two measures of the benefit from holding SDRs will, however, differ. Taking the former measure, and assuming that the alternative method of reserve acquisition is through the pursuit of expenditure-reducing policies, the size of the related income loss varies inversely with the value of the marginal propensity to import. For those imports that are of producer goods, this initial estimate of the impact on national income will have to be multiplied by the value of the marginal productivity of real resources. This approach to the measurement of benefit may also be used to estimate the benefit derived from using SDRs to pay off debts. Taking the latter measure, the benefit will further depend on the probability of a deficit occurring to the value of the accumulated SDRs.

The benefit from spending SDRs depends, in the first instance, on the way in which they are spent. If they are spent on consumer goods, the SDR value of the goods, exclusive of interest on the net use of SDRs, gives an approximate indication of the size of the benefit. If, however, they are spent on producer goods, the size of the benefit derived will depend on the rate of return on real resources, after deduction of the interest paid on the net use of SDRs and deflated by the social discount rate.

Calculations based on a more formal version of the above (Bird, 1979, 1988a) suggest that the welfare multiplier for LICs could reasonably be expected to exceed 1.5. At the very least, the value of the welfare gain may be significantly greater than the value of the SDR allocation itself.

If we now assume that an allocation of SDRs is made to LICs phased over five years, which, other things being constant, is designed to increase their reserve ratio up to 25 percent, an annual allocation of about SDR 1.6 billion is implied.[8] The annual welfare gain could, however, exceed SDR 2.5 billion annually.

These quantitative estimates are achieved on the assumption that the LICs' imports will continue to increase at approximately the same moving average rate as over the 1984–93 period, which would imply a 25 percent increase over the next five-year period, and that the addition to global expenditure implied by LICs spending extra SDRs has no discernible impact on world inflation. It is also assumed that the LICs' reserves do not change for any other reason.

It should also be noted that the estimates given above for the size of the SDR allocation assume that they are all added to reserves and not spent, whereas the estimate of the welfare gain mentioned earlier assumes that about half of them are spent. To this extent, the allocation discussed here would not lead *ex post* to a 25 percent reserve ratio. Assuming that there were to be no restriction imposed on net use, such as the reestablishment of the reconstitution clause, achieving a specific reserve-ratio target would mean that the size of the SDR allocation would have to move positively with the propensity of recipients to spend it. If LICs were to spend, say, 50 percent of the SDRs they received, and if the policy objectives were specifically to raise their reserve ratio to 25 percent, the size of the annual allocation would need to be twice that mentioned earlier.

An annual allocation of about SDR 1.6 billion would represent, even so, a significant financial contribution to the LICs, approaching 21 percent of their current-account balance-of-payments deficit in 1992. In dollar terms, it would represent an annual inflow from the IMF equivalent to about $2.25 billion. In contrast, and taking the entire 1984–91 period, LICs received negative net credit from the IMF's other accounts amounting to −$1.8 billion, an annual average *return* flow of $225 million. Although SDR allocations of the size discussed here would be large relative to the size of LIC balance-of-payments problems and other financial flows from the IMF, they would be extremely small relative to total global financing. Such allocations would represent a mere 0.2 percent of total official reserve holdings on an annual basis, with the percentage being lower if gold is valued at its market price.

But would the benefit to LICs from the SDRs they received be at a cost to others, or would it represent Pareto-efficient international financial reform? The answer to this question will have an important bearing on the political acceptability of an LIC link to the international community.

The costs to other countries

One might suppose that, if LICs gain real resources from spending an allocation of SDRs, other countries must be meeting the cost by losing resources. In a static sense, this is true, but a number of additional observations need to be made. First, to the extent that the marginal productivity of resources in LICs exceeds that in the countries releasing them (which may or may not be the countries acquiring the spent SDRs), world output will increase. This is no more than one of the conventional arguments for foreign aid. Second, and in the same vein, if the countries receiving the resources value them more highly than the countries that release them, world economic welfare will rise. Third, the countries that eventually acquire the SDRs spent by the LICs accumulate an asset that is a claim on resources in the future. Let us assume that it is indeed the country providing the real resources to the LICs that acquires their SDRs. Provided that the inflation-adjusted rate of interest equals the rate of discount, no sacrifice has been made in present-value terms, and, in this sense, there is no *permanent* resource transfer. There will still, however, be a net welfare gain. This follows because the LICs enjoy the benefit of additional resources now, and the countries that provide the resources are compensated by receiving SDRs, which are themselves a claim on future resources to an extent that the receiving country regards as equivalent. The LICs are better off and other countries are no worse off.

Instrumental in this analysis is the interest rate that is carried by the SDRs acquired. Just as an increase in the interest rate reduces the benefit from using an allocation of SDRs, so a fall in the interest rate shifts more benefits to net users but imposes costs on countries acquiring the SDRs. If the risk-adjusted interest rate on SDRs is equivalent to that on other reserve assets, other countries will be indifferent to how they hold their international reserves. As the interest rate on SDRs falls, however, countries holding SDRs rather than other reserve assets will incur an opportunity cost. They may be prepared to acquire low-interest SDRs from LICs as a way of assisting the LICs (psychic income may replace money income), but that is an issue of international political economy. Additionally, because the value of the SDR is determined by the weighted average value of a basket of five currencies, risk-averse countries may be prepared to trade off interest in return for the greater stability in value.

It must also be recognized that, although existing global real resources will be redistributed by allocating SDRs to LICs that then spend them to acquire real resources, redistribution will occur with any scheme that provides real aid to the LICs. If one of the basic purposes of the scheme is to provide help in the form of additional real resources to the LICs, it is hardly a criticism of the scheme that it does precisely that.

It is interesting that, when the link was discussed and rejected in the 1970s, its unacceptability to developed countries arose, not from the implications for the distribution of global resources, but from fears that it would prove inflationary. Related to this, but to a somewhat lesser extent, was the fear that the link would undermine the integrity of the SDR as an international reserve asset and would therefore prevent the SDR from becoming the principal reserve asset in the international monetary system. The erosion of monetary integrity, it was felt, would be associated with the excess creation of SDRs that would result from lobbying by developing countries anxious to ensure that SDRs were regularly created, as well as from the noncompetitive interest rate that SDRs would carry, which, it was assumed, developing countries would not want to see increased. What of these arguments now?

An allocation of SDRs linked as described above would be so small in terms of the total amount of international liquidity that it could not conceivably have any discernible impact on world inflation. In any case, one of the main routes through which SDR allocation was seen as inflationary was through the monetary relaxation in industrialized countries that would be induced by an increase in reserves; this mechanism does not apply in the case of an exclusively linked version.[9]

In a world in which international liquidity has become privatized and exchange rates have become flexible, critics of the SDR facility argue that official international reserves are completely unimportant. If so, how much less important will be a linked and limited allocation of SDRs to LICs. The logic of the argument that having fewer official reserves is not a problem – because private financing, financial innovation, and exchange-rate flexibility can adjust – may be turned around to say that having a small amount of additional reserves in the form of SDRs is equally insignificant.

In such a world, furthermore, the concern that the LICs will in some way cajole the IMF into creating excessive amounts of SDRs is nonsensical. To assume that the LICs have the sort of leverage that would persuade the IMF to create "excessive" amounts of SDRs credits them with a bargaining power that one suspects they only wish they had.

Within the LICs themselves, the receipt of SDRs would, in fact, be a less inflationary method than others of adding to reserves, because it would not affect the quantity of base money. A limited allocation of SDRs to LICs would not be significantly inflationary even in circumstances in which all linked SDRs were spent by LICs (which they would not be), the world economy were at full-capacity utilization of resources (which it is not), and the global aggregate supply schedule were perfectly inelastic (which it is not). With more realistic assumptions, the nonexistent threat of inflation recedes still further!

If inflation does not increase as a result of the link, it cannot damage the integrity of the SDR. In any case, we no longer need to worry much about its integrity, for the world long ago gave up the objective of establishing the SDR as the world's principal reserve asset.

It can be argued that abandoning this objective is in many ways unfortunate, but it is a *fait accompli*. Moreover, it releases the international community to use SDRs for other purposes (Bird, 1992), one of which could be to assist LICs. Unencumbered by the constraints of financial conservatism, the SDR becomes a more adaptable international financial instrument. But will the opportunity be grasped?

Considerations of international political economy

A number of conditions must be fulfilled to make the link a practicable possibility rather than a theoretical abstraction. First, there has to be a general *awareness of the problem* to be solved. Not only do the facts speak for themselves, but it seems that richer countries are beginning to listen and to recognize that the economies of LICs are in a fairly desperate state.

Second, there has to be a *recognized need for action*. If the performance of LICs has been poor over recent years, there is little prospect that it will improve in the short to medium term. The relative price of primary commodities is likely to continue to decline, export instability will continue to be a problem, LICs will not suddenly become credit-worthy, and the structure of their economies will continue to make adjustment costly, even though necessary. More narrowly in the context of the above discussion, holdings of international reserves will not rise to adequate levels. In other areas, the need for special treatment in the case of LICs has been recognized by the Toronto agreement on external debt and the establishment of the Structural Adjustment and Enhanced Structural Adjustment Facilities (SAF and ESAF) in the IMF. Special action has at the same time been taken to assist Central and East European economies in the process of transition to market-based systems. Meanwhile, various indicators imply some improvement in the economic performance and prospects of Latin American economies, which have, in any case, tended to be the principal beneficiaries of Brady-related debt relief. The position of the LICs, however, appears to remain intractable.

Although a perceived need to act has to exist, a third necessary condition is that there is a *means through which action may be taken*. In the case of the link there are in essence the "inorganic" and "organic" schemes discussed in the first section. As noted, the advantage of an inorganic link is that it does not require a change in the IMF's Articles of Agreement but simply an agreement among developed-country recipients to reallocate their SDRs to LICs. It is probably for this reason that Camdessus has emphasized voluntary schemes. However, if the IMF's major shareholders accept the argument for voluntarily reallocating SDRs to LICs, they may also be prepared to amend the Articles so as to modify the initial distribution of SDR allocations. Principles and pragmatism need not necessarily conflict.

Voluntary redistribution of SDRs could, of course, be limited to existing SDRs and would not then require a new allocation. This would circumvent the potential counterargument that there is no "global need" for additional SDRs. Yet, one of the advantages of much of the IMF's official language is that it is fairly broad and unspecific and can therefore accommodate a wide range of policies; "global need" can be interpreted to imply correcting global imbalances that exist in terms of the provision of international financing as well as in terms of the distribution of economic adjustment. Moreover, it may be recalled that Camdessus has argued that a global need exists. Where the desire to assist LICs is strong, additional finance could be granted by subsidizing the charge that LICs pay on the net use of SDRs. The subsidy could itself be financed by richer countries or by an income stream generated through sales of gold by the IMF.

A fourth and final condition is a *willingness to act* or, less ambitiously, not to impede the actions of others. Altruism may, of course, exist, but let us assume that the willingness of the IMF's major shareholders to accept a limited allocation of SDRs to LICs depends on the shareholders' perception of the direct and indirect costs of such a scheme on themselves. As shown above, the costs on the rest of world would be insignificant and could be adjusted through changing the precise form of link adopted. Although the claim that the 1970s version of the link would be inflationary actually lacked justification and empirical support, the inflationary threat was *perceived* as real, and it therefore affected the positions adopted by the inflation-averse industrial countries and the decisions finally taken. The situation now is fundamentally different. Again there is no prospect that the link will cause any discernible additional inflation; the difference now is that this is generally perceived to be true. Furthermore, the success that the industrial countries have had in reducing inflation since the 1980s, and the increasing preoccupation with global recession has had the effect of reducing the degree of inflation aversion.

The political and economic paradigms that underpin policies have also changed significantly in a number of influential economies. There is now less emphasis on completely free markets and more emphasis on (limited) intervention and economic management – as is reflected by the preference of the U.S. administration for greater international coordination of macroeconomic policy. Consistent with this trend, the adjustment programs supported by the IMF have begun to emphasize more heavily than in the past the protection of "vulnerable groups" and the provision of "social safety nets." Similarly, within the national welfare system of the industrial countries, there is growing concern with "targeting," endeavoring to concentrate assistance on those groups whose need is greatest (although this may clearly also be a means of reducing government expenditure on social security). In such an environment, the IMF's major shareholders may perceive LICs as an internationally vulnerable group and the link as a form of targeted social safety net.

A further global development that may make the international political economy of reform more conducive to the adoption of the link is changing East–West relations. Evidence suggests that, historically, much of the pattern of aid distribution can be explained in political, military, and strategic terms. Although it is unrealistic to assume that such considerations will suddenly evaporate (even though their precise configuration will change), it is realistic to assume that governments will reassess their aid policies and may, as part of this process, be persuaded to increase the relevance of economic and humanitarian factors.

Although there may be less opposition to the link now than in the early 1970s, there may still be resistance to its unconditional dimension – in spite of the observations made earlier in this chapter. Clearly, the link should be seen as a complement to policies that aim to improve conditionality and to make it more effective and efficient with respect to LICs. But there are various ways in which an element of conditionality can be attached to the link. Most straightforward would be to make the receipt of SDRs itself conditional upon the negotiation of a regular program backed by the IMF (or World Bank). Under this scheme, SDRs would represent a kind of financial "top up" to LICs. Although the SDRs would lose some attractiveness to recipients, they would involve no incremental conditionality. LICs would therefore receive more finance for the same conditionality, and this would surely be regarded as beneficial. Indeed, with additional finance, conditionality might be modified in ways that are more appropriate for LICs. To the extent that programs fail because they are inadequately supported financially, the link could, in this guise, have a positive impact on the completion rate of IMF-backed programs and could act as an incentive for countries to pursue policy reforms aimed at economic adjustment. Moreover, the "price" LICs would pay in having to accept conditionality could be offset by granting them a subsidy on their net use of SDRs. They could be offered a package of conditionality and reduced charge and, indeed, could be individually offered some choice in terms of the details of the package they accepted; some element of subsidy could be sacrificed to gain a lower degree of conditionality. The details of the scheme that emerged would depend on the bargaining strengths of "donors" and "recipients," but it seems feasible that arrangements deemed satisfactory by both parties could be reached.

Concluding remarks

The conclusion drawn from the above analysis is that an affirmative answer should be given to the question posed in the title of this essay. In a narrow and specific form, the link should be resurrected.

Low-income countries face massive economic problems that they are exceedingly unlikely to resolve on their own in the near to medium term. In their case, Keynes' dictum should perhaps be modified to read, "in the *medium run*, we are all dead." If the international community is not prepared to allow the financing gap to become an effective constraint condemning many millions of people to low, stagnant, and even falling living standards, some international action is needed.

The link provides a convenient and economically satisfactory mechanism through which action can be taken. The benefits to the recipients of SDRs would be substantial and the costs to others minimal, irrespective of whether one looks at the direct costs or the indirect costs through the link's systemic consequences. The link therefore meets both efficiency and equity criteria. An analysis of international political economy further suggests that the introduction of a link targeted on LICs would be acceptable to those governments the acquiescence of which would be needed; it also strongly confirms that the chances of adopting an LIC link now are very much higher than when the much broader version of the link was proposed in the early 1970s.

It may also be true that a case can be made, as Camdessus has attempted to do, for an SDR allocation to the FSU and former CMEA countries. It is certainly true that these countries, as nonmembers of the IMF, did not receive SDRs when they were previously allocated. It is also true that they face substantial financing and adjustment problems, which could be alleviated by receiving SDRs. The problem arises, however, if one is forced to rank needs, as would happen if the size of an SDR allocation were fixed in advance. In such circumstances, the needs of LICs are perhaps more pronounced than those of the FSU and former CMEA states. Would an SDR allocation to the latter countries crowd out SDRs to the LICs? International political economy is here again an important consideration. It may be that there would be greater political support for additional assistance to FSU states on the grounds that what happens in these countries constitutes the greater threat to international stability and the long-term interests of the IMF's major shareholders. At the same time, it might prove difficult to allocate SDRs to Central and East European states without allocating them to LICs as well. If this is true, an SDR allocation to the former would in practice crowd in an allocation to the latter. In this sense, the former CMEA countries would indeed offer "mutual economic assistance" to the LICs.[10]

Acknowledgements

Thanks are due to Tony Killick and an anonymous referee for comments on an earlier version of this essay. The usual disclaimer applies.

References

Aghevli, Bijan B., Mohsin S. Khan, and Peter J. Montiel, *Exchange Rate Policy in Developing Countries: Some Analytical Issues*, Occasional Paper No. 78, Washington, D.C., International Monetary Fund, March 1991.

Bienen, Henry S., and Mark Gersovitz, "Economic Stabilization, Conditionality, and Political Stability," *International Organization*, 40 (Autumn 1986), pp. 728–54.

Bird, Graham, "The Informal Link Between SDR Allocation and Aid: A Note," *Journal of Development Studies*, 12 (April 1976), pp. 268–73.

——, "The Benefits of Special Drawing Rights for Less Developed Countries," *World Development*, 7 (March 1979), pp. 281–90.

——, "The Demand for International Reserves in LDCs," in Graham Bird, *The International Monetary System and the Less Developed Countries*, London, Macmillan, 1978; 2nd ed., 1982a, pp. 82–113.

——, "Developing Country Interests in Proposals for International Monetary Reform," in Tony Killick, ed., *Adjustment and Financing in the Developing World: The Role of the International Monetary Fund*, Washington, D.C., International Monetary Fund, and London, Overseas Development Institute, 1982b, pp. 198–232.

——, "The Link Between SDRs and Aid," in Bird, *The International Monetary System*, 1982c, pp. 251–76.

——, "International Reserves: Supply, Demand and Adequacy," in Graham Bird, *World Finance and Adjustment*, London, Macmillan, and New York, St. Martin's, 1985, pp. 73–113.

——, "An Analysis of the Welfare Gains from Special Drawing Rights," *Economia Internazionale*, August–November 1978, pp. 177–85; reprinted in Graham Bird, *Managing Global Money: Essays in International Financial Economics*, London, Macmillan, 1988a, pp. 115–23.

——, "SDR Distribution, Interest Rates and Aid Flows," *World Economy*, 4 (December 1981), pp. 419–27; reprinted in Bird, *Managing Global Money*, 1988b, pp. 124–33.

——, "Global Environmental Degradation and International Resource Transfers," *Global Environmental Change*, 2 (September 1992), pp. 229–38.

——, *IMF Lending to Developed Countries: Issues and Evidence*, London, Routledge, 1995.

Chrystal, K. Alec, *International Money and the Future of the SDR*, Essays in International Finance No. 128, Princeton, N.J., Princeton University, International Finance Section, June 1978.

——, "International Reserves and International Liquidity: A Solution in Search of a Problem," in Graham Bird, ed., *The International Financial Regime: Surrey Seminars in Applied Economics*, London, San Diego, Sydney, and Toronto, Surrey University Press and Academic Press, 1990a, pp. 9–28.

——, "The Role of the Special Drawing Right in the International Monetary System," in Sidney Dell, ed., *The International Monetary System and Its Reform*, Part 5, Contributions to Economic Analysis No. 197, Amsterdam, Oxford, and Tokyo, North-Holland and the United Nations; New York, Elsevier, distributor, 1990b, pp. 703–27.

Coats, Warren L., Jr., "Enhancing the Attractiveness of the SDR," *World Development*, 18 (July 1990), pp. 975–88.

Frenkel, Jacob A., "International Liquidity and Monetary Control," in George M. von Furstenberg, ed., *International Money and Credit: The Policy Roles*, Washington, D.C., International Monetary Fund, 1984, pp. 65–109.

Grubel, Herbert G., "Basic Methods for Distributing Special Drawing Rights and the Problem of International Aid," *Journal of Finance*, 27 (December 1972), pp. 1009–22.

Haggard, Stephan, "The Politics of Adjustment: Lessons from the IMF's Extended Fund Facility," *International Organization*, 39 (Summer 1985), pp. 505–34; reprinted in Miles Kahler, ed., *The Politics of International Debt*, Cornell Studies in Political Economy, Ithaca, N.Y., and London, Cornell University Press, 1986, pp. 157–86.

Haggard, Stephan, and Robert Kaufman, "The Politics of Stabilization and Structural Adjustment," in Jeffrey D. Sachs, ed., *Developing Country Debt and the World Economy*, National Bureau of Economic Research Project Report, Chicago and London, University of Chicago Press, 1989, pp. 263–74.

Hawkins, Robert G., and C. Rangarajan, "On the Distribution of New International Reserves," *Journal of Finance*, 25 (September 1970), pp. 881–91.

Helleiner, Gerald K., "The Less Developed Countries and the International Monetary System," *Journal of Development Studies*, 10 (April–July 1974), pp. 347–73.

——, *The IMF and Africa in the 1980s*, Essays in International Finance No. 152, Princeton, N.J., Princeton University, International Finance Section, July 1983a.

——, "Lender of Early Resort: The IMF and the Poorest," *American Economic Review*, 73 (May 1983b), pp. 349–53.

Heller, H. Robert, "International Reserves and World-Wide Inflation," *International Monetary Fund Staff Papers*, 23 (March 1976), pp. 61–87.

Heller, H. Robert, and Mohsin S. Khan, "The Demand for International Reserves Under Fixed and Floating Exchange Rates," *International Monetary Fund Staff Papers*, 25 (December 1978), pp. 623–49.

International Monetary Fund (IMF), *World Economic Outlook*, Washington, D.C., International Monetary Fund, October 1992, October 1993, May 1994.

Kaufman, Robert R., *The Politics of Debt in Argentina, Brazil, and Mexico*, Institute of International Studies, University of California, Berkeley, 1988, processed.

Khan, Mohsin S., "The Macroeconomic Effects of Fund-Supported Adjustment Programs," *International Monetary Fund Staff Papers*, 37 (June 1990), pp. 195–231.

Killick, Tony, and Moazzam Malik, "Country Experiences with IMF Programmes in the 1980s," *World Economy*, 15 (September 1992), pp. 599–632.

Killick, Tony, Moazzam Malik, and Marcus Manuel, "What Can We Know about the Effects of IMF Programmes?," *World Economy*, 15 (September 1992), pp. 575–97.

Lizondo, Jose Saul, and Donald J. Mathieson, "The Stability of the Demand for International Reserves," *Journal of International Money and Finance*, 6 (September 1987), pp. 251–82.

Love, James, "Export Earnings Instability: The Decline Reversed?," *Journal of Development Studies*, 26 (January 1990), pp. 324–9.

Loxley, John, *The IMF and the Poorest Countries*, Ottawa, North South Institute, 1984, processed.

Nelson, Joan M., "The Politics of Stabilization," in Richard E. Feinberg and Valeriana Kallab, eds., *Adjustment Crisis in the Third World*, Overseas Development Council, U.S.-Third World Policy Perspectives No. 1, New Brunswick, N.J., Transaction Books, 1984, pp. 99–118.

——, ed., *Fragile Coalitions: The Politics of Economic Adjustment*, Overseas Development Council, U.S.-Third World Policy Perspectives No. 12, New Brunswick, N.J., Transaction Books, 1989, pp. vi, 161.

Park, Yoon S., *The Link between Special Drawing Rights and Development Finance*, Essays in International Finance No. 100, Princeton, N.J., Princeton University, International Finance Section, September 1973.

Stallings, Barbara, and Robert Kaufman, eds., *Debt and Democracy in Latin America*, Boulder, Colo., and London, Westview, 1989.

Williamson, John, *A New SDR Allocation?*, Washington, D.C., Institute for International Economics, March 1984.

Zulu, Justin B., and Saleh M. Nsouli, *Adjustment Programs in Africa: The Recent Evidence*, Occasional Paper No. 34, Washington, D.C., International Monetary Fund, 1985.

15
Debt Relief for Low-Income Countries: Is it Effective and Efficient?

Graham Bird and Alistair Milne

Introduction

In recent years religious bodies, campaigning groups, and parts of the media have made a strong moral case for debt relief, accusing creditors of imposing an excessive burden of debt on low-income countries and thereby forcing them to cut back in other areas of government expenditure such as education and health, with deleterious effects on poverty reduction and economic growth. The case for debt relief is also made from the other side of the political spectrum, most notably in the recent report of the International Financial Institution Advisory Commission sponsored by the US Congress (the 'Meltzer' report) which amongst other measures called for complete debt cancellation by the IMF and other IFIs.

Donors have responded with a series of measures, beginning with arrangements for debt relief under the Paris Club Toronto terms of October 1988 culminating in the current enhanced Heavily Indebted Poor Country (HIPC) initiative for the reduction of external debt.[1] These measures have attracted increasingly generous promises of funding from donors. Yet it is far from clear that even complete debt forgiveness, let alone the much more modest degree of debt relief offered through the HIPC initiatives, will transform the economic situation in low-income countries in the way that campaigners for debt relief seem to expect.

Discussion has tended to get carried away by the rhetoric of debt relief without troubling to analyse more carefully its implications for resource transfers and the conduct of economic policy in poor countries. Such analysis must confront two fundamental questions. First, should development assistance be offered to poor countries, and if so second, should this assistance be provided in the form of debt relief or in some other way? It is, in principle, possible to favour the idea of providing development assistance and yet be unenthusiastic about debt relief as a modality for organising it.

This chapter implicitly assumes that there is a role for development assistance and it has little to say about the first question. Instead, it focuses on the second question and, in a methodical fashion, explores the key issues surrounding debt relief as a way of providing development assistance.[2] Throughout, an attempt is made to keep a sharp distinction between rhetoric and reality. Again, much of the popular discussion surrounding debt relief mixes them up. While this may bring attention to the issue, in the long run it does not assist in designing appropriate policy. The ultimate objectives of development assistance are to help bring about economic, social and human development in poor countries by encouraging long-term economic growth and poverty reduction. This chapter investigates whether assistance offered in the form of debt relief can help deliver these objectives and whether it can deliver them better than conventional foreign aid. Is debt relief, in other words, effective and efficient?

It is tempting to try and short-circuit careful analysis by arguing that debt relief, in the form of the Brady Plan, was effective in alleviating the debt crisis in Latin America at the end of the 1980s, allowing countries in the region to achieve rapid economic growth in the first half of the 1990s, and that it will similarly help in the context of low-income countries, such as those in Sub-Saharan Africa. This approach is illegitimate. Apart from the scope for a reasonable debate about the role of debt relief in Latin America's economic recovery, there are also reasons to suggest that low-income countries are analytically different. The principal creditors of low income countries, unlike the case of the major Latin American debtors, are bilateral and multilateral donors not banks. Almost all the severely indebted low income countries countries, again unlike the Latin American case, continue to receive substantial net resources from their major creditors. It cannot be assumed, therefore, that policy can simply be exported from Latin America to Africa.

The layout of the chapter is as follows. The following section examines the available data on debt stocks and resource flows. The section on debt relief considers the resource implications of debt relief. The next section considers the economic consequences of transferring resources through debt relief, rather than through new lending or grants, taking account of issues such as debt overhang and moral hazard. The final section offers a few concluding remarks.

The data on debt

Table 15.1 presents data on the debt stock and associated flows for fifty-eight low-income countries. While this is standard data, our presentation is novel in one respect, distinguishing stocks and flows from official sources (such as the multilateral and bilateral donors) and private sources (such as banks).[3]

The figures for total debt confirm that both debt stocks and debt service payments are high, with total 1998 debt service payments for example

Table. 15.1 External debt and resource flows of low-income countries[a]

% GNP 1998	Stock (1)	Interest (2)	Amortisation (3)	New lending (4)	Net lending (5) = (4) − (3)	Debt service[b] (6) = (2) + (3)	Resource inflow (7) = (5) − (2)
Total debt[c]	39.6	1.4			−0.1	−3.4	−1.6
Long term[d]	33.4	1.2	2.1	2.5	0.4	−3.3	−0.8
Multilateral	9.2	0.2	0.3	0.8	0.5	−0.6	0.2
Bilateral	11.1	0.2	0.5	0.6	0.1	−0.7	−0.1
G'teed bank/bond[e]	5.5	0.3	0.4	0.7	0.3	−0.7	0.0
Other guaranteed[f]	2.1	0.1	0.3	0.1	−0.2	−0.4	−0.3
Non-guaranteed[g]	5.5	0.2	0.6	0.3	−0.3	−0.9	−0.6
IMF	1.1	0.0	0.1	0.4	0.3	−0.1	0.3
Short term	5.0	0.2			−0.9		−1.1
Grant[h]							0.6
FDI[i]							3.0
Portfolio[j]							0.1
Summary (excluding shot term)							
Official sources[k]	23.5	0.6	1.2	1.9	0.7	−1.8	0.7
Private sources[l]	11.0	0.5	1.1	1.0	0.0	−1.6	2.5

Notes: [a] Statistics for 58 low-income countries reporting to the World Bank (source Global Development Finance 2000 on CD-Rom). [b] Including the interest but not the amortisation of short term debt. The latter data are unavailable. [c] Total debt = Long term + IMF credit + short term. [d] Long term = multilateral + bilateral + supplier credits + other publically guaranteed + non-guaranteed. [e] 'G'teed bank/bond' is lending to the public sector and to publically guaranteed private sector borrowers via bank lending or bond issue. [f] 'Other guaranteed' is all other lending by private creditors either to public sector or to private sector borrowers supported by a public sector guarantee (typically export credit guarantee). [g] Non-guaranteed is debt finance from private sources to private sector borrowers without support of any public sector guarantee. [h] Grants are official development grants excluding technical co-operation. [i] FDI is net foreign direct investment. [j] Portfolio is net portfolio investment (purchase of equities and locally traded bonds). [k] Official sources = Multilateral + Bilateral + Other guaranteed + IMF + Grants. [l] Private sources = G'teed bank/bond + non-guaranteed + FDI + Portfolio.

averaging 3.4 per cent of GNP. The majority of this debt is held by official creditors but private sector creditors hold around one-third of the long-term debt stock. Because official creditors offer loans at less than market rates of interest, private creditors account for nearly half of debt service payments. However, debt service payments can be a misleading indicator of the burden of debt. In 1998 new lending (column 4) was a major offsetting inflow, reducing the overall resource outflow on total low income country debt (debt service minus new lending) to 1.6 per cent of GNP. Other significant resource inflows in 1998 to these countries were grants and foreign direct investment. The effect of adding these is to reverse the sign of total resource flows, resulting in total net resource inflows from all sources of just over 3 per cent of GNP in 1998.

The final two rows of Table 15.1 distinguish debt stocks and resource flows from official sources from debt stocks and resource flows from private sources. In 1998 there were positive resource inflows from both official and, to a greater extent, from private sources. New lending from official sources (1.9 per cent of GNP in 1998) and grants (0.6 per cent of GNP in 1998) were more than enough to offset debt service to official creditors. In the case of the private sector, while net lending was negative, substantial flows of FDI also led to a positive net resource inflow.

Table 15.2 has the same form as Table 15.1, but is restricted to the most severely indebted low-income countries.[4] This category includes all those countries that are eligible for debt relief under the current HIPC initiative. For the severely indebted countries stocks of debt are of course much higher, nearly three times higher in relation to GNP, than for low income countries as a whole. But most of this additional debt is associated with concessional lending from the official sector and as a result debt service payments are less than half as high again at 4.9 per cent of GNP. Private sector debt stocks are somewhat higher and private sector resource inflows somewhat lower than for all low-income countries.

Table 15.2 also highlights the fact that severely indebted low-income countries receive much greater levels of new lending from official sources and much higher levels of development grants, relative to other low income countries. In 1998 these favoured countries received new loans from official sources amounting to $4\frac{1}{2}$; per cent of GNP and grants of over 4 per cent of GNP. The most severely indebted low-income countries received nearly $3 in new lending and grants for every $1 of debt service payments and were therefore the beneficiaries of net developmental aid inflows amounting to nearly 6 per cent of GNP. Official creditors in effect provided the resources to service their own claims for the most severely indebted low-income countries.

Figure 15.1 compares debt stock and debt service for the twenty most severely indebted low-income countries, those with ratios of external debt to GNP in excess of 100 per cent. Given their limited tax capacity, these

Table 15.2 External debt and resource flows for severely indebted low-income countries[a]

% GNP 1998	Stock (1)	Interest (2)	Amortisation (3)	New lending (4)	Net lending (5) = (4) − (3)	Debt service[b] (6) = (2) + (3)	Resource inflow (7) = (5) − (2)
Total debt[c]	128.2	2.1			1.2	−4.9	−0.8
Long term[d]	111.3	1.8	2.9	4.7	1.9	−4.6	0.1
Multilateral	29.3	0.5	0.9	1.9	1.1	−1.4	0.6
Bilateral	57.1	0.5	0.6	0.8	0.2	−1.1	−0.3
G'teed bank/bond[e]	16.2	0.6	1.0	0.5	−0.5	−1.6	−1.1
Other guaranteed[f]	5.6	0.1	0.2	1.5	1.3	−0.3	1.2
Non-guaranteed[g]	3.1	0.1	0.2	0.1	−0.2	−0.3	−0.3
IMF	3.7	0.0	0.2	0.1	0.1	−0.3	0.1
Short term	18.8	0.3	0.3	0.4	−0.7	−0.3	−1.0
Grant[h]							4.2
FDI[i]							2.8
Portfolio[j]							0.0
Summary (excluding short term)							
Official sources[k]	95.7	1.1	1.9	4.5	2.6	−3.0	5.7
Private sources[l]	19.3	0.7	1.2	0.5	−0.7	−1.9	1.5

Note: [a] Statistics for 29 low income countries – all those defined as 'severely indebted' in Global Development Finance. [b-l] See Table 15.1.

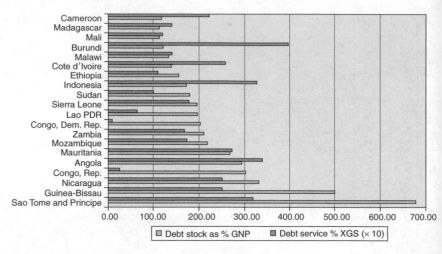

Figure 15.1 If Debt stock and debt service in the 20 most severely indebted low-income countries

countries would certainly be unable to service such high debt stocks on commercial terms. But in fact, while debt service payments (interest plus amortisation of principal) are a significant proportion of exports of goods and services (XGS), they are low relative to the magnitude of the debt, and there is no clear relationship between debt stock and the amount of debt service payments.

The most severely indebted countries tend to attract the largest inflows of new lending and grants. Figure 15.2a compares stocks of debt from official sources in 1995 with the average net inflow of resources over the years 1996–98 (official grants + new lending – debt service payments) for the severely indebted countries.[5] The only severely indebted country receiving negative net official resource transfers over this period was Nigeria.[6] A small number (Cameroon, Democratic Republic of Congo, Cote D'Ivoire, Indonesia, Sudan) received transfers of less than 2 per cent of GNP. The remaining twenty-three severely indebted countries all received positive net transfers in excess of 2 per cent of GNP. As the regression line in this figure suggests, from amongst the severely indebted low income countries it is those with the highest levels of debt stock which typically obtain the largest net official resource inflows. It seems that it pays to be indebted to official creditors. Figure 15.2b, comparing the stock of debt with net new lending, reveals a very different picture for debt owed to private creditors.[7] New lending is typically less than debt service, so net inflows are negative and there is no clear relationship between indebtedness and net inflows.

To summarise: low-income countries are carrying large stocks of external debt to GNP, with especially large amounts owed to official creditors by the

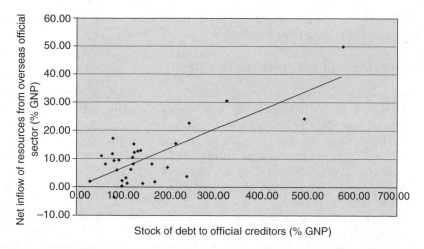

Figure 15.2a Official debt stocks (1995) and net inflow of official resources (1996–98)

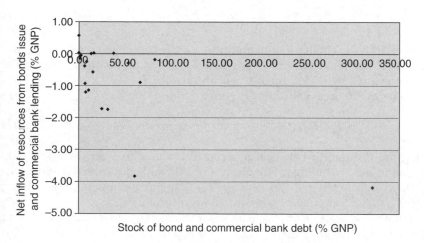

Figure 15.2b Private debt stocks (1995) and net inflow of private debt (1996–98)

most severely indebted countries. Debt service payments, relative to the magnitude of debt stocks, are much higher for borrowing from private creditors, compared to borrowing from official creditors. Finally and perhaps surprisingly, given the widespread perception that low income countries carry a substantial burden of debt service, inflows of official resources net of debt service payments are substantial and positive for virtually all the severely indebted low-income countries. The largest inflows go to those countries with the highest stocks of official debt. High debt stocks are a reflection of past aid dependency, but not indicative of any requirement to transfer borrowed resources back to official donors.

Debt relief and net resource transfers

Having looked at the data on debt, we may now examine the case for debt relief in terms of its impact on net resource transfers. It is sometimes suggested that debt relief can release additional resources for low-income countries without placing any additional burden on the taxpayers of donor countries.[8] This position can be quickly dismissed. The new resources have to come from somewhere and, in the case of official debt relief, this can ultimately only be from borrowing or the sale of assets by donors, or from increased taxation.

To explore the flow of resources arising from debt relief more carefully it is helpful to examine two accounting identities; one for the evolution of indebtedness and the other for the fiscal constraint of an indebted country. Thus,

$$\Delta D \equiv (S - P) + (L - W) \tag{1}$$

where ΔD is the change in indebtedness, S is the contracted debt service payments, P is actual debt service payments, and L is new lending. Debt relief is represented by W, although it will also reduce S.

As far as the fiscal constraint is concerned,

$$G \equiv I + N \equiv T + (L - P) + A \tag{2}$$

Here we distinguish between government expenditure on developmental expenditures, including infrastructure, health, and education (G) and a miscellaneous category (N). Tax revenue (T) is augmented by net new lending ($L - P$) and development grants-in-aid from abroad (A).

From these expressions we can see that the only direct impact of debt forgiveness is to reduce the stock of debt. The fiscal implications arise, if at all, only indirectly via the effects on P, L and A. It is quite possible for debt forgiveness to have no resource impact. For example, in the case where some debt service was not being paid prior to the granting of relief, and the relief only applies to this shortfall, that is, the difference between S and P, S is now reduced until it equals P. Debt relief of this sort will reduce the contractual stock of debt, but it will not strengthen the recipient's fiscal stance, unless it leads to new lending or more aid.

What if debt relief goes beyond this essentially cosmetic exercise and reduces both S and P? If the recipient was previously making all contractual debt service payments, such that $S = P$, then, other things being equal, debt relief will relax the budget constraint to the full extent of the fall in S. If, however, $P < S$, then the fiscal impact will be reduced accordingly, and will only occur to the extent of the fall in P (which will now clearly be less than the fall in S).

But, other things may not remain constant. If donors work to a target budget for the financial support of poor countries, the fall in S will be offset by a fall in L or A. Depending on the relative size of the fall in P, L and A, real resource transfers might not rise at all and might even fall. From expression (2), it may be seen that if A and L together fall by more than P, then the budgetary situation of the recipient will actually weaken rather than strengthen.

The immediate resource impact could be much worse than this. If for a moment we assume that donors forgive say \$100 m of debt and finance this out of a fixed aid budget. How will current resource flows to a recipient be affected? Assuming an interest rate of 3 per cent and an amortization rate of 2 per cent, the first-year resource gain from debt relief will be \$5 m. But the immediate resource loss from reduced aid inflow will be \$100 m. Thus where debt forgiveness is financed out of an equivalent amount of aid there will actually be a decline in net resource transfers during the first year of \$95 m. It is true that, because the debt is no longer being serviced, this decline will be offset by increased net resource transfers in future years. But this example makes clear that where economic development is constrained by the availability of external resources, the financing of debt relief out of current aid budgets could have a significantly adverse effect on the ultimate objectives articulated at the outset of this chapter.

This potential impact of debt relief has been recognised in the framing of the HIPC initiatives, which incorporate a principle of 'additionally': that is, that all debt forgiveness should be financed out of funds that are additional to current aid budgets. The need to do this reflects the basic resource constraint; any addition to net resource flows resulting from debt relief must be financed, ultimately by taxpayers in developed countries.

To the extent that debt relief crowds out conventional aid, from amongst low-income countries there will be gainers and losers from an initiative such as HIPC. The issue then becomes whether financial assistance channelled through debt relief is distributed in a way that it is in some sense preferable to the distribution of aid. There are sound reasons for believing exactly the opposite. Where debt relief goes to countries with amounts of debt that are deemed unsustainable, resources may in effect be directed towards countries with a history of economic mismanagement. To finance the debt relief, aid may be withdrawn from other low-income countries with greater 'need' and a better track record of economic management. To counter this problem HIPC eligibility is subject to strict conditionality in terms of the conduct of economic policy.

Another way of making the same basic points is by noting that:

$$F \equiv L + A - P \tag{3}$$

where F stands for total net resource transfers to an indebted poor country. A fall in P will only lead to additional transfers if L and A remain the same. If A and L together fall by the same amount as the fall in P, then from a resource transfer point of view, as well as from a fiscal point of view, the recipient of the debt relief will be no better off. Furthermore, an increase A and L equivalent to the debt relief shown by the fall in P *would* have resulted in additional resource transfers and a relaxation in the fiscal constraint.

Expression (3) also allows us to draw an important distinction between low-income countries and middle-income countries. At the end of the 1980s, and for the latter group of countries, $P > L + A$, and F was negative. Debt relief, provided through the Brady plan conversions and other mechanisms, reduced P, had relatively little effect on $L + A$, and therefore tended to have a positive effect on F. In the Brady plan 'additionally' was automatically provided by the reduction in interest income accepted by bank creditors.

As we have seen, in the case of almost all low-income countries on the other hand, $P < L + A$, and F is positive. Without additional resources, debt forgiveness financed out of current aid budgets, that is, out of reductions in $L + A$, will lead to an immediate decline in F which will take many years to offset.

In summary, what does this analysis tell us? It says that it is illegitimate simply to assume that debt forgiveness or even full debt cancellation will automatically strengthen the budgetary position of recipients or their net resource position. The crucial issue is the impact of debt relief on other flows. It is possible that debt forgiveness will leave the poor countries that receive it no better off. Indeed to the extent that aid flows to all low-income countries are used to finance debt forgiveness, those countries that receive aid but are not beneficiaries of meaningful debt forgiveness may well be left worse off.

One may argue that if additional resources are available for transfer to low-income countries, then the more efficient way of providing them is as conventional aid rather than debt relief. This is because conventional aid has a more high-powered short-run effect and also, as will be discussed in the next section, conventional aid may create better incentives for recipient countries to conduct policies which achieve the ultimate objectives of growth and poverty reduction.

Efficiency arguments for debt relief

The case for debt relief cannot be based on increased resource availability, since as we have seen increased resources can equally well be channelled through increased grants or new lending. The justification for debt relief must instead be that, independently of any impact on resource transfers, it helps achieve the ultimate objectives of improving growth rates and relieving poverty in low income countries.

One efficiency argument for debt relief which has featured significantly in the framing of the HIPC inititives is the desirability of reducing debt to *sustainable levels*. If debt service becomes unsustainable – that is, if the debtor country is unable to mobilise a sufficient proportion of external resources to service its external debt – then the consequence will be a shortage of international liquidity, a disruption of trade flows, and a consequent deterioration of economic performance. Debt relief can avoid both these costs and the associated costs of debt renegotiation and restructuring.[9] But is sustainability really a relevant issue in relation to the debt of low income countries?[10]

It might be claimed that the high levels of debt service in the most severely indebted countries shown in Figure 15.1, at sometimes about 40 per cent of export earnings, are indeed beyond the payment capacity of debtor countries. But this takes no account of the flow of development grants. Specific measures of debt sustainability therefore only make sense in the context of some particular level of aid flows.

If, as seems to be the case for virtually all the severely indebted low income countries, debtors can count on some given positive level of net resource inflows F then there would seem to be no effective limit on the sustainable level of debt. Debt service payments rising to 50 per cent of total exports or more could be matched by a corresponding increase in grants, and hence could always be financed. If there is no net burden of debt service, then any absolute level of debt is sustainable. Liquidity problems may emerge, but this will be because donors set limits on the total level of net resource transfer that they are willing to provide, not because debt stocks are unsustainably high.

An alternative efficiency argument for the provision of debt relief relates to *debt overhang*; the idea that the stock of debt acts as a disincentive to economic reform, since indebted countries perceive creditors to be the major beneficiaries from it while they – the debtors – carry the costs of economic adjustment. Debt acts as a tax on adjustment and investment.[11]

Of course, servicing any amount of debt involves an opportunity cost since the related resources will be unavailable for other purposes. But debt overhang goes further than this. While additional capital inflows may defray the costs of servicing existing debt, they wilt also lead to further accumulation of debt and will therefore increase the claims of external creditors on an indebted country's future resources. It is in the nature of debt overhang that it is the stock of debt that needs to be reduced. This is where debt relief fits into the picture.

But does official debt, which dominates the debt stock of the severely indebted low income countries, really induce debt overhang? This would only be true if higher levels of debt stock mean that debtors anticipate lower levels of net resource transfers from donors in the future. But as we have seen in the second section higher levels of outstanding debt are associated with higher, not lower, levels of net resource transfers from official sources.

Once again the key point is that it is not so much debt stocks that matter as expected levels of net resource transfers. If these are greatest for those countries with lowest per capita income, then countries which are successful in moving out of poverty will find that their share of limited aid budgets declines. This creates an obvious disincentive to pursuing growth and development.[12] The extent to which this "tax on development" alters policy choices in the poorest countries is unclear. But unless expectations of net resource flows are altered, reductions in the stock of debt will have no effect on incentives to engage in economic reform.

A related point, also of limited relevance to low-income countries, is the so called 'debt relief Laffer curve'. If there is a debt overhang then debt relief, by enhancing the domestic incentive to pursue economic reform and economic growth, can lead to a rise both in the secondary market price of debt and in the present value of expected debt repayments.[13] In this way creditors may gain from debt relief even though they have forfeited the option of full and complete repayment. In such a case debtors are to the right of the top of the Laffer curve. It was the concepts of debt overhang and the debt relief Laffer curve that were, in large measure, used to justify debt relief in the context of the Latin American debt crisis. But clearly if there is no equivalent debt overhang for low-income countries, there can be no equivalent debt relief Laffer curve.[14]

What about the efficiency arguments made against the provision of debt relief? The traditional case against relief of private sector debt is that of *moral hazard*. If private creditors expect that public funds, in the form of debt relief, will be used to bail out debtors in the event of their accumulating unsustainable debt, private capital markets will be encouraged to over-lend. As a consequence debt repayment crises will become more likely. But this moral hazard argument is a weak one when applied to debt relief for low-income countries. Relatively little of their debt comes from private sector creditors and current initiatives are designed for the relief of official debt.

There is another and somewhat different argument, confusingly also referred to as *moral hazard*, sometimes used to oppose the relief of official debt. This is that countries, rather like an individual anticipating escape from repayment by entering bankruptcy proceedings and racking up large and unsustainable credit card bills, will deliberately build up unsustainable levels of debt from official creditors in order to subsequently benefit from any additional resources flowing from official debt relief.[15] There are flaws with applying this argument to low-income countries. The analogy with an individual borrowing on a credit card is imperfect in that countries are not offered a large line of credit, which they can then utilise freely for whatever purposes they choose. In fact new lending is tightly controlled by donors and is usually conditional on the borrower pursuing appropriate policies. In any case altering debt stocks, as already discussed, has little impact on expected net resource flows so there are no obvious resource benefits to over-borrowing in this way.

A final argument that may in principle be made against relief of official debt is that, to the extent that it allows debtor countries renewed access to borrowing from private creditors, it may allow them to escape from the conditionally associated with official new lending and grants. Although the escape may well only be temporary, since they are likely eventually to exhaust their access to private sources of credit, in the meantime policies may be adopted that make economic growth and poverty reduction less likely in the long run.

This argument does not apply to the current HIPC initiative, since the degree of debt relief on offer has not been sufficient to allow low-income countries to gain access to private sector credit. Nonetheless it is true, in principle, that a sufficiently generous reduction of debt stocks could lead to a weakening of donor conditionality after the expiration of the debt relief scheme. To the extent that the objectives of donors and of debtor governments are in conflict, then there is a case for keeping debtors on a 'tight leash' through maintaining a sufficiently high level of debt to preclude access to private sector lending. Concerns about a loosening of conditionality also explain why qualification for HIPC is itself subject to strict criteria on debtor government policies and reform.

Overall we can conclude that the efficiency arguments for debt relief in low-income countries, just like the resource transfer arguments, have been very much overplayed. Sustainability of low income countries' official debt is not an issue in an economic sense. Since debt relief is unlikely to affect anticipated resource transfers, it will confer little benefit via debt overhang and the debt relief Laffer curve. But neither does it create any moral hazard. In the final analysis official debt relief seems to be little more than a bookkeeping exercise, irrelevant from both the perspective of resource transfers and economic efficiency. There is only one economic argument left. Were virtually complete forgiveness of official debt on offer, then access to private sector borrowing might allow debtors to escape from the conditionality associated with current developmental aid flows. But if debtor countries cannot to be trusted to set their own economic policies and work towards developmental goals, then this would be an undesirable outcome. The attraction of escaping from conditionality depends on its costs and benefits. Since these vary according to one's perspective, the perceived benefits and costs of debt relief may be expected to vary similarly.

Concluding remarks

It is understandable that pictures of poverty and starvation in Sub-Saharan Africa combined with discussion of the 'burden of debt' and expressions of the size of this burden relative to expenditures on health and education lead to the apparently natural conclusion that debt relief will help poor countries.

However, careful analysis of the budgetary and resource implications of debt relief reveals the weakness of this kind of argument. Net resource flows, that is, new lending and development grants less debt service, are substantially positive for all the most indebted low-income countries. The fact is that the world's most severely indebted low-income countries receive on average nearly 3 dollars of new money from official creditors, for every 1 dollar of debt service. Moreover, as we have emphasised, debt relief on its own does not create new resources. These resources have to come from somewhere and it is an open question as to whether new resources are best applied to the cancellation of official debt or to the more conventional form of new lending and development grants.

The principal economic argument for forgiveness in the form of debt relief rather than financing in the form of new inflows is debt overhang. This has been used in the past to justify debt relief for middle-income countries. But it turns out that this argument is irrelevant to low-income countries, for the simple reason that relief of their substantial stocks of official debt will have little impact on expected future resource flows. However, and by the same token, the opposing moral hazard arguments may also fail to apply to the relief of low-income country official debt.

If anything perhaps the balance of the remaining arguments goes against the provision of debt relief. There could be undesirable distributional effects with some poor countries losing out. Political pressures to offer debt relief may distort the allocation of resources. Moreover a complete relief of debt could result in an undesirable relaxation in donor conditionality. At best debt relief is a tidying up accounting exercise. From an economic perspective it may be largely irrelevant to the goals of growth and poverty reduction.

If the economic benefits of debt relief are minimal, why has it received so much attention? There are a number of potential explanations. First, even where the benefits are cosmetic in economic terms, they may be real in a political sense. Donor and recipient governments may wish to be able to claim that something is being done about the extreme poverty found in the world's poorest countries. Announcements of debt relief are an effective way for finance ministers and officials to grab the headlines, and appear generous, at no real economic or political cost. High profile initiatives such as HIPC imply that action is being taken. Indeed if donors are fundamentally uncommitted to increasing resource transfers an initiative that implies a lot and delivers only a little is ideal.

Second, the powerful symbolism of debt relief may create a political commitment in developed countries to increase resource transfers to low-income countries. Even if the transfer of resources through conventional aid is in fact a more efficient economic mechanism, providing resource transfers via a programme of debt relief may be needed to in order to mobilise these resources in the first place.

Third, and with some justification, debtors perceive that that they have lost sovereignty over the design of domestic economic policy. A large scale reduction of debt stocks could allow them to escape from what they see as the intrusiveness of IMF and World Bank conditionality. While conditionality may, in the short run, promote sounder policies, it is not obviously conducive to the development of domestic institutions and the practice of good governance. Over the longer term development and poverty reduction may therefore be better served by a transfer of sovereignty back to the governments of low income countries, facilitating political as well as economic development. However, this would require much larger scale forgiveness of debt to official creditors than is being contemplated under the HIPC iniative.[16]

In reality, however, aid is conditional tad is likely to remain so, especially as there is evidence to suggest that it is more effective in a sound policy environment. For as long as low-income countries are unable to access private capital markets, they will remain dependent upon aid provision. Debt relief will not therefore restore control into the hands of domestic governments, unless (perhaps) there is virtually complete debt forgiveness and this is a step which donor countries still seem reluctant to take.

References

Bird, G. (1989), 'Strategic Plans or Muddling Through: The Genetics of Third World Debt Policy', in G. Bird (ed.), *Third World Debt: The Search for a Solution*. Aldershot, Edward Elgar.

Bird, G. and N. Snowden (1997), 'From Banks to Bonds: A Problem Resolved? A Perspective from the LDC Debt Literature', *Journal of International Development*, **9**, 2, 207–20.

Boote, A. R. and K. Thugge (1999), *Debt Relief for Low Income Countries: The HIPC Initiative*. Pamphlet Series, **51**, Washington DC, IMF.

Claessens, S. (1990), 'The Debt Laffer Curve: Some Estimates', *World Development*, **18**, 12.

Cohen, D. (1990), 'Debt Relief: Implications of Secondary Market Discounts and Debt Overhangs', *World Bank Economic Review*, **4**, 1.

Cohen, D. (1996), 'The Sustainability of African Debt', *Policy Research Working Paper*, **1621**, Washington DC, World Bank.

Corden, W. M. (1989), 'Debt Relief and Adjustment Incentives', in J. A. Frenkel, M. P. Dooley and P. Wickham (eds.), *Analytical Issues in Debt*, Washington: IMF, 242–57.

Daseking, C. and R. Powell (1999), 'From Toronto Terms to the HIPC Initiative: A Brief History of Debt Relief for Low Income Countries', *IMF Working Paper*, WP/99/142, Washington DC, IMF.

Krugman, P. (1988), 'Financing vs. Forgiving a Debt Overhang', *Journal of Development Economics*, **29**, 253–68.

Sachs, J. (1984), 'Theoretical Issues in International Borrowing', *Princeton Studies in International Finance*, **54**.

Sachs, J. (1990), 'Introduction', in J. D. Sachs (ed.), *Developing Country Debt and Economic Performance. Vol. 2*, Chicago: Chicago University Press/NBER.

Samter, P. (2000), 'Debt Overhang and Debt Relief in Africa: A Case Study of Zambia', mimeographed.

Williamson, J. (1988), *Voluntary Approaches to Debt Relief*, Policy Analyses in International Economics, **25**, Washington DC, Institute for International Economics.

Notes

1 Conducting Macroeconomic Policy in Developing Countries: Piece of Cake or Mission Impossible?

1 New classical macroeconomics suggested that there was limited scope for governments to actively manage an economy. The top priority should be to avoid destabilising it, and this could be achieved by adhering to stable monetary growth.

2 While the first half of the 1980s saw a fall in the rate of inflation in industrial countries, it also saw a rise in the level of unemployment. The fact that new classical macroeconomics sought to explain this in terms of an increasing natural rate of unemployment, and as being consistent with their theories, did not make the additional unemployment any more palatable in political terms.

3 The argument here was that any pegged exchange rate system will lack credibility. It is only by adopting a single currency that credibility can be created.

4 For a summary of this see Page (1993).

5 In the liquidity trap there is a rate of interest at which the demand for money becomes infinitely elastic since no one expects it to fall further. Increases in the supply of money are willingly held and will not force down the interest rate.

6 See Easterly and Schmidt-Hebbel (1993) for a detailed review of the theory and evidence. Certainly developing countries have run fairly persistent fiscal deficits.

7 For a clear statement of this 'new structuralist' idea, as well as a brief overall summary of the new structuralist approach, see Fanelli et al. (1994).

8 Bird (1998a) provides a succinct presentation and evaluation of the nominal anchor approach to exchange rate policy, contrasting it with the alternative 'real target' approach.

9 For developing countries as a group, the rate of inflation as measured by percentage changes in consumer prices fell from 43% in 1991 to 9% in 1997. For developing countries in the Western Hemisphere, the reduction in inflation was even more pronounced and fell from 174% in 1991 to 11% in 1997, although this was still above the average for developing countries as a group.

10 Experience in Mexico provides a good example. Although inflation in Mexico fell sharply, the Mexican peso still appreciated in real terms and this contributed to the Mexican peso crisis in 1994. To a lesser extent, a similar story may be told about Thailand's economic crisis in 1997.

11 Whereas, following the adoption of generalised flexible exchange rates in 1973, about 10% of developing countries opted for a flexible exchange rate regime, by 1999 the percentage had increased to 60%.

12 However, working against this, while the Marshall–Lerner condition for industrial countries is that the sum of the import and export demand elasticities should be greater than one (because they price their exports in their own currency), for developing countries which price their exports in a foreign currency, such as the US dollar, the Marshall–Lerner condition is merely that the sum of the import demand elasticity and export supply elasticity must exceed zero. On this basis devaluation could be expected to be a relatively effective policy tool in developing countries and this is what the evidence suggests. See Kamin (1988).

13   Again the test for success was not merely that of reducing inflation but reducing it sufficiently to ensure that pegged exchange rates did not become progressively overvalued.

14   For a further discussion of this issue in the context of Latin America, see Bird and Helwege (1997).

15   For a presentation of some of the evidence see Sachs and Warner (1995) and Edwards (1998). But also see Mosley (2000) who argues that 'there exists no one unique set of good…policies. [this] takes on a different meaning in each developing or transitional country contingent on its structure, its stage of development and the external shocks to which it is subject' (p 614).

16   However, policies of economic liberalisation may not be effective in economies that are experiencing acute macroeconomic instability. Some degree of stabilisation to reduce inflation and eliminate currency misalignment may be a necessary precondition (Rodrik, 1996).

17   For a comprehensive discussion of the design of IMF programmes, see Edwards (1989), Killick (1995a) and Mussa and Savastano (1999).

18   See Edwards (1989), Conway (1994) and Killick (1995b).

19   In the period 1973–97 just over 65% of IMF programmes remained uncompleted in the sense that not all of the loan was disbursed.

20   The record of ESAFS is open to debate. While the Fund has claimed some success for them (Schadler *et al.*, 1993) others have maintained that there are indications suggesting otherwise (Killick, 1995a). For a more recent assessment, see Dicks-Mireaux *et al.* (2000).

21   A notable example is Summers (1999).

22   Both Conway (1994) and Killick (1995a) find that IMF programmes are associated with real exchange rate depreciation in a way that is statistically significant.

23   Conway (1994) and Killick (1995a) again provide evidence in support of this.

24   It is not just capital outflows that create problems for developing countries. Surges of capital inflows may also have effects which are macroeconomically destabilising. The problem here is that there is no straightforward way of dealing with the destabilising consequences of capital inflows. This is why measures to control them may be desirable (Bird, 1998a).

25   See Killick (1995a), Bird (1996) and Haque and Khan (1998) for reviews of the evidence.

26   Santaella (1995) shows that countries turning to the IMF for assistance had rates of monetary growth that were no faster in a statistically significant sense than those that did not.

2   External Financing and Balance of Payments Adjustment in Developing Countries: Getting a Better Policy Mix

1   For an explanation and evaluation of this "new" theory of the balance of payments see Corden (1991). Feldstein and Horioka (1980) provided early evidence suggesting a close relationship between saving and investment, although subsequent work has challenged their findings as well as the implications they draw (Ghosh, 1995).

2   It is also likely that the availability of external finance will be inversely related to the need for it. Countries experiencing an improvement in their terms of trade which strengthens their short-term balance of payments are likely to find that their creditworthiness also improves. Commercial lending may therefore be

inherently pro-cyclical with private lenders happiest to lend to countries that do not need to borrow, and least happy to lend to those that do.

3 For a more detailed analysis of IMF lending as well as an examination of the empirical evidence see Bird (1995).

4 While both rates fell in Africa, the Middle East and Europe and the Western Hemisphere after 1977–81, they rose in Asia. It is in Africa that the fall was most pronounced with the savings rate falling from 26.0% in 1977–81 to 15.7% in 1993, and the investment rate falling from 29.5% to 18.1% over the same period.

5 Where both the IMF and the World Bank have been simultaneously involved in developing countries it is difficult to identify the effects of their individual programs. Institutionally the Fund is typically more preoccupied with macroeconomic stabilization than is the World Bank and therefore the discussion in this paper is more heavily directed toward the Fund. In designing an appropriate mix of policies, however, it is important that the Fund and the Bank coordinate their involvement to ensure that their advice is consistent.

6 Evidence presented by Killick and Malik (1992) shows that most commonly it is a combination of domestic economic mismanagement and external shocks which leads countries to borrow from the IMF. In summing up a synthesis of case study findings they argue that, "in a high proportion of cases both exogenous shocks and domestic economic weaknesses are important in the circumstances leading up to adoption of a Fund programme. It is rare for either category of explanation to be materially absent ... our country studies suggest that natural disasters are a more frequent reason for programme adoption than is generally appreciated". They also emphasize "the singular vulnerability of countries heavily dependent on primary product exports, not only because of adverse terms of trade movements, but also due to mismanagement of short-term commodity booms" (p. 626). The latter observation reinforces concern that unconditional financing might be used as a substitute for adjustment. The findings confirm the need for structural adjustment.

7 Moreover, the Fund could play a role in helping to orchestrate debt reduction in developing countries, by providing an institutional structure for bringing debtors and creditors together, helping to formulate an adjustment program alongside creditor-based debt restructuring. Rather than providing finance in support of debt reduction, the Fund could seek to ensure that private creditors find debt relief more attractive, by essentially guaranteeing that the positive adjustment incentive provided by debt relief outweighs any negative incentive. There is clearly a danger that where the Fund provides its own resources to effectively bail out private lenders in conditions of crisis, it may inadvertently encourage imprudent lending in the future.

3   Where do we Stand on Choosing Exchange Rate Regimes in Developing and Emerging Economies?

1 See for example a report sponsored by the Council on Foreign Relations, dealing with reforming the international financial architecture advises developing countries to 'just say no' to pegged exchange rates. Similar advice was proffered by the International Financial Institution Advisory Commission (IFIAC, 2000).

2 There is a large literature on the effects of IMF programmes and we do not pursue the issue here. For a useful review see Killick (1995).

3   Similar issues arise in the case of advanced economies but it seems unlikely that the established regime of floating exchange rates between the Euro, the US dollar and the yen will be abandoned. The policy issue relates more normally to the exchange rate choices of developing and emerging economies, which are the ones that in any case are likely to be exposed to advice from the IMF.

4   Throughout the chapter 'dollarisation' is used to describe any regime in which a country replaces its national currency with the currency of another country. In principle this could involve the euro or the yen as well as the dollar.

5   This mirrors a conventional distinction between expenditure-switching and expenditure-changing policies for dealing with balance of payments disequilibria.

6   This raises another reason for distinguishing between advanced economies and developing ones. In the case of advanced economies that price their exports in their own currency, devaluation reduces the foreign currency price of exports as well as increasing the domestic currency price of imports. The domestic currency terms of trade deteriorate and if the sum of the import and export demand elasticities is less than one, in the short run the balance of payments on current account will weaken, giving the famous J-curve effect. In the case of developing countries that price their exports in foreign currency this adverse terms of trade effect is absent since domestic currency export prices rise alongside devaluation. The success of devaluation depends on the elasticity of supply associated with the change in the relative price of traded and non-traded goods, but there is no J-curve as such. Time is still important but devaluation should not weaken the current account.

7   The trick is to persuade labour markets that the government is firmly committed to its counter-inflationary policy. If labour believes that the peg will be defended whatever the circumstances then it will also be believed that inflationary wage claims that lead to balance of payments deficits will result in contractionary monetary and fiscal policy, which will increase unemployment in the future. The cost of higher wages now is therefore an increased probability of unemployment in the future. If the commitment to the peg is not believed then this cost evaporates.

8   Frenkel (1999) reports empirical evidence in support of the claim that closer integration is associated with a closer correlation of national income.

9   This touches on the important issue of sequencing. Problems may arise when the 'right' policies are pursued in the 'wrong' order. There is also the fairly conventional argument that balance of payments deficits under a pegged exchange rate regime will lead to greater protectionism, as imports cannot be reduced via devaluation. According to this view, flexible exchange rates are needed to defend liberal trade. However with pegged exchange rates that are part of a broader scheme of economic integration there will be other ways of both correcting and financing deficits, and protectionist measures will be ruled out in any case. There is also the counter-argument that flexible exchange rates can result in increased protectionism since they may fail to prevent the incidence of currency misalignment. Currency over-valuation may lead to accusations of unfair competition and de-industrialisation and to increased protection, which is not dismantled when the exchange rate depreciates. There may, in principle, be a ratchet effect on protectionism.

10   There is an interesting conundrum here since an advantage of pegged exchange rates has traditionally been seen as encouraging international trade and investment by reducing exchange rate risk. Now an argument seems to be that credible pegged exchange rates may lead to excessive capital flows. Should exchange rate instability or the possibility that it may occur therefore be welcomed in order to

offset the excess credibility of pegged exchange rates? This again sounds like a moral hazard problem. Would drivers drive more carefully without insurance?

11 The simple but rather unhelpful answer is that we are not sure. There are analytical arguments that point in different directions and there is some degree of empirical support for most points of vies. Again the lack of consensus makes the selection of an exchange rate regime that much more difficult.

12 While the consensus as described here can be reasonably said to exist, and while, significantly, Anne Krueger, the IMF's new First Deputy Managing Director, has gone on record as subscribing to it, mere are a number of economists who have sought to distance themselves from it. Notable amongst them are Williamson (1999), Frankel (1999) and Corden (2001). They raise and examine – often in detail – many of the issues discussed in this chapter. Corden, in particular, provides a thorough analysis of the choice of exchange rate regime and presents a wide-ranging case study application of the analysis upon which this chapter freely draws.

13 The author has already provided a related assessment of the 'nominal anchor' and 'real targets' approach to exchange rate policy in the light of events in Mexico, the Franc Zone and East Asia focussing on the apparent propensity of pegged regimes to break down (Bird, 1998).

14 Many issues, similar to those discussed here were involved, although clearly the pursuit of economic and monetary union in Europe made this something of a special case.

15 Of course it is not simply a question of wisdom but also information and priorities. The timing of crises and even to some extent their incidence is unpredictable. If devaluation is known to be politically unpopular, governments may rationally seek to postpone it for as long as possible. The possibility of a crisis at some imprecise time in the future may be subject to a high political discount rate. A policy decision which appears to have been a mistake where history has removed uncertainty may have appeared quite reasonable ex ante when less was known about how things would pan out.

16 The pros and cons of dollarisation and Ecuador's decision to dollarise have been more fully discussed by the author elsewhere (Bird, 2001).

17 An important part of exchange rate policy that is not discussed in detail here is indeed the exit strategy. If countries are to move between regimes how should they organise this? If a pegged rate is abandoned in a crisis the value of the currency is likely to fall precipitously and then overshoot its long run equilibrium. There is ample evidence from Latin America and East Asia to support this. Eichengreen *et al.* (1999) argues that for this reason a transition from a pegged exchange regime to a more flexible one should be made when the currency will appreciate as a result of capital inflows or a positive trade shock. While this makes sense, certainly if it helps to avoid crises and their costs, there is the problem that governments may be reluctant to lose international competitiveness and may prefer to build up international reserves especially if they see the capital inflows or terms of trade improvements as temporary. Although exchange appreciation may discourage capital inflows by highlighting exchange rate risk, there is also the danger that in markets dominated by short-term capital flows and elastic expectations the exchange rate may be driven up excessively to be followed by a collapse. This may then argue for managed flexibility. Also the transition in exchange rate regimes needs to be accompanied by an appropriate transition in terms of other policies. If a currency peg is abandoned some alternative form of nominal anchor will need to replace it.

18 There is the argument that the appreciation in the real effective exchange rates of East Asian economies which was associated with the rise in the value of the US dollar could have been mitigated by pegging to a basket of currencies. This is not to say that the suboptimality of pegging to the dollar was the root cause of the crisis. Capital inflows would in any event have led to real appreciation either via their direct effects on the nominal values of currencies or via their domestic monetary implications that sterilisation can only offset in the short run. Bird and Rajan (2000) provide a fuller analysis of the optimal peg in the context of East Asia, and briefly review exchange rate options for the region.

4   Is Dollarisation a Viable Option for Latin America?

1 In fact there was considerable domestic disagreement within Ecuador. The President favoured it largely on the grounds that since the relatively rich already used dollars, the relatively poor were the ones hit by the effects of devaluation. Devaluation was politically unpopular. Dollarisation meant 'dollars for all'. The central bank initially opposed the idea but condoned dollarisation provided an exchange rate of 25,000 sucres to one dollar was used rather than the 20,000-to-one exchange rate the President preferred.

2 Some claim that the seigniorage costs could be initially high as the stock of domestic currency would have to be bought with dollars either supplied by running down international reserves or by borrowing, and also high thereafter as future seigniorage earnings from supplying currency to meet the increase in the demand for money would be sacrificed. In Argentina, for example, domestic currency represents about 5 per cent of GDP and the annual increase in currency demand has averaged about 0.3 per cent of GDP. Countering this, others claim that financial innovation will reduce the need for currency and that higher interest rates from abandoning financial repression will reduce the demand for money. They therefore argue that the above figures seriously overstate the seigniorage loss. For a discussion of this issue – and others related to dollarisation – see Andrew Berg and Eduardo Borensztein (2000) 'The Pros and Cons for Full Dollarisation', *IMF Working Paper 00150*, Washington, DC: International Monetary Fund.

3 Ecuador has experimented with a whole range of exchange rate policies over the years and this raises doubts about whether it will stick with dollarisation. However, it is more difficult to abandon dollarisation since that would require the reintroduction of the national currency.

5   What Happened to the Washington Consensus?

1 For a discussion of the increasing overlap between the IMF and the World Bank see Feinberg (1988) and Bird (1994).

2 Tussie and Botzman (1990) provide a detailed analysis of this case. Observers of the Washington institutions do informally suggest that Fund–Bank relations reached something of a low ebb in the late 1980s.

3 Rodrik (1999a) discusses how the policy priorities of the Fund may lead rather than reflect opinion in private capital markets.

4 Thus the publicity accorded to the phrase may itself have encouraged policy-makers to modify their views. There may have been a herding tendency.

5 Polak (1991) and Killick (1989a) provide empirical evidence for this increase in conditionality.

6 Bird (1999) provides a brief summary of some of the research, which attempts to explain the surge of capital inflows towards some developing countries in the early 1990s. Generally, the WC is accorded little importance.

7 Data from the Development Assistance Committee of the OECD suggest that official development finance that, in current US dollars, had stood at $69.8 billion in 1990 had fallen to $69.4 billion by 1995.

8 The data in Table 5.1 show that a downside of the economic growth experienced in Latin America in the early 1990s was an increasing current account deficit, which may also have contributed to the economic problems that the region encountered in the mid-1990s. Evidence spanning a longer period also confirms that policies of trade liberalisation had met with little success in diversifying the export mix of Latin American economies (Puyana, 1994). Critics of the WC had maintained that there was a danger that a stronger outward orientation would lead to a fall in export prices and deterioration in the commodity terms of trade. The end result could be that export revenue would decline.

9 Calvo, Leiderman and Reinhart (1996) provide a succinct discussion of the potential effects of capital inflows and analyse the policy options available to governments. They demonstrate clearly that there are no easy solutions.

10 Fischer *et al.* (1998) present alternative views about the wisdom of capital account liberalisation. This demonstrates that there is no firm consensus in favour of it.

11 A number of reports on the international financial system and the international financial institutions reached the conclusion that developing countries should avoid pegged exchange rates. There seemed to be an emerging consensus on the exchange rate issue that appeared to be shared by the IMF and the World Bank. However, as soon as it emerged, it encouraged detractors to voice concern. See, for example, Williamson (1999), Frankel (1999), Bird and Rajan (2000). Capturing the general spirit of this critique of the emerging consensus Frankel entitled his Princeton Essay, 'No Single Currency Regime is Right for All Countries or at All Times'.

12 Examples of pro-openness evidence include Sachs and Warner (1995) and Edwards (1998). Examples of a more agnostic approach to trade liberalisation, and indeed liberalisation in general, include Rodrik (1999b), and Mosley (2000).

13 There is also the 'race to the bottom' argument that an export orientation which may work for a small number of countries may not work if all developing countries adopt it simultaneously since the related increase in world supply of developing-country exports will adversely affect their income terms of trade.

14 Killick (1989b) presents a clear and concise discussion of these issues. The WC view of the state was itself a reaction to claims that governments had become excessively large, but, according to Killick this reaction went too far. For a measured analysis of the role of the state in facilitating economic development particularly from the viewpoint of sustaining economic recovery in Latin America see Grindle (1994).

15 The vehemence of Stiglitz's attack on the Fund (Stiglitz, 2000) not only suggests a lack of consensus over macroeconomic policy but a deep divide and some animosity.

16 The ESAF is now renamed the Poverty Reduction and Growth Facility. Collier stresses the need for ownership – a theme originally investigated by the Bank rather than the Fund, and argues that it is important to explore the effects of economic adjustment on inequality since this will influence ownership. He argues that the Bank pays much closer attention to this than does the Fund (Collier, 1997; Collier and Gunning, 1999).

17   The emphasis here is on 'appears'. Certainly institutional changes have brought the Fund and the Bank closer on these issues; in particular the reformulation of the ESAF as the PRGF. However, informally and off-the-record, some Fund staff remain somewhat unenthusiastic about these reforms. Indeed, it is sometimes suggested that Fund staff are themselves uncomfortable about increasing overlap with the Bank and are not opposed to the redefinition of a clearer division of labour that some outside observers advocate. If this is the case then the idea of an emerging consensus around ownership is undermined. In the case of better-off developing countries in Latin America and East Asia, which are not eligible to use the PRGF, the Bank's criticism of the Fund's policies comes close to the argument made by some commentators that the Fund paid more attention to what was best for capital markets than what was best for the inhabitants of the countries in crisis. Critics point out that in the aftermath of the Fund's programmes in Korea, for example, output shrank by 6.7 per cent and unemployment rose by 6.8 percentage points.

18   The Reports were produced by the Council on Foreign Relations, the International Financial Institution Advisory Commission, and the Overseas Development Council. The recommendations they make are succinctly summarised in Williamson (2000).

6   Miracle to Meltdown: A Pathology of the East Asian Financial Crisis

1   Krugman (1994) argued that explaining East Asia's economic growth in terms of rapid factor accumulation rather than by rapid growth in factor productivity allowed comparisons to be drawn with the economic growth achieved in earlier years by the Soviet bloc. This comparison is interesting since it suggests that the nature of the 'Asian development model', relying on some degree of intervention in markets, is *per se* unlikely to be a significant factor in explaining the rapid economic growth achieved by East Asia.

2   The IMF's *World Economic Outlook*, May 1998 records Asian economic growth as averaging about 9.3% per year over the period 1992–95, compared with 7% per year over the period 1980–89. While Asia was growing at an annual rate of over 9%, Africa and Latin America were growing at annual rates of about 1.4% and 3.3%, respectively over the same 1992–95 period.

3   Malaysia, Singapore and Hong Kong were able to avoid turning to the IMF for assistance, whereas Thailand, Korea and Indonesia all arranged stand-by programmes with the IMF in the period from August to December 1997. The amounts of finance approved were SDR 2.9 billion for Thailand, SDR 7.3 billion for Indonesia and SDR 15.5 billion for Korea. As of March 1998, SDR 10.3 billion in total remained undrawn. The Philippines already had an extended arrangement in place, but negotiated a stand-by arrangement for SDR 1.02 billion in March 1998.

4   To a large extent the factors that influence economic sustainability are the same as those that were identified as influencing country risk in the context of the Third World debt crisis in the 1980s. See, for example, Bird (1989). A more recent analysis of current account sustainability that also identifies factors similar to those used here is Milesi-Ferretti and Razin (1996).

5 Empirical support for this explanation is found in Radelet and Sachs (1998) who test the strength of alternative risk indicators in predicting the onset of financial crises in the emerging markets over the period 1994–97. They find that a high ratio of short-term debt to reserves is 'strongly associated' with the onset of a crisis, even to the extent of being a necessary condition. Long-term indebtedness is not significant. A rapid build-up of claims by the financial sector on the private sector is relevant in some but not all cases. Large current account balance of payments deficits are found to be 'only weakly associated' with the onset of a crisis; they are neither necessary nor sufficient. Surprisingly, Radelet and Sachs find no empirical evidence to support the significance of real exchange rate overvaluation. This finding is at odds with other research which has systematically surveyed studies into currency crises (Kaminsky *et al.*, 1998) where, as a general rule, currency overvaluation is found to be important.

6 In early 1998 the IMF was estimating and forecasting a growth rate in Thailand that was barely positive in either 1997 or 1998. Before the crisis it had been predicting growth rates of 6.8% in 1997 and 7% in 1998. Growth rates for the Asian five in 1998, as predicted by the IMF in December 1997, were Indonesia, 2%, Malaysia, 2.5%, Philippines, 3.8%, Thailand, 0%, and Korea, 2.5%. The massive over-prediction of economic growth in East Asia by the IMF yet again illustrates the extent to which the crisis was unforeseen. It also suggests a measure of inconsistency within the Fund which, after the event, emphasised fundamental weaknesses in the East Asian economies. However, these did not discernibly reveal themselves in the Fund's own growth forecasts for the region before the crisis. The Fund's over-predictions of economic growth in the region also help explain to some extent the policy mistakes that were made under the auspices of the IMF in responding to the crisis.

7 The continuing crisis in East Asia contrasts with the apparently much shorter-term world financial crisis to which it contributed. Policy makers in the USA and Europe have been prepared to respond by relaxing monetary policy in an attempt to offset this contractionary overspill from East Asia and avert a major world economic recession. In October 1998 US equity prices rose by 14%, leading some Wall Street analysts to talk in terms of a financial market 'meltup' as opposed to 'meltdown'. The return of a bullish market mood in financial markets could improve the general lack of confidence, and influence consumer and investor behaviour in such a way as to sustain world economic activity. The domestic response of the USA and the UK to the world financial crisis may be contrasted with that adopted in East Asia, often under the auspices of the IMF.

7 The International Monetary Fund and Developing Countries: A Review of the Evidence and Policy Options

1 For a fuller discussion and analysis of these changes, see Bird, 1987, 93–107.
2 For more detailed evidence about developing countries' quasi-continuous engagement with the Fund, see Bird, 1995.
3 Killick, 1992.
4 For detailed evidence, see Bird, 1995.
5 For examples of such analyses, see Bird and Orme, 1981; Cornelius, 1987; Conway, 1994; Joyce, 1992; Knight and Santaella, 1994; and Bird, 1995, 142–50.

6 For a summary of available evidence, see Bird, 1995. For additional evidence concerning the Fund's various arrangements in seventy-eight developing countries during 1973–91, see Santaella, 1995.
7 The results reported herein are explored more fully in Bird, 1995 and Killick, 1995.
8 Bird, 1994c.
9 This, as well as other research, is reported in Bird, 1987, 60–2.
10 Bird, 1989.
11 For a review of these criticisms, see Bird, 1987, chap. 4. See also Killick, 1993.
12 See, for example, Killick, Malik, and Manuel, 1992. For more recent evidence, see Santaella, 1995.
13 Santaella, 1995.
14 For a good example of the neostructuralist critique, see Taylor, 1988.
15 For a forceful presentation of these points, see Edwards, 1989. A similar theme emerges in Sachs, 1989.
16 Killick, 1989.
17 See Finch, 1989; and Stiles, 1990.
18 For a brief review of the literature on the use of devaluation in developing countries, see Bird 1990. For a more recent review based on a World Bank-sponsored study, see Corden, 1993.
19 Killick, 1992.
20 Edwards, 1989.
21 Knight and Santaella, 1994, 18.
22 The results reported here are presented more fully in Killick with Malik, 1992.
23 World Bank, 1989.
24 Williamson, 1993. Other relevant references include Grindle and Thomas, 1991; Haggard and Kaufman, 1992; Haggard and Webb 1993; and Nelson, 1990.
25 See, for example, Salacuse, 1994.
26 See Cornia and Stewart, 1987; and Oxfam, 1993.
27 For more details on the sample, methods, and results, including the particular tests for statistical significance, see Killick with Malik, 1992.
28 Detailed reviews may be found in Killick, Malik, and Manuel, 1992; and Khan, 1990.
29 See Khan, 1990; and Pastor, 1987.
30 See Khan, 1990; Gylfason, 1987; and Doroodian, 1993.
31 Goldstein and Montiel, 1986.
32 See, respectively, Khan and Knight, 1982; and Khan and Knight, 1985.
33 Conway, 1994.
34 See Heller *et al.*, 1988; and Edwards, 1989.
35 See Killick, Malik, and Manuel, 1992; and Conway, 1994.
36 See Edwards, 1989; Heller *et al.*, 1988; and Zulu and Nsouli, 1985.
37 For a summary of the evidence of adjustment on poverty and for individual sources, see Bird and Killick, 1995. For an examination of the effects of the IMF on political stability, see Siddell, 1988.
38 Schadler *et al.*, 1995, 10.
39 For an interesting discussion of the role of the state in facilitating economic adjustment in Latin America, see Grindle, 1994.
40 See, for example, Bleaney and Greenaway, 1993; and Cardoso, 1993.
41 A more detailed version of this idea may be found in Bird, 1987, chap. 8.
42 Bird, 1994b.

43 See the communiqué of the Halifax meeting of the G-7 leaders in June 1995.
44 For a wide-ranging discussion on institutional reform, see Bretton Woods Commission, 1994. For a more structured analysis of the division of labor between the IMF and the World Bank, see Bird, 1994a.
45 A more detailed analysis of the political economy of the G-7 proposals can be found in Bird, 1995.

8 Remodeling the Multilateral Financial Institutions

1 See Harold James, *International Monetary Cooperation Since Bretton Woods* (New York: Oxford University Press, 1996), for a history of the international monetary system; and A. F. P. Bakker, *International Financial Institutions* (London: Addison Wesley, 1996), for a survey of multilateral financial institutions.
2 For a more detailed and structured discussion of the circumstances under which fundamental reform to the international monetary system may and may not take place, see Graham Bird, "From Bretton Woods to Halifax and Beyond: The Political Economic of International Monetary Reform," *World Economy* 19, no. 2 (1996): 149–72.
3 For example, Jeffrey Sachs, in *The Economist* (12 September 1998), writes about the shortcomings of global capitalism and the reforms necessary to make it work better.
4 Barry Eichengreen discusses many of the proposals that have been offered in the wake of the Asian crisis to reform the international financial institutions in *Toward a New International Financial Architecture* (Washington, D.C.: Institute for International Economics, 1999).
5 The benefits and risks of international capital flows are examined in IMF Occasional Paper No. 172, *Capital Account Liberalization: Theoretical and Practical Aspects* (Washington, D.C.: IMF, 1998).
6 The experiences of commercial lenders in trying to organize their own conditionality in the case of Peru in 1976 are nicely summarized in Dani Rodrik, "Why is there Multilateral Lending?" in Michael Bruno and Boris Pleskovic, eds., *Annual World Bank Conference on Development Economics 1995* (Washington, D.C.: International Bank for Reconstruction and Development, 1996), pp. 167–93.
7 See, for example, Roland Vaubel's use of the public choice approach in "The Political Economy of the International Monetary Fund: A Public Choice Analysis," in Roland Vaubel and Thomas D. Wilett, eds., *The Political Economy of International Organizations* (Boulder: Westview, 1991), pp. 204–44.
8 Anne O. Krueger, "Whither the World Bank and the IMF?" *Journal of Economic Literature* 36, no. 4 (1998): 2016. Krueger derives this estimate for Bank lending to areas outside of Africa.
9 Mohsin Khan summarizes the evidence on the impact of Fund-supported adjustment programs in "The Macroeconomic Effects of Fund-Supported Adjustment Programs," *IMF Staff Papers* 37, no. 2 (1990): 195–231; "Do IMF-Supported Programs Work? A Survey of the Cross-Country Empirical Evidence," with Nadeem Ul Haque, IMF Working Paper No. 98/169, 1998.
10 The increase in conditionality is explained in Jacques J. Polak, "The Changing Nature of IMF Conditionality," *Essays in International Finance*, No. 184, Princeton University, 1991.
11 Tony Killick, Moazzam Malik, and Marcus Manuel examine the reasons for noncompletion of IMF programs in "What Can We Know About the Effects of IMF Programmes?" *World Economy* 15, no. 5 (1992): 575–97.

12 Graham Bird analyzes the political economy of policy reform in "The Effectiveness of Conditionality and the Political Economy of Policy Reform: Is it Simply a Matter of Political Will?" *Policy Reform* 1, no. 1 (1998): 89–113.

13 An excellent analysis of policy-based lending by the World Bank is provided by Paul Mosley, Jane Harrigan, and John Toye in their *Aid and Power: The World Bank and Policy-Based Lending* (London: Routledge, 1998).

14 For an analysis of IMF programs, see Tony Killick, *IMF Programmes in Developing Countries: Design and Impact* (London: Routledge, 1995).

15 For a fuller discussion of this general theme, see Graham Bird, "How Important is Sound Domestic Macroeconomics in Attracting Capital Inflows to Developing Countries?" *Journal of International Development* 11, no. 1 (1999): 1–26.

16 Graham Bird and Dane Rowlands, investigating whether involvement with multilateral institutions has a positive catalytic effect for a country, find evidence for such an effect only in the case of official lending. See Bird and Rowlands, "The Catalytic Effect of Lending by the International Financial Institutions," *World Economy* 20, no. 7 (1997): 917–91.

17 For a more detailed discussion of these ideas, with supporting evidence, see Graham Bird, "External Financing and Balance of Payments Adjustment in Developing Countries: Getting a Better Policy Mix," *World Development* 25, no. 9 (1997): 1409–20.

18 See Killick, *IMF Programmes in Developing Countries*, for evidence on this issue.

19 See, for example, Jeffrey D. Sachs, Aaron Tornell, and Andrés Velasco, "Financial Crises in Emerging Markets: The Lessons from 1995," *Brookings Papers on Economic Activity*, no. 1 (1996): 147–98; and Graciela L. Kaminsky and Carmen Reinhart, "The Twin Crises: The Causes of Banking and Balance-of-Payments Problems," *American Economic Review* 89, no. 3 (1999): 473–501. Barry Eichengreen, *Toward a New International Financial Architecture*, provides further justification for this point of view.

20 For recent examination of this idea, see Graham Bird, "Economic Assistance to Low Income Countries: Should the Link Be Resurrected?" *Essays in International Finance*, No. 193, Princeton University, 1994.

21 For a brief analysis of capital account liberalization, see Graham Bird, "Convertibility and Volatility: The Pros and Cons Liberalizing the Capital Account," *Economic Notes* 27, no. 2 (1998): 141–56.

22 See Roland Vaubel, "The Moral Hazard of IMF Lending," *World Economy* 6, no. 3 (1983): 291–303.

23 Adam Lerrick presents the case for IMF borrowing from the private sector in *Private Sector Financing for the IMF: Now Part of an Optimal Funding Mix* (Washington, D.C.: Bretton Woods Committee, 1999).

24 The Fund has moved to greater use of external evaluators. See, for example, *External Evaluation of the ESAF* (Washington, D.C.: IMF, 1998).

25 U.S. treasury secretary Larry Summers recently advanced his own proposal for reforming the IMF, which included a reduction in the number of the Fund's lending facilities (*The Economist*, 18 December 1999), p. 123.

9 How Important is Sound Domestic Macroeconomics in Attracting Capital Inflows to Developing Countries?

1 The issues presented in this chapter can be viewed from a number of perspectives. The one adopted here is to approach them from the viewpoint of developing

countries anxious to maximize their access to private capital flows. An alternative favoured by one of the referees is to look at them from the viewpoint of investors. In terms of substance it makes little difference which approach is adopted. However, the context for this chapter is to consider the extent to which potential capital importing countries can influence capital inflows by modifying the conduct of macroeconomic policy.

2 Examples of this literature include Calvo and Reinhart (1996); Calvo *et al.* (1993; 1996); Chuhan *et al.* (1993); Claessens *et al.* (1995); Daveri (1995); Fernandez-Arias (1996); Fernandez-Arias and Montiel (1996); Goldstein *et al.* (1991); Montiel (1995); Obstfeld (1995); Schadler *et al.* (1993); Taylor and Sarno (1997).

3 Open economy macroeconomics also helps provide a theoretical framework within which to discuss private capital flows to developing countries. With high return to investment and high private (and social) discount rates developing countries may be expected to show an excess of private investment over private saving and to demand capital imports to cover the related current account balance of payments deficits. Similarly, with growing domestic expenditures in the form of consumption, investment and government expenditure running ahead of domestic output, import demand will tend to rise and weaken the current account balance which is then financed by importing capital. Asset market models emphasize the potential role of interest rate differentials which may be opened up to the advantage of developing countries either by domestic interest rate increases (a pull factor) or by falling interest rates in capital exporting countries (a push factor).

4 This approach to explaining capital flows starts from an attempt to specify the investor's objective function. While for most investors, utility may generally be seen as a positive function of return and a negative function of risk, more precise specification requires detail on the degree of risk aversion as well as the investor's time preference rate. In principle, the source of capital, whether banks, mutual funds or multinational companies will be important if they have different degrees of risk aversion and time preference.

5 Policy-makers may be required to change their policy stance as the duration of capital inflows extends. Early on, policies of sterilized intervention in the foreign exchange market may be sensible whereas in the longer run it may be wiser to allow the nominal exchange to appreciate and pursue contractionary fiscal policy (Calvo *et al.*, 1996). Moreover the design of the policy response may depend on the causes of the inflows, with those related to outside push factors requiring a compensatory response and those related to domestic pull factors requiring a direct policy change (Ferrandez-Arias and Montiel, 1996). Different capital-importing countries have been assessed to have dealt with capital inflows with different degrees of success and failure. Do foreign investors therefore need to form a view as to how countries will deal with capital inflows as part of their decision making regarding foreign investment?

6 For this reason as well as others Easterly *et al.* (1993) conclude that a country's performance in terms of economic growth may be more to do with good luck than good judgement and good policy. This is not, of course, a justification for pursuing bad policy, but it does suggest that good policy may not be enough.

7 This issue opens up the entire debate over why some countries grow faster than others. Recently this has found expression in terms of trying to explain the economic success of the so-called East Asian tigers, although, in this context, no firm consensus has emerged even in terms of characterizing the policies that they have pursued. Although some observers have presented the East Asian success as

evidence to support the superiority of market friendly policies (World Bank, 1991), others have strongly challenged this view both as a depiction of East Asian policies and as evidence for their success (Fanelli *et al.*, 1994). The inability to easily explain the success of the Asian Tigers is reflected in the tendency to refer to it as a 'miracle', but see Young (1995), who attributes it to factor accumulation rather than increases in total factor productivity, implying that endogenous growth theory is largely irrelevant in this context. Mankiw (1995) also doubts the contribution of endogenous growth theory in practical terms.

8 A related observation is that some form of macroeconomic policy rule is superior to *ad hoc* discretion. Having a rule may be more important than the precise nature of the rule itself. On this basis either a monetary target or an exchange rate target is better at controlling inflation than no target at all.

9 The shift from a situation that was perceived as sustainable to one perceived as unsustainable occurred in the case of the Asian financial crisis in 1997 and 1998. Although their significance varied across countries, key components related to the extent to which exchange rate targets and the largely unregulated growth of the domestic financial sector were deemed unsustainable by market agents. Analyses of the Asian crisis have in particular emphasized the importance of the lack of financial regulation and supervision, liquidity constraints, and unhedged exposures, as opposed to the more conventional emphasis on the exchange rate; although this was certainly a factor in Thailand (Krugman, 1998; Radelet and Sachs, 1998). Similar elements were to be found in the Mexican peso crisis of 1994–95 (Calvo, 1996, Garber, 1995).

10 Williamson (1993) argues that portfolio investment in developing countries will be particularly sensitive to their policies on the repatriation of profits.

11 It may also be noted that in a full survey of foreign private capital flows that pre-dated the surge of capital flows to Latin America, Cardoso and Dornbusch (1989) have very little to say about the causes of capital flows except in the context of capital flight. Foreign investment, and in particular foreign direct investment will of course be influenced by factors similar to those that influence domestic invest-ment, although clearly in the case of foreign investment the exchange rate will be relatively more significant (Greene and Villaneuva, 1991). The expectations of foreign investors can become self-fulfilling. The decision not to invest constrains domestic macroeconomic policy and performance. To the extent that economic growth falls below what it would otherwise have been, investors may see this as retrospectively vindicating their decision not to invest. An additional problem is that rapid economic growth may be seen by capital markets as a precursor of inflation and rising interest rates and may have a negative effect on investment.

12 In the case of Latin America, Krugman (1995) argues that there was a self-perpetuating but eventually almost self-destructive momentum at work as foreign investors showed over-optimism for market-based policies. However, as noted in the text, other studies have shown that, to a significant extent, it was the coexistence of policy change in Latin America alongside economic recession and low rates of interest in North America that redirected financial resources south (Calvo *et al.*, 1993).

13 For an interesting discussion of the Mexican peso crisis, see Sachs *et al.* (1995).

14 Thailand, of course, became a source of contagion effects in 1997 as the Thai crisis spilled over into other (but not all) countries in the region. An analysis of the Asian financial crisis of 1997–98 lies outside the scope of this chapter and occurred after the chapter had initially been written and revised. However,

at a superficial level it provides further empirical support for the chapter's basic theme. Economic analysis has been much better at explaining the crisis *ex post* than predicting it *ex ante*. The significance of the private financial sector in the Asian case has highlighted a dimension of sustainability that had previously often been ignored, or at least given secondary status. According to many 'conventional' macroeconomic indicators the 'crisis' was not anticipated.

15 Following the Asian crisis private sector balance sheets will receive as much attention as the public sector's budgetary position, and fiscal deficits will need to be assessed in the context of the private sector's financial position.

16 The Asian crisis presents the IMF in a damage limitation role, where Fund involvement attempted to provide stability in the depths of a financial crisis, applying a tourniquet to potential capital outflows.

17 A recent example of a government apparently getting the macroeconomics unambiguously wrong seems to be Turkey, where the Refah led government shortly after coming to power in 1996 announced pay increases of 50 per cent for civil servants financed by the sale of state lands, a possible cap on interest rates, a near doubling in the minimum wage, pay bonuses to the security forces and the writing-off of interest on agricultural debt, and a substantial increase in the predicted budget deficit. Financial analysts were quoted as responding by suggesting that 'the government is doing everything to hit rock bottom', and that 'if this kind of populism continues the cumulative impact will be devastating' (reported in *The Wall Street Journal*, 16 July 1996).

18 Krugman (1994) makes a similar point suggesting that conviction politicians are content to base policies on the unsubstantiated and simplistic notions of 'policy entrepreneurs'. The lack of a strong scientific consensus extends beyond macroeconomics and also applies to privatization and trade reform. The observations made here about macroeconomics may apply with equal force to the other elements of the Washington-consensus, and foreign investors will therefore find little firmer guidance by moving outside macroeconomics. For contrasting views on the wisdom of trade liberalization in developing countries, see, for example, Dornbusch (1992), and Rodrik (1992).

10 Convertibility and Volatility: The Pros and Cons of Liberalising the Capital Account

1 The evidence on capital flows is reviewed briefly in Bird (1999).

2 Bird (1999) discusses in some detail the links between domestic economic policy and capital flows. In part the problem lies in offering any precise definition of 'sound' economic policy.

3 Massad (1998) discusses the use of capital controls in Chile.

4 Haq, Kaul and Grunberg (eds) (1996), provide a detailed discussion of the issues raised by the Tobin tax proposal.

11 Coping with, and Cashing in on, International Capital Volatility

1 The US, with foreign aid constituting an extremely low 0.08 per cent of GNP has the lowest share, while France, with a share of 0.45 of GNP has the highest. Even France though had a lower share than the 1 per cent target by 2000 set by the

United Nations General Assembly and the Development Assistance Committee (DAC) (Tinbergen, 1990; White and Woestman, 1994).

2 See Lundborg (1998) for a formalization of this issue.

3 The IMF (1998) does caution that the distinction between portfolio and FDI flows in the balance of payments can be somewhat arbitrary and that the proportion of FDI flows in aggregate capital flows may be overstated. Conversely, FDI may actually be understated in some instances. For instance, some part of the recorded short-term borrowing by Thailand was actually FDI and intra-banking transfers (Ostry, 1997).

4 Note the difference between the East Asian and Mexican crises. In the latter case, short-term portfolio flows experienced the sharpest decline, as opposed to debt flows. Indeed, the sharp rise in borrowing from international capital markets in the wake of the Tequila crisis may have led to a substitution towards commercial bank lending.

5 To be specific, the top twelve countries (in descending order of magnitude of capital inflows) are China, Brazil, Mexico, Thailand, Indonesia, South Korea, Argentina, Malaysia, India, Turkey, Hungary and Russia (Lopez-Mejia, 1999).

6 Given the limits to sterilization of capital inflows over the medium- and long-term (see the next note), the reasons for the relatively high (and sustained) interest rate premium offered in an economy that has undertaken financial deregulation (even after accounting for potential default and devaluation risk premia) remains a relatively under-researched area. Fisher (1993) suggests a number of microeconomic imperfections, such as the oligopolistic structures of the finance industries and excessive interlocking ownership between financial, industrial and commercial firms as relevant factors. Rajan (1999b) develops a banking sector model that rationalizes the persistent interest rate premium in emerging markets within a context of a perfectly competitive framework.

7 A nominal appreciation due to inflows of funds may be precluded initially through sterilized intervention in the foreign exchange (forex) market which keeps the domestic money supply in check. However, sterilization is still only a short-term/ temporary option. First, sterilization leads to a hike in domestic interest rates, which in turn perpetuates portfolio capital inflows into the country. Second, the monetary authorities will be faced with mounting losses (quasi-fiscal costs), as accumulating forex reserves provide a lower return than the domestic debt issued. Conversely, allowing a nominal exchange rate appreciation helps to control inflationary pressures. See Calvo *et al.* (1995), Schadler *et al.* (1993) and World Bank (1999) for overviews of general issues and Glick and Moreno (1994) for a discussion of capital flows and monetary policy in the specific context of East Asia.

8 Given that the current account must always equal the difference between national savings and investment ex post, government policies that raise private or public savings (the latter through fiscal consolidation) may preclude a current account deterioration. The East Asian economies have generally been acknowledged as pursuing such policies. In addition, until recently, these economies ensured that capital inflows were channelled into productive investments, thus leading to a virtuous cycle of high growth and further capital inflows (Rajan, 1999a).

9 A study by Kaminsky and Reinhart (1996) found that of the twenty-five banking crises under investigation, in eighteen cases financial liberalization had been undertaken some time during the previous five years. Significantly, while there was no apparent link between balance of payments crises and banking crises in the 1970s when financial markets were highly regulated, they did become very closely

linked in the 1980s, a period which involved large-scale financial deregulation. Some of these issues are formalized in Rajan (1999b).

10 The adjustment process described in the text is not unlike the classic 'Dutch Disease' phenomenon, which may lead to a loss of economic competitiveness from a temporary and large mineral discovery, or favourable but transitory terms of trade movements.

11 This chapter does not discuss capital controls in any detail because they do not have the implications for revenue that form our focus. Dooley (1995) provides a useful review of the theory behind them and the evidence on their effectiveness. Analysis generally suggests that market-based regulatory mechanisms are superior in welfare terms to direct controls.

12 This paragraph and the next draw from Krause (1991). The references to the historical works can be found therein.

13 There are other models of this flavour. DeGrauwe *et al.* (1993) develop a model showing how the interaction between chartists and fundamentalists is capable of generating a chaotic behaviour of exchange rates. The complex non-linearities in their model preclude manual solutions, and necessitate computer simulations. Focusing on financial assets in general, De Long *et al.* (1989) develop an overlapping generations model in which noise traders are not chased out of the market by fundamentalists (in contrast to the efficient market hypothesis).

14 With specific reference to the model detailed in the appendix, such a tax could help reduce Var(s) by raising w or lowering f_s.

15 For instance, see Mathieson and Rojas-Suarez (1993) and Reinhart and Todd-Smith (1997).

16 There may be scope for considering the formation of a World Tax Organisation as suggested by Tanzi (1998) to deal with issues regarding the application of universal taxes (such as the Tobin tax), international tax evasion, tax competition and such.

17 Davidson (1997) also challenges Tobin's claim that 'this simple, one parameter tax would automatically penalize short-horizon round trips, while negligibly affecting the incentives for commodity trade and long term capital investments' (Tobin, 1996, p. xi). Davidson argues that, in so far as agents engaged in international trade in goods and services, FDI and other productive cross border activities hedge their financial transactions while speculators do not, the Tobin tax could provide a greater disincentive to the former than the latter. In addition, Davidson (1998) has pointed out that it is important to draw a distinction between the *volume of trading* and the *degree of volatility*. Through the law of large numbers, a currency tax that successfully reduces the volume of trading may in some circumstances increase volatility.

18 For formal confirmation of this intuitive point see Felix and Sau (1996).

19 Similarly, a Tobin tax will be of limited use if the objective is to increase the autonomy of national authorities to undertake discretionary monetary policy (one of the original objectives of James Tobin in proposing a currency transaction tax). This objective – of overcoming the 'impossible triad' – is probably better served by quantitative capital restraints, as suggested by Krugman (1998) and as undertaken recently by Malaysia. Quantitative restraints, of course, raise a range of other issues.

20 As noted earlier, Kaul and Langmore (1996) discuss some ways in which the revenue from a Tobin tax could be used, along with some of the underlying political economy issues, but they do not make the analytical point that links the

relationship between elasticity, volatility and revenue generation upon which we focus in this chapter.

21 If there is a moral hazard problem, it is more prevalent in the case of *creditors* than *debtors* (given the harsh economic and political costs involved in a crisis and IMF-led 'bailout'), and among creditors, *international* rather than *domestic* ones (as the former rarely have had to take a 'haircut' of any significance).

22 The distinction between financing a new ILLR and helping to finance the IMF becomes blurred if the Fund is envisaged as developing into an ILLR. Fischer (1999) provides a useful summary and discussion of the issues distinguishing between the *crisis-lending* and *crisis-managing* roles of the ILLR. The inadequacies of financing, even with the revenues from a Tobin tax, much more heavily constrain the lending function. Without becoming a fully-fledged ILLR, the IMF could take on a more important and systemic crisis management role (Bird, 1999). This would be facilitated by a share of the revenue from a Tobin tax.

12   The Catalytic Effect of Lending by the International Financial Institutions

1 Dhonte (1997) stresses the argument that by endorsing IMF conditionality, borrowing countries can establish credibility, enhancing the predictability of their policies, and that the demand for IMF endorsement is inversely related to policy credibility. It is by the self imposition of external restraints on their discretionary powers that countries seek to allay market anxiety. In a summary of Dhonte's paper, the *IMF Survey*, Vol. 26, No. 6 (24 March 1997) claims that, 'markets want proof not only of the technical merit of policies but also of the authorities' will to sustain them. IMF financing vouches for this will, and conditionality helps countries signal their determination to act predictably, in accordance with prior commitments '*Markets clearly respond to such signals*' (italics added).

In a recent UK Treasury Committee report on the IMF (Treasury Committee, 1997) the minutes of evidence contain the following question from one of the Committee's members. 'But is there not an all pervasive conventional wisdom that if you do sign up to an IMF programme you get the Good Housekeeping Seal of Approval and away you go!', p. 30. The same member reports that the 'drift of the evidence' received by the inquiry from 'people who claim to know' was 'a lot about catalytic effects and a lot about public leverage of private money ... it is just a very commonly held view', p. 30.

2 Killick (1995) also suggests that the tendency not to complete programmes increased towards the end of the 1980s and during the early 1990s and may have reached levels as high as 70 per cent.

3 In this context Dhonte (1997) argues that it is important for countries involved with the IMF not merely to change policies, but also to change the way in which policies are made, by 'capacity building' in the form of strengthening budgetary control and improving information networks and national expertise, and by 'strengthening the entire civil administration', and the scope for 'good governance'. However, since these changes may take a long time to achieve, is it reasonable to assume that there will be a short-run catalytic effect? Dhonte talks up the catalytic effect by, in large measure, ascribing improved economic fundamentals which then induce capital inflows to IMF involvement. While

improvements in economic performance according to basic indicators may enhance a country's credit-rating (Ul Haque and others, 1996), the available evidence does not allow a strong claim to be made that the Fund is instrumental in bringing about such improvements (see Bird, 1996, for a brief review).

4 Though it should be noted that in some (perhaps many) cases there are elements within a government (typically residing in the Ministry of Finance, Central Bank, or their equivalents) which do support the standard IFI programme. The idea of a unified government may be misplaced.

5 Ul Haque, Mathieson and Sharma (1997) provide a useful brief discussion of the causes of capital inflows, distinguishing between 'pull' and 'push' factors. Although they identify variables over which IFI programmes may be expected to exert an impact, such as exchange rates and interest rates as being potentially important, they do not isolate the negotiation of IFI-backed programmes as a significant event; indeed they do not mention it at all. As noted earlier Dhonte (1997) emphasises the signalling role of IMF conditionality by implicitly assuming a significant causal connection between IMF involvement and the variables which influence creditworthiness; a connection which is largely unsubstantiated by the empirical evidence.

6 The data set was unbalanced in the sense that the number of observations for each country was not always equal because of data availability.

7 It should be noted that in the case where the dependent variable was not itself scaled, a fifth domestic variable, GNP, was added to the list of explanatory variables to reflect scale effects.

8 Though when they occur during a year could have an effect on the analysis, this situation is not explicitly corrected for in the estimation.

9 The one exception to this generalisation is that the interest rate variable consistently switched signs between the early and late periods. In the early and full period estimations, the estimated coefficient was negative and significant. In the later period (1982–1989) the coefficient estimate was positive and significant.

10 Relevant again in this context is the observation that capital inflows to Latin America in the first half of the 1990s have largely been associated with varying interest rates in the US, and, perhaps, the perceived commitment of governments to economic reform, rather than IMF involvement *per se*. The latter observation suggests that the role of the IMF may be more significant in the longer run to the extent that it changes attitudes towards domestic economic policy. In the short run IMF conditionality may conflict with ownership and obscure the degree of governmental commitment to policy reform, exerting an adverse effect on credibility.

11 Indeed capital inflows may create problems for macroeconomic management and may, in excess, undermine exactly those policies favoured by the IMF (Ul Haque and others, 1997).

13 The Political Economy of Foreign Aid: Fatigue or Regeneration?

1 Table 13.2 shows that in percentage terms the decline in ODA was sharper in both Finland and Italy than in the US. But in absolute terms the reduction in US aid was more significant. It is also noteworthy that while 15 members of DAC increased their expenditure on technical co-operation between 1994 and 1995 in current prices, the US cut its TC budget.

2   White (1992) provides a comprehensive review of the theory and evidence relating
    to all these factors showing, on balance, that fear about the potentially adverse con-
    sequences of aid are not without justification. On the issue of fungibility, for exam-
    ple, Heller (1975) discovered a tendency for aid to be used to reduce taxation,
    although Pack and Pack (1990, 1993) found that the extent to which aid was used
    to support fiscal deficits associated with current expenditure varied between coun-
    tries. Feyzioglu *et al.* (1996) report evidence that from every US$1 of ODA about
    75 cents goes to governments' current expenditures. However, they also test aid
    fungibility across public spending categories finding that concessionary loans given
    to transport and communication are fully non-fungible, whereas, loans to the
    energy sector, agriculture and education are fungible. Empirical support for Dutch
    disease effects in Africa comes from van Wijnbergen (1986) and more recently
    Younger (1992) covering the case of Ghana. Although White (1992) is critical of the
    methodology used by van Wijnbergen, he also argues that the effect of aid on the
    real exchange rate may be significant for economies that are highly aid reliant, and
    cites other evidence of the effect in Sri Lanka (White and Wignaraja, 1991).

3   Representative is a quote from Mosley (1987); 'there appears to be no statistically
    significant correlation in any post war period, either positive or negative, between
    inflows of development aid and the growth rate of GNP in developing countries
    when other causal influences on growth are taken into account,' p. 39; although
    he goes on to warn against drawing too many quick conclusions from this in terms
    of the effectiveness of aid, since the impact of aid is too multi-faceted to be cap-
    tured adequately by a single relationship. Mosley also analyses the micro–macro
    paradox, which is a theme discussed by Cassen *et al.* (1994) and by White (1992).
    For further more recent evidence of the apparent macro ineffectiveness of aid see
    Boone (1994), and Brewster and Yeboah (1994) Snyder (1996) discovers a negative
    relationship between ODA and private investment across thirty-six developing
    economies which is particularly strong in the case of low income countries.

4   Again Mosley (1987) finds little evidence to support the claim that aid benefits the
    poorest; a conclusion broadly consistent with the one reached by Riddell (1987).
    While Cassen (1994) points out that the poor may benefit from aid directed
    towards rural projects and raising agricultural output, it appears that aid is at its
    least effective in these areas (World Bank, 1989).

5   Evidence presented by Killick (1991) suggests that aid has been at its least effective
    in Africa according to a range of criteria. He juxtaposes this with the fact that at
    the same time a higher proportion of aid has been directed towards Africa.

6   There is even evidence that donors may design their aid policies in order to assist
    the foreign policy objectives of other countries in order to indirectly favour their
    own (Katada, 1997).

7   The principal recipients of aid from France in 1994–95 were (in descending order)
    Côte d'Ivoire, Egypt, New Caledonia, French Polynesia, Cameroon, Senegal,
    Morocco, Congo, Algeria, Gabon, Vietnam, Madagascar, Niger, Indonesia and
    Burkina Faso. In the case of the UK the principal recipients included India, Zambia,
    Bangladesh, Uganda, Malawi, Pakistan, Zimbabwe, Kenya, Ethiopia, Rwanda,
    Mozambique and Tanzania.

8   Burnside and Dollar also discover that in a sound policy environment aid attracts
    private investment whereas in a poor policy environment it displaces it.

9   It is interesting to note that the micro–macro paradox has to some extent been
    reduced by the fact that the micro effectiveness of aid seems to have fallen over
    recent years. The Bank's Portfolio Management Task Force: Key to Development

Impact, Washington, World Bank, September 1992, reported that 37.5 per cent of projects in 1991 had an economic return of less than 10 per cent. The success of World Bank projects fell from 87 per cent over 1979–81 to 65.7 per cent in 1989–91. The Bank's own analysis was that the decline in performance was associated with the 'pressure to lend', which tended to create a preference for large scale projects.

10 However, the danger that aid will become conceptualised as a long term substitute for private capital flows, with the associated moral hazard and aid-dependency problems, needs to be countered by visibly pursuing a policy by which there is greater willingness to redistribute aid, favouring those developing countries that demonstrate a commitment to and progress with economic reform. In the long run aid recipients should be envisaged as graduating to a status where their creditworthiness is increased and they gain access to private capital. There are various ways in which multi-lateral aid could be directed towards low income countries (for examples, see Bird, 1983, 1994).

11 The view that 'the key role of multilateral agencies in foreign aid is their provision of conditionality' (Rodrik, 1996) has to be treated with caution.

12 Various ideas have been canvassed including that of a 'development contract', which would involve reciprocal obligations between donors and recipients. Donors would commit themselves to a certain level of assistance, while recipients would commit themselves to certain policies. Aid, alongside debt relief and trade would therefore form part of the contract (Ofstad *et al.*, 1991; Jayawardene, 1993; Stokke, 1996; and on a similar theme, Hyden, 1995). The problem would probably be in determining what happens when contracts are broken.

13 This conclusion is not inconsistent with Mosley and Hudson's finding that aid has become more effective over a period of time when conditionality has been increasing. Aid recipients may have become more aware of and committed to economic reform independently of World Bank conditionality. As Mosley and Hudson (1997) point out it may be the policy dialogue that negotiations with the World Bank have involved rather than the World Bank conditionality itself which has improved the quality of economic policy. Given the criticisms of conditionality as a modality for fostering economic reform, redesigning it could improve the quality of implemented policy still further. This conclusion is also consistent with Burnside and Dollar's observation that policy reform 'is largely driven by domestic social and political forces' (1997a, p. 6).

14 Economic Assistance to Low-Income Countries: Should the Link be Resurrected?

1 Under the SDR scheme, recipients holding 100 percent of their allocation in effect pay and receive the same amounts. Net users of SDRs, however, pay a charge on their net use, and net acquirers of SDRs receive interest on their net acquisitions. The charge and interest rate have conventionally moved in tandem. In principle, the two could be different, although a difference would have implications for the financial status of the SDR account within the IMF.

2 The IMF classifies forty-five countries as *small low-income countries*. Excluding China and India, these are countries in which GDP per person, as estimated by the World Bank, did not exceed the equivalent of $425 in 1986. They are Afghanistan, Bangladesh, Benin, Bhutan, Burkina Faso, Burundi, Cambodia, Central African Republic, Chad, Comoros, Equatorial Guinea, Ethiopia, The Gambia, Ghana,

Guinea, Guinea-Bissau, Guyana, Haiti, Kenya, Laos People's Democratic Republic, Lesotho, Madagascar, Malawi, Maldives, Mali, Mauritania, Mozambique, Myanmar, Nepal, Niger, Pakistan, Rwanda, Sao Tomé and Principe, Senegal, Sierra Leone, Somalia, Sri Lanka, Sudan, Tanzania, Togo, Uganda, Vanuatu, Viet Nam, Zaire, and Zambia.

3 A brief critical analysis of the ratio of reserves to imports as a measure of reserve adequacy may be found in Williamson (1984) and Bird (1985).

4 Bird (1982a) contains a review of the empirical evidence and a more detailed analysis of the theory of the demand for international reserves as it applies to developing countries. More recent analyses include Frenkel (1984), Lizondo and Mathieson (1987), and Chrystal (1990a).

5 Discussion of the political costs of stabilization may be found in Bienen and Gersovitz (1985), Haggard (1985), Nelson (1984, 1989), Kaufman (1988), Haggard and Kaufman (1989), and Stallings and Kaufman (1989).

6 By 1992, at least seven of ten countries in arrears could be classified as low income. The data suggest, moreover, that low-income countries more than any other group have quasi-continuous drawings from the IMF over protracted periods of time. Critical analyses of the IMF's role in LICs may be found in, for example, Helleiner (1983a), Loxley (1984), and Zulu and Nsouli (1985).

7 A major study of the IMF and developing countries that incorporates a detailed investigation of the effects of IMF programs has been completed at the Overseas Development Institute by the author and Tony Killick. For a full presentation and interpretation of the results relating to conditionality, see Killick and Malik (1992) and Killick, Malik, and Manuel (1992). The statements made in the text here draw empirical support from these studies.

8 Here and throughout, "billion" is a thousand million. Note also that some of the numbers in this and the next paragraph reflect calculations made with preliminary reserve data for 1990 to 1993, rather than the data given in Table 14.2. Use of the more recent data would alter the calculated outcomes, but not by significant amounts.

9 Although early studies appeared to find a causal connection running from international reserves to inflation (Heller, 1976), later studies have discovered "no significant relationships" and have found no support for "international reserve monetarism" (Chrystal, 1990a). If this is true for international reserves in total, it will be even more true for a small allocation of SDRs in which the total stock of SDRs accounts for less than 5 percent of the world's international reserves. Although allocating SDRs to the LICs may lead to some relaxation in LIC domestic monetary policies, it will not have a significant impact on global inflation.

10 If, however, SDRs were to be allocated simultaneously to LICs and to FSU and former CMEA states, it might be appropriate to modify the details of the allocation (in terms, for example, of the extent of the subsidy on net use) to reflect different economic circumstances.

15 Debt Relief for Low-Income Countries: Is it Effective and Efficient?

1 A good overview of debt relief for low income countries may be found in Daseking and Powell (1999). Boote and Thugge (1999) provide a comprehensive description of the HIPC initiative. This give a very useful summary of the institutional details that we omit from this chapter.

2   For attempts to place debt relief in the context of other policies for dealing with indebtedness, see Bird (1989) and Bird and Snowden (1997). An overview of the economics of debt relief in the context of the Third World debt crisis in the 1980s may be found in Williamson (1989).

3   There is a technical difficulty in making this distinction using the World Bank data on which this table is based. This date contains a category of other public sector and publicly guaranteed long-term lending (the row in Table 15.1 labelled 'other guaranteed') which cannot be clearly divided between official and private sources. We understand that this data includes a large component of supplier credit supported by export credit guarantees and we have therefore allocated this as an official rather than a private source of finance. The alternative of allocating it as a private source of finance would not significantly alter the conclusions drawn from either Table 15.1 or Table 15.2.

4   Other than Indonesia. Indonesia is a large economy only recently reclassified from middle to low income and with a very different debt structure than other severely indebted low income countries. Its inclusion would greatly distort the conclusions drawn from Table 15.2.

5   The allocation of debt and net resource flows between official and private sources used for Figures 15.2a and 2b is made on exactly the same basis as for the final two rows of Tables 15.1 and 15.2.

6   The refusal to provide resource inflows was presumably a conseqence of the international opprobrium of the Sunni Abacha regime.

7   The net inflow in Figure 15.2 excludes foreign direct investment.

8   The suggestion that debt relief must automatically release resources for health, education, and other developmental expenditures is made to seem plausible by campaigns which focus on the outflow of gross debt service payments rather than on net resource transfers.

9   There are very few attempts in the literature to assess the costs of debt relief to creditors. For one such attempt, see Daseking and Powell (1999).

10 For an attempt to model debt sustainability in the context of low income countries, see Cohen (1996).

11 The initial idea of a debt overhang is usually attributed to Sachs (1984). Other useful discussions of the idea, *inter alia*, are Krugman (1988), Corden (1989) and Sachs (1990).

12 Analagous to the disincentive effects arsing from welfare payments to low income households.

13 The debt relief Laffer curve is thoroughly discussed in Williamson (1989); but also see Krugman (1988). For an attempt to test for its existence, see Claessens (1990).

14 Claessens (1990) estimates a debt Laffer curve using cross section data from 1986 to 1989 for twenty-nine countries. He concludes that only Bolivia, Sudan, Peru, Nicaragua and Zambia are on the 'wrong side' of the curve. However, methodologically there are problems with the study since there are difficulties in measuring the 'price' of debt for poor countries. Cohen (1990) finds no support for a debt Laffer curve. Subsequent work by Samter (2000) again finds little support for a debt Laffer curve in Sub-Saharan countries over 1990–94. He does find, however, that the ratio of debt service payments to obligations is positively related to aid per capita, suggesting that aid has enabled low-income countries to meet their debt obligations.

15 Although such behaviour might be regarded as immoral, this is not moral hazard in the sense developed in the literature on insurance contracts under asymmetric information.

16 Complete debt forgiveness could lead to a related and genuine resource saving. Released from the costs of debt negotiations and constant rescheduling and, perhaps more pertinently with their balance sheets greatly shrunk, the IMF and World Bank, for example, could be forced to substantially reduce their operating costs and pass this benefit on to poor countries.

Index

absorption 145, 148
'additionality' principle 281–2
adverse selection 128, 258
aid fatigue 235, 238–40, 244–6
aid programs 64, 101, 128, 130, 141–2, 174, 182–3, 194, 204, 210–11; economics of 235–8; empirical evidence on 227–35; politics of 238–40, 246; public support for 243–4; regeneration of 241–6
Argentina 44–7, 51, 55–7, 61, 163

balance of payments: asset market model of 206–7; deficits on current account 14–23, 26, 31, 38–40, 49, 133, 136, 141, 147, 151–3, 208, 253–8; monetary model of 105
bankruptcy procedures 86, 88–9, 284
Baumol, William 188
Bhagwati, Jagdish 179
bond markets 154–7, 170
Boone, P. 237–8
Brady Plan 274, 282
Brazil 44–5, 53, 66, 94, 126, 158–63
Bretton Woods Commission 92
Bretton Woods system 46, 249
bureaucracy, theory of 179
Burnside, C. 241–2, 244

Calvo, S. 158–9
Camdessus, Michel 107, 251–2, 267–8, 270
capital account liberalization 169–80; arguments for and against 171–6; political economy of 178–80
capital controls 46–8, 89–90, 175–80, 187
capital flows 64–7, 81–2, 85–9, 101, 125–6, 141–66; empirical evidence on 157–65
catalytic effect of IMF and World Bank programs 103–4, 112, 116, 119, 132, 137, 156, 166; empirical evidence on 212–19; theoretical basis for 204–12

chaebols 78–9
Chile 45–6, 158, 176
China 46, 87
Chuhan, P. 157
Cold War, ending of 239–43
Collier, P. 70, 245
Colombia 158
conditionality 10–11, 20–3, 26, 29–32, 35, 61, 63, 70, 93, 98–109, 116–22, 126, 129–32, 135–9, 156, 179, 204–11, 220–3, 245, 250, 261–2, 269, 285–7; 'hidden' 171
contagion effects 20, 76, 82, 89, 101, 126, 129–30, 140, 154, 158–9, 164–6, 173–6
Conway, Patrick 116
costs and benefits of particular policies 150
Council on Foreign Relations 51, 53
crawling peg system 37, 39, 44–7
credit rationing 19–20
creditworthiness 16, 99, 101, 103, 128, 135, 146, 148, 157–8, 173–4, 261
crony capitalism 79
'crowding out' effects 4, 69, 118, 148–51, 235–7, 262–3, 281
currency boards 36, 39, 44–9, 51, 54, 68, 82
currency unions 36, 39–42

Davidson, P. 191
debt: corporate 78, 84–90; sovereign 5
debt overhang 258, 283–6
debt relief 273–87; efficiency arguments for 282–5
deflation 26, 130, 133
demand management 2, 22, 27, 31, 115–16, 133, 219–20, 258, 262
devaluation 6, 11, 24, 26, 38–40, 44–9, 53–4, 58, 82, 86, 106–7, 110, 115–17, 148, 153, 207, 256, 258
developing countries: macroeconomic policy in 3–8, 141–2; net resource flows 182–6